THE KINGDOM OF THE ISLES

SCOTLAND'S WESTERN SEABOARD, *c*.1100–*c*.1336

SCOTTISH HISTORICAL REVIEW

MONOGRAPHS SERIES

No. 4

THE KINGDOM OF THE ISLES

Scotland's Western Seaboard, *c*.1100–*c*.1336

R. ANDREW MCDONALD

TUCKWELL PRESS

First published in Great Britain in 1997 by
Tuckwell Press Ltd
The Mill House, Phantassie, East Linton, East Lothian, EH40 3DG
Scotland

Reprinted 1998

ISBN 1 898410 85 2

British Library Cataloguing-in-Publication Data. A catalogue
record for this book is available on request from the British Library

Typeset in 10/12 Baskerville by
Aligra Lancaster
Printed and bound in Great Britain by
The Cromwell Press, Trowbridge, Wiltshire

for
MY FATHER AND MOTHER

Contents

Illustrations

between pp. 144 and 145

Abbreviations

Ann. Conn.	*Annála Connacht: the Annals of Connacht, AD 1224–1544*, ed. A. M. Freeman (Dublin, 1944; repr. 1970)
Ann. Four Masters	*The Annals of the Kingdom of Ireland by the Four Masters*, ed. J. O'Donovan (2nd edn, Dublin, 1856)
Ann. Inisf.	*The Annals of Inisfallen (MS Rawlinson B 503)*, ed. S. Mac Airt (Dublin, 1951; repr. 1977)
Ann. Loch Cé	*The Annals of Loch Cé*, ed. W. M. Hennessy (Rolls Ser., 1871)
Ann. Tigernach	*The Annals of Tigernach*, ed. W. Stokes, in *Revue Celtique*, xvi–xviii (1895–7)
Ann. Ulster	*Annals of Ulster*, ed. W. M. Hennessy and B. McCarthy (Dublin, 1887– 1901)
APS	*The Acts of the Parliaments of Scotland*, ed. T. Thomson and C. Innes (Edinburgh, 1814–75)
Barbour, *Bruce*	[John Barbour], *Barbour's Bruce*, ed. M. P. McDiarmid and J. A. C. Stevenson (STS, 1980–5)
Beauly Chrs.	*The Charters of the Priory of Beauly with Notices of the Priories of Pluscardine and Ardchattan*, ed. E. C. Batten (Grampian Club, 1877)
Book of Dean of Lismore	*Scottish Verse from the Book of the Dean of Lismore*, ed. W. J. Watson (Scottish Gaelic Texts Soc., 1937)
CDS	*Calendar of Documents relating to Scotland*, ed. J. Bain *et al.* (Edinburgh, 1881– 1986)
Chron. Bower	Walter Bower, *Scotichronicon*, ed. D. E. R. Watt (Aberdeen, 1987–)
Chron. Bower (Goodall)	*Joannis de Fordun Scotichronicon cum Supplementis et Continuatione Walteri Boweri*, ed. W. Goodall (Edinburgh, 1759)
Chron. Fordun	John of Fordun, *Chronica Gentis Scotorum*, ed. W. F. Skene (Edinburgh, 1871–2)
Chron. Holyrood	*A Scottish Chronicle known as the Chronicle of Holyrood*, ed. M. O. Anderson (SHS, 1938)

Chron. Lanercost (Maxwell)	*The Chronicle of Lanercost, 1272–1346*, trans. H. Maxwell (Glasgow, 1913)
Chron. Man	*The Chronicle of Man and the Sudreys*, ed. P. A. Munch and Rev. Dr Goss (Manx Soc., 1874)
Chron. Melrose	*The Chronicle of Melrose* (facsimile edn), ed. A. O. Anderson *et al.* (London, 1936)
Chron. Wyntoun (Laing)	Andrew Wyntoun, *The Orygnale Cronykil of Scotland*, ed. D. Laing (Edinburgh, 1872–9)
Clanranald Bk.	*The Book of Clanranald*, in A. Cameron, *Reliquiae Celticae: Texts, Papers and Studies in Gaelic Literature and Philosophy*, ed. A. MacBain and J. Kennedy (Inverness, 1894)
CPL	*Calendar of Entries in the Papal Registers relating to Great Britain and Ireland: Papal Letters*, ed. W. H. Bliss *et al.* (London, 1893–)
Diplom. Norv.	*Diplomatarium Norvegicum*, ed. G. R. Unger and H. J. Huitfeldt (Kristiana, 1849–1919)
Donaldson, *Scot. Hist. Docs.*	*Scottish Historical Documents*, ed. G. Donaldson (Edinburgh, 1970)
Durham Liber Vitae	*Liber Vitae Ecclesiae Dunelmensis*, ed. J. Stevenson (Surtees Soc., 1841)
ER	*The Exchequer Rolls of Scotland*, ed. J. Stuart *et al.* (Edinburgh, 1878– 1908)
ES	*Early Sources of Scottish History, 500 to 1286*, ed. A. O. Anderson (London, 1922; repr. Stamford, 1990)
ESC	*Early Scottish Charters prior to 1153*, ed. A. C. Lawrie (Glasgow, 1905)
Foedera	*Foedera, Conventiones, Litterae et Cuiuscunque Generis Acta Publica*, ed. T. Rymer (Record Commission edn, 1816–69)
Hakon's Saga	Sturla Thordarsson, *Hakon's Saga*, in *The Saga of Hacon and a Fragment of the Saga of Magnus with appendices*, trans. G. W. Dasent (Rolls Ser., *Icelandic Sagas*, iv, 1894).
HP	*Highland Papers*, ed. J. R. N. Macphail (SHS, 1914–34)
Inchaffray Chrs.	*Charters, Bulls and Other Documents Relating to the Abbey of Inchaffray*, ed. W. A. Lindsay *et al.* (SHS, 1908)
OPS	C. Innes *et al.* (eds.), *Origines Parochiales Scotiae: The Antiquities, Ecclesiastical and Territorial, of the Parishes of Scotland* (Bannatyne Club, 1851–5)
Paisley Reg.	*Registrum Monasterii de Passelet*, ed. C. Innes (Maitland Club, 1832)

Palgrave, *Docs.* *Hist. Scot.*	*Documents and Records illustrating the History of Scotland*, ed. F. Palgrave (London, 1837)
PSAS	*Proceedings of the Society of Antiquaries of Scotland* (1851–)
RCAHMS	*Royal Commission on the Ancient and Historical Monuments and Constructions of Scotland*
RMS	*Registrum Magni Sigilii Regum Scotorum*, ed. J. M. Thomson *et al.* (Edinburgh, 1882–1914)
Rot. Scot.	*Rotuli Scotiae in Turri Londinensi et in Domo Capitulari Westmonasteriensi Asservati*, ed. D. Macpherson *et al.* (London, 1814–19)
RRS, i	*Regesta Regum Scottorum*, vol. I: *The Acts of Malcolm IV, King of Scots, 1153–1165*, ed. G. W. S. Barrow (Edinburgh, 1960)
RRS, ii	*Regesta Regum Scottorum*, vol. II: *The Acts of William I, King of Scots, 1165–1214*, ed. G. W. S. Barrow (Edinburgh, 1971)
RRS, v	*Regesta Regum Scottorum*, vol. V: *The Acts of Robert I, King of Scots, 1306–1329*, ed. A. A. M. Duncan (Edinburgh, 1988)
RRS: Handlist Alexander III	*Regesta Regum Scottorum: Handlist of the Acts of Alexander III, The Guardians, John, 1249–1296*, comp. G. G. Simpson (Edinburgh, 1960)
SAEC	*Scottish Annals from English Chroniclers, 500 to 1286*, ed. A. O. Anderson (London, 1908)
Scot. Stud.	*Scottish Studies*
SHR	*Scottish Historical Review*
SHS	Scottish History Society
SRS	Scottish Record Society
Stevenson, *Documents*	*Documents Illustrative of the History of Scotland, 1286–1306*, ed. J. Stevenson (Edinburgh, 1870)
STS	Scottish Texts Society
TGAS	*Transactions of the Glasgow Archaeological Society*
TGSI	*Transactions of the Gaelic Society of Inverness*
Watt, *Fasti*	D. E. R. Watt, *Fasti Ecclesiae Scoticanae Medii Aevi ad annum 1638: second draft* (SRS, 1969)

Preface

The aim of this book is to shed some light on the western seaboard of Scotland (Argyll, the Hebrides, and the Isle of Man) during a fascinating and formative, but nevertheless obscure, era: the period from the rise of Somerled of Argyll (*c*.1100) to the beginnings of the Lordship of the Isles (1336). It is nearly half a century since anything approaching a main historical survey of the region has been attempted (namely, Colin MacDonald's *History of Argyll*, published in 1950, and the essay by A. A. M. Duncan and A. L. Brown on 'Argyll and the Isles in the earlier Middle Ages', in 1956). Given the advances in scholarship since then, the time seems right for such a volume.

The book has been written with the needs of an ordinary, informed reader in mind, one who does not know much about the history of the western seaboard in the Middle Ages but would like to know more. Although I have utilised references to permit readers to follow up on sources or ideas, I have attempted to keep them to a manageable number, and they are not, for the most part, discursive. I have also quoted translations of medieval texts rather than citing them in the original. The historian of medieval Scotland is fortunate to possess the translations of various sources published by A. O. Anderson in his *Early Sources of Scottish History, 500 to 1286* and *Scottish Annals From English Chroniclers, 500 to 1286*. Many other important sources are available in translation, too, including the *Chronicle of Man*, John of Fordun's *Chronica Gentis Scotorum*, and Walter Bower's *Scotichronicon*. Although these translations are by no means a substitute for reading the medieval sources in the original (which I have endeavoured to do, and, when necessary, have adapted the translations accordingly), I have chosen to reference them wherever possible since they are available in standard editions that are readily accessible. For documents which are not available in translation I have provided my own summaries or translations. The one exception to these guidelines is Barbour's *Bruce*, where I have followed the normal practice of quoting the original Scots.

On the matter of names, I have agonised greatly over whether to utilise Gaelic versions or their modern English (Scottish) equivalents. In the end I have settled upon the latter, partly in order to be consistent with other standard works; and partly because, by the middle of the thirteenth century at least, it is by no means certain how the west-coast bearers of names such as Alexander or John would have rendered them. As a general guide I have followed versions of Scottish names given in A. A. M. Duncan's *Scotland: The Making of the Kingdom*, while Irish names have been modelled on the forms used in the *New History of Ireland*. I use the designation 'MacSorleys' to refer collectively to the descendants of Somerled. From about the second half of the thirteenth century I utilise either the surnames (MacDonald, MacDougall, MacRuairi) or the territorial designations (of Islay, of Argyll, of Garmoran) to distinguish the different branches descended from Donald, Dugald, and Ruairi respectively. Since the spelling of names prefixed by *Mac* (son) is so variable, it is difficult to be entirely consistent. I have endeavoured to use a capital letter for all forms following the prefix, whether a patronymic or a surname.

This work has benefited from the help and encouragement of many people. Archie Duncan read the entire book in manuscript form, saved me from many errors, and gave me much to consider. Ted Cowan has endured many discussions about the Western Highlands over the years, and I appreciate his willingness to share his knowledge with me. I am also grateful to Seán Duffy, who read and offered advice on parts of the manuscript relating to the Isle of Man. I have corresponded with John Bannerman, Rees Davies, Sandy Grant, David Sellar, Brendan Smith, and Keith Stringer, and their advice as well as their printed works have greatly influenced the present study. I must also thank the Manx National Trust, which provided me with information on Peel. My colleagues at Trent University have provided further guidance and support, and I am particularly grateful to David Page and Sarah Keefer. Finally, I would like to record my debt to two former instructors, John Gilchrist of Trent University, and John Trueman of McMaster University, who introduced me to the study of medieval history. Although all these people must share in whatever merits the work possesses, they are by no means to be held accountable for whatever errors remain.

Sharon Bosnell, Inge Lovell, and Anita Erschen at the Interlibrary Loans Office of the Bata Library at Trent University obtained many of the sources used in the preparation of this book; without their efforts it would have been much longer in the making. Donna Beaudin, Tracey O'Donnell and Lynn McIntyre at the University of Guelph xeroxed documents for me at short notice and never once complained. Cory Richards read early drafts of several chapters, while Karen Park and Tammy McGregor helped with the proofs, and they have saved me from some potentially embarrassing blunders.

A year as a resident don at Otonabee College, Trent University, in 1995–6 provided a comfortable environment in which to work, and I would like to thank the college head, administration, and my fellow dons for helping to create this setting. My secretary, Shirley Alguire, deserves special thanks for tolerating my demands on her time. The enthusiasm and interest of my students and former students for the topic has been a great inspiration to complete this book. I hope that it will answer their questions, and perhaps prompt them to ask some more.

I am very grateful to Alison Grant for typesetting the book and for drawing the map; and I am also grateful for her and Sandy Grant's advice on content and style. Their hospitality, too, was most gracious! Thanks are also due to John and Val Tuckwell at Tuckwell Press, who have been a pleasure to work with and who were instrumental in securing the illustrations.

I have received some funding toward research from Trent University's professional development fund for part-time instructors, and I am grateful to Historic Scotland, the National Monuments Record, and the Conference of Scottish Medievalists for permission to reproduce copyrighted material. Thanks also to the Communications Office at Trent University for preparing the genealogical tables.

My two cats, Islay and Erin, have also had a hand (or a paw) in the production of this book. Without their diligent assistance at the keyboard, it might have been completed a few months earlier.

Without question, however, my greatest debt is to friends and family. Bill and Laura MacGregor, Shane Aitken, and Heather Hall braved midges, mist, and mud to visit many of the sites with the author. Jacqueline Buchanan has helped with many facets of the work, but without her unwavering encouragement at a critical juncture it might have taken much longer to complete. My mother and father, Norma and Hugh, and my brother, Jeffrey, have always provided support, encouragement, and understanding for my choice of careers, and I hope that this volume offers some compensation. Finally, Margaret McDonald lived with this project for several years, and it owes much to her friendship, patience, and many sacrifices on my behalf. These people better than any others know how much of my time has been spent in the past at the expense of the present, and I am certain they would agree with Cicero: *Vulgo enim dicitur: Iucundi acti labores.*

R. A. McD.

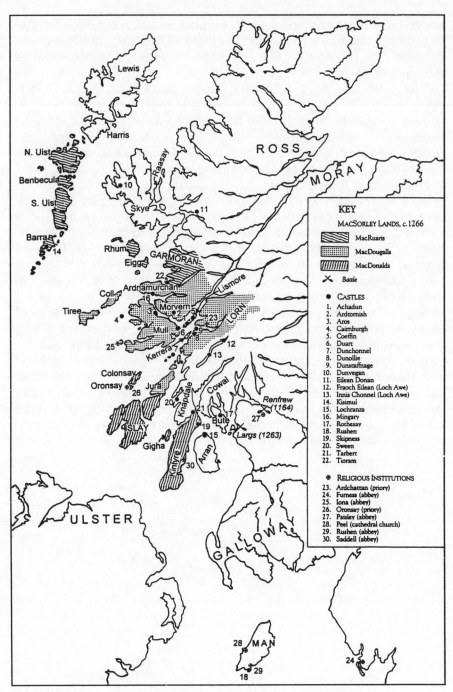

Map: *The Western Seaboard in the Central Middle Ages*

Introduction

> There are also many islands, both great and small, at the back of
> Scotia, between it and Ireland, separated from the Orkneys by a
> great intervening firth ... These ... islands, as well as many others,
> lie scattered about in the sea, on the western confines of Scotia,
> between it and Ireland; and some of these, to the north-west, look
> out upon the boundless ocean; whence it is believed that the
> inhabited world is bounded by this region of Scotia [John of
> Fordun, c.1385].[1]

Dr Samuel Johnson, perhaps one of the more eminent travellers to the
western islands of Scotland (between Donald Monro in the mid-sixteenth
century and the present-day tourists who board Caledonian MacBrayne
ferries for the Isles at Oban pier), remarked of the Hebrides that, 'Of
these islands it must be confessed, that they have not many allurements,
but to the mere lover of naked nature.'[2] No one would dispute that the
Hebrides are rich in natural beauty, but to these attractions Dr Johnson
could easily have added historical ones. Indeed, despite his remarks,
Johnson and his travelling companion, James Boswell, were quick to
appreciate the historical monuments they observed during their famous
tour in 1773. At Iona, a destination that Boswell, 'had thought on with
veneration' as long as he could remember, the two friends embraced
cordially upon arrival. Dr Johnson said:

> We are now treading that illustrious island, which was once the
> luminary of the Caledonian regions, whence savage clans and
> roving barbarians derived the benefits of knowledge, and the
> blessings of religion. To abstract the mind from all local emotion
> would be impossible, if it were endeavoured, and would be foolish if
> it were possible ... That man is little to be envied, whose patriotism
> would not gain force upon the plain of Marathon, or whose piety
> would not grow warmer upon the ruins of Iona![3]

Although few today might subscribe to his interpretations of the early
medieval inhabitants of what would become Scotland, Johnson, along
with Boswell, was clearly quite well aware of the historical significance of
the ruins that lay before him. While staying with MacLean of Lochbuie

---

1 *Chron. Fordun*, i, pp. 43–4; ii, pp. 39–40.
2 Samuel Johnson, *A Journey to the Western Islands of Scotland*, ed. P. Levi (Harmondsworth, 1984; with Boswell, *Tour to the Hebrides*), p. 146. An interesting study of
  travellers to the Hebrides is E. Bray, *The Discovery of the Hebrides: Voyagers to the Western
  Isles, 1745–1883* (London and Glasgow, 1986).
3 James Boswell, *The Journal of a Tour to the Hebrides*, ed. P. Levi (Harmondsworth,
  1984; with Johnson, *Journey to the Western Isles*), pp. 365–6.

on the Isle of Mull, Johnson pondered the castles of the Hebrides and their sea-girt locations, unable to discern the purposes for which they had been constructed, but impressed by them nonetheless. And, while enjoying the hospitality of the English-bred and educated chieftain Sir Alexander MacDonald, at Armadale in Skye, Dr Johnson nevertheless seems to have taken great pleasure in rebuking Sir Alexander for his abandonment of his Celtic heritage: 'Were I in your place, sir, in seven years I would make this an independent island. I would roast oxen whole, and hang out a flag as a signal to the Macdonalds to come and get beef and whisky.'[4] Unknowingly, perhaps, Johnson had harkened back to an age when not only Skye, but the rest of the western seaboard, too, could rightfully be called an independent kingdom of the Isles. It is this kingdom of the Isles that forms the focus of the present book.

The book deals with the history of the western seaboard of Scotland – the Hebrides, Argyll, and the Isle of Man – in an era which was formative, yet which remains obscure: that of the central Middle Ages, between *c.*1100 and *c.*1336. The period possesses more than just an artificial unity. From about 1100, a powerful new dynasty, that of Somerled MacGillebrigte, rose to power in the western seaboard, and wrested control over many of the islands from the Scandinavian rulers of Man. Somerled and his descendants, the MacDonalds, MacDougalls, MacRuairis, and others, would hold power in the West in one guise or another until 1493, when the MacDonald Lordship of the Isles was finally forfeited to the Scottish Crown. Yet within the continuum of dominance by the MacSorleys (as the descendants of Somerled can collectively be known), 1336 marks a significant development. In that year, John of Islay, a great-great-great grandson of Somerled, first utilised the style *dominus Insularum* or Lord of the Isles, and this date is consequently taken by historians as marking the beginning of the Lordship of the Isles. The date 1336, therefore, serves as a convenient terminal point for the present study, although it would be misleading to view the central Middle Ages as entirely disconnected from what preceded and what followed. The origins and ancestry of Somerled were rooted in the Scandinavian period, and, similarly, the MacDonald Lords of the Isles in the fourteenth and fifteenth centuries traced their ancestry from Somerled.

It is perhaps worth while asking why the central Middle Ages should be singled out for special attention, particularly since the period is often addressed within the context of Scandinavian or Viking Scotland.[5] Quite simply, by comparison both with what precedes it (Viking-Age Scotland), and with what follows it (the Lordship of the Isles), this era remains

---

[4] Ibid., p. 242.
[5] See, e.g., A. Ritchie, *Viking Age Scotland* (London, 1993), chap. 7.

poorly known and relatively obscure.[6] In contrast to Viking-Age Scotland and the Lordship of the Isles, both of which are well served by recent historical works, academic and popular, no comprehensive survey of the western seaboard in the central Middle Ages has, to my knowledge, ever been written. This book, therefore, will fill an obvious *lacuna* in Scottish historiography.

That said, there is quite a considerable amount of secondary literature to be taken into account. Many aspects of the history of the Isles in this era have been discussed in more general studies, by scholars such as Donald Gregory (in the introduction to his *Western Highlands and Isles of Scotland, 1493–1625*),[7] W. F. Skene (in his groundbreaking *Celtic Scotland* and *Highlanders of Scotland*),[8] E. W. Robertson, D. Mitchell, R. L. Bremner, W. C. MacKenzie,[9] C. MacDonald (whose *History of Argyll* is still very useful),[10] and, most recently, Geoffrey Barrow (in a chapter in his *Kingship and Unity*).[11] Moreover, specialist articles on various aspects of the history of the region, including architecture, archaeology, and genealogy, are continually appearing in both academic and popular journals. One article that especially deserves to be singled out is that of A. A. M. Duncan and A. L. Brown, on 'Argyll and the Isles in the earlier Middle Ages',[12] perhaps the most comprehensive and scholarly survey of the region during the period in question yet published.

This book deals with three major, and closely interrelated, themes: first, the existence of the Isles and coastal mainland of the region as a Kingdom of the Isles between 1100 and 1265; second, the rulers of the region, Somerled and his descendants, the MacSorleys; and third, the multiple and often very complex relations among the Hebrides, Scotland, Ireland, England, and – to 1266 – Norway. These three themes lend a certain unity to the region and to the time period in question, but there are other subthemes that also guide the present study: the development of the Church and monasticism, and the nature of the society of the western seaboard during the central Middle Ages. In both cases the fragmentary surviving evidence throws only fitful light upon these

6 See, e.g., I. Armit, *The Archaeology of Skye and the Western Isles* (Edinburgh, 1996), pp. 205–7.
7 Donald Gregory, *History of the Western Highlands and Isles of Scotland from AD 1493 to AD 1625* (2nd edn, London and Glasgow, 1881).
8 W. F. Skene, *Celtic Scotland: A History of Ancient Alban* (Edinburgh, 1876–80); W. F. Skene, *The Highlanders of Scotland*, ed. A. MacBain (Stirling, 1902).
9 E. W. Robertson, *Scotland under her Early Kings* (Edinburgh, 1862); D. Mitchell, *A Popular History of the Highlands and Gaelic Scotland from the Earliest Times to the 'Forty-Five* (Paisley, 1900); R. L. Bremner, *The Norsemen in Alban* (Glasgow, 1923; now hopelessly out of date in its interpretations); and W. C. MacKenzie, *The Highlands and Isles of Scotland: A Historical Survey* (Edinburgh and London, 1937).
10 C. MacDonald, *The History of Argyll* (Glasgow, 1950).
11 G. W. S. Barrow, *Kingship and Unity: Scotland, 1000–1306* (London, 1981), chap. 6.
12 A. A. M. Duncan and A. L. Brown, 'Argyll and the Isles in the earlier Middle Ages', *PSAS*, xc (1956–7). See also the remarkable recent review article by J. E. A. Dawson, 'Argyll: the enduring heartland', *SHR*, lxxiv (1995).

themes, but some attempt to squeeze the sources for information must nevertheless be made. For this purpose, a third subtheme is particularly important: the monuments of the western seaboard, especially the castles, monasteries, and parish churches and chapels. These physical remains are often held to be the preserve of the archaeologist and of the architectural historian, but as historical sources they have much to tell us; and they are also among the most visible (and often the most spectacular) of the legacies left behind by the society of the western seaboard. Indeed, for the modern visitor to the Western Isles, these monuments prompt fundamental questions: who built them, and why? It is my hope that this book will provide answers to those questions, and set those answers within a broader historical context.

Historical Sources and Historical Perspectives

With the central Middle Ages, historians of the western seaboard encounter a rather surprising paradox in the contemporary sources. As we move from the early medieval period into that from the eleventh to the fourteenth centuries, there is a gradual shift in both the quantity and the provenance of our historical documentation. Between about 500 and 1100, most of the surviving source material actually seems to display a bias towards the Highlands.[13] Up to the mid-eighth century, the Irish Annals, for example, have been shown to contain material derived from an Iona chronicle, now lost; the lives of saints like Columba are rich in Highland material; and there is even the remarkable administrative document known as the *Senchus fer nAlban* ('History of the men of Alba'), the core of which dates from the mid-seventh century and pertains to the western seaboard. By contrast, the Highlands and Islands, in the period between 1100 and 1300, are poorly served with historical documentation, at a time when the emphasis in the sources shifts to the Lowland regions. Thus, just as we are able, almost for the first time, to construct a relatively comprehensive history of the Scottish kingdom itself, the peripheral regions of the kingdom – that is to say, most of the Highlands and Islands – begin to fade into the background. Not only does the interest of the historian shift to the better-documented Lowland regions, but the sources for the history of the western Highlands become less amenable to analysis. It is no exaggeration to say that the twelfth and thirteenth centuries are among the most obscure in the whole history of the Highlands.

Our knowledge of the western seaboard in the central Middle Ages must be gleaned from a diverse, patchy, and often confusing array of chronicles, annals, sagas, charters, poems, genealogies, and clan histories of Scottish, Irish, Norse, Manx, and English provenance, written in Latin,

[13] G. W. S. Barrow, 'The sources for the history of the Highlands in the Middle Ages', in L. MacLean (ed.), *The Middle Ages in the Highlands* (Inverness, 1981), pp. 11–23.

Gaelic, Scots, and Norse languages. Not all are contemporary with the events that they purport to describe, nor are they of equal authority; and the use of sagas, genealogies, and clan histories is the subject of considerable debate. It will, therefore, be useful to draw a brief sketch of the types of sources that must be utilised in order to reconstruct the history of the western seaboard in the Middle Ages.

There were really only two strictly contemporary Scottish chronicles for the twelfth and thirteenth centuries: the Chronicles of Melrose and Holyrood. Both were composed in monasteries at the heart of the Scottish kingdom, by foreign elements in Scottish society, and neither took much interest in events on the kingdom's periphery. Neither was written specifically as a history of Scotland, nor even as history in general, but were records of recent significant events; both were more concerned with religious, than secular, affairs; and both exhibit the usual characteristics of medieval annals: a lack of context for events; a lack of explanation; and a lack of interest in causation. The mid-thirteenth-century *Chronicle of Man*, composed, it is thought, at the Cistercian monastery of Rushen on the Isle of Man, is the closest that we come to an indigenous account from the Isles during our period. But, important as it is, it is also, at best, a confused source; its chronology has been called into question on many occasions, and, as is pointed out in Chapter 2, it tends to be hostile toward the descendants of Somerled. Sources of Irish, Norse, and English provenance are also crucial to our investigation. Of the Irish sources, the most important are without doubt the Irish Annals, many of which, by the twelfth century, were contemporary with the events they described. They share the drawback with the Scottish and Manx chronicles that much of the information they record is incidental and external, but they have the attribute of viewing Scottish society, especially the periphery, from a Gaelic perspective, and they also record island events. The Norse evidence, consisting largely of two sagas, is based upon oral tradition written down after 1200. The *Orkneyinga Saga*, which takes as its focus the powerful Orkney earldom between its formation and the twelfth century, is important because the Northern Isles were closely connected with the Hebrides and Argyll during our period, and, accordingly, this saga provides valuable information on events in the Isles. For the momentous events of the thirteenth century in the Hebrides, Sturla Thordarsson's *Hakon's Saga* is a valuable, although not unbiased, account. It throws much light on the thirteenth-century descendants of Somerled and their dilemma of divided allegiances, and it has the added advantage that it seems to sympathise with the Hebrideans; what is not clear is the saga's historicity.[14] English writers, like Ailred of Rievaulx (d. 1166) and Matthew

[14] See E. J. Cowan, 'Norwegian sunset – Scottish dawn: Hakon IV and Alexander III', in N. H. Reid (ed.), *Scotland in the Reign of Alexander III, 1249–1286* (Edinburgh, 1990), pp. 103–10, which addresses the problem of the document's historical value.

Paris (c.1200–59), also shed some light on the Isles in the central Middle Ages, but most of the information they record is incidental and often without context, and they generally remain unsympathetic because they regarded Scotland and its inhabitants – particularly those of the remote regions like Argyll and Galloway – as backward and barbaric.[15]

Another category of source material is the later medieval and post-medieval. This embraces non-contemporary Scottish chroniclers such as John of Fordun (c.1380), Andrew of Wyntoun, Prior of Loch Leven (c.1415), and Walter Bower, Abbot of Inchcolm (c.1445), whose works are also crucial to our understanding of the western seaboard. Our knowledge of the central Middle Ages is not so great that we can ignore these writers altogether, especially since they sometimes provide the only account of events otherwise unrecorded, and they undoubtedly had access to sources of information that are now lost. While it would be wrong to accept their statements wholly on trust, we should not dismiss them out of hand, either, and often their version of events can be buttressed by other circumstantial evidence provided by charters or architecture. Finally, although far removed from the events they purport to describe, the late medieval and post-medieval genealogical information and the clan histories, discussed at greater length in Chapter 2, are increasingly regarded as preserving fossilised oral tradition, and these sources often illuminate regions and problems which are otherwise virtually unrecorded.

Two other types of evidence must be mentioned briefly: charters and non-documentary sources. From the late eleventh century, the use of written titles to land has left many charters, the evidence of which greatly enhances the extant narrative sources. A charter was a 'formal and legal record of a grant of land and rights'; it is not the conveyance itself, but rather a record of this, drawn up for posterity.[16] The earliest Scottish charters, recording grants of land to Durham Cathedral, date from the very end of the eleventh century, but before long the use of the charter was increasingly common in Scotland. Nevertheless, for the twelfth and thirteenth centuries, the geographical distribution of this material, like the narratives, is heavily biased towards the Lowland regions, and documentation relating to the margins remains scarce. The earliest charters relating to the western seaboard date from the middle of the thirteenth century, and even though King Robert I (1306–29) is known to have made many grants of land that pertained to the West,

---

[15] Although it is only fair to point out that Matthew Paris takes a particularly sympathetic stance toward Ewen of Argyll; see below, chaps. 3–4.

[16] B. Webster, *Scotland from the Eleventh Century to 1603* (London, 1975), p. 70. On this subject, see also G. W. S. Barrow, 'The Scots Charter', in *Scotland and Its Neighbours in the Middle Ages* (London, 1992), chap. 5.

only a few survive in full, though others are known in outline form from an index of now-lost materials.

Finally, there is the unwritten evidence: the physical remains of the past, and the very structure of the landscape itself. 'Documents and texts by themselves are not enough', writes Bruce Webster. 'Before we can understand them we need to use our imagination, our eyes and our feet, tramping the countryside, to learn about the land itself, and about the remains of the past that lie on every side.'[17] Although it is difficult to visit the remains of a medieval monastery, or castle, without being influenced either by the Romantic movement of the eighteenth century or by the finely trimmed lawns and didactic presentations of the present-day heritage industry, there is a considerable corpus of archaeological, architectural, and topographical evidence which enhances our know-ledge of the period in question. Indeed, Argyll and the Isles are rich in historical monuments.[18] Moreover, the study of place-names also yields much fruitful evidence. But medieval stone walls and place-names carry no dates, and the historian seizes uncritically upon the conclusions of archaeologists or toponymists at his peril; they must be used with caution and a certain amount of understanding – especially where all-important questions of dating are concerned.[19]

It is, perhaps, worth while at this point considering some of the limitations of the work, which have been imposed largely by the nature of the source material. The book is primarily about the politics of the western seaboard in the central Middle Ages, the ruling families of the West, their foreign and domestic relations, battles, and treaties. If the emphasis throughout is on the elite of the islands, it is a focus imposed by the sources; we simply do not possess information about those who worked the soil, raised the animals, and fished in the depths of the sea-lochs, to write with knowledge about their way of life. Medieval chroniclers and annalists said nothing of the daily rhythms of life, and the charter and material evidence is too sparse to shed much light on this otherwise dark corner of the history of the Isles in the central Middle Ages.

Another difficulty, and one that may well surprise the reader more familiar with the modern era, is the fact that our chronology is often, of necessity, very vague. We do not always know the exact year in which an

---

[17] Webster, *Scotland from the Eleventh Century*, p. 95.

[18] Dawson, 'Argyll: the enduring heartland', *passim.*

[19] On the Scottish sources in general, see Webster, *Scotland from the Eleventh Century*; on the English sources, see A. Gransden, *Historical Writing in England, c.550 to c.1307* (London, 1974); and on *Hakon's Saga*, see M. Magnusson, *Hakon the Old – Hakon Who?* (Largs and District Historical Soc., 1982), and H. Pálsson, 'Hakonar Saga: portrait of a king', in *Orkney Miscellany: King Hakon Commemorative Number* 5 (1973), pp. 49–56. A good general discussion of medieval historical writing is B. Smalley, *Historians in the Middle Ages* (London, 1974).

event transpired: the expedition of Alexander II to Argyll, for example, may have taken place in 1221 or 1222, or there may have been a campaign in each year; such is the state of the source material that we cannot be sure. The difficulties with chronology will also become apparent in discussing the lives and careers of the MacSorleys. Lacking records of their birth and, in many cases, of their death, their dates are most often best expressed by an approximate range in which they were active – a *'floruit'*. The death of Ranald, the son of Somerled, for instance, can be placed with certainty only in the first quarter of the thirteenth century; that of his son, Donald, the ancestor of the Clan Donald, is similarly uncertain. The MacSorleys, then, flit in and out of historical documentation like moths around a flame; many of them remain shadowy figures about whom relatively little can ever be known. In short, the reconstruction of the history of the Western Isles in the central Middle Ages requires, 'a creative historical imagination, as well as a determination to use every scrap of evidence that exists, whatever form it may take'.[20]

If the state of the historical sources is partly responsible for the fact that no full-scale history of the Isles in our period has ever been undertaken, it does not completely explain the lack of a comprehensive study of the western seaboard. Much of the neglect of the Hebrides in the Middle Ages by modern writers stems from the constraints implicit in most modern historical writing: to put it simply, we are too well conditioned to thinking in terms of national history. When the foundations of modern historical writing were laid in the nineteenth century, history was primarily an account of how the great powers of the world had come into being. Such notions sprang, in turn, from Darwinian models of biological evolution, each nation having its own character and destiny, with, consequently, a teleological emphasis upon its development into a nation-state. Scotland, which might be deemed to be an example of an 'unsuccessful' nation-state because of the effects of the Union with England in 1707, nevertheless possesses enough national identity to allow its history to be written in this same tradition. But kingdoms, states, or lordships which did not succeed in becoming European powers, did not warrant study. Thus, they are all too often ignored in the tradition of historical writing.

As a prominent Irish scholar has put it: 'The writing of national history as a genre has had the unfortunate result of obscuring entities once important in their own right that have not survived as nation states or even as geographical units.'[21] This is particularly true apropos the

[20] Webster, *Scotland from the Eleventh Century*, p. 232.
[21] F. J. Byrne, 'The trembling sod: Ireland in 1169,' in A. Cosgrove (ed.), *Medieval Ireland, 1169–1534* (*A New History of Ireland*, vol. II; Oxford, 1987), p. 18. See also the comments of S. Reynolds, *Kingdoms and Communities in Western Europe, 900–1300* (Oxford, 1984), pp. 250–3.

kingdom of the Isles, which, superficially, at least, had a most tumultuous history, and which did not evolve into a nation-state. The deaths of Godred Crovan in 1095 and Somerled in 1164 removed powerful, stabilising elements, and gave way to periods of confusion and turbulence. Following the partition of the kingdom between the sons of Somerled and the Manx kings in 1156 and 1164, there were numerous power struggles between the two sides, which contributed significantly to the tumultuous conditions in the Hebrides. Finally, in 1266, both the Isle of Man and the Hebrides were ceded to Scotland; this fact notwithstanding, Edward I seized control of the strategically important Isle of Man in 1290, and it took the Scots about another twenty-five years to recover it, albeit briefly. In short, for around fifty years in the late thirteenth and early fourteenth centuries, the Isle of Man was little more than a bone poised between the snarling jaws of the two most 'successful' states of medieval Britain: England and Scotland.

The fate of the Isle of Man between 1266 and 1333 neatly exemplifies the fate of the kingdom of the Isles at the hands of modern historians. As rulers on what British historians have come to term the periphery, or margin, of the Scottish kingdom, the descendants of Somerled, as well as their relatives and rivals, the Manx kings, have fallen between the cracks in modern historical writing. Most recent Scottish historical writing, for example, takes as its central theme the 'making of the kingdom' – the development of the Scottish monarchy and the territorial consolidation of the kingdom – and has paid relatively little attention to the peripheral regions. Where these regions are discussed, it is seldom in their own right, but rather in the context of the so-called 'winning of the West,' the process whereby the Hebrides and Argyll in the west, Galloway in the south-west, and Moray in the north were brought under the authority of the Scottish king. Hence, the Hebrides and their rulers, the MacSorleys, are thrust into the mould of nationalistic historical writing, which relegates them to the margins of Scotland and Ireland; they are seldom, if ever, viewed in a maritime context in their own right.[22] Even R. H. Kinvig, in his *History of the Isle of Man*,[23] had surprisingly and disappointingly little to say of Somerled and his descendants, while a more recent biography of King John of England ignores his dealings with the Manx kings in the context of his relations with native rulers of the British Isles.[24] More promising is the current trend towards a holistic British historiography, which is less concerned with old-fashioned nationalist history than with comparative, trans-national and cross-border themes.[25]

22 But see Dawson, 'Argyll: the enduring heartland', esp. p. 78.

23 R. H. Kinvig, *History of the Isle of Man* (2nd edn, Liverpool, 1950).

24 R. V. Turner, *King John* (London, 1994), pp. 135–46.

25 See, e.g., R. Frame, *The Political Development of the British Isles, 1100–1400* (Oxford, 1990); R. R. Davies (ed.), *The British Isles, 1100–1500: Comparisons, Contrasts and Connections* (Edinburgh, 1988); R. R. Davies, *Domination and Conquest: The Experience of*

This approach offers the most potential for lifting the sea-kingdom of the Isles from out of its crack between two national histories, and placing it into its proper setting: that of a maritime, multi-ethnic milieu. In short, the traditional perspectives need to be turned upside down: the periphery should become the core; the core should become the margin. To the MacSorleys and the Manx kings, as well as to others who plied the western seas in their war-galleys, these seaways defined their core; Scotland, Ireland, and England were their periphery.[26]

'A sea-coast inhabited by highlanders': Topography and Geography

The Hebrides stretch in a double archipelago lying parallel to the west coast of Scotland – over 500 islands of varying size and shape, shielding the mainland from the battering of the Atlantic. In total, these islands curve for nearly 250 miles, through three degrees of latitude, from the Mull of Oa in the south to the Butt of Lewis in the north. Most are tiny and uninhabited, but about twenty or thirty larger islands form two main groups: the Outer and Inner Hebrides. The Outer Hebrides – Lewis and Harris, Berneray, the Uists, Benbecula, Barra, and others – lie thirty-five to fifty miles from the mainland, a narrow and compact group stretching for some 130 miles, which, at some point in their distant past, formed a single island. Indeed, they are so closely connected that the whole chain is sometimes referred to as 'the Long Island'. These outer islands overlap for some sixty miles with the inner islands. The Inner Hebrides, generally more scattered and stretching for about 150 miles, lie closer to the coast, and can be divided into three major groups. In the north, Skye with the adjacent islands, including Raasay, Rhum, Eigg, and Muck, is separated from the mainland by part of the Minch, the Inner Sound, Kyleakin, the mouth of Loch Alsh, and the Sound of Sleat. The islands south of Ardnamurchan can be divided into two groups: the Mull group, stretching from Ardnamurchan to the Firth of Lorn, and the Islay group, stretching from the Firth of Lorn to Kintyre. The Mull group includes Mull, Lismore, Kerrera, Iona, Staffa, Ulva, the Treshnish Isles, and Coll and Tiree. The Islay group contains Islay, Jura, Scarba, Gigha, Colonsay and Oronsay. The traditional definition of the Hebrides excludes those islands that lie deeply within the arms of the Scottish mainland, such as the islands of the Firth of Clyde, as well as the Isle of Man. For the purposes of this book, however, these islands will be encompassed by the terms Hebrides or Western

---

Ireland, Scotland and Wales, 1100–1300 (Cambridge, 1990); and, originally, G. W. S. Barrow, *Feudal Britain* (London, 1956).

26 See the stimulating comments of Armit, *Archaeology of Skye and the Western Isles*, pp. 5–6, on 'an island-centred geography'.

Isles; as the following pages will make clear, their history is intricately bound up with that of the rest of the western seaboard.

The Hebrides exhibit a very diverse topography. They range from great 'fangs of rock 600 feet high, like St Kilda, to flat pancakes like Tiree; from close-packed mountains that tower out of the water, like Rhum or Skye, to the low monotonous line of Coll'.[27] Generally speaking, the outer Isles are lower to the sea, hilly and gently rolling (except Harris). Their eastern shores are rocky, or dominated by cliffs and skerries, while the western shores, facing the Atlantic, are often charac-terised by sandy beaches and stretches of meadowland. The inner Isles, on the other hand, share many characteristics with the adjacent mainland: they rise higher from the water, display great peaks and valleys, and often possess long sea inlets. Thus, while Clisham on Harris rises to about 2,600 feet and is the highest hill in the outer Isles, the Cuillins on Skye rise to some 3,200 feet, and Ben More on Mull to 3,170 feet.[28]

During the period covered by this book, the Hebrides were closely connected to the neighbouring region of the Scottish mainland, Argyll. Medieval Argyll was much more extensive than the modern region of the same name; it embraced the whole area from the Mull of Kintyre and the Clyde in the south to Loch Broom and beyond in the north. The seventeenth-century *Book of Clanranald* several times refers to Argyll as encompassing the lands from Dumbarton to Caithness, or from Dingwall to the Mull of Kintyre. This vast and rugged region with its extensive coastline was commonly divided into two areas: North Argyll, the region between Glenelg and Loch Broom, which pertained to Moray and to Ross in the Middle Ages, and South Argyll, stretching from Knoydart to the Mull of Kintyre, known as 'Ergadia que pertinet ad Scociam' ('Argyll which pertains to Scotland');[29] it is the latter region with which this work is principally concerned. The eastern boundary of Argyll was the natural barrier of the mountain range known as Drumalban, the Spine of Britain. The twelfth-century tract *De Situ Albanie* referred to it as 'the mountains which divide Scotia from Argyll', and its use to distinguish the west from the central and eastern regions dates back to the time of St Columba.[30] These mountains cut off the Atlantic coast from the rest of Scotland,[31] and throughout the period covered by this book, travel from

27 W. H. Murray, *The Islands of Western Scotland* (London, 1973), chap. 1, quotation on p. 30; see also W. H. Murray, *The Hebrides* (London, 1966).

28 Murray, *Islands of Western Scotland*, pp. 31–2. See also F. H. Groome, *Ordnance Gazet--teer of Scotland: A Survey of Scottish Topography* (new edn, London, 1895), iii, pp. 253–63.

29 *APS*, i, pp. 372, 447: 'Ergadia que pertinet ad Moraviam'; 'terra Comitis de Ros in Nort Argail'.

30 'De Situ Albanie', in *ES*, i, p. cxvi; see also G. W. S. Barrow, *The Kingdom of the Scots* (London, 1973), p. 365.

31 W. Orr, *Discovering Argyll, Mull and Iona* (Edinburgh, 1990), pp. 1–6, outlines the geography and topography of Argyll. See also G. Ritchie and M. Harman, *Discovering*

Argyll and the Isles by sea to Norway was easier than the overland route, through heavily forested mountains, to the Scottish court at Edinburgh, Perth, or Stirling.

This vast coastal region has been historically divided into several distinct sections: Kintyre and Knapdale, Cowal, Lorn, Ardnamurchan, and Morvern. Kintyre, along with its northern link of Knapdale, forms a long, narrow peninsula jutting south from Crinan for about fifty-five miles to its southern-most extremity, the Mull of Kintyre. Because the sea-loch of West Loch Tarbert penetrates to within a mile of East Loch Tarbert, Kintyre is all but an island, which means that its history is closely linked with that of the western seaboard, rather than with the mainland. Cowal, separated from Knapdale by Loch Fyne, is bounded on the east by Loch Long and the Clyde estuary; it reaches out to embrace the Isle of Bute, which is separated from it by the Kyle of Bute. Despite its proximity to Glasgow, it remains, even today, largely remote and inaccessible, because it is heavily cut into by sea-lochs with steep mountain ridges in between. Lorn, perhaps the best-known region of Argyll, is very extensive; the modern-day territory stretches from Loch Fyne northwards to Loch Leven, and eastward to Rannoch. It is notable for its varied physical features which include a scenic sea-coast, jutting sea-lochs like Crinan, Craignish, or Melfort, and mountains like Ben Cruachan or Buachaille Etive Mor. This was the heart of the Mac-Dougall, and later the Campbell, lordships, and it is liberally dotted with historic monuments. Finally, there is the Ardnamurchan–Morvern region, a large, detached, and very scenic territory on the west side of Loch Linnhe. It is a roughly triangular-shaped peninsula that is nearly bisected by Loch Sunart, which separates Ardnamurchan from Morvern.[32] Remote and inaccessible by automobile even today, the sea-girt castles which helped to define and defend this region are sufficient reminder that the highway of the seas helped integrate even Ardnamurchan and Morvern into the kingdom of the Isles. It seems clear that, when people of the Middle Ages thought of Argyll and Kintyre, they tended to associate them with the Isles rather than with the Scottish mainland: Matthew Paris's map of Britain, c.1250, labels Argyll 'a sea-coast inhabited by highlanders'.[33] In geo-political terms, then, mainland Argyll belonged not to the heart of the Scottish kingdom, but rather to the maritime world of the western seaboard from the eleventh to the late thirteenth century – a theme to which we shall return shortly.

Medieval writers were surprisingly well informed about the geography and topography of the western seaboard of Scotland. Perhaps the most

---

Scotland's Heritage: Argyll and the Western Isles (rev. edn, Edinburgh, 1990), pp. 9–15; N. Tranter, *Argyll and Bute* (London, 1977), esp. pp. 13–19; and Groome, *Ordnance Gazetteer of Scotland*, i, pp. 69–71.

[32] On these regions see Tranter, *Argyll and Bute*, pp. 15–19.

[33] Barrow, *Kingdom of the Scots*, p. 365.

definitive of the late medieval works of topography was written in 1549, when the newly appointed archdeacon of the Isles, Donald Monro, travelled through many of the islands and subsequently wrote his comprehensive topographical essay on the western islands: the *Description of the Western Isles of Scotland*. Beginning with the Isle of Man in the south, and concluding with Rona in the north, Monro described or mentioned some 250 islands in total, only a small handful of which remain to be identified today.[34] Despite the value of his account, Monro was not, however, the first to compile a description of the islands, and it is worthwhile considering exactly what medieval people knew of the lands and seas of the western seaboard.

Despite their position on the periphery of the Scottish kingdom and, indeed, on the margins of Europe in general, the western islands were not *terra incognita*. Robert of Torigni, the abbot of Mont St Michel in Normandy (1154–86), and the author of a chronicle for the years 1112–86, noted that the kingdom and the bishopric of the Isles contained thirty-two (unnamed) islands; he may have obtained his information directly from a bishop of the Isles. Reginald of Durham, who compiled an account of the miracles of St Cuthbert in the mid-twelfth century, also included a brief description of the Isles, which began with Uist and Lewis, included Coll, Tiree, Colonsay, and Skye, and ended with Islay, Iona, and Mull. It is an intriguing question as to how a monk of Durham should come to possess detailed information on the Western Isles; one possible solution is that such knowledge was obtained from the rulers of the West, the MacSorleys themselves, since in 1175, Dugald, the son of Somerled, and his clerk visited Durham and made a gift to St Cuthbert.[35]

By the early thirteenth century, we possess both further literary descriptions and topographical information contained, in official documents. Gerald of Wales (d. *c.*1220) included a brief passage on the northern and western islands in his *Topography of Ireland*:

> In the Northern Ocean beyond Ulster and Galloway are a number of islands, namely the Orcades and the Incades, and many others. Almost all of them are held by, and are subject to the Norwegians. For even though they lie nearer to other regions, nevertheless the Norwegians, who keep their eyes ever on the ocean, lead, above any other people a piratical life. Consequently, all their expeditions and wars are decided by naval engagements ...
> Among the smaller islands there is one of fair size that is now

---

[34] R. W. Munro (ed.), *Monro's Western Isles of Scotland and Genealogies of the Clans, 1549* (Edinburgh, 1961).

[35] 'Robert of Torigni', in *SAEC*, p. 245; *Reginaldi monachi Dunelmensis libellus de admirandis beati Cuthberti virtutibus*, ed. J. Raine (Surtees Soc., 1835), p. 251. See also Barrow, 'Sources for the history of the Highlands', pp. 12–13.

called the Isle of Man ... They say that it is equidistant from the
north of Ireland and Britain.[36]

A papal privilege for Iona Abbey, in 1203, provides evidence of some
topographical knowledge; it listed possessions in the Outer Isles, Mull,
Iona, Colonsay, Oronsay, Canna, and other individual churches and
lands. It was probably drawn up from written documents, perhaps
charters given by Ranald, the son of Somerled, and other benefactors of
the monastery. There is also a papal bull for the bishops of the Isles,
purporting to have been issued in 1231 but in fact most likely a forgery
of between about 1340 and 1505. It contains a fairly comprehensive
listing of the islands, from Bute and Arran to Skye; the last six names on
the list are difficult to read and identify, but they might correspond to
the 'Long Island' with its division into Barra, Uist, Harris and Lewis.[37]
Finally, the treaty of Perth (1266) which transferred the Western Isles to
Scotland from Norway, referred to 'Man with the rest of the Sudreys
and all other islands on the west and south of the great sea.'[38] This can
hardly be characterised as a detailed topographical description of the
Hebrides, but the cession of the Western Isles to Scotland paved the way
for the Scottish government to acquire a sound knowledge of the
western seaboard by the late thirteenth century. Thus, when the first
Parliament of John Balliol in 1293 created three new sheriffdoms in the
West, it was possible to outline in some detail the territorial divisions of
these sheriffdoms, and to name the principal landholders in each.[39]

By the fourteenth and fifteenth centuries the integration of the
western seaboard into the Scottish kingdom meant that very detailed
and comprehensive topographical knowledge was available. John of
Fordun (c.1380), who began his chronicle with a portrait of the land and
peoples of Britain, included a description of the islands of western
Scotland. This represents the earliest such description in a Scottish
source. 'There are also many islands', he wrote, 'both great and small, at
the back of Scotia, between it and Ireland, separated from the Orkneys
by a great intervening firth.' Beginning with the Isle of Man in the
south, Fordun then worked his way northwards through the islands,
listing forty-five of them, including Arran, Bute, Islay, Colonsay, Jura,
Mull, Iona, Kerrera, Lismore, Coll and Tiree, Barra, Uist, Rhum, Skye,
Lewis and St Kilda. He then concluded with the comment that

---

[36] Gerald of Wales, *The History and Topography of Ireland*, trans. J. J. O'Meara
(Harmondsworth, 1951; rev. edn, 1982), pp. 65–7.

[37] *Diplom. Norv.*, vii, pp. 4–5 (1203 Iona privilege); R. L. Poole, 'The Scottish islands in
the diocese of Sodor', *SHR*, viii (1911), pp. 258–63 (1231 papal bull); see also
W. W. Scott, 'John of Fordun's description of the Western Isles', *Scot. Stud.*, xxiii
(1979), pp. 1–13; and B. R. S. Megaw, 'Norseman and native in the Kingdom of the
Isles: a re-assessment of the Manx evidence', *Scot. Stud.*, xx (1976), pp. 1–44, esp. 29–34.

[38] *APS*, i, pp. 420–1; trans. in Donaldson, *Scot. Hist. Docs.*, pp. 34–6. See also chap. 4.

[39] *APS*, i, p. 447; see below, chap. 5 for further discussion.

The above-mentioned islands, as well as many others, lie scattered about in the sea, on the western confines of Scotia, between it and Ireland; and some of these, to the north-west, look out upon the boundless ocean; whence it is believed that the inhabited world is bounded by this region of Scotia.[40]

Fordun's list of islands has been called an 'elaborate essay in topography',[41] but the source of his information is not clear. The suggestion that Fordun had written his description after visiting the islands is not now in favour; a more recent explanation is that the chapter was based upon the alleged papal bull of 1231 discussed above, of which Fordun might have obtained a copy. But a careful examination of Fordun's description of the Isles, its attention to secular sites, and its relative ignorance of ecclesiastical ones, has led to the conclusion that his source was not of Manx or Iona provenance, but rather an informant in, or close to, royal circles of the late fourteenth century.[42] The fifteenth-century chronicler Walter Bower, Abbot of Inchcolm, incorporated much of Fordun's material in the early books of his *Scotichronicon*, including the description of the Western Isles. But Bower also made many small additions to Fordun's topographical sketch, revealing what his modern editor calls 'an unexpected knowledge of the west coast';[43] this is especially true when Bower discussed Scotland's 'famous lochs and very broad stretches of water containing a large number of islands ...'[44]

Bower's discussion of the famous lochs of Scotland returns us to the essentially maritime context of the region; just as the sea dominated the topography of the region, so too did it dictate the politics. There is perhaps no more vivid illustration of this theme than the events of 1098, when King Magnus Barelegs of Norway sailed to the west to exact tribute from the troubled Kingdom of Man and the Isles. In the course of his expedition, he came to an agreement with the king of Scots, whereby Magnus should be allowed to have 'the islands off the west coast which were separated by water navigable by a ship with the rudder set'. The *Orkneyinga Saga*, which describes this agreement, goes on to relate how, when King Magnus reached the Kintyre peninsula, 'he had a skiff hauled across the narrow neck of land at Tarbert, with himself sitting at the helm, and this is how he won the whole peninsula'.[45] Whether the feat was historical or not, it is clear that Norwegian claims to Kintyre

40 *Chron. Fordun*, i, pp. 43–4; ii, pp. 39–40.
41 Barrow, 'Sources for the history of the Highlands', p. 12.
42 Scott, 'John of Fordun's description of the Western Isles', *passim*.
43 *Chron. Bower*, i, pp. 187–91, 343–51; editor's quotation on p. 344. For further examples of medieval knowledge of the Highlands, see Barrow, *Kingdom of the Scots*, pp. 370–3.
44 *Chron. Bower*, i, p. 191.
45 *Orkneyinga Saga: The History of the Earls of Orkney*, trans. H. Pálsson and P. Edwards (Harmondsworth, 1978), cap. 41.

never seem to have been recognised. But what is really important is that the whole arrangement, which attempted to distinguish between mainland and insular territory, was quite impractical, particularly in a region of Scotland where it is difficult to tell if land is insular or mainland. As Barbara Crawford has remarked, 'the saga tale of King Magnus' attempts to include Kintyre in his lot no doubt reflects a realisation that to separate Kintyre from the islands to which it is linked by water made no sense in politico-geographical terms'.[46]

Whether the feat of Magnus Barelegs at Tarbert in 1098 was historical or not – and some historians have doubted its authenticity – it nevertheless demonstrates how the sea acted as the unifying factor between mainland Argyll and the islands. Indeed, the western seaboard of Scotland was part of a single cultural zone during the central Middle Ages; the basis of this culture was its maritime orientation, and it was the highway of the western seas that lent unity to the kingdom of the Isles. Some of the most remarkable geographical features of Argyll and the Hebrides are the deep sea-lochs and inlets stretching far inland. Notable sea-lochs include Loch Sunart, which penetrates eastward between Ardnamurchan and Morvern. The Sound of Mull separates Morvern from Mull, and from it Loch Aline branches north-eastward. Loch Linnhe stretches north-east from the south-eastern end of the Sound of Mull, and separates Morvern from Appin. From the junction of the Sound of Mull and Loch Linnhe, the Sound of Lorn reaches southward, separating Mull from Lorn, and embracing Kerrera, while Loch Etive branches off to the east. Loch Awe, in the heart of Lorn, was described by Bower as 'twenty-four miles long, where there are three castles'. From the southern reaches of the Sound of Lorn, the Sound of Jura opens; Loch Craignish and Loch Crinan run off to the north-north-east and the east-south-east respectively. The Sound of Jura separates Knapdale from Islay and Jura, and is joined on its lower part by three virtually parallel Lochs: Sween, Caolisport, and West Loch Tarbert. On the other side of Kintyre, the Firth of Clyde at its widest extent, separates the southern part of Kintyre from Ayrshire, while Kilbrannan Sound, an arm of the Firth of Clyde, separates Arran from Kintyre. Loch Fyne, a continuation to the north of Kilbrannan Sound, penetrates the mainland deeply, first in a north-north-westerly direction and then north-north-east; it separates Cowal from Kintyre, Knapdale, and Lorn, and from its north-western extremity reaches Loch Gilp. Loch Long, jutting northwards from the Firth of Clyde, separates Cowal from Lennox.

So serrated is the coastline of Argyll that no part of the interior lies more than about twelve miles from either the open sea or a sea-loch. This fact of geography is appropriately reflected in the name of the region Morvern, which probably derives from the Gaelic *a' Mhuir-*

---

[46] B. Crawford, *Scandinavian Scotland* (Leicester, 1987), p. 25.

bhearna, meaning 'sea-cleft' or 'sea-gap', and refers to its many indentations, which include Loch Teacuis, Loch Aline, Loch a Choire and the river of Gleann Dubh with Loch Uisge.[47] Many of the Hebrides, like Mull, Skye, and Lewis, are similarly indented with deep lochs; it has, for example, been estimated that no point on the Isle of Skye is more than five miles from the shore, and that these inlets, bays, and arms of the sea give the Hebrides a total coastline approaching 4,000 miles.

The importance of the sea as a highway and a line of communication is easily overlooked, particularly by peoples who are conditioned to thinking in terms of terrestrial civilisations and empires. In the Middle Ages, most of western Europe inherited this pattern of thought from the Roman Empire. 'All roads lead to Rome', goes the old axiom; it neatly emphasises the terrestrial organisation of the Roman Empire, which is often symbolised by its vast system of overland communication, and its physical frontiers (*limes*) in the sweltering deserts of Syria or the cold and damp hills of Northumbria. The Romans possessed a fleet, it is true, but it was the legions upon which the glory of the Empire was based. The ideas of terrestrial empire were perpetuated and spread by the Christian church, which carried them well beyond the old frontiers of the Roman Empire, in the course of the conversion of the Germanic peoples, and they were inherited by early medieval rulers like Charlemagne (768–814), whose efforts at reviving the Roman Empire created one with land-bound limitations.

One of the few early medieval peoples who used the seaways extensively, as a means of communication and settlement, were the Scandinavians. Their advanced shipbuilding technology and navigational methods allowed them, from the end of the eighth century, to plunge land-bound Europe into a state of terror and confusion (see Chapter 1). That the assault from the sea was as unexpected as it was novel, is indicated by a letter written by the Northumbrian scholar Alcuin to Ethelred, the king of Northumbria, in 793, in which he described the Viking onslaught. 'It is nearly 350 years that we and our fathers have inhabited this most lovely land', he wrote, 'and never before has such terror appeared in Britain as we have now suffered from a pagan race, nor was it thought that such an inroad from the sea could be made.'[48] Four hundred years later, Gerald of Wales, whose comments have already been noted, also remarked on the sea-going nature of the Scandinavians.

Of course, the western seaways had served as a line of communication for centuries before the Vikings arrived to dominate them. It has been demonstrated that the shorelands of the Irish Sea were united under a single cultural stimulus, and that they were linked with lands even

---

[47] H. C. Gillies, *The Place-Names of Argyll* (London, 1906), p. 102; W. J. Watson, *The History of the Celtic Place-Names of Scotland* (Edinburgh and London, 1926), p. 123.

[48] *English Historical Documents*, vol. I: *c.500–1042*, ed. D. Whitelock (London, 1955), i, no. 193.

further abroad, from at least three millennia before the Christian era. Although the Roman occupation of Britain between AD 43 and about 400 weakened this network of lines of communication, the end of Roman Britain saw its gradual revival. One of its greatest expressions came in the early Christian period, when what has been described as a 'Celtic Christian Thalassocracy' extended from Iceland to Spain.[49] Among those who contributed to the formation of this civilisation were the *peregrini*, the pilgrim saints of the early Church in Ireland, Wales, and Scotland like Donnan (martyred in 618), whose travels were almost exclusively by sea. These Celtic saints were seasoned mariners, as the *Voyage of St Brendan*, which describes the maritime wanderings of a famous saint, makes clear. This same source describes the vessel used by the Celtic saints in their travels – the coracle:

> Brendan and his companions made a coracle, using iron tools. The ribs and frame were of wood, as is the custom in those parts, and the covering was tanned ox-hide stretched over oak bark. They greased all the seams on the outer surface of the skin with fat and stored away spare skins inside the coracle, together with forty days' supplies, fat for waterproofing the skins, tools and utensils. A mast, a sail and various pieces of equipment for steering were fitted into the vessel.[50]

Vessels like this carried the early saints far abroad. Dicuil, an Irish monk and scholar writing *c*.825, observed that 'There are many other islands in the ocean to the north of Britain ... on these islands hermits who have sailed from our Scotia (Ireland) have lived for roughly a hundred years.'[51] This passage is thought to refer to the Faroe Islands, and it is believed that sea-faring Irish hermits had reached Iceland, too, long before the Vikings arrived on the scene.

Given these precedents, it should come as no surprise that, following the Scandinavian invasions and settlements in the Isles in the ninth and tenth centuries, and the intermarriage between Scandinavians and Gaels that came to characterise relations between the two peoples there (see Chapter 1), the sea continued to remain an important line of communication. If we seek some indication of the importance of ships in the maritime culture of the western seaboard, we need look no further than some of the place-names of Argyll and the Hebrides. The Old Norse word *skip* (ship) has lent itself to place-names like Skipness in

---

[49] E. G. Bowen, *Saints, Seaways and Settlements in the Celtic Lands* (Cardiff, 1977), quotation on p. 79. Another useful work is A. R. Lewis and T. J. Runyan, *European Naval and Maritime History, 300–1500* (Bloomington, Indiana, 1985), esp. chap. 5.

[50] *The Voyage of St Brendan*, in *The Age of Bede*, ed. D. H. Farmer (rev. edn, Harmondsworth, 1988), pp. 211ff.; quotation at p. 214. See T. Severin, *The Brendan Voyage* (London, 1978), for the modern construction and sailing of a leather coracle like St Brendan's.

[51] Cited in F. D. Logan, *The Vikings in History* (2nd edn, London and New York, 1991), p. 78.

Kintyre, Skipport (ship-fjord) in Uist, and Port Sgibinis in Tiree and Colonsay, while Loch Long in Argyll was known as *Skipa-fjordr* (ship-firth) to the Norse.[52] The place-name Tarbert is also a common one on the western seaboard; it is derived from *tairm-bert*, (an over-bringing), and means an isthmus over which ships could be dragged. There are examples in Harris, in the north of Kintyre (over which King Magnus had himself hauled in 1098), in Gigha, and between Loch Long and Loch Lomond (which was utilised by King Hakon IV of Norway in 1263 when ships were pulled from Loch Long into Loch Lomond where they plundered).[53] Even Monro, writing his *Description of the Western Isles of Scotland* in 1549, after the final forfeiture of the Lordship of the Isles, still noted those islands which provided good harbours for 'heiland Galayis', and he also observed that the sea around the Treshnish islands was 'very perillous for schippis be reason of the starkness of the stream'. Other, less orthodox, evidence also demonstrates the importance of the ship to west Highland society. The outer wall of the old parish church on Luing preserves pre-Reformation graffiti, some of which represent late medieval galleys, possibly carved by children obsessed with 'the best racers of their day'.[54]

Thus, the culture of the western seaboard in the Middle Ages was a maritime one. For the inhabitants of Argyll and the Isles, the sea was not a barrier, but a link, a line of communication, and a means of efficient transportation. The geographical framework within which this book is set, then, is a maritime one. Few of the events which occurred in the western seaboard between 1098 and 1336 were not dictated by its essentially maritime orientation, from Magnus Barelegs having himself hauled across the Kintyre peninsula, in a skiff with the sails and rudder set, at the beginning of our period, to the great invasion fleet that Hakon IV of Norway assembled in 1263 with which to expel the Scots from the Isles, to the activities of John MacDougall as Admiral of the Western Seas in the early fourteenth century. What has been said of Scandinavian Scotland is therefore equally applicable to the period of the Kingdom of the Isles:

the Northern and Western Isles and the northern and western Scottish coasts were controlled by a people whose outlook was

---

52 Watson, *Celtic Place-Names of Scotland*, p. 45.
53 Ibid., pp. 505–6; Gillies, *Place-Names of Argyll*, p. 20.
54 RCAHMS, *Inventory of the Ancient Monuments of Argyll* (Edinburgh, 1971–92), ii, no. 356; quote from Dawson, 'Argyll: the enduring heartland', p. 85. For an interesting account of a modern attempt to design, build, and sail a 16th-century Hebridean galley, see W. Clark, *The 'Lord of the Isles' Voyage: Western Ireland to the Scottish Hebrides in a 16th-century Galley* (Kildare, 1993), which recounts the 1991 voyage of the *Aileach* from Co. Clare to Stornoway.

seaward, whose way of life was dominated by the sea, and whose political structures were based on sea power.[55]

The importance of the sea and its mastery by the peoples of the western seaboard is summed up effectively in two works of the late twelfth, and of the fourteenth, or fifteenth century, respectively. Gerald of Wales, in the context of his discussion of the Northern and Western Isles, noted quite deliberately that, 'the Norwegians, who keep their eyes ever on the ocean, lead, above any other people a piratical life. Consequently, all their expeditions and wars are decided by naval engagements.' Gerald's use of the term 'piratical' perhaps echoes his land-locked perspective,[56] but a different tone is struck in a poem, possibly of fourteenth-century date, among those in the *Book of the Dean of Lismore*.[57] The Gaelic verses celebrate the 'Tryst of a fleet against Castle Sween', probably in 1310, and they beautifully capture the ethos of the maritime culture of the western seaboard:

Tall men are arraying the fleet, which swiftly holds its course on the sea's bare surface: no hand lacks a trim warspear, in battle of targes, polished and comely ... They have a straight stern-wind behind them ... their dappled sails are bulging, foam rises to the vessels' sides.

[55] Crawford, *Scandinavian Scotland*, p. 11.
[56] Walter Bower, in his *Scotichronicon*, outlined the submission of the king of Man to Alexander III in 1264, and used the term 'pirate-type galleys' (*galeis piraticis*) to describe the vessels the Manx king was required to provide for the king of Scots. Despite his interest in the western regions already noted, the use of this term might also reflect Bower's landlocked perspective: *Chron. Bower*, v, pp. 347–9.
[57] *Book of Dean of Lismore*, pp. 6–13, 257–9.

CHAPTER ONE

Celts, Norsemen, and *Gall-Gaedhil* in the Isles: The Historical Background to 1100

King Magnus was making his way north along the Scottish coast when messengers from King Malcolm of Scotland came to offer him a settlement: King Malcolm would let him have all the islands off the west coast which were separated by water navigable by a ship with the rudder set [1098, *Orkneyinga Saga*].[1]

The history of Scotland is inextricably bound up with Argyll and the adjacent western islands, for this was the birthplace of the Scottish kingdom and its monarchy. Sometime in the late Roman or early medieval periods, the *Scotti* of Dál Riata, an Irish kingdom in the north-eastern corner of the island (in what is now County Antrim), emigrated the twelve miles across the North Channel to the western seaboard of Scotland. In view of the establishment of Irish colonies elsewhere in Britain in the same period, it would be surprising if the inhabitants of Dál Riata had ignored the western regions of Scotland, parts of which are visible from their homeland, as an area for settlement. The date of this migration is unknown. Traditional accounts suggest that it began as early as the third century, and modern scholarship has demonstrated that there were close connections between northern Ireland and western Scotland, and gradual cross-Channel settlement for several centuries before AD 500, the date around which the kings of Dál Riata in Ireland took up residence in the new colony. The ruler most closely associated with the dynastic transfer from northern Ireland to western Scotland is Fergus Mór, son of Erc, who was said to have been accompanied by his supposed brothers Loarn and Oengus. With this migration, the name of Dál Riata was transferred across the North Channel, and the two parts were ruled from Scotland until the seventh or the ninth century.

The extent of this new kingdom in north Britain can be deduced from careful study of early historical sources. By the eighth century, Dál Riata in Britain extended from Ardnamurchan to the Mull of Kintyre, and included the Hebrides from Coll and Tiree to Bute and Arran. Other, less reliable records, suggest that it may have extended even further east and north, and it is possible that there were Scotic colonies on the isles of Raasay and Skye as well. Four major defended sites within Dál Riata are

[1] *Orkneyinga Saga* (Pálsson and Edwards), cap. 41.

known from the Irish Annals: Dunollie (Dun Ollaigh), on a headland overlooking Oban Bay; Dunadd (Dun Att), on a hill rising from a boggy flatland south of Kilmartin; Tarbert (Tairpert Boittir), on the isthmus between Knapdale and Kintyre; and Dunaverty (Aberte) on a rock jutting into the sea near the Mull of Kintyre. Dunadd and Dunollie receive mention in the Irish Annals as places that were attacked periodically, which suggests that they were centres of power among the Scots, an interpretation which has been borne out by archaeological excavations.

By the middle of the seventh century, three chief peoples or kindreds are attested in Dál Riata, although it is possible that the divisions among them were not as clear cut as the sources might suggest. The Cenél nOengusa (kindred of Oengus) seems to have inhabited the island of Islay. More important than this kindred were the Cenél nGabráin (kindred of Gabran) and the Cenél Loairn (kindred of Loarn), which were competing with one another for supremacy by the beginning of the eighth century. The former apparently occupied Kintyre, Cowal, and Bute, and possibly Gigha, Jura, and Arran; while the latter seem to have inhabited the district of Lorn (which preserves their name), Colonsay, Ardnamurchan, Mull, Coll, and Tiree. The language of the Scots was Gaelic, which eventually became the language of almost all of Scotland. Indeed, the very word 'Argyll' is itself derived from the Gaelic *Airer Goidel* (coastland of the Gael), and commemorates the early occupation of the region by the *Scotti*, while Dál Riata itself may be said to represent the embryonic kingdom of the Scots.

The geography of western Scotland clearly influenced the development of the kingdom of Dál Riata. The heartland of Dál Riata, both islands and mainland, was linked by a series of waterways which provided an ideal means of communication. In addition to the lochs, rivers, and firths which serrate the western seaboard of Scotland, two passages between the west coast and the interior were also important in the history of Dál Riata and the subsequent history of the West. These were the Firth of Clyde, long used as a route between northern Britain and Ireland, and the Great Glen, which linked Ireland and the western seaboard with the northern Highlands of Scotland. The eastern boundary of Dál Riata was the north–south range known as the 'ridge of Alba', and it was this geographical feature which separated the Scots from their neighbours in North Britain, the Picts.

The Picts have been called 'the mystery people of early Britain'.[2] Thanks to a dearth of contemporary documentation, little is known directly of either their political or their social organisation; indeed, by the twelfth century, English chroniclers could claim that the Picts had disappeared without a trace, while Norwegian writers regarded them as

[2] B. T. Hudson, *Kings of Celtic Scotland* (Westport, Conn., and London, 1994), p. 8.

magical pygmies, who performed wonders in the morning and evening, but had to disappear into their underground cities at midday. Over the past fifty years, however, historians, archaeologists, linguists, and art historians have unravelled many of the mysteries that once enshrouded the Picts, and have ensured that they are better known today. One of the major themes of modern Pictish studies is that of relations between the Picts and their new neighbours, the Scots of Dál Riata.

Given the close proximity of the two peoples in North Britain, conflict between the Scots and the Picts was virtually inevitable, and the first efforts of the Scots to conquer their eastern neighbours took place in the late sixth and early seventh centuries. Although the Scots suffered a period of sustained Pictish aggression in the first half of the eighth century, when chronicles recorded 'the overthrow of Dál Riata' in 741, within a century Kenneth, son of Alpin, already king of the Scots of Dál Riata, had also become king of the Picts (*c.*843). This takeover of Pictland by the Scots is often regarded as the result of either military conquest or genealogical connections, although a recent study by Benjamin Hudson has argued that it comprised a drawn-out, complex, and largely peaceful process, which owed little to either one individual (Kenneth MacAlpin), or one dynasty (the Cenél nGabráin), and may have provoked so little comment because it was so unremarkable. Although the exact nature of the Pictish takeover remains shadowy, one thing is certain: following the triumph of the Scots in Pictland, the Dál Riatan centres of power, both secular and ecclesiastical, were shifted eastward. Kenneth himself transported some relics of St Columba from Iona to Dunkeld, possibly as early as 849, and first Forteviot, and then Scone, rather than Dunadd, served as the *caput* or chief place of the new 'United Kingdom' of Picts and Scots. The unification of the Picts and the Scots had dramatic implications for both peoples. It resulted in the Scoticisation of the Picts to such an extent that they disappeared from the stage of history after about 900; while for the Scots it meant that their western homeland would now assume second place to the old Pictish centres of power in the East.[3] The winning back of the West and

---

[3] There is a wealth of modern work on the Picts, less for the Scots. General introductions dealing with both peoples include S. Foster, *Picts, Gaels and Scots* (Edinburgh, 1996); A. P. Smyth, *Warlords and Holy Men: Scotland, AD 80–1000* (London, 1984) [although it should now be read with W. D. H. Sellar's review, 'Warlords, holy men and matrilineal succession', *Innes Review*, xxxvi (1985), pp. 24–43, close to hand]; and A. A. M. Duncan, *Scotland: The Making of the Kingdom* (Edinburgh, 1975). For the Picts, a good introduction is A. Ritchie, *The Picts* (Edinburgh, 1989); see also F. T. Wainwright, *The Problem of the Picts* (Edinburgh, 1955); I. Henderson, *The Picts* (London, 1967); J. G. P. Friell and W. G. Watson (eds.), *Pictish Studies: Settlement, Burial and Art in Dark Age Northern Britain* (Oxford, 1984); and A. Small (ed.), *The Picts: A New Look at Old Problems* (Dundee, 1987). On the Scots a good introduction is D. Breeze and A. Ritchie, *Invaders of Scotland* (Edinburgh, 1991), which also deals with other early medieval peoples of Scotland; see also J. Bannerman, *Studies in the History of Dalriada* (Edinburgh, 1974) [a collection of scholarly articles]; and M. O. Anderson, *Kings and Kingship in Early Scotland* (Edinburgh, 1973). One book which incorporates both

the re-establishment of Scottish royal authority are prominent themes of Scottish history between the twelfth and early fourteenth centuries, the period covered by this work.

The rise of Kenneth MacAlpin as king of both Scots and Picts and the subsequent shift of power from west to east, owed much to pressure from a new wave of people making their way into the western seaboard of Scotland: the Vikings. As one leading Viking scholar has put it, 'no part of Great Britain was more directly affected by the Scandinavian invasions than the elaborate complex of islands that stretches from the tip of Shetland south-west around the coast of Scotland into the Irish sea'.[4] For three centuries, beginning shortly before 800, most of north-western Europe was subjected to attacks by Scandinavian raiders. The British Isles, due in large measure to their geographical location *vis-à-vis* Scandinavia, were among the first regions of Europe to feel the onslaught of the Vikings. The causes of Viking expansion, which are related to conditions within Scandinavia itself, have been well treated elsewhere and need not detain us here.[5] Whatever the causes of this impressive phenomenon, it was an advanced ship technology that ensured Viking domination of the seaways of western Europe. The Viking ship had been evolving for centuries, in the Scandinavian countries, before the first raids in the late eighth century. The most eloquent testimony to the nature of this ship technology was unearthed at Oseberg and Gokstad, in the late nineteenth and early twentieth centuries, where two ninth-century Viking ships were uncovered in a near perfect state of preservation. While the shape and size of Viking vessels varied according to their purpose as warship, merchant vessel, or royal yacht, certain characteristics make them almost instantly identifiable. The symmetrically ended hull with curved bow and stern stems, and the curving top line of planking, gave these vessels their graceful lines, but it was their flexible clinker-built construction and shallow keels which allowed them to take a pounding on the open ocean or to slip up shallow rivers and outlets with equal efficiency. The longships, built for war, were able to operate semi-independently of the wind, and their main source of power was the oar. To contemporaries, these ships glided through the water like dragons or serpents. They were highly prized, and Scandinavian kings and chieftains built formidable fleets to emphasise their authority. The saga of Olaf Tryggvason relates how

> King Olaf ... ordered a large ship built underneath the Hlathir Cliffs which was much larger than any other ship in the country ...

peoples between its covers is L. and J. Laing, *The Picts and the Scots* (Stroud, 1993), and there is much of value in Hudson, *Kings of Celtic Scotland*.

[4] H. R. Loyn, *The Vikings in Britain* (London, 1977), p. 108.

[5] On this topic there is a vast literature. See, among others, G. Jones, *A History of the Vikings* (rev. edn, Oxford, 1984), pp. 182–203; J. Graham-Campbell, *The Viking World* (London, 1980); and Logan, *Vikings in History*.

The vessel was both long and broad, stood high out of the water, and was constructed of big timbers ... It was constructed as a dragon ship, on the model of the Serpent which the king had taken along from Halogaland; only it was much larger and more carefully wrought in all respects. He called it the Long Serpent, and the other one, the Short Serpent. The Long Serpent had thirty-four compartments. The head and the tail were all gilt. And the gunwales were as high as those on a seagoing ship. This was the best ship ever built in Norway, and the most costly.[6]

The advanced boat-building and associated maritime skills of the Vikings meant that Scotland, hitherto perched on the periphery of Europe, suddenly found itself in the forefront of Scandinavian assault and settlement. Moreover, with the Viking settlement the history of the western seaboard became inextricably linked with Ireland, the Isle of Man, the Northern Isles, and Norway – all part of the Viking World. Throughout the period covered by this book, the sea formed an important highway which lent unity to the otherwise disparate topography of the western seaboard, and whoever would effectively rule this region must first have control of the sea.

The Vikings are first mentioned in a British context in 793, when they plundered and destroyed the island monastery of Lindisfarne on the north-east coast of England. The following year, an Irish annalist noted the 'devastation of all the islands of Britain by the gentiles'. In 795 'Skye was pillaged and devastated', and Iona, the venerable and important monastic community established by St Columba in or around 563, also felt the ravages of the Vikings, although these were unlikely to have been the first raids on Scotland. The position of Iona on the western seaways, however, meant that it was particularly vulnerable to sea-borne invaders. In 802 it was plundered again, and then in 806, 'the community of Iona was slain by the gentiles, that is to say, sixty-eight [inhabitants]'. In the wake of this raid, the abbot of Iona fled to Kells in Ireland; yet despite these hardships, the monastic community never entirely disappeared: 'It struggled on with a token community of zealous monks willing to face martyrdom at the hands of the heathen.'[7] In 825 one of those zealous monks, Blathmac, who had deliberately come to Iona in the hope of being martyred, gained his wish when he hid the shrine of St Columba from the raiders and was killed after refusing to disclose its location under vigorous interrogation. Iona was raided in

6 Snorri Sturluson, *Saga of Olaf Tryggvason*, in *Heimskringla: History of the Kings of Norway*, trans. L. M. Hollander (Austin, Texas, 1964), pp. 220–1. For secondary literature on the Viking ships, see A. W. Brøgger and H. Shetelig, *The Viking Ships: Their Ancestry and Evolution* (new edn, London, 1971); Jones, *History of the Vikings*, pp. 182–94, with a good bibliography at p. 183, note 2; Graham-Campbell, *Viking World*, pp. 36–63.

7 Smyth, *Warlords and Holy Men*, p. 147.

845, 878, and 986, which suggests that there was still something there worth plundering, and a small community survived into the eleventh century, when Queen Margaret reportedly rebuilt the monastic buildings and endowed the monks there.[8]

In assessing the Scandinavian expansion into the Hebrides and the Irish Sea, several fundamental points need to be stressed. First, the Viking involvement in the Hebrides was only part of a much larger movement that carried the Norsemen as far afield as England, Ireland, the Carolingian Empire, Russia, Iceland, and eventually North America. Once across the open stretch of water that separates Norway from Shetland, the Vikings could sail within sight of land all the way to Ireland, Scotland, England, France, Spain, and the Mediterranean. The string of islands off Scotland's west coast provided a 500-mile-long set of stepping-stones on this sailing route, as well as offering an attractive haven for Scandinavian settlement; just as the Orkney islands provided a convenient jumping-off point for travel down both coasts of Britain. Because of the sea-culture of the Scandinavians, Viking Scotland cannot be viewed in isolation: it maintained contacts with Ireland, Cumbria, the Isle of Man, and Norway. However, as Anna Ritchie remarked, that point reflects the historian's grand overview: to the individual boat-load of Vikings the pattern was smaller, more personal, and certainly more local, and there was no grand design or master-plan behind the raiding and settling process. Moreover, although when viewed in isolation these attacks appear to be devastating by comparison with the raids on Ireland or the Anglo-Saxon kingdoms, it appears that the Scots suffered no more and, indeed, perhaps less, than their neighbours – though this may be due in part, at least, to the fact that there is no source for Scotland comparable to the *Anglo-Saxon Chronicle*, from which so much of our knowledge of the Viking impact on England is derived. And, although they are most often portrayed as raiders and plunderers, with the initial phase of Viking activity in Scotland seeming to have been primarily piratical, the Vikings were also farmers, fishermen, and settlers. The boundaries between such distinctions were, in fact, by no means clear, as this passage from the thirteenth-century *Orkneyinga Saga*, about the way of life of Svein Asleifarson, a twelfth-century Orkney Viking, demonstrates:

> This is how Svein used to live. Winter he would spend at home on Gairsay, where he entertained some eighty men at his own expense. His drinking hall was so big, there was nothing in Orkney to compare with it. In the spring he had more than enough to occupy him, with a great deal of seed to sow which he saw to carefully himself.

[8] See *ES*, i, pp. 255–8; and also A. MacQuarrie and E. M. MacArthur, *Iona Through the Ages* (2nd edn, Society of West Highland and Island Historical Research, 1992), pp. 8–13.

Then when that job was done, he would go off plundering in the Hebrides and in Ireland on what he called his 'spring trip', then back home just after mid-summer, where he stayed till the corn-fields had been reaped and the grain was safely in. After that he would go off raiding again, and never came back till the first month of winter was ended. This he used to call his 'autumn trip'.[9]

This account is neatly corroborated, and the various roles in which an individual Viking might operate are illustrated by a Viking grave that was explored at Kiloran Bay on Colonsay in 1882–3. The grave, possibly a ship-burial, was found to contain human and equine remains, as well as a number of artefacts. Alongside the male burial, a sword, knife, shield-boss, axehead, spearhead and arrowheads, all of iron, were discovered, clearly the accoutrements of a Viking warrior. But a balance, pans, and lead weights were also uncovered, which point to trade and commercial activities; and so, perhaps, do two Anglo-Saxon copper coins of early to mid-ninth-century date. Finally, although the burial itself was pagan in nature, slabs with crudely incised crosses were found at either end of the stone enclosure, which suggests that this Viking or his comrades had at least rudimentary contact with Christian ideas.[10]

This is not the place for a complete examination of the Vikings in Scotland. There are, however, three major themes of interest for the present study: the date of Scandinavian settlements in Scotland; the nature of these settlements, especially their density; and the interactions between the Vikings and the Gaelic inhabitants of western Scotland.[11]

It is difficult to say when Viking settlement began in the Hebrides, or Sudreys (seen from Norway, the Hebrides are 'southern islands' as opposed to the 'northern islands' of Orkney and Shetland). Settlement in the Outer Hebrides may have begun as early as 800, perhaps even in the last quarter of the eighth century, and continued in successive waves until the end of the ninth, when the Norse earldom of Orkney was established. The limits of Scandinavian settlement in Scotland must be defined through the study of archaeological and linguistic evidence, given the almost total absence of contemporary written sources. Because of their location relative to Norway, the Northern Islands (Shetland and Orkney) received the earliest and densest colonisation. There, Scandinavian houses and settlement sites, such as Jarlshof and Birsay, have been recognised and studied in increasing numbers, and Scandinavian toponymy accounts for about 99% of place-names. Indeed, these islands

---

9 *Orkneyinga Saga* (Pálsson and Edwards), cap. 105.
10 Ritchie, *Viking Age Scotland*, pp. 79–84.
11 For what follows, see Armit, *Archaeology of Skye and the Western Isles*, chap. 10; Ritchie, *Viking Age Scotland*, esp. chaps. 4–5; Smyth, *Warlords and Holy Men*, chap. 5; and Duncan, *Making of the Kingdom*, chap. 4.

were so densely colonised that they became an integral part of the Norse world, and they would remain so politically for five more centuries.

The settlement of the western seaboard, on the other hand, appears in a different light. Unlike Orkney and Shetland, where several important Viking sites are known to archaeologists, the Hebrides have produced few sites that attest to the Viking presence in material terms, and much of it was discovered so long ago that it is of limited value today. Viking graves are known from Lewis, Tiree, Colonsay, Oronsay, Islay, and the Isle of Man, while the single most important excavated settlement site in western Scotland comes from Udal on North Uist. Here, a pre-Norse settlement was replaced in the middle of the ninth century by Norse buildings and artefacts, although its occupation was apparently a short one. The linguistic evidence in the Hebrides also contrasts with the Northern Isles: although ninety-nine of 126 village names on Lewis represent Norse forms, and about two-thirds of the settlement names on the Trotternish peninsula in Skye are Scandinavian, the proportion of Norse settlement-names declines gradually from north to south through the Hebrides. Thus, on Islay only about 30% of settlement names represent Norse forms, and the proportion is very much lower on Arran. Moreover, Scandinavian place-names along the coast of mainland Scotland primarily identify topographical features, rather than farms and settlements, and this has been taken as evidence that these areas were on the fringe of the areas settled by the Norsemen, representing a sphere of influence, rather than a region that was directly colonised. The lack of Scandinavian grave-goods from western mainland Scotland also suggests a lack of permanent settlement. In short, the Scandinavians were never successful in stamping their imprint on these islands as extensively as they did in Orkney and Shetland. Nonetheless, from the perspective of the inhabitants of Scotland, the Norse impact on the Western Isles was significant enough to warrant the coining of a new name for them: from some point in the ninth century they were known as *Innse Gall*, the 'Islands of the Foreigners'. And those 'Foreigners' were the Scandinavians.

The interaction between the Norse and the inhabitants of the islands is complex, and has provoked considerable debate among archaeologists and historians. Although only a relatively small number of Scandinavian sites have been fully excavated, many of those that have been extensively studied seem to tell the same story: rather than the extermination or enslavement of the native population, blending and integration of Norse and Gaelic culture appears to have been a common occurrence. At Buckquoy in Orkney, which was extensively excavated in 1970–1, a Norse farm was found to overlay an earlier Pictish structure. Yet this Norse structure contained no distinctively Norse artefacts; instead, pins and combs of Pictish style were discovered. The pottery, too, was Pictish, and the only objects of arguably Norse origin were several stone gaming boards. This implied that the Vikings were able to obtain domestic items from a native population which had clearly not been annihilated. As one authority has put it:

> The inference seems to be that the early settlers at Buckquoy simply took over and assimilated the native culture they found there, and presumably the natives as well, since it was not too alien to them ... The Buckquoy excavation demonstrated, for the first time, a startling degree of cultural admixture between the new settlers and a sophisticated native population.[12]

The conclusions of archaeology are reinforced by historical investigations and analogies with Ireland and the Isle of Man. Evidence of mixed Irish-Norse names in the Irish annals suggests that the Vikings took native wives, although the earliest of these hybrid names ironically reveals that the individual concerned had a Norse mother and an Irish father. His name is Godfrey MacFergus, and he was the ruler of Airgialla (Oriel), in northern Ireland. Although there are some difficulties with this entry, which occurs in a late text, as one authority has put it, there is 'nothing inherently impossible about the marriage of a Norse woman into an Irish princely family' in the early ninth century.[13] Similar evidence is provided by the lack of female pagan graves on the Isle of Man, which has been interpreted as meaning that the Vikings intermarried with local women.

Further evidence of intermarriage and integration between Norse and Gael in the Isles comes in the form of a group of warriors of mixed blood, who first appear on the record in the middle of the ninth century. These warriors are the *Gall-Gaedhil*, which means literally the 'Foreign Gael' or 'Scandinavian-Gael'. The term is generally applied to a population of mixed Norse and Gaelic descent, active in Ireland and the Hebrides from the middle of the ninth century. Irish sources described them as Scots fostered by Norsemen, who were notorious for perpetrating even greater atrocities than the Vikings, and modern historians have regarded them as renegades, freebooters, or mercenaries, who posed an equal threat to Irish, Scots, and Hiberno-Norse alike. Their homeland was almost certainly the Hebrides, as this was the only place where such a people of mixed ethnic background could have emerged as early as the mid-ninth century. The settlement of the *Gall-Gaedhil* in the south-west of Scotland has often been suggested, on the assumption that this explains the name 'Galloway', but it is not now universally accepted. The importance of the *Gall-Gaedhil* in the present context is their multiethnic makeup, and the fact that they could only have come into being

---

[12] M. Magnusson, *Viking Expansion Westwards* (London, 1973), p. 46. But Crawford, *Scandinavian Scotland*, pp. 139–40, sounds a more cautious note.

[13] Ibid., p. 47.

in areas where Norse domination was not total, and where there was interaction and assimilation between the two peoples.

One of the ninth-century leaders of the *Gall-Gaedhil* was 'Caitill Find', who was defeated on a rampage in Munster in 857. The very name of 'Caitill Find' is also in keeping with the mixed origins of the *Gall-Gaedhil*, as it represents a combination of Norse and Gaelic forms. It consists of the Old Norse *ketill* and the Old Irish *find* (fair). This individual has been identified, by A. P. Smyth, with the Ketil Flatnose of the later Icelandic sagas. Although this identification remains uncertain, tradition does associate Ketil with the Hebrides. His daughter, Aud, married Olaf, king of Dublin, and there is also evidence that his family was strongly influenced by the Gaelic society of western Scotland in the form of Christianity. What all of this amounts to is that intermarriage must have taken place between the Norse and the Christian Gaels in the Hebrides, and that Ketil's rule did not mean the annihilation or displacement of native elements in this region.[14] Rather, it appears that the Hebrides were characterised by peaceful communities of mixed Norse-Gaelic blood, and quite possibly Christian observances. The western islands thus entered into a long period, extending into the thirteenth century, in which both Gaelic and Norse were spoken throughout their length. Although the islands became known to the Gaels as *Innse Gall*, in reality the 'Islands of the Foreigners' belonged to both the Celtic and Scandinavian worlds, a fact which was to become increasingly apparent in the twelfth and thirteenth centuries, and which forms a major theme in the history of the kingdom of the Isles.

By the middle of the ninth century, Norse domination of the western seaboard was an established fact. From the later ninth and tenth centuries, we enter an obscure period in the history of the Isles, but the most significant development in political terms was the rise of individuals bearing the title 'lord', or 'king', of the Isles. Godfrey MacFergus, the lord of Airgialla in northern Ireland, who has already figured in the narrative, was one of the earliest recorded bearers of the title. He died in *c*.853, and was called in his obit *toiseach Innse Gall* (lord of the Hebrides), by Irish chroniclers.[15] His association with Kenneth MacAlpin in 836, when he is said to have come to Scotland to assist Kenneth, has led some historians to argue that the Scottish king must have established him in this lordship, but, if this is true for Godfrey, it cannot be so for those who followed him as Hebridean kings, for, by then, the region had been wrested from the hands of the Scots. The first individual accorded the

---

[14] On the *Gall-Gaedhil* and Ketil Flatnose, see A. P. Smyth, *Scandinavian Kings in the British Isles, 850–880* (Oxford, 1977), pp. 114–16, and chap. 8; Smyth, *Warlords and Holy Men*, pp. 154–63; Jones, *History of the Vikings*, p. 206, note 1; Duncan, *Making of the Kingdom*, p. 89; and D. Brooke, 'Gall-Gaidhil and Galloway', in R. D. Oram and G. P. Stell (eds.), *Galloway: Land and Lordship* (Edinburgh, 1991), pp. 97–116.

[15] *ES*, i, pp. 267, 284.

title *rí Innse Gall* (king of the Hebrides), is Godfrey, the son of Harold. He appears in Welsh sources as having ravaged Anglesey and Dyfed in the 970s and early 980s; in 987, he is recorded as having been a participant in the 'battle of Man'; and *Njal's Saga* portrays him as involved in conflict with Earl Sigurd of Orkney. Upon his death at the hands of the men of Dál Riata in 989, Irish sources referred to him as 'king of the Hebrides', and his sphere of influence seems to have encompassed Man and the Isles. His brother, Maccus or Magnus, also held power in the Isles. In 971, he ravaged Anglesey, and, in 974, he plundered 'Inishcathy' (Scattery Island) in Ireland. In 973, he is recorded as one of the several British kings who rowed the Anglo-Saxon King Edgar on the River Dee, and the same source calls him 'king of very many islands'. The careers of Godfrey and Maccus neatly illustrate the contacts that existed within the Irish Sea world, among the Hebrides, Man, Ireland, and even Wales.[16] Of more interest is the use of the title 'king' (Old Norse *konungr*; Old Irish *rí*), since it is a notably non-Scandinavian feature of the Scandinavian and mixed Gaelic-Norse elite in the Isles. It has been shown to have developed through contact with Irish society, and it seems plausible that once the Norse arrived in Ireland and the Hebrides, they were given or adopted the title of 'king'. However, the extent and nature of this kingship was fluid, and there could be several kings in the region at once. Thus, at different times in the history of the Isles, we see kings of the northern Isles, the southern Isles, the Hebrides, and Man, while the kings of Dublin also exercised intermittent authority in the Isles.[17]

Following the demise of Godfrey and Maccus, the influence of the powerful earls of Orkney extended south into the Hebrides and apparently eclipsed the power of the Hebridean chieftains, although the line of Godfrey was not extinguished: Irish annals record the death of Ragnvald, Godfrey's son, 'king of the Islands', in 1005. However, the Orcadian influence in the Hebrides is attested by the fact that Islesmen, as well as Orcadians, fought alongside Earl Sigurd of Orkney against Brian Bóruma, at the battle of Clontarf in Ireland in 1014. In the sixty years following Clontarf, the kings of Alba, Dublin and Leinster, and Norway, together with the earls of Orkney, all vied for power in the Isles, and, in 1072, the *Annals of Tigernach* recorded the death of Diarmait mac Maíl na mBó, who is called king of the Hebrides, Dublin and Leinster.[18]

---

16 On Godfrey and Maccus, see *ES*, i, pp. 478–9, 494, 499–502, 521; *Brut y Tywysogyon or The Chronicle of the Princes: Red Book of Hergest Version*, ed. T. Jones (Cardiff, 1955), pp. 15, 17; and W. D. H. Sellar, 'The Western Isles *c*.800–1095', in P. McNeill and R. Nicholson (eds.), *An Historical Atlas of Scotland, c.400–c.1600* (St Andrews, 1975), p. 23.

17 On the question of kingship in the Isles, see Crawford, *Scandinavian Scotland*, pp. 191–2; and Barrow, *Kingship and Unity*, p. 107.

18 *ES*, ii, p. 42, and note 2.

The involvement of the King of Leinster in the Isles serves as a reminder that the Hebrides and Man enjoyed close connections with Ireland in the eleventh and twelfth centuries, beyond the mere facts of geography. The nature of these connections has been elucidated by Seán Duffy, who has demonstrated that, when control of Dublin passed to the Irish provincial kings in the middle of the eleventh century, these rulers also inherited the old Viking links between Dublin and the Isles. When Diarmait mac Maíl na mBó captured Dublin in 1052, he drove out the Hiberno-Scandinavian king and, rather than simply installing a compliant puppet, he assumed the kingship himself. This was a crucial step, and thereafter he was able to utilise both the Ostmen and the Leinster host on his expeditions; but it was not until 1061 that his son, Murchaid, invaded Man, defeated the exiled Hiberno-Scandinavian ruler of Dublin who had fled there after the events of 1052, and took tribute. Murchaid then ruled over both Man and Dublin until 1070. Duffy regards these events as 'the first clear insight we get into the way in which Irishmen were sucked into the politics of the Irish Sea as a result of their assertion of authority over the Ostmen'.[19]

Rivalry between the dynasties of Leinster and Munster over Dublin also extended into the Irish Sea, and many examples can be found to illustrate further the connections between Ireland and the kingdom of the Isles. A few will have to suffice. In 1073, two members of the Munster dynasty, descendants of Brian Bóruma, were killed in Man, while another member of this same dynasty ruled the Isles briefly from about 1111 to 1114. In 1152 or 1153, three Dubliners (nephews of the reigning king of Man, Olaf), invaded Man, assassinated their uncle, and divided the island among themselves, before going on to campaign in Galloway. Of course, if the rulers of Dublin were ambitious to exert their authority over Man and the Isles – the maritime hinterland of Dublin – then the reverse is also true, and ambitious rulers in the Isles were eager to add Dublin to their sea-kingdom. This is precisely what happened in 1091, when Godred Crovan, the king of the Isles and founder of the Scandinavian dynasty of Man that ruled until 1265, went to Dublin and assumed the kingship until he was driven out by a coalition of Irish forces in 1094. It was even possible for aid to flow from the Isles to Ireland. When, in 1171, Ruaidri Ua Conchobair, king of Ireland, besieged the Anglo-Norman invaders in Dublin, men of the Isles are recorded as having assisted him, because, Gerald of Wales tells us, of their fear of English domination.[20] Clearly the threat of English

---

19 S. Duffy, 'Irishmen and Islesmen in the Kingdoms of Dublin and Man, 1052–1171', *Ériu*, xliii (1992), p. 100. See also A. Candon, 'Muirchertach Ua Briain: politics and naval activity in the Irish Sea, 1075 to 1119', in G. MacNiocaill and P. Wallace (eds.), *Keimelia: Studies in Medieval Archaeology and History in Memory of Tom Delaney* (Galway, 1988), pp. 397–415, for further Irish involvement in the Isles.
20 [Gerald of Wales]: Giraldus Cambrensis, *Expugnatio Hibernica. The Conquest of Ireland*, ed. and trans. A. B. Scott and F. X. Martin (Dublin, 1978), pp. 78–9.

domination in Ireland had wide-reaching implications for the rulers of the Irish Sea, and this episode also further illuminates the connections that existed between Ireland and the Isles in the eleventh and twelfth centuries.[21] There is thus a sense in which the Hebrides and the Irish Sea formed a single maritime sphere of influence, within which competition for dominance encompassed Irish, Scottish, Manx, Scandinavian, Hiberno-Norse and Hebridean elements.

It should be evident from the foregoing discussion that, in our period, the Hebrides were far from being 'isolated islands on the edge of the world'.[22] Their significance lay in the fact that they lined the western seaways, and formed a corridor to the Norse settlements in Ireland, Scotland, Cumbria, and Man. Pride of place within this Norse web of connections was accorded to the Isle of Man. With its safe harbours, rich agricultural land, long sandy beaches (which made good landing sites for longships), and position as the nexus of the Irish Sea, within reach of the harbours of Dublin and northern Europe, it is little wonder that Man came to hold great attraction for the Norse as well as the Irish, and that Norse settlement there was also intensive. In the tenth and eleventh centuries Man was prosperous, as evidenced by the appearance of Manx crosses and coin hoards, and it was also probably completely Norse in administration, Church (Man became Christian again sometime in the tenth century), and probably language.

A new chapter opened on the history of the Isles in about 1079, when Godred Crovan, called 'Gofraid mac mic Arailt' in one set of Irish annals, arrived in the Isle of Man with a great fleet of ships.[23] He is an obscure figure about whom little is known, but his importance should not be underestimated. His designation as 'mac mic Arailt' probably indicates that he was a son, or nephew, of Imar mac Arailt who ruled Dublin between 1038 and 1046, and who was in turn a nephew of Sitriuc Silkenbeard. The *Chronicle of Man* states that he was a son of Harold the Black 'of Ysland', and added that he was a veteran of the battle of Stamford Bridge in 1066, at which the Norwegian King Harald Hardrada, a claimant to the English throne, had been killed, and from which only a handful of survivors escaped.[24] His credentials were therefore impressive.

The Manx Chronicle goes on to tell the story of his conquest of the Isle of Man:

21 In addition to Duffy, 'Irishmen and Islesmen', see also S. Duffy, 'The Bruce brothers and the Irish Sea world, 1306–29', *Cambridge Medieval Celtic Studies*, xxi (1991), pp. 56–86, esp. 59–63.

22 Sellar, 'Western Isles', p. 24.

23 *ES*, ii, p. 43, note 6; *Ann. Tigernach, s.a.* 1091. The epithet *crovan* is derived from OI *crobh-bhan*, 'of the white hand': see Duffy, 'Irishmen and Islesmen', p. 106, and note 66.

24 *ES*, ii, pp. 43–5. In the notes to *Chron. Man*, pp. 143–8, it is argued that 'Ysland' represents neither Ireland, nor Iceland, but Islay. See Duffy, 'Irishmen and Islesmen', p. 106; and G. Broderick, 'Irish and Welsh strands in the genealogy of Godred Crovan', *Journal of the Manx Museum*, viii (1980), pp. 32–8.

Godred Crovan collected a great number of ships, and came to
Man. He fought a battle with the people of the land; but he was
defeated, and put to flight. Again he brought together an army and
ships, came to Man, fought with the Manxmen; was conquered, and
put to flight. A third time he assembled a plentiful multitude, and
came by night to the harbour that is called Ramsey; and he hid
three hundred men in the wood that was upon a steep brow of the
mountain called Snaefell. When the star of day arose, the Manxmen
formed their line of battle, and met with Godred in a great assault.
And when the battle was proceeding vigorously, the three hundred
men arose from their place of ambush, and began to weaken the
Manxmen from the rear, and drive them into flight. And when they
saw that they were defeated, and that no place of refuge was open
to them ... those who had still remained begged from Godfrey with
piteous cries that their lives should be spared ...

The Manxmen were probably led by Fingal, the son of Godfrey Sitriuc's
son, of whom it was said that he succeeded his father as king of Man in
1070. Godred's victory, however, was apparently total, and the chronicle
continued with a description of the aftermath of the conflict:

On the following day, Godred gave his army the choice either of
dividing Man among themselves, and living in it, if they preferred;
or taking the whole substance of the land, and returning home.
And it pleased them better to pillage the whole island, and to be
enriched by its goods, and so to return home. But to the few of the
islanders who had remained with him Godred granted the southern
part of the island; and to the rest of the Manxmen, the northern
part ...[25]

Remembered in Manx tradition as 'King Orry', Godred went on to
subdue Dublin, 'and a great part of Leinster' after his conquest of Man.
He was driven out of Ireland in 1094, and in 1095 he succumbed to a
plague, dying on Islay.[26] Godred Crovan's achievement was multi-
faceted. Not only did he found the Scandinavian sea-going dynasty of
Man and the Isles, and firmly establish 'an extensive island kingdom
which encompassed the western Scottish islands',[27] but when his
granddaughter, Ragnhild, married Somerled of Argyll, Godred became
the ancestor of a vigorous new race of Hebridean sea-kings, who would
eventually wrest authority in the Isles from his own Norse descendants.

The period from 1095 to 1114 was one of great confusion in the
history of the Isles, in which competition for the throne and internecine
strife disrupted the kingdom. Following Godred's death, Norse, Manx,

25 *ES*, ii, pp. 43–5.
26 Ibid., ii, pp. 43–5, 98. See also Kinvig, *History of the Isle of Man* (2nd edn), p. 51.
27 D. Freke, 'History', in V. Robinson and D. McCarroll (eds.), *The Isle of Man:
Celebrating a Sense of Place* (Liverpool, 1990), p. 113.

and Irish elements were all involved in this contest, including his son Lagman, a Norseman named Ingemund, and Donald MacTagd, the nephew of Muirchertach Ua Briain, king of Munster. The death of Ingemund (who may have been sent by King Magnus Barelegs of Norway to restore order) at the hands of the Hebrideans probably spurred King Magnus himself to action. In 1098, he embarked on an expedition through the Isles, in order to assert Norwegian royal authority in these troubled waters. He seized the earl of Orkney and installed his own son as earl, then plundered his way southwards through the Hebrides, from Lewis and Skye south to Man.[28] The wake of destruction that he left behind, as well as an intimate knowledge of the islands off Scotland's west coast, was graphically recorded in Bjørn Cripplehand's skaldic poetry:

> In Lewis Isle with fearful blaze
> The house-destroying fire plays;
> To hills and rocks the people fly
> Fearing all shelter but the sky.
> In Uist the king deep crimson made
> The lightning of his glancing blade;
> The peasant lost his land and life
> Who dared to bide the Norseman's strife.
>
> The hungry battle-birds were filled
> In Skye with blood of foemen killed,
> And wolves on Tiree's lonely shore
> Dyed red their hairy jaws in gore.
> The men of Mull were tired of flight;
> The Scottish foemen would not fight
> And many an island girl's wail
> Was heard as through the Isles we sail ...[29]

Strangely enough, Iona escaped destruction. Arriving at the holy island, King Magnus

> wished to open the small church of Columcille; and the king did not go in, but closed the door again immediately, and immediately locked it, and said that none should be so daring thenceforward as to go into that church ...'[30]

The 'church of Columcille' is probably the small structure now known as St Columba's Shrine, which stands to the north of the main west doorway of the abbey church; but what prompted Magnus to prohibit

---

[28] See R. Power, 'Magnus Barelegs' expeditions to the West', *SHR*, lxv (1986), pp. 115–16, which addresses the difficulties of the chronology for this period.

[29] *Saga of Magnus Barelegs* in *Heimskringla*, trans. Hollander, p. 675; Smyth's translation, in *Warlords and Holy Men*, p. 141, is used here.

[30] *ES*, ii, p. 108.

entry to the building remains a mystery. As this little building had quite
likely been the original site of St Columba's tomb,[31] it is tempting to
suppose that Magnus succumbed to the same curiosity that overcame
William the Conqueror at Durham in 1072, when that monarch ordered
the relics of St Cuthbert exhumed. According to the story related by
Simeon of Durham, as William was on the verge of having his wish
executed, he was stricken with an intense fever which forced him to
leave the church, and 'he hurriedly mounted his horse, and did not
draw bridle until he had reached the river Tees'.[32] Perhaps – and it can
be only speculation – Magnus nursed similar curiosities, and it is not
inconceivable that even a hard-nosed warrior like him was a little
reluctant to test the powers of an often vengeful saint, who acted as a
protector of the Hebrideans. Indeed, the vision of Alexander II, as he
lay dying at the head of an invasion force at Kerrera in 1249, may also
provide an instructive parallel (see Chapter 3 below).

Resuming his southward journey through the Hebrides, and arriving
at Man, King Magnus captured Lagman, the son of Godred, and
perhaps assumed the overlordship of the kingdom. He then sailed south
to Wales, where he fought a battle at the Menai Strait with two Norman
'earls of Wales' (Hugh the Stout of Chester, and Hugh the Bold of
Shrewsbury), and took possession of Anglesey, off the north-west coast of
Wales. On his return trip north through the Hebrides, he came to an
agreement with the king of Scots, Edgar (wrongly called Malcolm in the
Orkneyinga Saga, which records the treaty), whereby the king of Norway
should have 'all the islands off the west coast which were separated by
water navigable by a ship with rudder set'.[33] However, in negotiating this
agreement the two kings were ignoring the basic problem which had
necessitated the expedition in the first place, for they were partitioning
territories which neither effectively controlled.[34]

The *Orkneyinga Saga* described in detail how, upon reaching Kintyre,
Magnus 'had a skiff hauled across the narrow neck of the land at
Tarbert, with himself sitting at the helm, and this is how he won the
whole peninsula'. Kintyre, adds the sagaman, 'is thought to be more
valuable than the best of the Hebridean islands, though not as good as
the Isle of Man'.[35] Regardless of the historicity of Magnus's feat, modern
research suggests that Kintyre was not recognised as part of the territory

[31] J. J. Waddell, 'The chapel or oratory of St Columba at Iona', *TGAS*, new ser., x (1941).
[32] Simeon of Durham, *A History of the Church of Durham*, in *The Historical Works of Simeon
of Durham*, trans. J. Stevenson (Church Historians of England, 1855; repr. Llanerch,
Lampeter, 1988), p. 75. On saints as powerful protectors of their peoples, goods, and
territories, see B. Ward, *Miracles and the Medieval Mind: Theory, Record and Event,
1000–1215* (rev. edn, Philadelphia, 1987), pp. 61–6, which deals with the example of
St Cuthbert. For the miracles of St Columba, and his sometimes vengeful nature, see
Smyth, *Warlords and Holy Men*, chap. 3, esp. pp. 96–7.
[33] *Orkneyinga Saga* (Pálsson and Edwards), cap. 41.
[34] Duncan and Brown, 'Argyll and the Isles', pp. 193–4.
[35] *Orkneyinga Saga* (Pálsson and Edwards), cap. 41.

ceded to the Norwegians.[36] However, the episode is significant in that it demonstrates both the impracticalities of distinguishing mainland from offshore islands in this region of Scotland, and it also reflects an awareness that the separation of Kintyre from the islands off Scotland's western seaboard made little or no sense in political and geographical terms. The episode is best seen in the light of a political settlement, which reflected the principles of terrestrial empire and ignored the maritime culture of the west coast and the offshore islands.[37]

King Magnus Barelegs ultimately met his fate in 1103 in Ulster, while on yet another raiding expedition. Although he had succeeded in asserting his presence in the Isles, he had nevertheless done little to halt the steady erosion of Norwegian authority that was manifest. Yet, as a result of his expedition, the Isles did acquire a political identity with clearly defined boundaries, and, perhaps more importantly, they remained in close contact with the Norse world.[38] But Magnus's death, and the state of civil war in Norway among his descendants which followed, led to a corresponding lack of royal initiative in the Isles. No king of Norway would lead an expedition back to these islands until King Hakon IV's great invasion fleet set sail from Norway in the late summer of 1263. Following the death of Magnus, Lagman, the son of Godred Crovan, ruled in the Isles from 1103 to 1110 or 1111. In 1111 Donald MacTagd apparently took the Isles by force, and ruled briefly until 1114. In that year he returned to Ireland, and was killed in 1115 in Connacht. It was probably only now that Olaf, another son of Godred Crovan, took the Manx kingship. He was remembered by the Manx chronicler as a good and peace-loving king who 'had all the kings of Ireland and Scotland so in alliance with him that none dared to disturb the kingdom of the islands, during all his days'. Olaf ruled for forty years, dying in 1152 or 1153.[39]

Although a Scandinavian dynasty had been restored to the Manx kingship in about 1115, in the person of Olaf, these kings do not seem to have been able to exercise very effective control of the region. This fact, combined with a lengthy civil war in Norway which precluded any Norwegian royal presence in the region, as well as the disorder and confusion in the Isles in the early twelfth century, created a power vacuum – or, as it has also been called, a no man's land – into which an

---

[36] Duncan and Brown, 'Argyll and the Isles', p. 194. In about 1315, King Robert I performed a similar feat, when he had a track cut over the isthmus on East Loch Tarbert, where Kintyre and Knapdale meet, in order to facilitate the hauling of galleys between the Clyde estuary and the Western Isles. See R. Nicholson, *Scotland: The Later Middle Ages* (Edinburgh, 1974), p. 113; and G. W. S. Barrow, *Robert Bruce and the Community of the Realm of Scotland* (3rd edn, Edinburgh, 1988), pp. 291–2.

[37] Crawford, *Scandinavian Scotland*, p. 25.

[38] G. Donaldson, *A Northern Commonwealth: Scotland and Norway* (Saltire Soc., 1990), p. 74; Power, 'Magnus Barelegs', p. 130.

[39] *ES*, ii, pp. 133, 137; Power, 'Magnus Barelegs', p. 116; Kinvig, *History of the Isle of Man* (2nd edn), pp. 54–5.

aggressive new dynasty could carve out a sphere of influence. From about 1100 onwards, the kings of Man began to lose the race to fill this power vacuum to chieftains who had Norse names but were of mixed Scandinavian and Gaelic descent, and whose position was based upon their impressive control of the seas. The most prominent of these leaders in the twelfth century was Somerled MacGillebrigte.

CHAPTER TWO

The Age of Somerled, 1100–1164

A naval battle was fought between Godfrey and Somerled ... and great slaughter took place on either side. And when day dawned they made peace; and they divided the kingdom of the islands between them ... [1156, *Chronicle of Man*].[1]

No figure from the western seaboard of Scotland between the time of Kenneth MacAlpin and Godfrey MacFergus in the mid-ninth century, and the MacDonald Lords of the Isles in the fourteenth and fifteenth centuries, is as formidable as Somerled, the king of *Innse Gall*, who perished at the head of a multi-ethnic army in an attack on the Scottish mainland in 1164. Somerled steps on to the stage of Hebridean history in the first half of the twelfth century fully mature, and already a ruler of note in Argyll and the Isles. His early life, and rise to power, remain shrouded in mystery, while his career after the 1140s is only fitfully recorded. Yet with Somerled, a crossroads in the history of the western seaboard of Scotland is apparent. Not only is he the first Hebridean ruler whose activities are identifiable, beyond just the simple information provided by an obit, but he was also the ancestor of a number of kindreds, dominating the western seaboard for some three and a half centuries after his death.

Despite the invasions and settlements of the Norse in the ninth and tenth centuries, the western seaboard had ostensibly formed part of the Scottish kingdom until 1098. With the treaty of that year between Magnus Barelegs of Norway and King Edgar of Scotland, control of the Hebrides formally passed to the Norse. But, as the events of the previous century had demonstrated, this control could only be realised if the Norwegian kings maintained a strong presence in the Isles. This they proved unable to do, due in large measure to civil war in Norway, and no Norwegian king visited the Isles between the time of Magnus Barelegs and the formidable Hakon IV, over a century and a half later. Norwegian authority in the Isles in the twelfth century was therefore more illusory than real. This development might have opened the way for a waxing of Scottish power in the West, but the kings descended from Malcolm III 'Canmore' and Queen Margaret (both d. 1093) were simultaneously turning their attentions southwards, towards England

---

[1] *Chronicle of Man*, in *ES*, ii, pp. 231–2.

and the Continent, and were unable or unwilling to intervene in the
political affairs of the western seaboard. The ensuing power vacuum
allowed the dynasty of Somerled MacGillebrigte to flex its muscles, and
the story of the next two centuries in the Western Isles and Argyll is the
history of this vigorous line of sea-kings. It is therefore no exaggeration
to state that the history of the western seaboard in the Middle Ages
begins with Somerled.[2]

Perhaps the most important obstacle facing the historian of Somerled,
and indeed of the Hebrides in our period, is that of the sources. More
specifically, two interrelated problems present themselves. First, how
reliable are the medieval and post-medieval sources, especially the Gaelic
pedigrees and clan histories? Second, what is the proper balance
between these two types of source material? The answers are crucial to
our understanding of Somerled and his career.

There are four major contemporary sources upon which much of our
knowledge of the western seaboard in the time of Somerled rests: the
two Scottish chronicles of Holyrood and Melrose; the Manx chronicle;
and the Latin poem known as the *Carmen de Morte Sumerledi*. To these
may be added the Irish annals, but their entries are so sparse that they
do little more than corroborate the other sources. Nevertheless, their
value should not be underestimated: not only do they fill in crucial
details that are missing from other accounts, such as the name of the son
of Somerled slain at Renfrew, but they also provide important information on the composition of the Hebridean army of 1164 and the status of
Somerled. Yet, for all their value as contemporary documents, the four
major sources just mentioned are not without their difficulties. They are
jejune. They take no notice of Somerled before 1153, when he was
carving out territories for himself in Argyll and the Hebrides. And, most
significantly, they are uniformly hostile in their attitude to the Hebridean chieftain. It is worthwhile exploring in greater detail the nature of
this hostility, since it has considerably affected Somerledian historiography throughout the centuries.

Both the chronicles of Holyrood and Melrose were the product of
reformed monasteries, and both represent brief sets of annals rather
than extended narratives. But despite their importance to the historian
of medieval Scotland, these chronicles do possess serious limitations.
The most significant in the present context is simply that, as Webster has
so aptly stated, 'both were compiled by members of new monastic orders
which were introduced from outside Scotland by kings who were
anxious to modernise their kingdom'.[3] In short, then, these chronicles
were composed by writers who had many interests outside Scotland and
who represented alien elements in Scottish society; consequently, they
can hardly be expected to understand fully the structure and hierarchy

---

[2] MacKenzie, *Highlands and Islands*, p. 91.
[3] Webster, *Scotland from the Eleventh Century*, p. 38.

of native Scottish society. Moreover, the connection between the monastic centres at which these chronicles were produced and the kings of Scots is not insignificant: it meant that the chroniclers were very sympathetic to the cause of the kings descended from Malcolm III and Queen Margaret. The bias in the Scottish chronicles can be clearly seen in the 1164 entry for the Melrose chronicle. Somerled is said to have been 'wickedly rebelling' against King Malcolm, whom the chronicler regarded as his lord, and his death is attributed to divine vengeance.[4]

At first glance the *Cronica Regum Mannie et Insularum*, or the *Chronicle of Man*, as it is known, might appear to be less biased than either of the Scottish chronicles, since it was compiled on the Isle of Man in the thirteenth century and narrates the activities of the kings of Man and the Isles from *c*.1066 to *c*.1266. It therefore notes the doings of Somerled and his descendants in an insular context. But, because Somerled had wrested power from the Manx king in 1156, and had expelled him entirely in 1158 as he expanded his dominion over the Isles, the Manx chronicle is hardly objective and tends, like the chronicles of Holyrood and Melrose, to be unfriendly to Somerled and his descendants. Thus, when it discusses the partitioning of the kingdom between Somerled and Godfrey, the Manx king, in 1156, it notes that, 'this was the cause of the downfall of the kingdom of the islands, from the time when the sons of Somerled took possession of it'.[5]

Finally, there is the Latin poem called the *Carmen de Morte Sumerledi*. In many ways this is a remarkable document, describing the assault of Somerled on the Scottish mainland, and the fate of the attacking army as it was defeated by a local force. Perhaps the *Carmen*'s most remarkable feature is that it was composed by an eyewitness – William, a clerk of Glasgow – who claims to have seen and heard, at first hand, the events that he recounts. But the Glasgow provenance of the document ensures that it takes a profoundly hostile tone in treating the Hebrideans, who plundered the area around the city and cathedral: 'Gardens, fields, ploughed lands, were ravaged and laid waste; barbarous hands mastered and menaced the meek ... The people of Glasgow wounded fled from the sword-strokes ...' Thus, Somerled can be described by William as 'foul with treachery, the most cruel enemy, who was conspiring and striving against the Lord's servants', while his army is likewise described as treacherous.[6]

Despite the immense difficulties in utilising these sources to provide a balanced account of Somerled's activities, they are of the utmost value to the historian, for without them the history of the western seaboard in the central Middle Ages would be a virtual blank. But, since they are lacking in specific detail about Somerled's origins, ancestry, and rise to power, it

[4] *ES*, ii, pp. 254–5.
[5] Ibid., ii, p. 232.
[6] Ibid., ii, pp. 256–8.

remains to discover what the post-medieval sources reveal about these aspects of Somerled's career. The traditional genealogy of Somerled is preserved in at least fifteen accounts in Latin and Gaelic, ranging in date from the late fourteenth to the eighteenth centuries. The Clan Donald traditions about Somerled and his descendants are preserved in the books of Clanranald and by the sennachie Hugh MacDonald, both of seventeenth-century date.[7] The attraction of these sources is that they provide considerable detail on the early life of Somerled; the drawback – and some have argued that it is a fatal one – is simply the question of whether they can be held to possess any validity because of their late date, and because of the nature of their transmission. Recent research, however, has tended to show that, when utilised with caution, these sources can be made to divulge significant information. David Sellar, who has explored in great detail the Gaelic pedigrees of the West Highlands of Scotland, has shown that those of Somerled correspond remarkably well with one another, and with other extant sources like the annals, and that, 'there is a strong case for believing the pedigree from Somerled back to Fergus [ninth century] to be authentic in detail'.[8] As for the accounts of the clan historians, they are only beginning to be explored as fossilised oral histories, passed down for centuries by generations of sennachies, but here again Sellar's work has been instrumental in revealing their significance. He writes:

> These sources are not reliable, but they cannot be ignored. In later stages of Clan Donald history where facts can be cross-checked with contemporary evidence, the Clanranald historian and Hugh Mac-Donald are frequently wrong in matters of detail, yet in their narration of the general trend of events they are usually correct ... Their acount of the origins of Somerled is verifiable inasmuch as he does appear to have risen from obscurity and to have carved out for himself a principality in Argyll and the Isles ...[9]

The nature of the source material has spawned two disparate views of Somerled across the last seven centuries. Many modern historians, who relegate Somerled and his fellow rulers on the margins of Britain (like Fergus of Galloway, d. 1161) to the historiographical periphery in their treatment of the modernisation of the Scottish kingdom, rely heavily upon the laconic accounts of the medieval chroniclers. The result is often a portrayal of Somerled not unlike that presented in the medieval sources themselves: at best, he becomes an overmighty subject; at worst, he is portrayed as a rebel and a thorn in the side of the modernising

---

[7] Hugh Macdonald, *History of the Macdonalds*, in *HP*, i; see also *Clanranald Bk.*, ii.

[8] W. D. H. Sellar, 'The origins and ancestry of Somerled', *SHR*, xlv (1966), p. 137.

[9] Ibid., p. 124. On these narratives, see also the comments of Cowan, 'Norwegian sunset – Scottish dawn', p. 112, note 40; and in general, J. MacInnes, 'Clan sagas and historical legends', *TGSI*, lvii (1990–2), pp. 377–94. A negative view of their value is expressed in Duncan and Brown, 'Argyll and the Isles', p. 195.

kings of Scots.[10] An alternative view, often propagated in popular histories, clan histories, or nineteenth-century works, presents Somerled as a great Gaelic lord, heading a Celtic revival in the Isles, driving out the Norse, and perhaps intent on establishing an independent Gaelic kingdom in the West. He is also often elevated to semi-mythical status, as the ancestor of the Clan Donald. But, just as many modern historians rely upon the medieval sources for their view of Somerled, this view depends heavily upon the Gaelic pedigrees and the clan histories of the seventeenth century; indeed, in some instances, the episodes described by Hugh MacDonald and the *Book of Clanranald* are accepted uncritically, at face value, and presented as historical fact.[11] We are left, then, with two very disparate views of Somerled; neither view, as we shall see, is entirely adequate.

As E. J. Cowan has remarked,

> Hebridean history in the twelfth and thirteenth centuries is as complex, intricate and elusive as a Celtic artistic motif with tendrils snaking out to Ireland, England, the Northern Isles and occasionally Norway, but that history is above all obscure because large chunks of the pattern have been obliterated by the fragmentary nature of the historical evidence.[12]

This poignant statement reminds us of two important principles. First, our knowledge of the Hebrides in the period in question is so fragmentary that no scrap of evidence can be ignored. Medieval and post-medieval accounts must be woven together in order to attain a balanced synthesis. This means that while the post-medieval genealogies and clan histories are not reliable and cannot be used as historical narratives, they cannot be entirely dispensed with, either. Secondly, the metaphor of the Celtic artistic motif with tendrils extending to Ireland, England, the Northern Isles, and Norway is particularly apt: it serves as a reminder that the culture of the western seaboard was a maritime one, and that, as such, the Hebrides were intimately connected with Ireland, the Isle of Man, the Northern Isles and Norway. Indeed, as we have seen, the Hebrides, with the adjacent coastline of Argyll, were much more closely linked to these regions during the eleventh and twelfth centuries, than to the centre of the Scottish kingdom at Edinburgh, Perth and Stirling. In short, we must set aside the tendency, partly inherited from the chronicles of Holyrood and Melrose, to view Somerled from a purely Scottish perspective. Only when he is placed within a broader, maritime,

---

[10] See, e.g., Duncan, *Making of the Kingdom*, pp. 166–7; Barrow, *Kingship and Unity*, p. 48; and M. Lynch, *Scotland: A New History* (Edinburgh, 1992), p. 85.

[11] R. Williams, *The Lords of the Isles: The Clan Donald and the Early Kingdom of the Scots* (London, 1984), chap. 11, and *passim*, treats the 17th-century narratives uncritically, apparently as fact. See also I. F. Grant, *The Lordship of the Isles* (Edinburgh, 1935), pp. 163–4; and M. Campbell, *Argyll: The Enduring Heartland* (London, 1977), chap. 9.

[12] Cowan, 'Norwegian sunset – Scottish dawn', p. 111.

context do his true standing and significance as a sea king, and as a dominant force in the history of the western seaboard, become apparent.

The early life of Somerled is lost to history, and the subject of his ancestry and origins has provoked rigorous and lively debate. Nineteenth- and early twentieth-century historians and antiquarians were divided over whether his background was Norse or Gaelic. Somerled (Gaelic 'Somhairle'), is a Norse name meaning 'Summer Warrior', or 'Viking'. While originally denoting not a personal name, but rather an epithet for a Viking, by the end of the tenth century it had begun to appear as a given name, and there are on record an Earl Somerled of Orkney, who was the son of Earl Sigurd the Stout, and a Somerled, *rí Innse Gall*, who died in 1083.[13] Some historians, arguing on the basis of this evidence, and with a distrust of the relatively late genealogical evidence, viewed Somerled's background as primarily Norse. Others, following the genealogies, and pointing to the Gaelic names of his father and grandfather, Gilla-Brigde (Servant of St Bride), and Gilleadomnán (Servant of St Adomnán), have stressed the predominantly Gaelic nature of his background.[14] In 1966, however, Sellar demonstrated, in an article that has found widespread acceptance among historians, that the traditional accounts of Somerled's pedigree should be regarded as authentic in detail back to the ninth century; that is, through eight generations spanning about 300 years. These pedigrees agree in taking Somerled's descent back to Godfrey, the son of Fergus, the same mid-ninth-century chieftain who was styled *toiseach Innse Gall*, and who aided Kenneth MacAlpin in 836 (see Chapter 1); Godfrey may, suggests Sellar, have had a Norse mother. From Godfrey, the genealogy continues back to the mythical Colla Uais, many generations too short, but Sellar argues that the genealogy at this point represents merely a pointer to the tribe, or people, of the Airgialla from whom Godfrey was sprung. Somerled's pedigree thus shows connections with Derry and Dál Riada, Ireland and the Isles, and has Norse connections also.[15] Thanks to this painstaking research, Somerled's mixed Scoto-Norse extraction is now the most widely held view of his pedigree. Somerled's ancestry, therefore, places him firmly within the mixed Gaelic-Norse environment of the Hebrides, which was itself a result of some two centuries of Viking settlement, and interaction, with the native Gaels of the region.

Somerled's family connections also serve to reinforce his mixed Celtic-Norse heritage, and his place within a Hebridean milieu. Through

---

[13] *ES*, ii, p. 511; *Ann. Four Masters*, ii, p. 920. The Somerled of 1083 is possibly Somerled of Argyll, misplaced 81 years by the *Annals*, which make no mention of his death in 1164: see Sellar, 'Origins and ancestry of Somerled', p. 134.

[14] See, e.g., E. MacNeill, 'Chapters of Hebridean history I: the Norse kingdom of the Hebrides', *The Scottish Review*, xxxix (1916), pp. 254–76; see also MacDonald, *History of Argyll*, p. 73.

[15] Sellar, 'Origins and ancestry of Somerled', pp. 121–37.

marriage, he was able to establish ties with the leading figures of the western seaboard, and the Irish Sea, in the early twelfth century. Sometime before 1150, Somerled married Ragnhild, the daughter of King Olaf of Man, and the marriage produced a number of sons and at least one daughter. Although the date 1140 is often cited for this marriage, it rests on no firm contemporary evidence.[16] It is instructive to note, however, that this was not Somerled's first marriage. The clan historians mention several children from other unions, perhaps in the Celtic tradition of handfasting, or else perhaps simply from what contemporary reformers regarded as barbarous marriage customs. Here, it is worth while drawing parallels with Ireland, where kings married early and often, where concepts of illegitimacy were vague, and where divorce was easy for both parties.[17] Moreover, polygamy was practised in the Irish Sea in the twelfth century; the Manx chronicle noted, with disapproval, that Olaf, the son of Godred Crovan, 'indulged too much in the domestic vice of kings', presumably a reference to its earlier comment that he 'had many concubines'.[18] Polygamous or not, the marriages of Somerled are significant because they produced many offspring, making Somerled the founder of a vigorous race of sea-kings, who, until 1265, were in constant competition with the Manx rulers for kingship in the Isles.

In addition, Somerled's own sister married Malcolm MacHeth (d. 1168), a figure who is prominent in the history of the Highlands in the early twelfth century, but whose identity is rightly considered one of the most important unsolved mysteries of twelfth-century Scottish history. Although his pedigree is uncertain, and he has sometimes been identified as an illegitimate son of King Alexander I (1107–24), who had connections with the earldom of Moray or of Ross, he was probably related to the ruling families of those provinces, perhaps belonging to the Moray dynasty of Macbeth (1040–57) and Lulach (1057–8), which claimed descent from the Cenél Loairn.[19] This marriage must have been contracted before 1134, since, in that year, MacHeth was captured by David I, and he spent the next twenty-three years as a prisoner in Roxburgh Castle. (The imprisonment, rather than the execution, of MacHeth incidentally lends credibility to the argument that he was of

---

[16] See *ES*, ii, p. 255, note.

[17] On handfasting, see W. D. H. Sellar, 'Marriage, divorce, and concubinage in Gaelic Scotland', *TGSI*, li (1978–80), pp. 464–93; on Irish marriage customs, see Byrne, 'Trembling sod', pp. 41–2.

[18] *Chron. Man*, pp. 62–3.

[19] MacHeth's lineage and origins remain one of the great unsolved problems of 12th-century Scottish history. See *ES*, ii, p. 232, note 3; *Chron. Holyrood*, p. 129, note 1; *RRS*, ii, pp. 12–13; and R. A. McDonald, 'Kings and Princes in Scotland: Aristocratic Interactions in the Anglo-Norman Era' (Guelph University, Ph.D. thesis, 1993), pp. 128–43. On the often-ignored Cenél Loairn, and their role in Scottish history, see Hudson, *Kings of Celtic Scotland*, chap. 6.

royal descent.) Whatever MacHeth's family origin, a daughter of this
match was eventually to marry Harald Maddadsson (1139–1206), the
last of the great Orkney earls, who was also active in campaigns against
the king of Scots in the 1180s and 1190s.

In assessing what the marriage alliances of Somerled and his family
reveal about the politics of the western seaboard in the first half of the
twelfth century, it is instructive to note that medieval marriage was
seldom arranged for love, but was viewed, by nobility and royalty, rather
as an important political and social tool for building alliances and good
relations. As Georges Duby has noted: 'lawful marriage was first and
foremost a political weapon. The wife was moved from square to square
like a pawn. The stakes were high. They were honour, glory, and
power.'[20] Taken in this context, it is important to determine whether any
patterns emerge from the marriage alliances of Somerled and his kin.

At the same time as many of the prominent families of eastern
Scotland (like the earls of Fife, Dunbar, and Strathearn) were associating
themselves consciously, through marriage and other means, with the
Scottish kings and Anglo-Norman families, Somerled and other west-
coast rulers (like Fergus of Galloway) demonstrate an opposite trend.
They made no attempt whatsoever to forge links with the kings of Scots,
or with Anglo-Norman settlers, until the later twelfth and thirteenth
centuries. The most important marriage connections were those linking
Somerled and Fergus with the Norse dynasty of Man, entirely separate
from the Scottish kingdom, and with other families of the north and
west like the MacHeths. Indeed, while the geographical basis for such
marriage alliances must always be kept in mind, it is tempting to surmise
that the patterns of matrimony evident in the western seaboard in the
twelfth century represent a conscious policy of separation from the royal
family and its attendants in the east.

The marriage of Somerled's sister to Malcolm MacHeth is particularly
instructive in this respect. Although some scholars have seen it as
representing an honourable link between the kings of Scots and the
family of Somerled, this view hinges on the identification of Malcolm
MacHeth as an illegitimate son of Alexander I, an interpretation which is
highly unlikely. The match more probably demonstrates an alliance
between elements opposed, for one reason or another, to the kings of
the Canmore dynasty. It is no coincidence that many of those who led
uprisings against the Scottish kings in the twelfth century were related
by marriage, and it seems clear that matrimony was fundamental in
maintaining and perpetuating an alliance of princes in the northern and
western regions of Scotland who opposed the kings of Scots. There
existed, then, a community of kings and princes on Scotland's western
seaboard, of whom Somerled was the most prominent representative,

[20] G. Duby, *The Knight, The Lady and The Priest: The Making of Modern Marriage in Medieval France* (London, 1983), p. 81.

who were linked spiritually through resistance to the Scottish kings and connected physically through ties of matrimony.[21]

A common theme in the art and literature of the Middle Ages is the 'Wheel of Fortune': someone who is humble today will rise to greatness tomorrow, only to be cast down again. Somerled appears in the light of history riding the wheel to its pinnacle, but little is known about his upward climb to the summit. It seems certain that he rose from a position of relative obscurity, since in the contemporary sources he appears on the scene only with his marriage to Ragnhild. But the evidence for the rise to the summit of the wheel rests largely upon the seventeenth-century MacDonald historians. According to these sources, Somerled's ancestors held a position of importance in Argyll, before being either forfeited or displaced. Since little is known of these predecessors, other than their names, their status cannot be corroborated. And the exact means by which they lost their territory is not known, either. The *History of the Macdonalds* suggested that Argyll had been 'wrung out of the hands of his [Somerled's] father unjustly by MacBeath, Donald Bain, and the Danes'.[22] But these accounts cannot be verified, and it is more probable that the displacement of Somerled's ancestors corresponded with the rise to power of Godred Crovan in Man (*c.*1079–95), or else with Magnus Barelegs's royal expedition to reassert Norwegian authority in 1098, when he plundered his way south through the Hebrides to Man.[23] But so much is speculation, and there is no reliable account of how Somerled managed to win back his mainland territories. Although the MacDonald historians provide a lively account of his heroic exploits in this period, they cannot be assigned to the category of history in this detail. They do suggest, however, that it was in Argyll that Somerled's rise to power began. Contemporary evidence, and evidence from the thirteenth century, would seem to support these contentions. The *Chronicle of Melrose* styled him *regulus* of Argyll, the Latin equivalent of the Gaelic *rí Airer Goidel* (king of Argyll). There is good reason for thinking that this title was bestowed upon his son, Dugald, and in the thirteenth century the MacDougalls of Lorn took the territorial designation *de Ergadia* (of Argyll) (see Chapter 3). Whatever may have been the case, Somerled's activities on the mainland were quickly eclipsed by those in the Hebrides, and with this expansion the title of *rí Innse Gall*, or 'king of the Hebrides', seems to have eclipsed that of *rí Airer Goidel*.

21 R. A. McDonald, 'Matrimonial politics and core-periphery interactions in twelfth- and early thirteenth-century Scotland', *Journal of Medieval History*, xxi (1995), pp. 227–47.

22 Macdonald, *Hist. Macdonalds, HP*, i, p. 6; *Clanranald Bk.*, p. 155. Grant, *Lordship of the Isles*, p. 165, notes that in the *Book of Clanranald* the term 'Dane' is used loosely, and evidently means 'Scandinavian'.

23 *Orkneyinga Saga* (Pálsson and Edwards), cap. 41. See also Power, 'Magnus Barelegs' expeditions', pp. 107–32.

There are further reasons for thinking that Somerled's rise to power
in Argyll must have taken place in the decades between about 1120 and
1140 – perhaps in the 1130s – when the political climate in the Scottish
kingdom would have been favourable to such an enterprise. In 1135,
King Henry I of England died without a male heir, and Stephen of Blois
seized the English throne. In the following year, civil war broke out
between Stephen and Henry's daughter, Matilda, to whom many of the
magnates had sworn fealty as rightful heir to the throne. King David of
Scotland, who had been the first lay magnate to take the oath to Matilda,
his niece, seized the opportunity presented by the civil war to press
territorial claims in northern England, and succeeded in capturing
Carlisle and Newcastle, the strategic centres of Cumbria and Northumbria. Despite the first Treaty of Durham in 1136, relations between
Stephen and David quickly deteriorated, and the Scots invaded
Northumberland in early 1138, ravaging the countryside with fire and
sword. In late summer of that year, the Scottish forces were defeated at
the Battle of the Standard, fought on 22 August at Cowton Moor near
Northallerton, but even so David was still in a strong enough position to
obtain favourable terms in a second Treaty of Durham in 1139.[24] With
King David's attention deflected toward the south, it seems probable that
Somerled took full advantage to extend further his sphere of authority.
In the account of the MacDonald historian, Somerled made himself the
master of Lorn, Argyll, Kintyre, and Knapdale even before his marriage
to Ragnhild, and had already subdued Mull and Morvern. Somerled's
marriage to the daughter of King Olaf of Man also provides proof of his
stature in the eyes of contemporaries, and suggests that the phase of
expansion on the mainland was complete. It must be noted, however,
that there is no evidence that Somerled and David were enemies, or that
Somerled seized power in Argyll in spite of the king. No chronicle
mentions war between the two men, and Islesmen are even recorded as
forming part of the Scottish contingent at the battle of the Standard in
1138. When Ailred of Rievaulx, a northern English chronicler and an
important source for the events of 1138, described the Scottish order of
battle, he noted that, 'The men of Lothian formed the third rank, with
the islanders and the men of Lorn.'[25] Ailred, unfortunately, does not
mention whether Somerled himself was present, although some modern
historians have suggested that he may well have been the leader of this
contingent from the Isles and Lorn.[26] But if Richard Oram is correct in
arguing that the Galwegian forces who participated in the battle were
mercenaries, then it may be that the Hebrideans were also hired troops,

---

[24] See K. J. Stringer, *The Reign of Stephen: Kingship, Warfare and Government in Twelfth-
century England* (London, 1993), esp. chap. 3, which deals with David I and northern
England.
[25] *SAEC*, p. 200.
[26] Duncan, *Making of the Kingdom*, p. 166.

rather than levies, and it is not necessary to assume that Somerled was present.[27] It was not until after the death of David I, and the succession of Malcolm IV, that Somerled's relations with the Scottish monarchs of the Canmore dynasty soured.

In 1153, both David I of Scotland and Olaf of Man died – the former an old man at Carlisle, having ruled vigorously for nearly thirty years, the latter killed by his nephews, who had come from Dublin to demand a share of his kingdom. David's successor was his twelve-year-old grandson, Malcolm IV (1153–65); Olaf's son, Godfrey, was in Norway doing homage at the time of his father's death, and returned to deal with the killers of his father. The situation which had been kept stable by the might and influence of both those powerful rulers was upset, and 'in these troubled waters Somerled fished assiduously'.[28] From 1153 until his death in 1164, it is necessary to follow Somerled's actions through two separate, but not entirely unrelated, spheres of influence. On the one hand, he was engaged in conflict with the king of Scots from 1153 to 1157 or 1160, and again in 1164. On the other hand, the period from 1154 to 1158 saw him extend his power and gain authority in the Isles: it might fairly be said that these years saw Somerled ride the 'Wheel of Fortune' to the pinnacle of success.

It was in the affairs of the mainland of Scotland that Somerled first became entangled, after the death of David I in 1153. In November of that year the *Chronicle of Melrose* recorded how 'Somerled and his nephews, the sons of Malcolm [MacHeth], having allied themselves with very many men, disturbed and disquieted Scotland in great part.'[29] Since Malcolm MacHeth himself had been a prisoner at Roxburgh Castle since 1134, it has been assumed, probably correctly, that the support given to the MacHeths in 1153 by Somerled was on behalf of their father, Somerled's brother-in-law, a situation which certainly requires some explanation. Above all, it must be suggested why the *status quo* was upset by Somerled in 1153.

That the rising of 1153 coincided with the death of the old king is not conclusive proof that its causes were dynastic: the death of a king, and the succession of a minor, was always an explosive combination and a potential recipe for danger. But when the timing of the rising is combined with the fact that the disaffected elements were clearly the MacHeths, and that the successor to David I was his grandson, Malcolm IV, it is difficult to escape the conclusion that the 1153 conflict was sparked by dynastic considerations.

At this point, the difficult subject of succession to the Scottish royal office must be introduced. From the ninth to the eleventh centuries in

27 R. D. Oram, 'Fergus, Galloway and the Scots', in Oram and Stell, *Galloway*, pp. 123–4.
28 Duncan and Brown, 'Argyll and the Isles', p. 196.
29 *ES*, ii, pp. 223–4.

Scotland, a system operated which can be described as alternating succession, whereby two related but rival dynastic segments took turns in the kingship, so that each held power in succeeding reigns. On the whole, under this system, sons did not succeed fathers; it was a largely inclusive system, by which it was more likely for grandsons, cousins, or even brothers to succeed. However, in the tenth and early eleventh centuries, Kenneth II (971–95) and Malcolm II (1005–34) attempted to restrict the kingship to their nearer descendants, thus creating confusion within the segmentary system of succession. These attempts to alter the succession reveal one of the great problems inherent in such an inclusive system: the threat of strife as various segments are excluded from competing for the prize of the royal office. And this is precisely what happened during the long reign of Malcolm II, which ended with two mature candidates for the kingship: Malcolm's grandson, Duncan (1034–40), and Macbeth (1040–57), a representative of the Cenél Loairn. Seventeen years after slaying Duncan, Macbeth was himself slain by Duncan's son, Malcolm (1058–93), in what one historian has called an episode in the 'war of the macAlpin succession'.[30] Indeed, between 858 and 1034, there were no fewer than fourteen Scottish kings, and, of those fourteen, five reigned for five years or less, while a further four reigned ten years or less; the average reign length was only twelve years. Strife resulting from this succession pattern is also evident in the turbulent years between 1093 and 1097, when no fewer than three different groups were in competition for the royal office. They were Malcolm III's brother, Donald bán (1093–4; 1094–7); Duncan II (1094), the son of Malcolm III by his first wife; and the sons of Malcolm III by his second wife, Margaret.

Ultimately, of course, it was the offspring of Malcolm and Margaret who emerged as the dominant segment by the end of the eleventh century, as much by accident as by the deliberate design of Malcolm III. Edgar (1097–1107) was followed in the kingship by his brother, Alexander (1107–24), who was in turn followed by the youngest of the brothers, David I (1124–53). But it was not merely the accession of these so-called MacMalcolm kings that disrupted the tradition patterns. Because Edgar and Alexander had died without issue, the succession of the eldest surviving brother was acceptable under both the kin-based system and that of primogeniture. But at the same time as these kings were consolidating their hold on the kingship, profound changes were overtaking this segment of the Scottish royal kin: it was becoming organised as a lineage. This meant that it had a sense of identity, and a self-consciousness, and that it increasingly identified itself with the kingdom it ruled. Above all, however, the organisation of the MacMalcolms as a lineage meant that there was a sense of familial order

[30] Lynch, *Scotland*, p. 47.

that bridged the gap created by the death of a ruler. In essence, in late eleventh- and early twelfth-century Scotland, as elsewhere in Europe, royal and aristocratic family structures were evolving so that it became acceptable that the natural heir was the king's eldest son or next brother. In certain charters, from about 1145, King David's son, Henry, was styled *rex designatus*, or king designate, which suggests that he was the heir apparent, according to the principle of primogeniture, and was recognised as such.

But the transition from a kin-based system of succession to a system governed by primogeniture was bound to create difficulties, and, although it may be true that after 1153 the hereditary principle of succession was generally accepted in Scotland, as late as the early thirteenth century, there were always disaffected elements waiting for the right moment to press their own claims to the royal office under the older, kin-based, system. That this is so may be seen as early as 1124, when, shortly after the succession of David I, Malcolm MacHeth made a bid for the kingship. There was a follow-up attempt in 1130, when Malcolm enlisted the assistance of Angus, the mormaer[31] of Moray (some Irish sources call him king), and then, in 1134, there followed the capture and subsequent imprisonment, of MacHeth at Roxburgh.[32] These uprisings look like the attempts of a discarded dynastic segment to press its claims on the royal office, and (as remarked already) MacHeth was only imprisoned, and not executed, in 1134, which strongly suggests that he had at least some legitimacy to his claims.[33]

Thus, a discussion of Scottish succession practices brings us back to the uprising of 1153, which begins to resemble yet another chapter in the struggle of the discarded dynastic segment represented by the MacHeths against that of the MacMalcolms, who were exercising a hereditary hold on the kingship. The 1153 uprising may therefore be regarded as an example of Gaelic conservatism, not perhaps unlike that which brought Macbeth to the kingship a century earlier, and which represented an ongoing struggle between the Cenél Gabráin and the Cenél Loairn for the kingship – the 'war of the MacAlpin succession'. That Somerled should prove to have been a major player on the twelfth-century stage in this conflict should not be surprising: he was related by marriage to MacHeth, and apart from the dictates of kin, it was natural that his nephews would seek the resources of their uncle in launching a claim on the kingship.[34]

---

31 *Mormaer* (= 'great steward') is the term used, from the 10th to the 12th centuries, for the provincial rulers of Scotland (subsequently the earls). See K. Jackson, *The Gaelic Notes in the Book of Deer* (Cambridge, 1972), pp. 102–10.

32 *ES*, ii, pp. 173–4, 183.

33 It may be instructive here to recall the example of Donald bán: although deposed and blinded in 1097, he was not killed.

34 The foregoing discussion is based upon the following sources: Smyth, *Warlords and Holy Men*, pp. 218–28; Barrow, *Kingship and Unity*, pp. 24–6; Frame, *Political*

There is, unfortunately, no evidence for the course of the uprising, although it did not proceed favourably for the Somerled/MacHeth cause. From 1154 to 1156, Somerled's attention was diverted to the Hebrides, where he was invited to establish his son, Dugald, as king of the Isles, which ultimately resulted in a bloody naval battle between the forces of Somerled and the Manx king on the night of 5–6 January, 1156.[35] The diversion of Somerled's attention towards the Irish Sea, as well as an almost inevitable withdrawal of forces from the mainland, must be related to the capture of Donald MacHeth (the son of Malcolm MacHeth) at Whithorn, and his subsequent imprisonment at Roxburgh, also in 1156.[36] These events almost certainly contributed to the collapse of the uprising. The *Chronicle of Holyrood* stated that Malcolm MacHeth was reconciled with the king of Scots in 1157, and, since he appears on record in 1168 as earl of Ross, the logical conclusion is that he received that earldom at this time, perhaps in compensation for abandoning whatever his claim might have been upon the Scottish kingship.[37] An important question is therefore whether the rising continued after 1157. By then it had lost one of its leaders, Donald MacHeth; its primary supporter, Somerled, had shifted his attention to the Western Isles and Man; and Malcolm MacHeth had been reconciled with the king of Scots. There would appear to have been little left to sustain any uprising. Nonetheless, there is no mention of a truce between Somerled and Malcolm IV until 1160, when a charter of King Malcolm to Berowald the Fleming was dated 'in Natali Domini proximo post concordiam Regis et Sumerledi' ('at the next Christmas after the agreement between the King and Somerled').[38] It is difficult to assess which party – Somerled, or the king – gained most from this agreement. Its terms are not known, and it is not mentioned in any of the contemporary narrative sources. It is, however, as difficult to sustain the thesis that King Malcolm forced the terms on Somerled as it is to maintain that Somerled forced the agreement on the king. There is an otherwise uncorroborated account in one of the clan histories that a Gilchrist, who is called 'thane of

---

Development of the British Isles, chap. 5; Hudson, *Kings of Celtic Scotland, passim*, and esp. chap. 6, on the Cenél Loairn; W. C. Dickinson, *Scotland from the Earliest Times to 1603*, 3rd edn, revised by A. A. M. Duncan (Oxford, 1977), p. 66; Barrow, *Feudal Britain*, pp. 131–42; Lynch, *Scotland*, chap. 4; and for Irish material, see D. Ó Corrain, *Ireland Before the Normans* (Dublin, 1972), pp. 37–42; and now D. Ó Cróinín, *Early Medieval Ireland, 400–1200* (London, 1995), chap. 3. There is also much of value on lineages and aristocratic family configurations in A. W. Lewis, *Royal Succession in Capetian France: Studies on Familial Order and the State* (Cambridge, Mass., and London, 1981).

[35] *ES*, ii, pp. 231–2.
[36] Ibid., ii, p.183.
[37] Ibid., ii, p. 232. A parallel circumstance may be provided by the earls of Fife, who probably abandoned their claims to the kingship in return for the honour of inaugurating the kings of Scots: J. Bannerman, 'MacDuff of Fife', in A. Grant and K. J. Stringer (eds.), *Medieval Scotland: Crown, Lordship and Community. Essays Presented to G. W. S. Barrow* (Edinburgh, 1993), pp. 20–38.
[38] *RRS*, i, no. 175.

Angus', was sent against Somerled sometime in the course of the uprising, but

> Sommerled [sic], making all the speed he could in raising his vassals and followers, went after them; and joining battle, they fought fiercely on both sides with great slaughter, til night parted them ... Being wearied, they parted and marched off at dawn of the day, turning their backs to one another.[39]

While there is no contemporary evidence for such a battle, it should be noted that no details are known about the military campaigns of the rising, and that some such conflict is not beyond the realms of possibility. But if the circumstances of the time favour a conflict, what of the identification of Somerled's opponent?

A man called Gilchrist is recorded as earl of Angus, but the first reference to him is not until about 1198, much too late for him to have been actively campaigning against Somerled in the 1150s. Gilchrist's father was Gillebrigte, who appears frequently in charters and other documents in the 1150s. Yet it does not seem inherently likely that Gilchrist should be confused with his father, Gillebrigte. There is, however, another candidate for Somerled's opponent, who is viable in terms of his name, chronology, and geography: Gilchrist, the earl of Menteith. Although little is known of the early earls of Menteith, Gilchrist is first mentioned in about 1164 and was dead by 1198, so it is not impossible that he was active in the late 1150s. But would an earl of Menteith have been more likely to campaign against the ruler of Argyll than an earl of Angus? Here the strategic position of Menteith, which shared a common frontier with Argyll, makes it quite possible that an earl of Menteith might well have fought against Somerled. In this context, it is also interesting to note that the rulers of Menteith seem to have exercised intermittent authority over Cowal and Kintyre, although how they acquired such authority remains unknown.[40] While the credibility of the seventeenth-century source must, again, arouse our scepticism, there is some circumstantial evidence which suggests that a battle between Somerled and an earl named Gilchrist might well have occurred. If, as the clan historian relates, the battle ended in a draw, with neither side emerging clearly victorious from the field, then peace may have been mutually agreed upon.

Whether or not we accept the possibility of a conflict between Somerled and the earl of Menteith, there were compelling reasons for the Scottish king to desire peace with his powerful western neighbour in 1160. Earlier in that year King Malcolm had been besieged by some of his native magnates at Perth – the so-called 'Rebellion of the Earls' –

---

39 Macdonald, *Hist. Macdonalds, HP*, i, p. 8.
40 'Ancient earls of Menteith', in J. B. Paul (ed.), *Scots Peerage*, vi (Edinburgh, 1904–14), pp. 124–5.

and, after emerging unscathed from the crisis, Malcolm vented his rage upon Fergus, the powerful and independent ruler of Galloway in the south-west. Whether this should be taken as an indication that Fergus was implicated in, or was perhaps even the leader of, the conspiracy of 1160, or whether it should simply be taken as evidence of border raids from Galloway into Scotland proper, cannot be solved on the basis of the available evidence. What is certain is that in late 1160 or early 1161, King Malcolm conducted a series of military operations in Galloway which eventually brought Fergus to heel, and forced his retirement to the Augustinian abbey of Holyrood, where he died in 1161.[41] Sound strategic sense would dictate that Malcolm did not engage in hostilities on two fronts at once, and so the peace of 1160 would have come at a particularly opportune moment, as the Scots king marshalled his forces against Galloway. But, if the agreement of Christmas 1160 guaranteed temporary peace between the western seaboard and the Scottish kingdom, the campaigns of Malcolm IV against Galloway in 1160/61 may also have laid the seeds for the more formidable rising that Somerled orchestrated in 1164, to which we shall turn shortly. First, however, it is necessary to consider Somerled's activities in the Hebrides and the Irish Sea.

The *Chronicle of Man* said of King Olaf: 'He was a man of peace, and was in such close alliance with all the kings of Ireland and Scotland, that no one ventured to disturb the kingdom of the Isles during his time.'[42] If the might of King Olaf of Man had kept Somerled in check in the Isles, then his death in 1153, and the succession of his son Godfrey, opened the way for Somerled's expansion into the Hebrides. At the time of the murder of his father, Godfrey was in Norway, doing homage to the King of Norway for Man and the Islands. After dealing with the killers of his father, and undertaking an adventure in Dublin, Godfrey returned to Man. The *Chronicle of Man* records that:

> When he [Godfrey] saw his kingdom established, and that none could oppose him, he began to employ tyranny against his chiefs; he disinherited some of them, others he cast down from their dignities.[43]

This event set the stage for the expansion of Somerled's power into the Isles. In 1155 or 1156 one of the disinherited chiefs, Thorfinn MacOttar, sent word to Somerled of Godfrey's behaviour, and invited him to send his son, Dugald, 'in order to appoint him king over the islands'.[44] It was

---

[41] *ES*, ii, pp. 245, 247. See also D. Brooke, *Wild Men and Holy Places: St Ninian, Whithorn, and the Medieval Realm of Galloway* (Edinburgh, 1994), chap. 4.

[42] *Chron. Man*, p. 61.

[43] *ES*, ii, p. 231.

[44] Ibid.

this event which may have prompted Somerled to abandon his support for the MacHeths on the mainland. Hostages to secure the good behaviour of the Islesmen were taken, but one discontented chief escaped to warn Godfrey of what had taken place, and the inevitable conflict followed.

The overture of Thorfinn to Somerled, and the sequence of events as outlined by the *Chronicle of Man*, raise more questions than they answer. Who was Thorfinn, and why did he invite Somerled to set up his son in the kingship of the Isles? In order to answer these questions, it is necessary to delve into the confusing, and often obscure, politics of the Irish Sea in the first half of the twelfth century. One of the major themes in the history of the region between about 1050 and the later twelfth century, is the close connections that existed between Dublin and Man, and the competition between the rulers of each to obtain overlordship of the other. It is difficult to escape the conclusion that it was this Dublin–Manx axis that engulfed Somerled in the mid-1150s.

From about 1112 Dublin and Man had been ruled by separate kings, but the politics of the Irish Sea continued to be dominated 'by a clique of aristocrats with a foot in both camps'.[45] In 1152, there had been an attempt by the men of Dublin to invade the Isle of Man; in 1157, Godfrey of Man had reciprocated in an attempt to assume the overlordship of Dublin. According to the *Chronicle of Man*, which may be confused in its chronology at this point, Godfrey fought a fierce battle with Muirchertach mac Lochlainn, the king of Ulster – although Irish sources are silent on any such encounter.

Thorfinn, described in the Manx chronicle as a chieftain of the Isles 'more powerful than the rest', has been identified as a relative of Ottar, an Islesman who seized power in Dublin in 1142 and held on to it until his assassination in 1148. In 1154, Muirchertach mac Lochlainn assumed the overlordship of Dublin, and it is from Muirchertach's reign that connections between Dublin and the Hebrides become apparent. The *Four Masters* record a naval conflict between mac Lochlainn and Toirrdelbach Ua Conchobair of Connacht, also in 1154, and mac Lochlainn's fleet is said to have included ships from Galloway, Arran, Kintyre, Man, and the 'shores of Scotland', presumably a reference to Argyll and the Hebrides.[46] In a neat reversal of this naval co-operation, Somerled's fleet of 1164, with which he attacked the Scottish mainland, included warriors and ships from Dublin.

Somerled's expansion into the Isles must be fitted into the context of these intrigues, counter-intrigues, and conflicts. But the chronology of the Manx chronicle is difficult to accept; although it places Godfrey's invasion of Dublin, his return to Man and ensuing tyranny, and Thorfinn's overture to Somerled in 1157, the subsequent naval battle

[45] Duffy, 'Irishmen and Islesmen', p. 126.
[46] *ES*, ii, pp. 226–7.

between Godfrey and Somerled is placed in 1156. But what the politics of the Irish Sea in the mid-twelfth century make clear is the following: that there was a connection between Dublin and the Hebrides, and between Muirchertach mac Lochlainn and Somerled, from at least 1154; and that Muirchertach mac Lochlainn and Godfrey of Man were rivals for the overlordship of Dublin and Man from about the same time. These polarisations would therefore have made Somerled the opponent of Godfrey of Man in the mid-1150s. Thorfinn's role in these events remains unclear: could he have been an envoy of Muirchertach, or was he pursuing his own agenda, perhaps in a bid to revive his family's fortunes in Dublin, with Somerled's assistance? Regardless of Thorfinn's motives, one thing seems certain: the chronicle's explanation – that Thorfinn and the other chieftains were simply reacting against Godfrey's tyranny – cannot be accepted at face value. The ongoing competition between Dublin and Man had expanded to include a new element, and Somerled had been sucked into the swirling vortex of Irish Sea politics in the 1150s. But the results were probably more than either side had bargained for.[47]

Godfrey, upon hearing the news of Somerled's attempted coup, collected a fleet with which to challenge his rival. On the night of the Epiphany, 1156 (5–6 January: although, as we have seen, the chronicle may be in error on this date), Somerled's fleet of eighty vessels met, and defeated, Godfrey's galleys. The chronicle says that there was great slaughter on both sides, but 'when day dawned they made peace; and they divided the kingdom of the islands between them, and the kingdom became bipartite from that day to the present time'.[48] There is no evidence for the precise nature of the partition in 1156, but, working backwards from the division of the later twelfth and thirteenth centuries, it would appear that Somerled (or his sons) seems to have taken control over the Southern Isles, comprising the islands south of the point of Ardnamurchan: Islay, Jura, Mull, Iona, Kintyre, Coll, Tiree, and possibly Arran and Bute. The islands north of Ardnamurchan – Skye, Lewis, and Harris – were apparently retained by Godfrey, along with Man itself. But the peace which followed the battle of the Epiphany was short-lived. Only two years later, in 1158, Somerled returned to Man, this time with fifty-three ships, and defeated Godfrey again, perhaps more decisively, forcing the latter to flee from the Isles altogether. After

---

47 On the connections between Dublin and Man in the 11th and 12th centuries, see Duffy, 'Irishmen and Islesmen', *passim*; on Somerled's involvement in the Irish Sea, see R. A. McDonald, 'Causa Ruine Regni Insularum': Somerled MacGillebrigde and the rise of a new dynasty in the Isles, *c*.1100–1164', in S. Duffy (ed.), *A New History of the Isle of Man*, vol. III: *The Medieval Period, 1000–1405* (Liverpool University Press, forthcoming).

48 *ES*, ii, pp. 231–2. There is a discussion of the site of the battle in Clark, *'Lord of the Isles' Voyage*, pp. 20–2; it is highly speculative but Clark notes that the weather conditions must have been exceptionally good to permit a naval battle at this time of year.

seeking, and apparently being refused, aid from both the Scottish and English kings in order to recover his kingdom, Godfrey fled to Norway, where he remained until Somerled's death in 1164.[49] Somerled – or his son – now became king of the Isles, and presumably of Man as well. There is no reliable evidence that Godfrey returned to the Isles before 1164, and so, in 1158, Somerled would have added Man to an island domain that already included the southern Hebrides, making him the master of most of the western seas. A new power had come of age on the western seaboard of Scotland.

An important question is why the Islesmen had asked for Somerled's son, and not Somerled himself, to rule over them. The most likely explanation is that Somerled, for some reason, was not acceptable to the Islesmen, and that the descent of Dugald from Ragnhild, the daughter of King Olaf of Man, lent the son credibility, which Somerled himself may have lacked, perhaps because of his relatively recent rise to power on the western seaboard. On the other hand, the practice of setting up a son as king under the overlordship of the father was not unusual in societies which recognised grades or degrees of kingship. As recently as 1098–9, in the wake of his expedition to the Isles, Magnus Barelegs of Norway had married his nine-year-old son to the five-year-old daughter of the king of Munster, and had set him up as ruler over the Hebrides and the Orkneys, with the title of king.[50] It may be that Somerled nursed similar aspirations in the mid-1150s. However, two facts seem noteworthy in this context. First, no source mentions Dugald as holding kingship in the Isles – indeed, nothing more is known of him until 1175, when he appears at Durham cathedral (see Chapter 3). Second, Irish sources, which noted Somerled's demise in 1164, styled him *rí Innse Gall & Cind Tire* (king of the Hebrides and Kintyre) so that in their perception, at least, it was Somerled, and not his son, who was king of the Isles – a perception no doubt reinforced in 1158, when Somerled expelled Godfrey entirely.

The motivation behind Somerled's expansion in the Hebrides and the Irish Sea has been a subject of considerable debate. The seventeenth-century historians saw the ousting of the Norse as something akin to racial hostility, and they praised Somerled as a great Gaelic lord heading a Celtic revival in the Isles. Such a view was also favoured by some nineteenth-century historians, who believed Somerled's aim to have been the establishment of an independent Gaelic kingdom. There is, in fact, little evidence for either theory. As we have seen, Somerled's ancestry was mixed Gaelic-Norse, and his family connections had brought him into close contact with the Norse dynasty of the Isles. It makes little sense to suppose that Somerled entertained racial hostility towards his neighbours and kinsmen. Moreover, the political situation in

49 *ES*, ii, pp. 248–9; Duncan and Brown, 'Argyll and the Isles', p. 196, note 5.
50 *ES*, ii, pp. 116–18; Duffy, 'Irishmen and Islesmen', p. 112.

the Irish Sea goes far towards explaining Somerled's intervention in Manx affairs in the 1150s. The answer to Somerled's policies in the Isles is to be found rather in sheer opportunism: he had been invited to Man, after all, and took full advantage of the opportunity that this presented. As one scholar so aptly puts it: 'this was ... the time for men with sharp swords and ruthless ambition to carve out spheres of power and profit for themselves'.[51] Indeed, the submission of Man and the Hebrides to Somerled's son does not appear to have been voluntary, for the *Chronicle of Man* records that hostages were taken.[52]

At this point, it is worth while attempting to discern the position held by Somerled, both on the mainland and in the Isles, and his status within twelfth-century society. One source styled Somerled *regulus*, 'kinglet', of Argyll, suggesting a nearly independent position, but also implying subordination.[53] This raises the question of just how autonomous he was. Most historians have viewed him as a mormaer, or provincial ruler, making him at worst a vassal, and at best a semi-independent, or an overmighty, subject of the Scottish king.[54] It may just be, however, that, in styling Somerled *regulus*, the *Chronicle of Melrose* was deliberately downplaying his regal status – no doubt because it did not accord with the model of a single monarchy within that kingdom, which the kings of Scots wished to uphold. Irish sources, on the other hand, are quite explicit in assigning a royal dignity to Somerled and his descendants. In his 1164 obit in the *Annals of Tigernach*, he was referred to as *rí Innse Gall & Cind tire* (king of the Hebrides and Kintyre).[55] But what did these terms mean in a twelfth-century context; and, more importantly, what do they suggest about the relationship between Somerled and the king of Scots?

Medieval society was acutely aware of questions of status and social hierarchy. This is made clear from literature, law codes, and official documents, all of which reflect the medieval obsession with status. Unfortunately, one obstacle is the difficulty of translating accurately the terms used by the chroniclers to describe status. It would, for instance, be anachronistic to translate the Latin *princeps* as the modern word 'prince'; a more accurate rendering might be simply 'ruler', 'chief', or 'lord'. *Regulus*, too, is difficult to translate: although 'kinglet' might be appropriate, 'under-king' or 'ruler' also seem to fit. In general, though, the terms utilised by the English and Scottish chroniclers to describe Somerled really only indicate that he was a ruler. From a contemporary perspective he comprised part of a large group (including kings, but not made up exclusively of kings), who, as *principes*, determined the fate of

51 J. MacInnes, 'West Highland sea power in the Middle Ages', *TGSI*, xlviii (1972–4), p. 522.
52 *ES*, ii, p. 231.
53 Ibid., ii, p. 254. On the difficulties of translating these terms, see Reynolds, *Kingdoms and Communities*, p. 260.
54 Duncan and Brown, 'Argyll and the Isles', p. 196; Barrow, *Kingship and Unity*, p. 110.
55 *Tigernach's Continuator*, ed. W. Stokes, in *Revue Celtique*, xviii (1898), p. 195.

their subjects, and the church, in their territories.[56] So, while this larger grouping of *principes* included kings, there is nothing in the terminology used by the Scottish chroniclers to denote a definite royal status for Somerled, although semi-independence and importance are certainly implied. But this bias in the Scottish sources is remedied by turning to the Irish sources, which clearly regarded Somerled as a king (Gaelic *rí*). In twelfth-century Ireland, the term *rí* was usually reserved for those rulers whose domain encompassed a significant area, and it also had territorial connotations.[57] Thus, while sources composed on the Scottish mainland were reluctant to accord Somerled a title which clearly implied royal dignity, the Irish sources were not. This was not merely the hibernicisation by Irish chroniclers of a closely related society.

There had been 'lords', or 'kings of the Isles', since the ninth and tenth century, and the title was probably a borrowing from Irish society which, like other Gaelic societies, recognised degrees of kingship ranging from tribal kingship up to provincial kingships. By the time the Norwegian kings asserted control in the Isles, the title was so well established that it was virtually impossible to suppress it, and the mid-twelfth-century situation in Norway was not conducive to restoring royal authority, nor to disciplining rulers like Somerled.[58] Moreover, Somerled was not unique in holding this title, for it was accorded to other powerful figures on the Scottish periphery. Somerled's contemporary, Fergus of Galloway, was called *princeps* of Galloway by one chronicler and styled himself *rex* in one of his charters, while the rulers of Moray in the tenth and eleventh centuries were sometimes styled kings in the Irish sources. To contemporaries within the Gaelic world, Somerled and his descendants possessed regal dignity, and it is doubtful that his 'constitutional position' (to use an anachronism) differed from that of the Irish provincial kings, the Welsh princes of Gwynedd, Powys, and Deheubarth, or the Norse kings of Man. When viewed from the broader British perspective, part of the problem is simply that kingship on the periphery of Britain was contracting in the twelfth, and especially the thirteenth, centuries, as Scottish and English kingship expanded.[59] Moreover, not only did Gaelic notions about multiple kingship not fit into the contemporary ideas of kingship that were finding expression in England and Scotland, but there was also a good deal of confusion about the terminology of status in the twelfth century.

Much of the debate over the status of Somerled evaporates when viewed in the light of the relationship between Gaelic and Latin titles in the sources. The terminology is often so confusing because the eleventh

56 K. F. Werner, 'Kingdom and principality in twelfth-century France', in T. Reuter (ed.), *The Medieval Nobility: Studies on the Ruling Classes of France and Germany from the Sixth to the Twelfth Century* (Amsterdam, 1979), p. 244.
57 See K. Simms, *From Kings to Warlords* (Woodbridge, 1987), p. 11.
58 Crawford, *Scandinavian Scotland*, p. 192.
59 See Frame, *Political Development of the British Isles*, esp. chap. 5.

and twelfth centuries in Scotland were a time of transition, when Latin scribes were struggling with Gaelic vocabularies that were alien to them. This problem has been illuminated by John Bannerman, who has undertaken a comprehensive examination of the terminology of the kin-based society in the early Gaelic, and later Latin, sources. He has been able to demonstrate how the terminology of the kin-based society was translated into Latin terms that were acceptable to feudal society. Thus, the *toiseach* of the Gaelic sources became, in Latin sources of *c.*1100, the *thenus*, or more familiar *thane*. In similar fashion, the *rí tuath* or *ruiri*, who was both the ruler of his own 'tuath' and the overlord of others, became in Latin documents either *dominus* or *regulus*. It was only the *rí ruirech* of Gaelic society who was accorded the title of *rex* in the Latin sources. This suggests that, when confronted with an alien social hierarchy consisting of many different levels of kingship, Latin scribes did their best to describe that society in their own terms, and to make it conform with a society that was familiar to them. But Somerled, as we have seen, was not a product of feudal society; his relations were not governed by feudalism, and the Irish sources which call him *rí* are the most accurate measure of his status in contemporary eyes. Even if the Irish sources relating to Somerled were somehow lost, Bannerman's detective work would permit us to work backwards from the Latin sources, and would allow us to deduce the status of Somerled within the kin-based society.[60]

Two entries in the Manx chronicle suggest that not only Somerled, but also his sons, had some stake in the kingdom of Man after the events of 1156–8. When it mentions the marriage of Somerled to Olaf's daughter, the chronicle states that 'she was the downfall of the whole kingdom of the isles; for he begot by her four sons'. The 1156 entry goes on to explain that 'this was the cause of the downfall of the kingdom of the islands, from the time when the sons of Somerled took possession of it'.[61] While not only betraying the outlook of the chronicler, this statement has also led scholars to believe that Somerled's sons must have had some share in the kingdom before his death.[62] Although Godfrey rapidly re-established himself in Man and the Sudreys, following the death of Somerled in 1164, as late as 1231 the kingdom was still regarded as being divided between the kings of Man and Somerled's descendants.[63] The rise of Somerled had implications that stretched far beyond just the west coast of Scotland proper, into the rest of the Irish Sea world.

---

[60] See J. Bannerman, 'The Scots language and the kin-based society', in D. S. Thomson (ed.), *Gaelic and Scots in Harmony: Proceedings of the Second International Conference on the Languages of Scotland* (Glasgow, 1990); and E. J. Cowan, 'The historical MacBeth', in W. D. H. Sellar (ed.), *Moray: Province and People* (Edinburgh, 1993), p. 119.

[61] *ES*, ii, pp. 137, 231–2.

[62] Duncan and Brown, 'Argyll and the Isles', p. 197.

[63] *ES*, ii, pp. 471–2.

Between the years 1160 and 1164 Somerled disappears from the historical record. G. W. S. Barrow thinks that, although his name is not present in contemporary documents, Somerled may have been among those who kept the Christmas feast of 1160 at Perth with Malcolm IV, where he may have confirmed his agreement with Malcolm in some fashion. Perhaps, as Barrow suggests, it was this occasion which led to a clerk of Glasgow giving Somerled the epithet 'sit-by-the-king'.[64] Whatever may have been the case, if the terms of this agreement were kept, peace should have prevailed between the king of the Isles and the king of Scots. But then, in 1164, Somerled orchestrated a massive invasion of the Scottish kingdom. According to the chronicles (though their numerical estimates should not always be believed), a fleet of 160 galleys full of warriors from the Hebrides, Argyll, Kintyre, and Dublin sailed up the Clyde as far as Renfrew; the *Carmen de Morte Sumerledi* records the event in graphic detail: 'The enemy slew and injured with fire and sword their miserable victims. Gardens, fields, ploughed lands, were ravaged and laid waste; barbarous hands mastered and menaced the meek ... The people of Glasgow wounded fled from the sword-strokes.' According to the same source, the Hebridean army was defeated in battle by a hastily assembled, and numerically inferior, force (albeit with a bit of supernatural help from St Kentigern):

> Hear a marvel! To the terrible, the battle was terrible ... And in the first cleft of battle the baleful leader fell. Wounded by a spear, slain by the sword, Somerled died. And the raging wave swallowed his son, and the wounded of many thousand fugitives ... and very many were slaughtered, both on sea and on land ... Rout and slaughter were made of thousands of the traitors; while none of their assailants was wounded or killed.[65]

Some traditions suggest that the landing took place at Renfrew, with the battle occurring near the Knock, an elevation halfway between Paisley and Renfrew. Others suggest a landing near Greenock and a battle near Inchinnan. In 1772 the traveller Thomas Pennant was shown at the Knock a mound or tumulus with a stone on the top, which he was told indicated the spot where Somerled had died; but by 1895 no trace remained of this monument.[66] Another tradition, which first arose in the seventeenth century and is frequently perpetuated, maintains that Somerled was assassinated through the treachery of King Malcolm's Anglo-French nobles:

---

64 *RRS*, i, pp. 14–15; *ES*, ii, p. 256.
65 Ibid., ii, pp. 256–8.
66 On the traditions of the battle, see W. M. Metcalfe, *A History of the County of Renfrew* (Paisley, 1905), pp. 29–30; and J. A. Dunn, *History of Renfrew* (Paisley, n.d.), p. 30. On the absence of the mound on the Knock in 1895, see Groome, *Ordnance Gazetteer of Scotland*, v, p. 241.

There was a nephew of Sommerled's, Maurice MacNeill, his sister's son, who was bribed to destroy him. Sommerled lay encamped at the confluence of the river Paisley into Clyde. His nephew taking a little boat, went over the river, and having got private audience of him, being suspected by none, stabbed him, and made his escape ... The rest of Sommerled's men hearing the death and tragedy of their leader and master, betook themselves to their galleys.[67]

It is difficult to say how such a tradition arose. But since the contemporary sources, both Irish and Scottish, all agree in either stating that there was a battle or suggesting that Somerled's death occurred in battle, this seems to be the most likely explanation of how the king of *Innse Gall* met his death. Indeed, the *Carmen* records that 'A priest cut off the head of the unfortunate leader Somerled, and gave it into the bishop's hands.' The *Annals of Tigernach* name the son that was killed with him as Gillebrigte.[68] Although nineteenth-century MacDonald tradition held that Somerled's final resting place was Saddell Abbey in Kintyre, the seventeenth-century sources, relying upon a chronicle now lost, stated – probably correctly – that his body was carried to Iona for burial (possibly in St Oran's chapel), which may have been constructed by Somerled, or his sons, to serve as a mausoleum.[69]

The motivation behind the 1164 attack, has long puzzled historians, and the matter is not helped by the fact that the earliest attempts to explain it are confused, and probably inaccurate. John of Fordun, writing in the fourteenth century, thought that Somerled aimed at nothing but plunder. George Buchanan, writing in the sixteenth century, believed that his aim was the throne of Scotland, while one of the seventeenth-century clan historians implied that Somerled had been provoked to invade because 'the nobles were still in [King Malcolm's] ears, desiring him to suppress the pride of Sommerled', so that they could divide his kingdom among themselves.[70] Writers of the past century have generally agreed that Somerled's aim was the establishment of an independent Gaelic kingdom, and only seldom is the 1164 rising attributed to Celtic conservatism.[71] The motives of the assault only become intelligible when viewed within both the framework of Somerled's position as a Scoto-Norse ruler on the periphery of the Scottish

---

67 Macdonald, *Hist. Macdonalds*, *HP*, i, pp. 9–10. This view was popularised by Nigel Tranter in his novel: *Lord of the Isles* (London, 1983).

68 *ES*, ii, p. 254.

69 See R. A. McDonald, 'The death and burial of Somerled of Argyll', *West Highland Notes and Queries*, 2nd ser., viii (Nov. 1991), pp. 6–10. The suggestion that St Oran's was built as a mortuary chapel is made by J. G. Dunbar and I. Fisher, in *Iona* (RCAHMS, 1983), p. 12.

70 *Chron. Fordun*, i, p. 257; ii, p. 251; George Buchanan, *The History of Scotland*, trans. J. Aikman (Glasgow, 1827), i, pp. 359–60; Macdonald, *Hist. Macdonalds*, *HP*, i, p. 8.

71 See MacDonald, *History of Argyll*, p. 79; Barrow, *Kingship and Unity*, p. 48.

kingdom (which has already been assessed), and that of the modern-isation of Scotland under the successors of Malcolm Canmore.

The sequence of events, which culminated in Somerled's invasion in 1164, commenced in late 1160 and early 1161, when King Malcolm invaded Galloway three times, and forced Fergus to retire to Holyrood Abbey in Edinburgh, where a watchful eye could be kept on him by the king, and where he died in 1161.[72] This episode demonstrates the fate that awaited traditionally independent native princes at the hands of the young king and his supporters. Another passage in the *Chronicle of Holyrood* shows that Galloway was not the only province to feel the iron fist of Malcolm IV; it states that in 1163, possibly following a disturbance in the northern province of Moray, King Malcolm moved, or subsequently transferred, the men of that province ('rex Malcolmus Murevienses transtulit').[73] To Fordun, that meant that Malcolm removed the inhabitants of Moray, 'so that not even one native of that land abode there'.[74] But the vagueness of the wording of the original chronicle entry makes it difficult to interpret, and various suggestions have been offered on the meaning of this passage, including a transplantation of the natives of the region, or the transferral of the bishopric of Moray.[75] While some allowance must be made for the ambiguous nature of the statement, and for exaggeration on the part of Fordun, this should not cause us to dismiss it lightly. Indeed, the passage may well be related to a continued policy of colonisation of the Moray region by King Malcolm, and, in this context, it may be no coincidence that, as recently as 1160, the king had granted lands in Moray to Berowald the Fleming from Lothian.[76] On the other hand, it may be that the transferral was prompted by some otherwise unknown rebellion in Moray, always a hotbed of dissent and a rallying-point for those who would oppose the Canmore dynasty. Whatever may have been the case, the events of the years between 1160 and 1164 illustrate that not only did King Malcolm appear to be striking less of a balance between old and new than had his grandfather, David I, but also that the native Scottish elite was being alienated at an alarming rate. Somerled's attack on the Scottish mainland in 1164 must be seen as a natural development out of this background of alienation and suppression.

An important question is just how this alienation would have manifested itself, and in order to answer it we must consider the process whereby the Scottish kingdom underwent modernisation, or Norman-isation, as it is sometimes called, in the course of the twelfth century.

[72] *ES*, ii, pp. 245, 247.
[73] *Chron. Holyrood*, p. 142; *ES*, ii, p. 251.
[74] *Chron. Fordun*, i, pp. 256–7; ii, pp. 251–2.
[75] See, e.g., *Chron. Holyrood*, pp. 142–3, note; Duncan, *Making of the Kingdom*, p. 191; and D. P. Kirby, 'Moray in the twelfth century', in McNeill and Nicholson, *Historical Atlas of Scotland*, p. 49.
[76] *RRS*, i, no. 175.

Although Macbeth had utilised some Norman mercenaries who had been exiled from England in the early 1050s, foreign influence in Scotland may be said to have begun with a trickle in *c*.1070, when Malcolm III married the Anglo-Saxon princess Margaret. According to Turgot's *Life of Margaret*, she attempted to modernise the life of the court, and she also made moves towards the reform of the Scottish Church. While the civil strife which followed the deaths of Malcolm and Margaret in 1093 included the expulsion of 'all the English who had been with King Malcolm' from Scotland, the year 1097 saw the establishment of Malcolm and Margaret's eldest son, Edgar, in the Scottish kingship, with the assistance of the Norman king of England, William Rufus.

Edgar may well have been simply a client-king of the Norman kings of England, but with his reign there began nearly sixty years of rule for Scotland by three sons of Malcolm and Margaret. Since they had all spent significant periods of their lives at the court of the Norman kings of England, it was only natural that aspects of that culture would begin to permeate Scottish society. Alexander, who succeeded Edgar in 1107, took a more independent line, and his reign saw the introduction of some castles and the foundation of several houses for the reformed monastic orders. But it was not until the reign of the youngest son, David (1124–53), that Scotland really moved into a new epoch – what Barrow has called the 'Davidian experiment'.[77] Under King David, lands began to be granted to his followers in return for military service. What this process, which continued throughout his reign and well beyond, amounted to was the beginning of the transformation of Scottish society south of the Forth–Clyde line, and along the Lowland plain of the east coast, into Moray. As lands were granted out, in return for military service, society became feudalised; the motte-and-bailey castle and the mounted knight – the symbols of Anglo-Norman feudalism – became increasingly common; burghs and coinage signalled an economic transformation. It must be noted, however, that this expansion did not proceed uniformly throughout Scotland. Indeed, it was to be a century and a half before royal authority even began to be extended in the western seaboard, and there was also little settlement in Galloway proper before the last quarter of the twelfth century.[78]

[77] Ibid., i, p. 4.
[78] On the feudalisation, or Normanisation, of Scotland, see the recent work of D. Walker, *The Normans in Britain* (London, 1995), chap. 4; works dealing more specifically with Scotland include R. L. G. Ritchie, *The Normans in Scotland* (Edinburgh, 1954); Duncan, *Making of the Kingdom*; Barrow, *Kingship and Unity*; and G. W. S. Barrow, *The Anglo-Norman Era in Scottish History* (Oxford, 1980). The term 'feudalism' engenders much debate at present. A precise definition is difficult, because, as R. A. Brown has observed, 'having been invented by writers of a later age to describe a state of affairs already past, it tends to mean different things to different people': *The Normans and the Norman Conquest* (London, 1969), p. 85. Depending upon the training and outlook of the writer it can be interpreted very narrowly, or in such

By the middle of the twelfth century (about the same time that Somerled upset the *status quo* of the 1130s and 1140s, and became locked in conflict with the kings of Scots), the heart of the Scottish kingdom was being insulated from the autonomous regions of Galloway and Argyll by a buffer zone of fiefs, which had been slowly expanding westward from the middle of the 1120s. Although this expansion took place piecemeal, rather than at one fell swoop, and its chronology remains elusive, there can be no doubt that this represented a deliberate act of policy aimed at building up a barrier between the increasingly feudalised core of the kingdom and the peripheral regions on the western seaboard, which both frightened and fascinated the Scottish kings and their English and French followers. The process began early in the reign of David I, with the grant of Annandale and its castles at Annan and Lochmaben. Next came Walter fitz Alan's investiture with Renfrew, Strathgryfe and Mearns, and the northern half of Kyle, which tightened the noose in the west and south-west. In addition to these vast Stewart holdings, the de Moreville family also acquired significant lands in the west of Scotland, comprising Cunningham, which bordered on the Stewart holdings of Renfrew, and Kyle Stewart. This policy of granting land meant that the most important Anglo-Norman officers in the kingdom were enfeoffed in such a way that their holdings interposed themselves between the unruly margins and the Normanised core of the kingdom. As Barrow has noted:

> we should remark the symmetrical arrangement by which the four districts of Renfrew-Strathgryfe, Cunningham, North Kyle and South Kyle, important for the defence of the realm against attack from Galloway or the west, were held respectively by the Steward, the Constable, the Steward and the Crown.[79]

The conflict of 1164, in which Somerled lost his life, should probably be seen as conservative opposition to the rapidly expanding group of Anglo-Norman fiefs pushed westward by David I and Malcolm IV, and especially to the growth of the Stewart lordship around Renfrew. The westward thrust of these fiefs, with their Anglo-Norman lords, knights, and motte-and-bailey castles, must have been viewed with increasing interest and suspicion by the rulers of the south and west, like Somerled

broad fashion that it becomes all-encompassing; other historians, however, would expunge it from our vocabulary altogether on the basis that it is an artificial construct: E. A. R. Brown, 'The tyranny of a construct: feudalism and the historians of medieval Europe', *American Historical Review*, lxxix, no. 4 (1974); and S. Reynolds, *Fiefs and Vassals: The Medieval Evidence Re-interpreted* (Oxford, 1994). In treating of feudalism, I accept the commonly used definition: 'An institution based on the holding of a fief, unusually a unit of land, in return for stipulated honourable service, usually military, with a relationship of homage and fealty existing between the grantee and the grantor': C. W. Hollister, *The Military Organization of Norman England* (Oxford, 1965), p. 11, note 3.

[79] *RRS*, i, p. 39; see also Barrow, *Robert Bruce*, p. 20.

and Fergus of Galloway. In short, although the surviving sources suggest that Somerled was the aggressor, from his perspective as an independent ruler of the western seaboard, it would have been the Stewarts, and the feudal society of which they were a part, who were cast in that role. Somerled's actions should therefore be seen as a pre-emptive strike against the expanding Stewart lordship in the west of Scotland.

This hypothesis is supported by the geographical setting for Somerled's landing, for Renfrew was the *caput* of fiefs held by Walter fitz Alan, one of King Malcolm's closest Anglo-Norman advisors. Moreover, it was only part of a far-flung feudal lordship that stretched from northern England to the southern shores of the Clyde. It is certainly no coincidence that Somerled chose Renfrew as the beachhead of his landing. With its castle (first documented between 1163 and 1165) and burgh, Renfrew symbolised Anglo-Norman penetration as far west as the Clyde, surely bordering too closely for comfort on Somerled's own island kingdom. It is also significant that, while these fiefs had been initially granted by David I, Malcolm IV rapidly expanded knights' feus and baronies in the Clyde valley, in the process confirming his grandfather's grants to Walter fitz Alan in 1161 or 1162. And one of the most remarkable developments in the Firth of Clyde, in the later twelfth century, was the dynamic growth of the Stewart lordship from its original centre at Renfrew. Whether or not the presence of Walter fitz Alan at Renfrew was perceived as a threat to Somerled must remain a matter of conjecture, but the landing at Renfrew does support the proposed motive for the invasion: the elimination, or at least reduction, of Anglo-Norman influence in the West, and hence the threat to his territory.[80] While it is not known whether the king of Argyll was met in battle by Walter fitz Alan himself, it does seem likely, given the nature of the threat. And there would be a certain dramatic, if not historical, satisfaction, had Somerled and Walter fitz Alan faced one another on the field of battle at Renfrew, the former representing the forces of Celtic or Scoto-Norse conservatism, the latter the face of the 'Brave New World' of Scoto-French feudal society.

In the span of the four years from 1160 to 1164, the 'Wheel of Fortune had brought Somerled crashing down from the pinnacle of his success. After the forces of the Islesmen were routed at Renfrew, the body of Somerled was carried to the island of Iona for burial. It is certainly ironic that a prince whose main interest clearly lay in the Isles, was killed on the mainland, but it is also fitting that one whose career was based upon the sword perished in battle. It is also entirely appropriate that Somerled should have been buried on Iona, in both the

---

[80] See the fuller argument presented in R. A. McDonald and S. A. McLean, 'Somerled of Argyll: a new look at old problems', *SHR*, lxxi (1992), pp. 1–20. The best work on the Anglo-Norman families remains Barrow's *Anglo-Norman Era* (for Renfrew, p. 339); see also Barrow, *Kingship and Unity*, pp. 47–8 and 87–8.

religious, and political, centre of his kingdom. Whether we are inclined to regard Somerled as a semi-independent client-king, or as an independent ruler in the Hebridean tradition, his legacy in the western seaboard was profound. First, he had succeeded in carving out an island kingdom, which stretched from the Isle of Man to the Isle of Skye, and from Kintyre to the point of Ardnamurchan, the unity of which was based upon the highway provided by the western seas themselves, and the galleys that plied its waves. The solidarity of this kingdom was very real. It is reflected in the title accorded to Somerled in one of the Irish annals, *rí Innse Gall & Cind tire*, which suggests the political cohesion of the area as a territorial unit. This political unity is further reinforced by the composition of the army that Somerled mustered in 1164 for his ill-fated invasion of the Scottish mainland. Various sources state that Somerled was able to call on warriors from Argyll, Kintyre, the Hebrides, and Dublin, and it would hardly be surprising if the army had contained men from Galloway, Moray, or even the Orkneys, as well. This only reinforces the point that rulers from one region of the Irish Sea world were able to recruit troops from others, and it reminds us of the trans-national nature of this maritime culture of the Irish Sea as late as the twelfth century. On at least one other occasion, we see the men of Argyll and the Isles acting in concert: when, in 1164, an attempt was made to reform or revive the church at Iona, it was undertaken 'by the counsel of Somerled, and the men of Argyll and of the Hebrides'.[81] Moreover, although there is no evidence to suggest that Somerled and David I were ever at odds with one another during the 1150s and 1160s, in the reign of Malcolm IV, the relations between the periphery and the core of the Scottish kingdom took a definite turn for the worse. Somerled himself perished in an invasion of the Scottish mainland, foreshadowing one of the major themes of the century following his demise: the ambivalent relations between his descendants and the Scottish kings. Finally, while it is true that, with the removal of Somerled from the scene in 1164, the southern half of his sea-kingdom was recovered by the Manx kings, and that most of the northern half was divided among his own warring descendants, the greatest legacy of this twelfth-century prince was that from him sprang the families which would dominate the western seaboard for some three and a half centuries following his death, and it is to these descendants that we must now turn.

[81] *ES*, ii, pp. 253–4; see also below, chap. 7.

CHAPTER THREE

'A Good Family': The MacSorleys, 1164–1249

> Then came from west beyond the sea Ewen, Duncan's son, and Dugald, Ruairi's son; and they both endeavoured after this, that the king [Hakon IV of Norway] should give them the title of king over the northern part of the Hebrides [1247–8, *Hakon's Saga*].[1]

The decades spanning the years between 1164 and 1249, from the fall of Somerled at Renfrew to the death of Alexander II at Kerrera, are paradoxically both crucial and obscure ones in the history of the western seaboard. They are obscure because, even by the standards of the Western Highlands and Islands, the period after 1164 is particularly ill-served by historical sources. While there is a dearth of evidence for Somerled, even less is known with much certainty about his descendants (often called the MacSorleys) and the division of his island kingdom among them. On the other hand, these decades are crucial because two key themes run through them. The first is the continued independence and autonomy of the region under the MacSorleys, no less marked for the divisions within their own ranks and their recurring conflicts with one another. The second, and perhaps the more important, is the increasing interest paid to the region by both the kings of Scots and the kings of Norway, and the increasing tension as the Hebrides were caught between the pull of two powerful magnets: the expanding monarchies of Scotland and Norway. By 1249, the descendants of Somerled were finding themselves ground between these upper and lower millstones of royal authority, and were faced with a dilemma of divided allegiances which would eventually force them to throw in their lot with either Norway or Scotland. The plights of Ewen of Argyll and his cousin, Dugald MacRuairi, great-grandsons of Somerled, neatly encapsulate the difficulties that faced the rulers of the western seaboard, in the uncertain times of the thirteenth century.

King Malcolm IV followed Somerled to the grave in 1165. His successor was his brother, William (1165–1214), whose long reign has been divided into several distinct parts by modern historians. Although the first seven or eight years of the reign were marked by peace at home and good relations with the king of England, the year 1173 was the

---

[1] *Hakon's Saga*, in *ES*, ii, p. 548.

beginning of the lowest ebb of the reign, when Scotland was subjected to fifteen years of English overlordship. This turn of events owed much to William's fervent desire to recover the northern English counties, in pursuit of which the Scots undertook three incursions across the Border in 1173–4. It was in the course of the third invasion that the king and many of his followers were captured at Alnwick in July 1174; and the Scots were further humiliated by the terms of the Treaty of Falaise in 1175. Clearly, the Scots king had other concerns than the West, and it was fortunate for Argyll, in its weakened state, that William did not decide to crush Somerled's sons.[2] Little effort was therefore expended on the subjugation of Argyll or the Isles by William I, although there was a good deal of campaigning in the North against other foes in the late 1170s, the 1180s, and the 1190s. The last years of the reign were dominated by poor relations with England, uprisings by the MacHeths and the MacWilliams, and by the king's advancing age and ill-health.[3] These factors, combined with a lengthy and bitter civil war in Norway from 1130 to 1204, meant that for much of the twelfth and early thirteenth centuries the western seaboard was left to its own devices – and troubles – by both Scotland and Norway.

This non-interventionist attitude toward the western seaboard, which persisted for over fifty years, must be seen as crucial in allowing the MacSorleys to retain their autonomy. It has been observed how, in a kin-based society like that of Ireland and Scotland, divisive tendencies appeared during a period of expansion, particularly when control at the top was weakened.[4] Nowhere can this process be seen more vividly than in the Western Isles during the second half of the twelfth century, when the sons of Somerled fell to quarrelling with one another over their father's patrimony, and the Clan Somairle separated into three important divisions. Somerled was the first and the last of his house, with the possible exception of his great-grandson, Ewen, to rule such a far-flung sea-kingdom. He had at least five sons: Dugald, Ranald, Angus, Olaf (of whom nothing more is known) and Gillabrigte (who perished with his father at Renfrew), a daughter, Bethag (anglicised as Beatrice, first abbess of the Augustinian nunnery on Iona), and possibly several other sons, born either out of wedlock or by other marriages, whose historicity remains contentious.[5] Upon his death, Somerled's sons partitioned their father's kingdom among them, according to Gaelic practice,[6] and, while

2 MacDonald, *History of Argyll*, p. 84.

3 A good introduction to William's reign is to be found in *RRS*, ii, pp. 1–28; and, now, in D. D. R. Owen, *William the Lion, 1143–1214: Kingship and Culture* (East Linton, 1997), *passim*.

4 K. A. Steer and J. Bannerman, *Late Medieval Monumental Sculpture in the West Highlands* (RCAHMS, 1977), appendix I, p. 202.

5 *Clanranald Bk.*, p. 157, mentions Gall MacSgillin; Macdonald, *Hist. Macdonalds, HP*, i, p. 11, mentions Somerled and Gillies.

6 A. J. G. MacKay, 'Notes and queries on the custom of Gavelkind in Kent, Ireland, Wales, and Scotland', *PSAS*, xxxii (1898), pp. 133–58.

each was much less powerful individually than Somerled himself had been, they nonetheless maintained both the regal dignity which they had inherited from Somerled and the autonomy of his western kingdom.

It is the division among Dugald, Ranald and Angus that is the most important. Unfortunately there is no contemporary evidence to shed light on how the territories were apportioned. While the holdings of Somerled's grandsons can be determined with greater certainty than those of his sons, it would be dangerous to assume that the same divisions existed in the later twelfth century, particularly because of the warfare between Dugald and Ranald, and between Ranald and Angus.[7] In general terms, though, there is little doubt that the sons of Somerled ruled on the mainland from Knoydart in the north to the Mull of Kintyre in the south, and held sway over the islands from Coll and Tiree to Islay, and possibly over Arran and Bute as well. The most widely accepted hypothesis for the distribution of Somerled's lands is that Dugald received the heart of Somerled's territory, namely Lorn, Benderloch, Lismore, Mull, Coll and Tiree (perhaps the ancestral lands), while Ranald's share was Kintyre, Morvern, Ardnamurchan, Islay, and Jura. The territory of Angus, less easy to identify, probably consisted of largely insular holdings, possibly including Bute and Arran, Skye, and perhaps Garmoran (Rhum, Eigg, the Uists, Benbecula, Barra, and, on the mainland, Moidart, Arisaig, Morar and Knoydart) as well.[8] However uncertain our knowledge may be of the exact allocation of Somerled's kingdom, one thing seems clear: in the understated words of A. and A. MacDonald, 'the division of the Somerledian possessions does not appear to have given unqualified satisfaction'.[9] By the beginning of the thirteenth century, in a process largely hidden by gaps in the evidence, Ranald had apparently greatly expanded his holdings; Dugald's authority was perhaps circumscribed; and Ranald's sons also appear to have obtained at least some of the territories of Angus on his death in 1210.

One of the important by-products of these internecine struggles among the MacSorleys was the resurgence of the Norse dynasty in Man. In 1156, Somerled and Godfrey, the Manx king, had divided the Isles between them, following the naval battle of the Epiphany. Then, in 1158, Somerled returned to Man, and defeated Godfrey in another engagement, this time forcing his opponent out of the Isles altogether. Following the demise of Somerled in 1164, however, Godfrey quickly re-established himself as king of Man and of at least some of the Isles, including Lewis, Harris, the Uists, Barra, and apparently also Skye. This meant that not only was Somerled's far-flung but short-lived sea-

[7] Duncan and Brown, 'Argyll and the Isles', p. 198; see also MacDonald, *History of Argyll*, pp. 84–5.

[8] Barrow, *Kingship and Unity*, pp. 109–10; Duncan and Brown, 'Argyll and the Isles', p. 198; MacDonald, *History of Argyll*, pp. 84–5.

[9] A. and A. MacDonald, *The Clan Donald* (Inverness, 1896–1904), i, p. 59.

kingdom seriously truncated, and the division of 1156 reopened, but also that there now existed, in close proximity, two rival but related dynasties in the Western Isles: the MacSorleys and the Godfreysons. Much of the strife in the Hebrides, noted by the thirteenth-century chroniclers, stemmed from the re-establishment of the Manx dynasty, and from the close proximity of these two rival sea-going dynasties in the islands.

The question of which of Somerled's sons, Dugald or Ranald, was the elder is a bristly one, complicated by the various claims, counterclaims, and rivalries of clan history.[10] It is perhaps essential to note two points at the outset: first, that in a kin-based society which did not practise inheritance by primogeniture, the question is largely irrelevant; second, that none of the contemporary sources stated the order of birth of Somerled's sons, and, accordingly, we are left to make deductions and speculations based upon the fragmentary evidence available. Current scholarly opinion favours Dugald as being the eldest surviving son, and Ranald and Angus as being his younger brothers. The late twelfth- or early thirteenth-century *Orkneyinga Saga* listed Somerled's sons as Dugald, Ranald, and Angus, in that order, but it is extremely confused in its account of Somerled and should not be regarded as authoritative in this regard. Of more significance are the events of 1155–6, when the chieftain Thorfinn MacOttar requested that Somerled send his son Dugald to be set up as king in the islands. This seems to suggest Dugald's seniority, and the case for his being the eldest son is further strengthened by the fact that the power-base of his descendants, the Clan Dugall, was located in the heart of mainland Argyll, which is usually taken to be Somerled's original territory. This may indicate that Dugald had succeeded his father in the headship of the kindred. It may well be, although it was never recorded, that Dugald was *rí Airer Goidel*, king of Argyll, in succession to his father. But since the kindred of Somerled was a rapidly expanding one, Dugald's brother, Ranald, was able to share in the expansion also, becoming *rí Innse Gall*, ruler of the Hebrides, a title acquired through conquest which ultimately eclipsed that of *rí Airer Goidel*. The claim that Dugald was *rí Airer Goidel* is further reinforced by the fact that his descendants, the MacDougalls of Lorn, took the title *de Ergadia*, of Argyll.[11]

Whatever may have been the case, contemporary records are remarkably, and frustratingly, silent on Dugald. Nothing is known, nor can anything be deduced, about his activities between 1155 and 1175. It is

---

[10] See MacDonald, *History of Argyll*, p. 89, and note 242, for further discussion of the problem.

[11] I am grateful to John Bannerman, who mentioned the possibility of Dugald being *rí Airer Goidel* to me in private correspondence. See also MacDonald, *History of Argyll*, pp. 89–90.

not known, for instance, whether he played a role in the administration of his father's kingdom while Somerled was still alive, although the events of 1155–6 might suggest that he did, perhaps ruling Man under his father's overkingship. It is also unknown whether he accompanied his father on the ill-fated Renfrew invasion of 1164, when Somerled and Dugald's brother, Gillabrigte, were killed. It is not until 1175 that Dugald emerges briefly into the light of historical documentation, this time not in the western seaboard at all but in northern England. A notice in a twelfth-century hand in the *Liber Vitae*, or *Book of Life*, of Durham Cathedral, recorded that:

> In the year from the Lord's incarnation 1175, in which king Henry the elder received allegiance and fealty from the Scots at York, Dugal, son of Somerled, and Stephen his chaplain, and Adam de Stanford received the brotherhood of our church at the feet of St Cuthbert on the vigil of St Bartholomew [23 August]; and the same Dugal offered there two golden rings to St Cuthbert, and promised that every year, so long as he lived, he would give one mark to the convent, either in money or its equivalent.[12]

This entry raises the intriguing problem of why one of Somerled's sons should appear in England at this time, and why he should appear as a benefactor of the monks of Durham. Since he was recorded as being at Durham a fortnight after King William and his barons had sworn fealty to King Henry II at York on 10 August 1175, in the wake of the defeat and capture of the Scottish king at Alnwick in 1174, it has been suggested that Dugald must have been one of those Scottish nobles who accompanied King William to York, and that he was in the king of Scots' peace at this time.[13] The major difficulty with this interpretation is that it supposes Dugald to have been more of a Scottish noble than the evidence would seem to warrant, although it is probably significant that Dugald's son, Duncan, was listed among the Scottish barons in a document of 1237, the only magnate of the West to be included. This might mean that the branch of the MacSorleys descended from Dugald had pro-Scottish leanings, although it would be dangerous to suppose that what was true in the thirteenth century was also true in the later twelfth. Colin MacDonald, on the other hand, thought that Dugald could not have been associated with William the Lion in this period,[14] but it does seem difficult to discount the coincidence of William's homage at York with the Scottish nobles, and the entry in the *Liber Vitae* a fortnight later which mentions Dugald. Perhaps Dugald was late in going to York, or perhaps the visit to Durham took place on the return trip. But whatever may have been the case, we should not be surprised

---

12 *Durham Liber Vitae*, p. 135; *SAEC*, p. 264.
13 Duncan and Brown, 'Argyll and the Isles', p. 198; Barrow, *Anglo-Norman Era*, p. 159.
14 MacDonald, *History of Argyll*, pp. 90–1.

that Dugald, in the company of a clerk with a French name, chose to stop at Durham: the shrine of St Cuthbert was a popular pilgrim destination, and St Cuthbert himself enjoyed a reputation as a powerful northern saint. As is so often the case in twelfth- and thirteenth-century Hebridean history, the sources raise more questions than they answer.

After his brief mention in 1175, nothing further is known of Dugald, and even the date of his death is unrecorded. He could well have lived on into the thirteenth century, as his brother Ranald almost certainly did, but this can only be speculation. Like his brother, however, Dugald was the founder of an important lineage. The names of three of his sons – Olaf, Duncan, and Ranald – are recorded in the Durham *Liber Vitae* along with that of their father.[15] Olaf and Ranald are otherwise unknown, but their brother Duncan, and another son of Dugald's named Dugald Screech, are mentioned in *Hakon's Saga*, where it was stated that they were 'very unfaithful' to Hakon, the king of Norway, in the first quarter óf the thirteenth century.[16] Duncan and Dugald Screech were to be prominent players in the events of the mid-thirteenth century in the western seaboard, and we shall return to their roles shortly.

Ranald, remembered in various traditions as a pirate, warrior, crusader and law-giver, and as a friend and benefactor of the Church, is the most notable of Somerled's sons. Although the sources for his life are, like those for his father and his brother, scarce, Ranald emerges on to the stage of Hebridean history as an almost larger-than-life figure. There is a story in MacDonald tradition that relates how Somerled made his two sons, Ranald and Dugald, swim from Oban to the island of Kerrera in order to determine who would inherit Somerled's title of 'king of the Isles'. Midway through the contest, according to the tale, Ranald, seeing the advantage pass to Dugald, severed his own hand and threw it onto the beach before his brother could wade ashore, thus claiming the right to their father's title in addition to lending a grisly title to the tale: 'the red hand'.[17] While the story appears in other contexts as well, and must be regarded as apocryphal, it does point to the existence of intense rivalry among the sons of Somerled, and highlights the internecine strife and struggle for power that followed his death. Ranald's role in this strife forms a central theme in the history of the successors of Somerled.

Ranald's share of his father's territories probably comprised Islay, Jura and Kintyre, as well as Morvern and Ardnamurchan. That he inherited some of his father's regal standing is evidenced by the use of the titles 'king oḟ the Isles and lord of Argyll and Kintyre', in a charter to

[15] *Durham Liber Vitae*, p. 4.

[16] *ES*, ii, pp. 464–5.

[17] A. M. W. Stirling, *MacDonald of the Isles* (New York, 1914), p. 23, note 1. A variant of the story relates how the ownership of Skye was settled by two of Somerled's descendants in the same manner.

Saddell Abbey, and 'lord of the Isles', in a charter to Paisley.[18] What is not clear is the process by which the title 'king of the Isles' in the Saddell charter became 'lord of the Isles' in the Paisley document, or why the title 'lord of Argyll and Kintyre' was not utilised in the latter. Much hinges on the date and provenance of the documents; Duncan and Brown regarded the Paisley charter as later than the Saddell grant, and they connected the dropping of the title 'king of the Isles' with Ranald's defeat at the hands of his brother Angus in 1192, or else with the expansion of his namesake, Ragnvald (Reginald), king of Man, after 1188.[19] Moreover, it is possible that the provenance of the Paisley document comes into play here as well, for, as a monastery established within the mainland territory of the great Stewart lordship, it is not impossible that Ranald's status as king of the Isles was deliberately downgraded by the cleric recording the grant, just as Somerled's status was deliberately downplayed by the chroniclers of Holyrood and Melrose. The use of the title 'lord of Argyll and Kintyre' by Ranald is equally problematic, as is its use in the Saddell grant, but not in the Paisley document: given the medieval obsession with status, this must be significant. Perhaps, since the dating of the charters cannot be established, the Paisley charter should be seen as earlier than its Saddell counterpart, and the use of the title attests to Ranald's aggrandisement, at the expense of his brother Dugald, on the mainland. Certainly much later, and therefore less reliable, MacDonald tradition also recorded how 'Reginald ... had several bickerings with Dugall of Lorn, his brother, about the Isles of Mull', and how his nephew John, placed under Ranald's tutelage, campaigned against the inhabitants of Moidart and Ardnamurchan, who had assisted Dugald in his struggle against Ranald.[20] This episode also seems to suggest conflict between Ranald and Dugald over mainland Argyll, for Mull is one of the large islands directly adjacent to the mainland.

Whatever may have been the case, further conflict among the sons of Somerled is recorded in 1192, when a battle took place between Ranald and his brother Angus, in which many men were slaughtered and Angus had the victory.[21] While it would be informative to know where the battle was fought, and under what circumstances, the sources are silent on these details. However, since some of Angus's share of his father's territories lay in the north, it may be that the battle represents a further attempt at territorial aggrandisement by Ranald, after he had acquired some, at least, of the holdings of Dugald. This would have brought Ranald into close proximity to Angus's territories, and would have

---

[18] *RMS*, ii, no. 3170; *Paisley Reg.*, p. 125.

[19] Duncan and Brown, 'Argyll and the Isles', p. 198. At the same time as Ranald made the grant to Paisley Abbey, his son Donald and his wife also made a similar grant; this may suggest that Ranald's charter came near the end of his life: ibid., note 8.

[20] Macdonald, *Hist. Macdonalds, HP*, i, p. 12.

[21] *ES*, ii, p. 327.

perhaps laid the context for the 1192 conflict. In any event, the battle of 1192 serves as a reminder that some modern portrayals of Ranald as a 'pacific and deeply religious man'[22] need to be balanced by his evidently warlike activities, even if it would be a gross oversimplification to portray him purely as a pirate. Certainly one of the characteristics that Ranald was noted for was his martial skill: the seventeenth-century *Book of Clanranald* hailed him as, 'the most distinguished of the Foreigners or Gael for prosperity, sway of generosity, and feats of arms'.[23]

Ranald MacSorley has thus far appeared in the guise of a Scoto-Norse Hebridean sea-king, expanding his territories and ruling as *rí Innse Gall*. But there is also some evidence for foreign influences beginning to permeate the upper strata of Hebridean society in this period, a generation or two earlier than is usually held to be the case. The evidence comes in the form of a seal used by Ranald, which was described in a fifteenth-century notarial instrument: 'In the middle of the seal on one side a ship filled with men at arms; on the reverse side, the figure of an armed man on horseback with a drawn sword in his hand.'[24] Although the seal does not survive, the nature of the document in which it was described attests to its authenticity, and the use of a seal by one of Somerled's sons deserves our attention for several reasons. Although the primary use of a seal was pragmatic – that is, it served to authenticate a document – the seal was also significant in symbolic terms. Seals are important to the historian because their iconography and symbolism offers insights into the status of their owners, and how they wished to be depicted; what can be deduced from the images on the seal of Ranald?

The galley was an important West-Highland motif, and many examples survive in later West-Highland stone carvings: the best known is probably that on the sixteenth-century tomb of Alexander MacLeod at Rodel, Harris.[25] Although A. and A. MacDonald published a rather fanciful reconstruction of Ranald's seal (including an imaginary legend) in their *Clan Donald*, a better idea of the appearance of the galley it portrayed may be gained by examining the seals of other contemporary, and later, rulers in Man and the Isles. Ship seals with round borders were common enough by the thirteenth century, and they were utilised by English and Continental trading ports. But it was probably the seals of the Manx kings that provided the model for Ranald's seal. Ranald's namesake, Ragnvald, king of Man (1188–1226, d. 1229), is said to have utilised a double-sided seal, with both the ship and knight on it, and King Harald (1237–48) is also known to have used a ship seal. Angus of the Isles,

---

22 Williams, *Lords of the Isles*, p. 127.
23 *Clanranald Bk.*, p. 157.
24 *Paisley Reg.*, p. 149.
25 See N. Fojut, D. Pringle, and B. Walker, *The Ancient Monuments of the Western Isles: A Visitor's Guide to the Principal Historic Sites and Monuments* (Edinburgh, 1994), pp. 52–3.

Ranald's grandson, had a seal (*c.*1292) which displayed a galley with four men seated and with its sails furled; this was a prominent aspect of the seals of the later MacDonald Lords of the Isles, Alexander and John.[26] Given the importance of the sea as a route of communication in this period, it is hardly surprising that the galley should form a prominent theme in the art of the West Highlands, and that an elaborate heraldry should have developed around its use in crests and coats of arms. The use of the galley on Ranald's seal and on those of other rulers in the Isles should hardly evoke any surprise: it was the indispensable tool of the rulers in the Isles, and represented the perfect expression of lordship in the islands, which was held together by the western seaways.

It is, however, the portrayal of Ranald on horseback with a drawn sword that is more significant, for this is the depiction of a knight, so common on the seals of the Anglo-Norman kings, nobles, and eventually knights of the eleventh to the thirteenth centuries. The cult of knighthood reached the zenith of popularity in Europe in the twelfth and early thirteenth centuries, and was imported into Scotland by the francophile Scottish monarchs descended from Malcolm III and Margaret. David I, Malcolm IV, William I, and the two Alexanders were all knighted, and Malcolm and William were particularly ardent devotees of the cult of knighthood. In 1159 the young King Malcolm IV followed Henry II of England all the way to Toulouse in the hope of winning his spurs, and William the Lion took part in the tournament that laid the foundations for the reputation of the great William Marshal in 1167. Indeed, by the early part of the thirteenth century, it was possible for one contemporary English chronicler to remark that 'more recent kings of Scots profess themselves to be rather Frenchmen, both in race and in manners, language and culture'.[27] Interest in knighthood, and in the Anglo-French culture of which it was part and parcel, was not just the preserve of the kings of Scots and their Anglo-Norman retainers, and it was also expressed by many members of the native Scottish elite – particularly the earls of Fife, Strathearn, and Dunbar – all of whom portrayed themselves as equestrians, with the accoutrements of knighthood on their seals. Indeed, knighthood was an important instrument in the process of cultural assimilation and blending, and it no doubt played an important role in the creation of a hybrid kingdom of Scotland by the thirteenth century.

But in the west of Scotland, the penetration of Anglo-French culture and ideals seems to have been much slower. As we have seen, Somerled's uprising in 1164 probably had much that was anti-feudal, or at least

---

26 H. Laing, *Descriptive Catalogue of Impressions from Ancient Scottish Seals* (Bannatyne and Maitland Clubs, 1850), nos. 450–4. For the Manx seals, see B. R. S. Megaw, 'The ship seals of the kings of Man', *Journal of the Manx Museum*, vi, no. 76 (1959–60), p. 79. I am very grateful to David Sellar for bringing this article to my attention.

27 Chronicle attributed to Walter of Coventry, in *SAEC*, p. 330, note 6.

conservative, about it. Of course, the use by Ranald of the mounted knight on his seal is not proof that he was knighted, and thereby inaugurated into the 'international world' of chivalry:[28] some Gaelic magnates are known to have used this device without having been dubbed knights. But this is to miss the point. In portraying himself as an equestrian, with the accoutrements of knighthood, Ranald, like other Scottish nobles of the time, was expressing a desire to be an up-to-date magnate, in an Anglo-Norman mould; and like his contemporary, Alan of Galloway, Ranald straddled two worlds. The use by Ranald (on opposite sides of the same seal) of the Highland galley – a Hebridean device – and the mounted knight – an Anglo-Norman, feudal one – suggests that Gaelic and feudal traditions were beginning to come to terms and merge in the western islands by the early thirteenth century. Indeed, Ranald's acknowledgement of the same feudal influences that his father had apparently rejected, may be one reason why King William did not intervene in western affairs during his long and troubled reign.

Finally, there is the double-sided aspect of the seal, which is most interesting and significant, for it was rare among magnate seals of the period. Impressions on both sides of the wax were first utilised by the English monarchs after 1066, and then copied by other sovereigns, who had themselves depicted as armed warriors on one side, and in majesty on the other. It is therefore possible, and indeed very likely, that the use of the double-sided seal by Ranald provides evidence of his kingly pretensions, and emphasises his title of *rí Innse Gall*. The replacement of the majesty aspect of the seal by the galley is certainly natural, given the Hebridean context and the precedent of the Manx kings.[29]

If the use of a seal portraying Ranald as a knight is evidence that he moved in a wider and more cosmopolitan world and was open to more far-reaching influences than the documentary sources might suggest, it is also possible that he undertook the greatest of medieval journeys: a pilgrimage or a crusade to the Holy Land. At first sight, the evidence does not inspire confidence, consisting as it does of MacDonald tradition, recorded in the *Book of Clanranald*, that Ranald 'received a cross from Jerusalem'.[30] There is, however, circumstantial evidence which lends credibility to the possibility, at least, that Ranald participated in a crusade, possibly late in life. The crusade had been preached in Ireland by John of Salerno in 1201–2, and John de Courcy, Lord of Ulster, departed for the Holy Land in 1204.[31] Given his Irish Sea connections, it is not impossible that Ranald learned of the crusade, and its promotion, in Ireland. A suitable context for his pilgrimage may be provided by his

28 Davies, *Domination and Conquest*, p. 51.
29 See R. A. McDonald, 'Images of Hebridean lordship in the twelfth and early thirteenth centuries: the seal of Raonall MacSorley', *SHR*, lxxiv (1995).
30 *Clanranald Bk.*, p. 157.
31 See A. MacQuarrie, *Scotland and the Crusades, 1095–1560* (Edinburgh, 1985), p. 33; *Ann. Loch Cé*, i, p. 235.

defeat at the hands of Angus in 1192, following which he could have left for the Holy Land, perhaps participating in the Third (1189–92), or, more probably, because of the 1192 battle, in the Fourth Crusade (1199–1204), which was deflected to Constantinople and never reached its intended destination. If this were the case, then perhaps the source simply records, in garbled fashion, the fact that Ranald made a vow to participate in a crusade: that is, that he took the Crusader's Cross. If it seems impossible to believe that Ranald made a pilgrimage to Jerusalem, or took part in a crusade without any contemporary chronicler taking notice of the fact, then it is surely instructive to recall that no details whatsoever survive surrounding the actions of the great William Marshal (d. 1219) in the Holy Land, despite his prominence, and the excellent contemporary account of his life.[32] If the actions on pilgrimage of such an important and well-documented man as the Marshal are elusive, then it is hardly beyond the realms of possibility that Ranald made a similar pilgrimage. He was certainly imbued with a piety typical of the age, since he was responsible for the foundation and benefaction of several religious houses (see Chapter 7, below), and in this context it would not be surprising to find him embarking on a crusade. Nevertheless, it is clear that little faith can be placed in the seventeenth-century account, without contemporary corroboration. However, Ranald's participation in a crusade or pilgrimage might explain the curious silence of the chronicles regarding his activities in the period following the conflict of 1192, when he was still alive, but when his activities are unknown. Whatever may be said about Ranald, one thing seems certain: 'we should be wrong to accept him as just the pirate depicted by the jejune annals which notice his life'.[33] And, whether or not he actually did participate in a crusade or undertake a pilgrimage, the evidence of his seal alone is sufficient to demonstrate that, by the early thirteenth century, the Hebrides were beginning to be opened up to the wider influences of western Christendom as a whole. The periphery was shrinking, and the Hebrides were coming in from the margins.

Considering how much of his life eludes the historian, it is scarcely surprising that even the exact date of Ranald's death is difficult to determine. It is generally held, following the *Book of Clanranald*, that he died in 1207.[34] Other dates have also been proposed, however, and the one given in the clan history is not definitive. Duncan and Brown argued that, since the *Book of Clanranald* placed the death of Somerled in 1180 – that is, sixteen years out – then if the date of 1207, which it gives for Ranald's death, is adjusted accordingly, that would bring us to 1191. This would seem to indicate that he was slain in the battle against the

[32] D. Crouch, *William Marshal: Court, Career and Chivalry in the Angevin Empire, 1146–1219* (London, 1990), pp. 51–2.
[33] Duncan, *Making of the Kingdom*, p. 198.
[34] *Clanranald Bk.*, p. 157.

forces of his brother, Angus, recorded in 1192.[35] However, the *Chronicle of Man*, which notices the conflict between the two brothers, does not give any hint that Ranald was killed there, when it could easily have done so. More recently, dates in the early thirteenth century have been proposed. The years 1209 or 1210 have been suggested for the demise of Ranald, on the basis of the strife in that year involving the MacSorleys, while a re-examination of the original Gaelic text of the *Book of Clanranald* suggests that a date of about 1227 would be more appropriate.[36] The case for 1209 or 1210 is attractive because, in recording a conflict between the sons of Ranald and the men of Skye, the *Annals of Ulster* make no mention of Ranald himself, which seems strange if he were still alive.[37] Simple chronology would seem to argue against 1227, which appears to be impossibly late for a man who was an adult in 1164. Lacking any better evidence, the best that can be offered for Ranald's obit is a broad spectrum of dates ranging from about 1192 to 1227, although the silence that envelopes him after 1192 is certainly puzzling. One clue to Ranald's fate may be provided by his charter to Paisley Abbey, which seems to indicate that he had entered into confraternity with the monks. If the charter were given towards the end of his life, as has been suggested, then it seems within the bounds of possibility that Ranald retired to Paisley and lived out his last days there. This was not an uncommon phenomenon among the nobles of the period, and although it is hard to say why Ranald might have chosen to enter Paisley Abbey instead of one of his own religious foundations (see Chapter 7), this tantalising clue might go some way towards explaining why Ranald disappears from the record after 1192.[38] Perhaps old age had removed him from the forefront of events, perhaps he had entered a religious house, or perhaps these years were occupied with a pilgrimage or crusade. Whatever may have been the case, it is certainly disappointing that the demise of Somerled's most prominent son evoked so little comment among contemporary writers.

The *Icelandic Annals* succinctly described the early thirteenth century as a time of 'warfare in the Hebrides'. The warring parties included the descendants of Somerled, the kings of Man, who had recently made good their re-entrenchment in the Isles, and also Norwegian and Scottish contingents. The details of these conflicts, often sketchy, are

---

[35] Duncan and Brown, 'Argyll and the Isles', p. 198.
[36] Cowan, 'Norwegian sunset – Scottish dawn', p. 114, proposes 1210; A. B. W. McEwen, 'The death of Reginald son of Somerled', *West Highland Notes and Queries*, 2nd ser., vi (1990), suggests 1227.
[37] *ES*, ii, p. 378.
[38] Ranald's charter: *Paisley Reg.*, p. 125. On confraternity, see C. H. Lawrence, *Medieval Monasticism: Forms of Religious Life in Western Europe in the Middle Ages* (2nd edn, London, 1989), pp. 99–100; on noble retirement to a monastery, see G. Duby *et al.*, *A History of Private Life*, vol. II: *Revelations of the Medieval World* (Cambridge, Mass., 1988), p. 26.

recorded in various annals which provide little more than a list of names and battles. Ranald's sons were Donald, who inherited Islay, southern Kintyre and the southern isles, and his brother, Ruairi, who seems to have acquired Garmoran after the death of Angus in 1210. From Donald were descended the Lords of Islay, while the Lords of Garmoran were descended from Ruairi; both families were to play a prominent role in the history of the Isles in the later thirteenth century. In 1209 Ranald's sons fought a battle with the men of Skye, 'and slaughter was made of them [the men of Skye] there'. Although it is unfortunate that this laconic entry did not locate the battle (a conflict with the men of Skye need not have taken place on Skye itself), it might be a reasonable assumption that this contest represented an attempt, on the part of the sons of Somerled, to extend their territory at the expense of the kings of Man, for Skye at this time seems to have been a possession of the Manx kings. On the other hand, the conflict could have been an attempt, on the part of the Manx kings, to re-acquire parts of their domain, which had been lost in the previous half-century. Whatever the case, in the following year, 1210, Angus, the son of Somerled, was killed along with his three sons, and Iona was plundered. Given the date, it is tempting to connect the death of Angus with King John's expedition to Ireland, or else with his invasion of Man, both in the same year.[39] Whether or not this was so, the western seaboard remained disturbed. In 1212, Thomas, the son of Roland of Galloway and younger brother of Alan of Galloway, along with Ranald's sons, plundered Derry in Ireland with a fleet of seventy-six ships; and in 1214 he returned with Ruairi, Ranald's son, and 'took the treasures of the community of Derry, and of the north of Ireland, besides, from inside the church of the abbey'.[40] The raid of 1212 has been linked with the attempts of John de Grey, the justiciar of Ireland (1208–12), to establish King John's presence in the north of Ireland, and it has been suggested that the attack on Derry by Thomas and the MacSorleys must have taken place with the connivance of de Grey.[41] Perhaps it was this chronic unrest in the West, during the late twelfth and early thirteenth centuries, that prompted the construction, in 1197 by King William of Scotland, of a new castle between the Doon and Ayr.[42] But whether or not this new castle was constructed with a view to insulating the heart of the kingdom from the turmoil of the western seaboard, it is very clear that the rulers on the Scottish periphery were using the power vacuum, created by the absence of Scottish and Norwegian royal authority, to further their own ends. Moreover, as the very fact of the construction of the castle at Ayr demonstrates, these

[39] *ES*, ii, pp. 383–4; 387–8.

[40] Ibid., ii, pp. 378, 381–2, 387, 393, 395. *Ann. Ulster, s.a.* 1212, call Thomas Uhtred's son, but this is an understandable error.

[41] F. X. Martin, 'John, Lord of Ireland, 1185–1216', in Cosgrove, *Medieval Ireland* (Oxford, 1987), pp. 146–7.

[42] *ES*, ii, p. 348.

conflicts on the western seaboard could all too easily spill over into the mainland kingdom proper.

In 1214, King William I of Scotland died. He was by then an old man, and the last years of his reign had been plagued by persistent uprisings in the remote northern reaches of his own realm, led by the descendants of Malcolm MacHeth and Donald MacWilliam. Like Malcolm MacHeth, the contemporary and ally of Somerled, Donald MacWilliam is a shadowy character. The MacWilliams take their name from William fitz Duncan, the son of Duncan II (ruled briefly 1094) and grandson of Malcolm Canmore by his first wife, Ingebjorg. From *c.*1180 to *c.*1230 they were one of those families distinguished by their resistance to the kings of Scots in the far northern reaches of the kingdom.[43]

The nature of this resistance has proved elusive, but there is little doubt that it was primarily dynastic, and that it represented opposition from the kin-based society to the feudal transformation of the twelfth and early thirteenth centuries. Donald's father, William fitz Duncan, displays his Norman affinities clearly enough, in both the form of his name, and in his close attendance on King David I. But, while he may have been happy to achieve accommodation within feudal society, and to let his claims to the kingship lapse, the same cannot be said for his son, Donald MacWilliam. The form of Donald's name betrays a Gaelic upbringing, possibly through fosterage in the Isles or in Ireland, as does the fact that he does not appear in the charters of the period, as he surely would have done had he grown up at court. His claims to the kingship are the subject of some contention among modern scholars, but were almost certainly derived from the kin-based system of succession, under which he would have been considered the most likely successor to David I. While it is true that no claim is known to have been put forward by Donald on the death of David I in 1153, he was active by the early 1180s, if not earlier, when he 'landed in Scotland with a numerous armed host'. It required the efforts of Roland of Galloway, with some 3,000 men, to hunt down MacWilliam and put an end to his claims in 1187, when he was slain at an unknown site called Mam Garvia, and described as 'prope Muref' ('near Moray').[44]

Despite the removal of MacWilliam from the scene in 1187, his descendants, also obscure figures, continued to cause trouble for the Scottish kings in the north. In 1211–12 Godfrey MacWilliam ravaged

43 See my comments in McDonald, 'Kings and Princes in Scotland', chap. 3.
44 On the MacWilliams, see: *ES*, ii, pp. 313, 389, 404, 471; *SAEC*, pp. 278–9, 330; *Chron. Fordun*, i, p. 268; ii, p. 263; *Chron. Melrose*, p. 96; Bannerman, 'MacDuff of Fife', p. 36, note 1; Ritchie, *Normans in Scotland*, pp. 400–1; *ESC*, pp. 271–2; and *RRS*, ii, pp. 12–13. The site of the battle is unidentified, but since *Chron. Holyrood* placed it *apud Ros* and the Melrose chronicle located it *prope Muref*, it probably took place in southern Ross. See G. W. S. Barrow, 'The reign of William the Lion, king of Scotland', in J. C. Beckett (ed.), *Historical Studies VII* (London, 1969), p. 31, for the convincing suggestion that it was fought in Strath Garve, about a dozen miles west of Dingwall.

the north, before being captured and killed by King William's son, Alexander, the future King Alexander II. When King William died in 1214, it was the signal for a new round of rebellions. In 1215 an uprising led by Donald bán (the son of MacWilliam), Kenneth MacHeth, and 'the son of a certain king of Ireland' had to be put down, this time by Farquhar 'Maccintsacairt' (*Macc an t-sacairt*, son of the priest), one of the native magnates of Ross, who, in an interesting turn of affairs, was knighted for his loyal service. Farquhar presents an intriguing case indeed, for with him we see a member of the northern Scottish nobility throwing in his lot with the modernising kings of Scots, and being rewarded with a knighthood; he has rightly been called 'something of a phenomenon'.[45] Nevertheless, even Earl Farquhar's efforts did not prevent further disturbances in the far north. In 1223, 'some wicked men of the race of MacWilliam, namely Gillescop and his sons and Roderick, appeared in the furthest limits of Scotland'.[46] Still another rising was recorded in 1228, in which part of Inverness was burned and royal lands in the north were plundered. The final episode in the MacWilliam family saga came in 1230, when the MacWilliams and 'Roderick' again rallied a large number of men to their cause, with the intention of taking the kingdom by force. Like all the previous attempts, this one, too, fell victim to the superior forces of the king. The *Chronicle of Lanercost* recorded the fate dealt out to the last of the MacWilliams, an infant girl, by knights loyal to the king of Scots:

> a somewhat too cruel vengeance was taken for the blood of the slain: – the same MacWilliam's daughter, who had not long left her mother's womb, innocent as she was, was put to death, in the burgh of Forfar ... her head was struck against the column of the [market] cross and her brains dashed out.[47]

These MacWilliam uprisings in the north were closely connected with the western seaboard and Ireland. The 'Roderick' mentioned by the chronicles in their accounts of the 1228 and 1230 uprisings is almost certainly Ruairi, the son of Ranald. The association of Ruairi with the MacWilliams argues that the latter had been obtaining aid from the Hebridean chieftains of the line of Somerled, in their struggle against the MacMalcolm kings, thus continuing both the tradition of resistance to the Scottish kings inaugurated by Somerled and the links forged between the western seaboard and the northern provinces, when Somerled's sister married Malcolm MacHeth nearly a century earlier. Moreover, Irish armies constituted the backbone of at least three of these uprisings, and Irish kings are stated to have participated in two of

---

[45] Duncan, *Making of the Kingdom*, p. 197.
[46] See *Chron. Fordun*, i, pp. 278–9; ii, p. 274; *ES*, ii, pp. 403–4; and *Chron. Bower*, v, p. 143, for these northern disturbances.
[47] *ES*, ii, p. 471.

them. As Seán Duffy has so aptly put it, 'there were always men in Ireland ready and willing to throw their military muscle about in Scotland and in the islands ... The underdog, the pretender, and the malcontent in Scotland all found Irish support.'[48] We are reminded, yet again, of the extensive political connections and maritime culture which spanned the Irish Sea and transcended 'national' boundaries, as late as the first decades of the thirteenth century.

Considering the unrest in the Isles, which was spilling over into the Scottish kingdom, and especially the probable involvement of the kindred of Somerled in the northern insurrections of the MacWilliams, it is little wonder that the new king, Alexander II (1214–49), the son of William I, turned his attention to Scotland's western seaboard in the early 1220s. That he was able to do so must be attributed, in large measure, to the fact that he enjoyed better relations with England than his father had, and also, perhaps, to the fact that the kings of Scots were finally discovering how to build or commandeer the galleys which were a prerequisite for serious campaigning on the western seaboard.[49]

John of Fordun, writing in the later fourteenth century, recorded that in 1221, King Alexander raised an army from Lothian and Galloway, and sailed for Argyll, but was forced to turn back when a storm arose. The comment on the composition of the army is interesting, since it indicates a joint sea and land attack force – which suggests that the Scots kings were finally learning to deal with the rulers of the Hebrides on their own terms. The following year, says Fordun:

> he [King Alexander] led the army back into Argyll, for he was dis-pleased with the natives for many reasons. The men of Argyll were frightened: some gave hostages and a great deal of money, and were taken back in peace; while others, who had more deeply offended against the king's will, forsook their estates and posses-sions, and fled. But our lord the king bestowed both the land and the goods of these men upon his own followers, at will; and thus returned in peace with his men.[50]

Andrew Wyntoun, prior of Loch Leven, writing in the 1410s, recorded a single, successful expedition in 1222 which proceeded by land, and in the aftermath of which, confiscated territories were distributed to loyal Argyllsmen.[51] Although the vague nature of both accounts, as well as discrepancies in detail, have caused some scholars to reject these writers as sources for this expedition, it seems likely that

[48] Duffy, 'Bruce brothers', p. 63.
[49] Barrow, *Kingship and Unity*, p. 113. See also MacInnes, 'West Highland sea power', pp. 525–6.
[50] *Chron. Fordun*, i, pp. 288–9; ii, p. 284.
[51] *Chron. Wyntoun* (Laing), iii, p. 240.

both Fordun and Wyntoun used earlier annals – now lost – as the basis for their narratives.[52] But it remains to be determined whether there were one or two expeditions to Argyll in 1221–2. It has been suggested that Fordun may have confused two different accounts of the same expedition for two separate expeditions in 1221 and 1222, but a study of the king's itinerary has shown that two expeditions are in fact possible: one in the autumn of 1221 and a second in the early summer of 1222.[53] But what were the repercussions of this expedition, or these expeditions, for the western seaboard?

This is difficult to answer, due in large measure to the sparse nature of the source material, but one probable result was a forced redistribution of lands between Ruairi and Donald, by which Kintyre was taken from the former and given to the latter, or his sons.[54] Ruairi appears, in charters of the early thirteenth century, to hold lands in Kintyre. But then, between 1241 and 1249, Angus, son of Donald of Islay, granted the church of Kilkerran, 'in my land which is called Kintyre', to Paisley Abbey, and, although the MacDonalds are well attested as landholders in Kintyre in the later thirteenth century, nothing further is heard of Ruairi or the MacRuaris there. This suggests that there was a forced transfer of land in the wake of the campaign of 1221 or 1222.[55] If Ruairi had been providing assistance to the MacHeths and MacWilliams, enemies of the kings of Scots, in the 1210s, then his forfeiture seems very likely indeed. And, while his appearance in the north in 1223 cannot be taken as sure proof of his earlier complicity with the northern rebels, it may well be connected with this redistribution of lands and his forfeiture in Argyll; Ruairi as well as the MacWilliams may have had an axe to grind with the Scottish monarchs. Moreover, a royal charter from July of 1222 erected a burgh at Dumbarton, with a trading area that extended to the head of Loch Long. Thus, 1222 has been seen as representing the pacification of the Clyde estuary, and the expedition of that year should probably be regarded as having been aimed at Arran, Bute, and the east shore of Kintyre.[56] Finally, it was also probably around this time that Cowal was granted to Walter Stewart and a castle was built for him at Dunoon, while the first phase of building on the royal stronghold at Tarbert may also have followed in the wake of Alexander's first western campaign.[57] The picturesque castle at Eilean Donan, located on a small islet at the junction of Loch Duich, Loch Alsh,

---

52 MacDonald, *History of Argyll*, p. 100, rejected these accounts; but Duncan and Brown, 'Argyll and the Isles', p. 199, argued convincingly for their authenticity.

53 Compare ibid., p. 199, and J. G. Dunbar and A. A. M. Duncan, 'Tarbert Castle: a contribution to the history of Argyll', *SHR*, l (1971), pp. 2–3.

54 Duncan and Brown, 'Argyll and the Isles', p. 200.

55 *RMS*, ii, no. 3136 (= Duncan and Brown, 'Argyll and the Isles', appendix IV); *Paisley Reg.* p. 128; Duncan and Brown, 'Argyll and the Isles', p. 200.

56 *RMS*, vii, no. 190 (1); Dunbar and Duncan, 'Tarbert Castle', pp. 2–3.

57 Barrow, *Kingship and Unity*, pp. 114; Ritchie and Harman, *Argyll and the Western Isles*, no. 34; Dunbar and Duncan, 'Tarbert Castle', pp. 7–13.

and Loch Long, although much rebuilt and altered in subsequent centuries, also seems to date in its earliest stages from the early thirteenth century, and so it, too, should probably be connected with these campaigns to tame the western seaboard.[58] For the first time, Scottish royal authority was making itself felt in the western seaboard: it was an ominous sign for the descendants of Somerled, and the storm clouds were clearly upon the horizon.

Following Alexander's expedition in the early 1220s, the peace of the Hebrides was further disrupted by a civil war in the Isle of Man.[59] When Godfrey, the king of Man, died in 1187 he left three sons, Ragnvald, Olaf, and Ivar. Although Godfrey had appointed Olaf as heir to the kingdom, following his death the Manxmen chose Olaf's brother Ragnvald instead, 'because he was a vigorous man, and of a hardier age'; Olaf was only ten years old at the time. According to the *Chronicle of Man*, Ragnvald allowed Olaf to rule under him in Lewis, 'leading a sorry life'. When the resources of Lewis proved insufficient to maintain Olaf and his followers, they approached Ragnvald to request a share of the islands. Ragnvald's response was to seize his brother and send him off to Scotland, where King William kept him in prison for seven years. When William died in 1214, Alexander II freed Olaf, who went on pilgrimage to Compostela and then returned to be received on good terms by his brother, to marry Ragnvald's wife's sister, Lavon, 'the daughter of a certain noble of Kintyre', and to settle once more in Lewis. But the old rivalry flared up again, when the bishop of the Isles declared this new marriage null and void on the grounds of consanguinity. Olaf repudiated Lavon and instead married Christiana, the daughter of Earl Farquhar of Ross. This insult to her sister so offended the wife of Ragnvald, that she sent a letter in the name of her husband to her son Godfrey in Skye, 'bidding him seize Olaf, and kill him'. But Olaf got wind of the plot and escaped with some followers to his father-in-law. A few days later, Olaf, Farquhar, and a 'sheriff [*vicecomes*] of Skye named Paul Baliki's son (who had refused to condone the murder of Olaf), came to Skye and fought Godfrey, whom they defeated, blinded and emasculated.

The next summer, having taken hostages from Skye, Olaf sailed with a fleet of thirty-two ships to Man, and forced Ragnvald to come to terms; the two brothers then divided the northern Hebrides, although Ragnvald, we are told, retained the title of king. This second truce was broken when Ragnvald, along with Alan of Galloway (called by the saga-

---

58 On Eilean Donan, see J. Close-Brooks, *Exploring Scotland's Heritage: The Highlands* (Edinburgh, 1986), pp. 97–8; and R. Miket and D. L. Roberts, *The Mediaeval Castles of Skye and Lochalsh* (Isle of Skye, 1990), pp. 74–92. The latter work contains a discussion of the legends surrounding Eilean Donan's foundation, as well as a summary of the early remains.

59 For what follows, see *Chron. Man*, pp. 82–92; and *ES*, ii, pp. 456–60, 465–6.

man 'the greatest warrior at that time'), sought to repossess Olaf's share
of the divided kingdom, perhaps with the sanction of the Scottish king,
who had sided with Ragnvald. But, the chronicle records, 'because the
Manxmen would not fight against Olaf or the islanders, because they
loved them, Ragnvald and Alan ... effected nothing, and returned
home'. Fortune now favoured Olaf, who had in the meantime gained
the support of the English king.[60] Shortly thereafter Ragnvald was
deposed, and Olaf recovered his inheritance, the kingdom of Man and
the islands. Olaf reigned for two years, from 1226 to 1228. In 1228,
however, he sailed with many of his nobles to the islands. Alan of
Galloway, his brother Thomas, the earl of Atholl, and Ragnvald took this
opportunity to invade Man with 'a great army'. Following the plundering and devastation of the island, Alan left bailies in Man, who were
promptly defeated by Olaf upon his return. Ragnvald returned from
Galloway under cover of night, and, according to the Manx chronicle,
'drew to himself the minds of all the islanders who were in the southern
part of Man, and allied them to himself'; while Olaf collected support in
the north. The final conflict came on St Valentine's day in 1229, when
the two opposing armies met at Tynwald, and Ragnvald was killed in the
fighting.

The fact that both Somerled and Godfrey, the king of Man, each had
a son whose name was Latinised as Reginald, has occasionally vexed
historians. As one early twentieth-century writer on the period noted:

> Not a little confusion exists in the history of this period in the west
> from the fact that with the death of Godred of Man in 1187, and
> the accession of his son Reginald, there came to be two Reginalds, a
> Celtic one and a Norwegian one, to whom the title King of the Isles
> was contemporaneously applied.[61]

Like his namesake the son of Somerled, Ragnvald, the king of Man, was
one of the most important and formidable figures in the Isles in the later
twelfth and early thirteenth centuries. He was not only one of the
longest reigning of the Manx kings, but also one of the most vigorous.
What is known of his career derives largely from the Manx chronicle
and from English sources; the Irish annals took remarkably little notice
of him, although a Gaelic poem in praise of his exploits survives, which
suggests he inspired awe in Ireland, too. In about 1180 Ragnvald's
sister, Affreca, married John de Courcy, that energetic warrior who
carved out a principality for himself in Ulster between 1177 and 1181.
The Manx alliance not only provided him with access to the formidable
Manx fleet and protected his right flank, but also sucked Ragnvald into

---

[60] *Foedera*, i (1), p. 104. A document of 1235 calls Olaf 'amicum nostrum': p. 117.
[61] Mitchell, *Popular History of the Highlands and Gaelic Scotland*, p. 235. Despite its early
date of publication, this work is full of important observations on the western seaboard during the period in question.

the swirling vortex of Irish politics. When de Courcy was driven out of Ulster in 1204, it was natural that he would look to his brother-in-law for help. And when, in the following year, de Courcy landed at Strangford and besieged the castle of Moira in an attempt to recover his lost territories, he was accompanied by Ragnvald and 100 Manx warships. Clearly the king of Man was a potent ally and a formidable enemy. However, as an Irish annalist observed, 'No profit resulted from that fleet, but that the land was destroyed and plundered; and they went away ... without obtaining power.'[62] The Gaelic praise-poem in Ragnvald's honour suggested that he might become king of Ireland – 'You will obtain, o noble son of Sadhbh, speech from the flagstone on the side of Tara.'[63] While this need not be taken seriously, it is possible that some hope was entertained that Ragnvald would invade Dublin, thereby re-establishing the old links between Dublin and Man that had existed in the days of Godred Crovan. Indeed, it has been noted that the Manx kings had a long history of often unfriendly relations with east Ulster, and that de Courcy's invasion of Ulster might well have been utilised by the king of Man as a means of settling old scores.[64]

Ragnvald's Irish campaign on behalf of his brother-in-law also entangled him in relations with the English kings, John and Henry III. In February 1205, King John took Ragnvald and his lands and vassals under his protection, and a few days later he issued letters of safe-conduct so that the Manx king and John de Courcy could attend him in England during the fortnight after Easter. In May 1212 Ragnvald became the vassal of King John, and in 1213 he received land in Carlingford for the service of one knight, as well as 100 measures of corn yearly from the English king. It is worth noting that this grant to Ragnvald provided him with a fine harbour for his galley-fleet in Carlingford Lough. Ragnvald appears to have been in King John's good books in 1214, when the English monarch prohibited mariners of Ireland from entering the king of Man's territory. But this goodwill does not appear to have been continuous, and in 1218, Henry III demanded that Ragnvald perform homage, as well as make amends, for 'the excesses committed upon our Lord the King, as well in England as in Ireland, by men of his land'.[65] It would seem, then, that Ragnvald had been causing trouble in Ireland, a suggestion that might be reinforced

---

[62] *ES*, ii, pp. 363–4, and note 4.

[63] 'A poem in praise of Raghnall, King of Man', ed. B. O Cuiv, *Eigse*, viii (1956–7), stanzas 10, 19, and p. 286 [adapted by the author]. On John de Courcy, see M. Dolley, *Anglo-Norman Ireland* (Dublin, 1970), pp. 84–8, 91–103, 105–8; F. X. Martin, 'Overlord becomes feudal lord, 1172–85', in Cosgrove, *Medieval Ireland*, pp. 114–16; and S. Duffy, 'The first Ulster Plantation: John de Courcy and the men of Cumbria', in T. D. Barry, R. Frame and K. Simms (eds.), *Colony and Frontier in Medieval Ireland: Essays presented to J. F. Lydon* (London, 1995).

[64] Duffy, 'Bruce brothers', pp. 67–8.

[65] 'Poem in praise of Raghnall', ed. O Cuiv, p. 286 [adapted by the author]; *ES*, ii, p. 439, note 1.

by references in the praise-poem to the plundering of the Irish coast, and the taking of cattle. But it is certain that in September 1219 the king of England issued a proclamation informing his subjects that the king of Man had come into his faith and service, and had done homage. At the same time, the justiciar of Ireland was instructed to give Ragnvald his protection.[66] The relations of the kings of England with the Manx rulers need to be viewed in the context of the loss of Normandy and Anjou by King John, following which the English kings were able to devote themselves more fully to the task of forming their insular lands into a coherent state. Part of that policy was the exercise of lordship over native kings and lords, including the Irish kings, Welsh princes, and even the Scottish monarchs; thus the Manx kings were by no means unique in their relations with the English kings.[67]

Ragnvald of Man reigned in the Isles for nearly forty years, during which time he gained a reputation as a formidable warrior. The Gaelic praise-poem is full of allusions to his prowess in battle – 'Your red spear on your palm, every man becomes weak before its smooth point; you thrust it, o Raghnall, into the navel until its point is through his clear back' – and to his fearsome fleet of war galleys – 'You are the man of the speckled ships, unlucky the strand to which you will come ...'[68] But perhaps the best epitaph to this remarkable sea-king comes from the *Orkneyinga Saga*, which described Ragnvald as 'the greatest fighting man in all the western lands. For three whole years he had lived aboard longships and not spent a single night under a sooty roof.'[69]

Given the events of the civil war in Man, it is scarcely surprising that, in the summer of 1229, the chroniclers reported 'a great dispeace' wracking the Hebrides.[70] But this was not a new state of affairs: as early as 1224, *Hakon's Saga* relates how, while King Hakon was at Bergen, 'Gillecrist, and Ottar, Snaekoll's son, and many Hebrideans, came to meet him there, from west beyond the sea: and they had many letters concerning the needs of their land.'[71] These emissaries may have gone to Norway as a result of the perception on the part of the Islesmen that King Alexander of Scotland, after his campaign in Argyll in 1221 or 1222, was preparing to launch a follow-up campaign against the

---

[66] Ibid., ii, p. 439, note 1. Many of the documents that deal with Ragnvald's relations with the English kings are to be found in *Foedera*. A recent study of King John has nothing to say of his dealings with the Manx kings: Turner, *King John*.

[67] See Frame, *Political Development of the British Isles*, pp. 44–7; and Davies, *Domination and Conquest, passim*.

[68] 'Poem in praise of Raghnall', ed. O Cuiv, stanzas 22–3.

[69] *Orkneyinga Saga* (Pálsson and Edwards), cap. 110. On Ragnvald, see also Kinvig, *History of the Isle of Man* (2nd edn), pp. 54–6. It is to be hoped that the forthcoming *New History of the Isle of Man* will have more to say on this important and interesting figure.

[70] *ES*, ii, p. 463.

[71] Ibid., ii, p. 455.

Hebrides.[72] Or they may have been responding to the increased unrest in the Isles. In any case, Hakon was too engaged in his own kingdom over the next few years to offer any aid to the ambassadors from the West. The events of 1228–9, however, seem to have spurred him to action. The saga-writer recorded that:

> the kings of the Hebrides, who had come of Somerled's race, were very unfaithful to king Hakon. The kings in the Hebrides were Dugald Screech, and his brother Duncan, the father of John [Ewen], who was king afterwards. These were the sons of Dugall, Somerled's son.[73]

Also mentioned were Uspak, 'a man who had long been with the Birchlegs [supporters of Hakon IV]', of whom 'it came out that he was a son of Dugall', and Somerled, yet another kinsman. It may well be that the MacSorleys had been attacking lands held by the Manx kings in an attempt to expand further their territories, while the civil war raged between the brothers Olaf and Ragnvald; or they might have been supporting Alan of Galloway in his incursions into the Isles. Either of these activities would surely qualify as unfaithfulness to King Hakon in Norwegian eyes. One thing seems clear, however: the MacSorleys were regarded by the Norwegian king as the main culprits in the Isles during the 1220s.

By 1229, events in the Isles had finally tried Hakon's patience to breaking point, and, more significantly, the domestic situation in Norway finally permitted the king to turn his attention to this troublesome region. By the time King Olaf of Man arrived in Norway to report 'many disputes in the west', including another impending campaign against Man by Alan of Galloway, Hakon had already ordered the outfitting of an expedition to go 'west beyond the sea', led by a certain Uspak. The identity of this individual is problematic. The *Chronicle of Man* refers to him as Uspak, Ogmund's son, while *Hakon's Saga* calls him a son of Dugald, and adds that he was favoured with the royal name, Hakon. But the Manx chronicle is frequently unreliable, and there is no reason why Dugald could not have had a son named Uspak. The name Uspak is Scandinavian, and it is relevant to bear in mind that Somerled himself bore a Scandinavian appellation, but A. A. M. Duncan thinks that Uspak might be a Norse attempt at rendering the Gaelic name Gillespec.[74] On the other hand, since name changes are by no means uncommon in the sagas, Uspak, who spent a considerable period of time in Norway, could have acquired a new name there, even if he had been known by a different designation.[75] Neither name is ultimately inconsis-

72 Cowan, 'Norwegian sunset – Scottish dawn', p. 114.
73 *ES*, ii, pp. 464–5.
74 Duncan, *Making of the Kingdom*, p. 547.
75 Cowan, 'Norwegian sunset – Scottish dawn', p. 114.

tent with Uspak being a son of Dugald, and it seems inconceivable that
Hakon would have risked alienating the MacSorleys, unless Uspak had a
claim to the kingship of the Isles which would be universally recognised.[76] This, more than anything, may argue for his MacSorley
pedigree.

The *Chronicle of Man*, the *Chronicle of Lanercost*, and the *Icelandic
Annals* all state that Uspak was given the kingship over the Hebrides.
The saga states that Hakon favoured Uspak with the title of king and
gave him a force with which to campaign in the Western Isles.[77] Setting
out with twelve ships from Norway, the expedition added twenty more
to its numbers at Orkney, before sailing south to the Sound of Islay.
Here, Uspak and his followers were met by his probable brothers,
Duncan and Dugald Screech, and by their kinsman Somerled, with 'a
great and fair army'. Distrust prevailed between the Hebridean and the
Norwegian forces, however. The Hebrideans invited the Norwegians
who had accompanied Uspak to a feast, which they (probably sensibly)
declined. The following morning the Norwegians fell upon the MacSorleys,
slew Somerled, and captured Duncan and Dugald Screech. Uspak, the
saga informs us, was not party to the attack; once apprised of it, he let
Duncan escape and took Dugald under his protection. The force, by
now numbering eighty ships, sailed round the Mull of Kintyre to Bute.
Here Uspak besieged the stronghold held by a 'certain steward' –
presumably Rothesay Castle, which at that time probably consisted of a
circular curtain-wall some ten metres high and three metres thick,
constructed by Walter Stewart (1204–41). The attackers are said to have
hacked away at the soft rock of the defensive wall with axes, despite the
showers of boiling pitch that were dumped on their heads by the
defenders. Eventually, the commander of the castle was killed, and the
Norwegians stormed its walls, capturing much treasure 'and one Scottish
knight, who ransomed himself for three hundred marks of refined
silver'. When word arrived that Alan of Galloway was advancing with a
fleet of nearly 200 ships, the Norwegian forces abandoned Bute, but
Uspak fell ill and subsequently died (according to one source having
been wounded in the fighting for Rothesay). Following his death, the
expeditionary force broke up; the fleet returned to Man for the winter,
then plundered Kintyre in the spring before returning to Norway by
way of Lewis and the Orkneys.[78]

Sturla, the author of *Hakon's Saga*, writing of Uspak's 1230 expedition, proudly boasted that, 'the king's honours had been won in this
expedition, in the west beyond the sea'.[79] While some allowance must be

[76] Ibid.
[77] *ES*, ii, pp. 471–3.
[78] Ibid., ii, pp. 475–8. On Rothesay Castle, see R. Fawcett, *Scottish Castles and Fortifications*
    (Edinburgh, 1986), pp. 40–1; and S. Cruden, *The Scottish Castle* (London, 1963),
    pp. 29–36.
[79] *ES*, ii, p. 478.

made for the poetic licence of the saga-man in this case, the 1230 expedition nevertheless remains of great significance in the history of the western seaboard. First, it showed that King Hakon was prepared to intervene actively in the affairs of the Isles – something that he had been either unwilling, or unable, to do five years earlier. It also showed either that he sought the return of Bute, or that the MacSorleys had used their influence in an attempt to have it obtained for them.[80] The objective of the expedition seems to have been the establishment of order where there had previously been chaos, and the mechanism by which this was to be achieved was the establishment of a kingdom for Uspak in the Hebrides. Since Olaf, the king of Man, was said to have 'held manfully' under Hakon,[81] this kingdom was probably meant not to deprive Olaf, but rather to extend over the territories of Somerled's descendants, and to secure their allegiance, something which was presumably made easier for the MacSorleys to tolerate by the fact that Uspak was a kinsman. Thus, Uspak's intended kingdom would have comprised Argyll, Kintyre, and the Inner Isles.[82] Even though the scheme was nullified because of Uspak's death, the importance of the 1230 expedition, and the motives behind it, should not be underestimated. Hakon IV was now ready and willing to take an active role in the politics of the Western Isles, and 'it was only a matter of time before King Alexander reciprocated this interest'.[83]

The history of the western seaboard in the early thirteenth century was dominated by the descendants of Somerled and the Manx kings. But there were other prominent figures in the political saga playing itself out in the West, and it would be negligent not to discuss perhaps the greatest of their number, Alan of Galloway. Alan was lord of Galloway from 1200 until his death in 1234, and was something of a phenomenon in both the history of Scotland as a whole, and of the western seaboard. The son of Roland of Galloway (d. 1200), and the great-grandson of Fergus of Galloway, *rex Galwitensium*, the contemporary of Somerled who died in 1161, Alan had a mother of Norman descent, and was one of the greatest magnates in the Scottish kingdom. Yet, while he was a feudal noble and held the title of Constable of Scotland, he was also the hereditary chieftain of the semi-independent province of Galloway. In a masterly study, Keith Stringer has demonstrated how Alan operated simultaneously within both the inner, feudalised, zone of the Scottish kingdom and the rugged, outer or peripheral Atlantic zone. The bicephalous aspect to Alan's power is neatly encapsulated by the military forces at his disposal. Although in his role as Constable he was respon-

---

[80] Duncan, *Making of the Kingdom*, p. 548.
[81] *ES*, ii, p. 464.
[82] Duncan and Brown, 'Argyll and the Isles', pp. 201–2.
[83] Duncan, *Making of the Kingdom*, p. 548.

sible (along with the earls), for leading the royal army, his personal resources were also formidable. He was prone to regard the common army of Galloway as a private fighting force, and the Icelandic author, Sturla, put his strength at 150–200 ships, which would suggest an army of 2–3,000 men. Armed with such forces, Alan's greatest ambition was clearly that of lording it over part of the western seaboard, which included Ulster, Man, and Cumbria, as well as Galloway itself.[84]

It has been shown how Alan's activities on the periphery of the Scottish kingdom, while taking place in a region generally outwith the direct authority of the Scottish king, were nevertheless sanctioned by the Crown. Alan's acquisition of extensive lands in Ulster, probably in 1212 at the hand of King John of England, for example, also served the Scottish king by closing off a potential source of manpower for the troublesome MacHeths and MacWilliams, who utilised Ireland as a recruiting centre for their risings against the Canmore dynasty. It was this acquisition of lands in Ulster, as much as his position as Lord of Galloway, that enabled Alan to become entangled in the affairs of the western seaboard.

The involvement of Alan of Galloway in the affairs of the western seaboard in the 1220s, and especially in the Manx civil war, stems from a combination of personal ambition, as well as an indirect attempt to exert Scottish royal authority in this troubled area. Alan's activities in the western seaboard were at least partially driven by dynastic considerations, for after the death of his only legitimate son at a young age, he had fathered only three daughters, and a son born out of wedlock named Thomas, who was, by contemporary rules of inheritance, barred from the succession to Galloway. As Stringer has convincingly argued, much of Alan's activity on the west coast must be seen in the light of his attempts to build an alternative power-base for his son. When Alan married Thomas to a daughter of Ragnvald, king of Man, in 1226, his intention seems to have been that Thomas should succeed his father-in-law as king of Man. The scheme was brought to nothing, however, when this Galwegian interference was opposed by many of the Manx, who transferred their allegiance to Ragnvald's rival, Olaf. It is not therefore unreasonable to regard Alan's career as 'that of a great sea-captain in the Gaelic society of the western seaboard, intent upon acquiring territories in Ireland, Man, and the Isles, territories which must be linked by dominance of the sea-routes'.[85] On the other hand, Alan's involvement in the political affairs of the Isles should not be regarded as falling entirely beyond Scottish crown authority. If the establishment of Alan's son, Thomas, in the Manx kingship had been successful, it would have

---

[84] K. J. Stringer, 'Periphery and core in thirteenth-century Scotland: Alan son of Roland, Lord of Galloway and Constable of Scotland', in Grant and Stringer, *Medieval Scotland*, pp. 82–113.

[85] Duncan, *Making of the Kingdom*, p. 530.

represented a major triumph for Scottish power in the western sea-board, and so it is likely that Alexander II was not totally opposed to Alan's activities. Alan only seems to have incurred the king's displeasure after the events of the late 1220s had brought his ambitions to naught. In Alan of Galloway we therefore glimpse a man who was of two worlds: at home in the troubled waters of the western seaboard as much as in the castles of the feudal kingdom. In his time, he was an important participant in the maritime affairs of the western seaboard, and the best epitaph for him remains that of the saga-writer: 'He was the greatest warrior at that time. He had a great army and many ships. He plundered about the Hebrides.'[86]

The Irish Sea and the Hebrides also attracted the attention of Alan's younger brother, Thomas, who was responsible for plundering Derry in 1212 and 1214. In 1209 he had married Isabel of Atholl and became earl of Atholl, but it has been said that 'his inclinations were mainly sea-faring'.[87] In 1205 he supplied war galleys to King John of England for his attempt to regain Normandy; he later fought with John in Ireland, and was rewarded with an estate for three knights' service. In short, the western seas were not the exclusive preserve of the MacSorleys and the Godfreysons. The rulers of Galloway and their war-galleys were no strangers to the maritime sea lanes of the West, and the descendants of Fergus also played a prominent role in the affairs of the Hebrides and Irish Sea.

The events of the 1230s also bring into the limelight the grandsons of Somerled. Duncan and Dugald Screech, the sons of Dugald, were active participants in the affairs of the 1220s. Nothing further is recorded of Dugald Screech, but his brother Duncan is comparatively well known and deserves some further attention. He first appears on the record in 1175, when his name was entered, along with those of his father and brother, Olaf, in the *Liber Vitae* of Durham. Considering that he lived into the late 1240s, he must only have been a child in 1175; it was not uncommon for the sons of nobles to appear in the record at the age of about five or six. In *c.*1224 Duncan witnessed a charter to Paisley Abbey, but he is better known for founding the priory of Ardchattan for the Valliscaulians on Loch Etive, four miles north of North Connel in the foot of the Benderloch hills, in about 1230. Along with Beauly and Pluscarden, this was one of only three houses for this order in Scotland, although little is known of its history before the sixteenth century (see Chapter 7). Ardchattan was apparently well endowed by Duncan, for it held lands in Benderloch, Appin, and Nether Lorn, as well as teinds or portions of teinds of the churches of Ardchattan (or Kilbodan), Kilninver,

---

[86] *ES*, ii, p. 464. See also Duncan, *Making of the Kingdom*, pp. 529–30; and Brooke, *Wild Men and Holy Places*, chap. 6, on Alan.

[87] Brooke, *Wild Men and Holy Places*, p. 130.

Kilbrandon in Lorn, Soroby in Tiree and Kilmaro in Kintyre and salmon fishings and shell nets at the end of Loch Awe, and at Port Verran at the head of Loch Etive. It may be that Ardchattan Priory was founded largely as a peace-offering to Alexander II on the part of Duncan of Argyll. Such motives for founding monasteries were not unknown in the Middle Ages, and, given Alexander's recent campaign on the west coast, the foundation of Ardchattan may have been intended to assure the king of Duncan's goodwill.[88]

Despite his involvement in the Norwegian expedition in 1230, he must have returned to the king of Scots' loyalty, for in 1237, as Duncan of Argyll, his name appeared on a document sent on behalf of the Scottish king and magnates to the Pope; he was the only individual from the western seaboard so named.[89] What this seems to indicate is that it was becoming increasingly uncomfortable for the princes of the west coast to continue their policy of professing obedience to either Scotland or Norway, while maintaining *de facto* autonomy. That Duncan was named in a document of this nature demonstrates that, by the middle of the thirteenth century, some of the elite of the western seaboard were being drawn into the Scottish society of the mainland.[90] This fact is further reflected by the construction by Duncan and his son, Ewen, of Dunstaffnage Castle in the most up-to-date design, using the most sophisticated military technology of the day (see Chapter 8).

The date of Duncan's death is not known with certainty, but must have been between 1237 and 1248, in which year his son, Ewen, appears in the forefront of events on the western seaboard. It seems likely that the *Annals of Loch Cé* refer to the death of Duncan when they record, under the year 1247, the death of 'MacSomhairle', king of Airer-Goidel, in a battle between Maurice fitz Gerald and the Cenél Conaill in Ireland. This entry is sometimes taken to refer to the death of Duncan's cousin, Donald, Ranald's son, but since Donald's territories included Kintyre, it is difficult to see how the annalist could have called him *rí Airer-Goidel*. Duncan therefore seems the more probable candidate for this obit, but the matter must remain contentious.[91]

Donald, the son of Ranald, Duncan's cousin, is a more elusive figure, but he too appears as a warlike and predatory figure: 'a man of blood and iron', as one modern account has called him.[92] We have already seen how he, along with Thomas, the brother of Alan of Galloway,

---

[88] On Ardchattan, see *Chron. Bower* (Goodall), ii, p. 539; RCAHMS, *Argyll*, ii, no. 217; and *Beauly Chrs.*, pp. 142–51. The Valliscaulian rule had close affinities with the Cistercian and Carthusian rules.

[89] *SAEC*, pp. 356–7.

[90] See the observations of Mitchell, *Popular History of the Highlands and Gaelic Scotland*, p. 243.

[91] *Ann. Loch Cé*, i, p. 377. Duffy, 'Bruce brothers', p. 68, argues that this entry refers to the death of Donald.

[92] MacDonald and MacDonald, *Clan Donald*, i, p. 79.

plundered Derry in 1212. His brother, Ruairi, had aided the MacWilliam and MacHeth risings in the north in the 1210s, and it is not unlikely that Donald was also involved in these insurrections, even if his name is not mentioned in connection with them. Perhaps paradoxically, at least to the modern observer, given his reputation as a pirate, Donald also appears in the contemporary record as a patron of Paisley Abbey, to which he confirmed his father's grant of eight oxen and two pence for each house from which smoke issued, and one penny per year thereafter.[93]

If the contemporary record is disappointingly silent on Donald, MacDonald tradition records how he travelled to Denmark after the death of his father, and how eventually 'King Alexander sent Sir William Rollock as messenger to him to Kintyre, desiring [him] to hold the Isles of him, which he now had from the King of Denmark.' Donald's reply was predictable: 'his predecessors had their rights of the Isles from the crown of Denmark, which were renewed by the present King thereof, and that he held the Isles of his Majesty of Denmark ...'[94] While it would be rash to accept this narrative at face value, and while the events outlined cannot be corroborated by contemporary sources, there may be kernels of truth preserved in these orally transmitted sagas. The purported trip to Denmark, for instance, may refer to a journey to Norway to obtain a formal grant or confirmation of his territories – and when the journeys of Duncan, Dugald Screech, Uspak, and later, Duncan's son Ewen, to Norway on similar endeavours are borne in mind, the possibility that Donald did so too should not be ruled out. Moreover, while the conflict with William Rollock cannot be confirmed, and even though the reply made by Donald to the demands of King Alexander bear great similarity to the reply made by Somerled to the demands of Malcolm IV some fifty years or more earlier, some such demands may well have been made. This tradition, however, would seem to be difficult to reconcile with what little is known about the redistribution of lands following the 1221 or 1222 campaign, since it appears that Kintyre was taken from Ruairi and given to Donald or his sons. Donald is also said to have received messages from Ireland to the effect that he should 'take the government of Innsigall and of the greater part of the Gael'. Although the source is late and untrustworthy, it is worth noting that Donald had allied himself with Thomas of Atholl to undertake expeditions in Ireland, and that he had also headed the army of the Irish of Ulster against Anglo-Norman intrusion into their kingdom.[95]

Even the date of Donald's death is not known with any certainty. MacDonald tradition placed it in 1289, but this seems impossibly late, and various dates from 1247 to 1269 have been proposed as more likely,

---

[93] *Paisley Reg.*, p. 126.
[94] Macdonald, *Hist. Macdonalds, HP*, i, p. 13.
[95] *Clanranald Bk.*, p. 157; Duffy, 'Bruce brothers', p. 68.

but apparently rest on no good authority.[96] As we have seen, the reference to the death of a MacSorley in Ireland in 1247 probably refers to the demise of Donald's cousin, Duncan MacDougall. However, when King Hakon IV of Norway sailed through the Hebrides in 1263, and collected the allegiances of the MacSorleys, it was Donald's son, Angus Mór, rather than Donald himself, who was in the forefront of events, and it seems safe to conclude that Donald was either dead by that time, or else had retired from active affairs. However little is known about Donald, though, he must 'hold an undisputed place in Scottish hearts and in the story of the Scots the world over, for almost all Macdonalds, Macdonnells, and MacConnels are named after him and descend from him'.[97] Moreover, it was from the line of Donald that the Lords of the Isles were descended. The MacDonald sea-girt lordship, which was not abolished until 1493, dominated the history of the western seaboard in the later Middle Ages, and played a not inconsiderable role in Scottish history.

If it was only a matter of time before the king of Scots took a renewed interest in the western seaboard, following the abortive Norwegian expedition of 1230, this was very much dependent upon other factors, both internal and external. In particular, the political situation within Scotland, especially in Galloway, and the state of Anglo-Scottish relations, would help dictate the rate at which royal expansion westward could occur. No serious campaign could be mounted in the West until these issues had been addressed, and it is therefore necessary to examine the constraints faced by the king of Scots in the 1230s and 1240s.

In 1234, Alan of Galloway died. He left a son born out of wedlock and three daughters, and King Alexander ordered a partition of the lordship among the co-heiresses. When the Galwegians requested that the unity of the lordship be preserved, the king rejected their petition. The result was predictable: a Galwegian uprising on behalf of Thomas, Alan's son, ensued, which laid waste some of the king's nearby lands, so that, in the summer of 1235, King Alexander entered the region with an army. The army was attacked in the rear while setting up camp, and only the fortuitous arrival of Earl Farquhar of Ross brought about the defeat of the Galwegian army. Walter Comyn was left in charge of the occupying forces, and, although subsequent events are obscure, it appears that a brief recovery of the lordship by Thomas gave way to further campaigning which forced first Thomas's chief supporter, and then Thomas himself, to seek the king's mercy. These events brought to an end the semi-independent existence of the last great Celtic province of Scotland, a fact

---

[96] Williams, *Lords of the Isles*, p. 137; MacDonald and MacDonald, *Clan Donald*, i, p. 81. Duffy, 'Bruce brothers', p. 68, makes the most plausible case for 1247.

[97] Barrow, *Kingship and Unity*, p. 109.

which was to have tremendous implications for Argyll and the Isles. The suppression of Galloway effectively paved the way for Alexander II to press ahead with 'a final solution to the west highland problem',[98] but the nature of Anglo-Scottish relations dictated that the king could not divert his full attention to the West just yet.

It is an oversimplification to state that Anglo-Scottish relations in the thirteenth century were exclusively peaceful. The major issue of the recovery of the northern counties had driven William I to war in 1173–4, and the perceived duplicity of King John in his dealings with William and his son, Alexander II, led to further invasions of northern England (and indeed an expedition as far south as Dover!) by Alexander in 1215–17. In 1221, peaceful relations were restored by the marriage of Alexander II to Joanna, the sister of Henry III. Matches were also promised for three of Alexander's sisters, and for the youngest of them to marry Henry III himself. But, by the mid-1230s, Anglo-Scottish tensions were running high again, as Henry broke the agreement to marry Margaret, and instead she married Gilbert, Earl of Pembroke, a leader of the English baronial opposition. Although, by the Treaty of York in 1237, the matter was resolved, Scottish claims to the northern counties were abandoned, and the issue of the Border was settled by the Treaty of York in 1237, these issues had scarcely been dealt with when new ones brought the two kings to the brink of war. The immediate cause was the suspicion in late 1243 that the king of Scots was involved in intrigue with the king of France against Henry III. This problem was solved, and peace was restored, in 1244; and thereafter Anglo-Scottish relations remained generally good until the 1290s. Nevertheless, it can be said with certainty that the middle years of the 1230s represented a critical period in the reign of Alexander II, when the twin issues of Galloway and Anglo-Scottish relations were very much to the fore. It was only once those issues had been resolved, and the southern frontiers of the kingdom stabilised, that it became possible for the king of Scots to set his sights on the western seaboard, and on the securing of the western and northern frontiers.

Increasing royal interest in the western seaboard and a build-up of crown strength in Argyll were demonstrated, in an indirect manner, as early as 1240. In that year, King Alexander granted lands in mid-Argyll and Cowal to Gillascop MacGilchrist. Gillascop's father, Gilchrist, was the brother of Suibhne and Ferchar, who were the ancestors of the MacSweens and Lamonts respectively. The royal charter states that Gillascop owed homage and 'service in Argyll', but he was also bound to render Scottish service in exactly the same fashion as barons and knights on the north side of the Forth rendered for their lands. Since 'Scottish service' represented service due to the king for defence of the kingdom,

---

[98] *ES*, ii, p. 496–8; Duncan, *Making of the Kingdom*, pp. 530–2; quotation from Barrow, *Kingship and Unity*, p. 115.

it is clear that a new generation of nobles was emerging in the West –
nobles whose primary allegiance was to the king of Scots, and who were
thoroughly accommodated to feudal society.[99] The encroachments of the
1220s were therefore continued, as magnates answerable to the king and
bound to the core of the kingdom were placed in positions of authority
in the West.

In 1244 a diplomatic attempt at winning the West was made when
King Alexander sent ambassadors to King Hakon in Norway, 'to enquire
whether the king were willing to give up the dominion that king Magnus
Bareleg had acquired in the Hebrides with some unfairness, from the
Scottish king Malcolm, [Alexander's] relative'. The response was
predictable. King Hakon replied that:

> he knew that king Magnus and king Malcolm had arranged it all
> between themselves, what dominion the Norwegians were to have
> in the Hebrides, and he said that the Scots had no authority in the
> Hebrides when he acquired them from king Godfrey; and besides,
> Magnus said that he went to seek his own inherited lands.[100]

The saga goes on to relate how the Scottish king, thus rebuked, then
offered to buy the islands in question with refined silver. But Hakon
stated that 'he was aware of no such urgent need of silver that he needed
to sell those lands. Upon that, the messengers went away.' Further
envoys received the same answer. Clearly, Scottish interest in the
Western Isles was taking on new proportions in the 1240s, and it was
not long until the actions of Duncan's son, Ewen, gave Alexander an
excuse to mobilise against the western seaboard.

When, in the 1240s, the historical mists which enshroud the western
seaboard in the 1220s and 1230s finally lift, a new generation of
MacSorleys appears on the scene, at just the moment when Scottish
expansion was really beginning to gather momentum. Duncan of Argyll
was still alive in 1237, as we have seen, but, whether he died in 1247 or
some other time, he was gone from the scene by 1248, when his son,
Ewen (called John in the saga), along with Dugald MacRuairi, went to
Bergen, where 'they both endeavoured after this, that the king should
give them the title of king over the northern part of the Hebrides'. Ewen
and Dugald's voyage to Bergen is almost certainly related to Scandinavian politics in 1247–8. In the summer of 1247, King Hakon was
crowned,[101] and he may well have summoned Harald, the king of Man,
to do homage. It seems likely that Ewen and Dugald would have been
similarly summoned to perform homage to the newly crowned king.

---

99 The charter is printed in *HP*, ii, pp. 121–4, with a commentary on pp. 227–45. See
     also W. D. H. Sellar, 'Family origins in Cowal and Knapdale', *Scot. Stud.*, xv (1971),
     pp. 29, 33, for the background of Gillascop. See Duncan, *Making of the Kingdom*, pp.
     380–3, on Scottish service.
100 *ES*, ii, pp. 539–40.
101 Ibid., ii, p. 546.

Following the betrothal, and subsequent marriage, of Harald, King of the Isles, to Hakon's daughter in 1248, Hakon bestowed the title of king upon Ewen; we do not know why he, rather than his cousin, was rewarded with the title.[102] The islands sought by Dugald and Ewen (the 'northern Hebrides') cannot have included Skye and Lewis, which formed part of Harald's kingdom of the Isles. This would suggest that Ewen and his cousin were competing for a kingship in the western islands, and it is tempting to surmise that this kingship corresponded to that which Hakon had bestowed upon Uspak in 1230.[103] These proceedings, therefore, look like another attempt to create a stable political atmosphere in the Hebrides, and to extend Norwegian royal authority in that region. As one writer has put it: 'by marrying his daughter to the king of Man Hakon was surely signifying a strong presence in the islands and indicating that he would tolerate no further nonsense from Somerled's descendants'.[104]

Whatever Hakon's plans might have been, yet another untimely accident nullified them, as had happened in 1230. In September 1248, King Harald and his new bride were drowned at Sumburgh Roost, off Shetland, while returning to their kingdom. Although disastrous from the Norwegian point of view, the drowning of the Manx king and his wife presented golden new opportunities for the MacSorleys. When news of the accident reached Hakon in early 1249, Ewen was ordered to 'go west as quickly as possible, and be [the ruler] over the islands, until he made another plan for them'.[105] A. A. M. Duncan believes that this meant Ewen was given a temporary commission to rule over all the Isles. Alternatively, the new plan may have involved giving a portion, or all, of the Isles to Dugald, since the *Icelandic Annals* state that in 1249 'Dugald took kingship in the Hebrides.'[106] It seems more likely, however, that Duncan's interpretation is correct, and that Dugald's assumption of the kingship followed the campaign of Alexander II in 1249 and the subsequent displacement of Ewen for six years.

Ewen's voyage to Norway, where he almost certainly performed homage to King Hakon, had proved too much of a trial upon Alexander II's patience, and Ewen's kingship over the Hebrides no doubt placed far too much key territory in the hands of one man who was also, from the Scottish perspective at least, a baron of the kingdom. Directly, then, one of the objectives for Alexander's campaign was to bring Ewen of Argyll to heel; but indirectly, and by implication, the campaign was aimed against Norwegian authority in the western seaboard. Finally, it is also possible that Henry III of England had been intervening in the

102 Ibid., ii, pp. 548–9.
103 Duncan and Brown, 'Argyll and the Isles', p. 207.
104 Cowan, 'Norwegian sunset – Scottish dawn', p. 115.
105 *ES*, ii, pp. 554–5.
106 Ibid., ii, p. 554.

affairs of the Isles. In early 1248 he had allowed Walter Bisset to purchase supplies in Ireland for Dunaverty Castle, which Bisset had seized and was fortifying. Later that same year, Walter was captured when the castle was stormed by Alan, the son of Thomas of Galloway, but Bisset seems to have made good his restoration by early 1249, perhaps because he was able to disclose valuable information about the western seaboard to the Scottish king. It has been suggested that these facts, combined with the intercession of Henry III on behalf of Ewen in 1255, argue strongly that negotiations had been taking place between Ewen and the English king.[107]

Diplomatic negotiations for a Scottish purchase of the Isles, which had been going on since 1244, were terminated, as Alexander II assembled an army and prepared for what would prove to be his last expedition in the West. When Ewen returned to the Hebrides from Norway, he received word that the king of Scots wished to meet him. Details of the relations between the two kings are preserved both in *Hakon's Saga*, and in the *Chronica Majora* of Matthew Paris, the thirteenth-century chronicler of St Albans.[108] According to the saga, Ewen refused to meet the king until his safe-conduct had been assured by the pledges of four Scottish earls – a precaution which illustrates just how high tensions were running. When the two kings met, the Scottish king required Ewen to cede 'Biarnaborg' (probably Cairn na Burgh More) Castle in the Treshnish islands, and three other castles which he held of King Hakon, in addition to the rest of the territory that the king of Norway had granted him. It has been argued that the three unnamed castles may have been Dunstaffnage, and two castles associated with Cairn na Burgh More in fourteenth-century charters: 'Iselborg' and 'Dunchonnell'. Dunchonnell is the most northerly island of the Garvellach group, and contains extensive remains of a castle, while 'Iselborg' has not been satisfactorily identified.[109] If these conditions were met, King Alexander then promised that, in an attempt to win Ewen to the Scottish side, he would give him 'a much larger dominion in Scotland; and along with it, his friendship'. Although the terms of the settlement were pushed upon Ewen by his chief advisors, he refused to break his oath to the Norwegian king, and left the scene of the meeting.[110]

Matthew Paris gives an account which agrees in sentiment with, but differs in some essentials from, that of the saga. According to his account, the negotiations were carried out by an exchange of letters. Ewen replied to Alexander's charge of treason that 'he should render entire the service due both to the king of Scots and to the king of the

[107] Duncan, *Making of the Kingdom*, p. 550.
[108] *ES*, ii, pp. 554–7; *SAEC*, pp. 360–1.
[109] Duncan and Brown, 'Argyll and the Isles', p. 208. 'Iselborg' may be Cairn na Burgh Beg, also in the Treshnish group: see *The Acts of the Lords of the Isles, 1336–1493*, ed. J. and R. W. Munro (SHS, 1986), index, p. 328.
[110] *ES*, ii, pp. 555–6.

Norwegians', arguing in essence that it was possible to serve two masters. King Alexander replied that no one could serve two masters, to which Ewen retorted that 'one could quite well serve two masters, provided the masters were not enemies'.[111] Enraged, Alexander mobilised his army to attack Ewen, who, 'being loth to offend his lord the king of Scotland, besought him that a truce might be granted him so that he should resign to the king of Norway his homage ...' The king of Scots' response was to declare Ewen unfaithful, and to pursue him 'to near Argyll', where Alexander, in retribution for 'wishing to disinherit an innocent man', was taken ill and died.[112] The saga records in vivid detail King Alexander's dream on the eve of his death:

> When king Alexander lay in Kerrera sound, he dreamed a dream: and he thought that three men came to him. He thought that one wore royal apparel; this man was very frowning, and red-faced, and stout in figure. The second man seemed to him tall, and slender, and youthful; the fairest of men, and nobly dressed. The third was by far the largest in figure, and the most frowning, of them all. He was very bald in front. He spoke to the king, and asked whether he intended to go plundering to the Hebrides. He thought he answered that that was certain. The dream-man bade him turn back, and said to him that they would not hear of anything else.
>
> The king told his dream; and men begged him to turn back, but he would not do that. And a little later he fell ill, and died. Then the Scots broke up the levy, and conveyed the king's body up into Scotland. The Hebrideans say that these men who appeared to the king in his sleep must have been St Olaf, king of Norway; and St Magnus, earl of the Orkneys; and St Columba.

One of the messages of the dream, also emphasised in the chronicle of Matthew Paris, was that Alexander II was the aggressor and the one causing strife in the Hebrides. The English chronicler portrayed Ewen as an innocent man and described him as 'one of the noblest of his realm ... a vigorous and very handsome knight'. Alexander, on the other hand, was described as a king who reigned wisely for many years but who 'in his last days prompted by greed is said to have swerved from the path of justice'.[113] Sturla's portrayal of Alexander was similar, stating that the Scottish king was 'very covetous of dominion in the Hebrides'.[114] The convergence in viewpoint of the English and Icelandic authors is more than mere coincidence, and it has been argued that it might derive from a visit that Matthew Paris made to Norway in 1248, when he could well

---

[111] *SAEC*, pp. 360–1.
[112] Ibid., p. 361. D. J. MacDonald, *The Clan Donald* (Loanhead, 1978), p. 38, suggested that Ewen plotted Alexander's death, but there is no evidence for such a view, and the Scottish king's demise hardly worked to Ewen's advantage.
[113] *SAEC*, p. 360.
[114] *ES*, ii, p. 555.

have met Ewen, perhaps at the Norwegian court.[115] Although this is possible, and presents an attractive explanation, a more likely explanation for the concurrence of Matthew Paris and Sturla in condemning Alexander II is the fact that both were known to oppose centralising authority, the former probably being influenced by the events of the reign of King John of England, the latter by the imperialistic ambitions of Hakon IV in Iceland, which he had actively opposed.[116] Whatever may have been the case, the ultimate message of Alexander's abortive campaign in 1249 was that 'it would only be a matter of time before the Scottish monarchy exerted its full strength and annexed the Hebrides in spite of Norwegian opposition'.[117] Fate, or, as contemporaries saw it, the vengeance of St Columba, had prevented the tide of Scottish authority from overwhelming Ewen and the other MacSorleys in 1249. But the first waves had broken on the shore, and it was to be less than twenty years before what Alexander II had begun was completed by his son and successor, Alexander III, described by the saga-writer as 'a great chief'.[118]

---

[115] Gransden, *Historical Writing in England*, p. 356.
[116] On Matthew's outlook, see ibid., i, pp. 367–73; and on Sturla, see Cowan, 'Norwegian sunset – Scottish dawn', pp. 105–9: 'As an Icelander (and a one time activist) Sturla was clearly in sympathy with the plight of the Hebridean chiefs.'
[117] Barrow, *Kingship and Unity*, p. 116.
[118] *ES*, ii, p. 557.

CHAPTER FOUR

1266 And All That: The MacSorleys and the Dilemma of Divided Allegiances, 1249–1266

Magnus, King of Norway ... granted, resigned and quit-claimed ... for himself and his heirs forever, Man with the rest of the Sudreys and all other islands on the west and south of the great sea ... to be held, had and possessed by the said lord Alexander III, King of Scots ... [Treaty of Perth, 1266].[1]

Despite its dramatic and premature ending, King Alexander II's campaign of 1249 was a limited success. While it is true that it had failed to integrate the Western Isles into the Scottish kingdom, it did nonetheless send a powerful message that the Scottish kings were ready and willing to undertake military action in order to do so, and it also seems to have shaken up the *status quo* on the western seaboard through a redistribution of at least some MacSorley lands. The major difficulty was that the death of Alexander II created an environment in which it was not possible to undertake a swift follow-up campaign, and immediately to complete the subjugation of the MacSorleys to Scottish authority. Alexander II's successor was his eight-year-old son, also named Alexander, who was inaugurated in traditional fashion on 13 July, only a few days after the death of his father. But the situation was complicated by his youth, and a troubled minority of twelve years ensued, as various magnate factions strove to gain control of the young Alexander III. Not until 1260 or 1261 did the king take full charge of government, which enabled him to turn his attention to the West. The subjugation of the western seaboard, begun in the 1220s by Alexander II, was thus completed in the 1260s by Alexander III.

When Alexander II died at Kerrera on 8 July 1249, the army that had massed adjacent to Ewen's mainland territories dispersed. Although it would be easy to claim that the campaign had been a failure, it had in fact attained some measure of success. Following the events of the summer of 1249, Ewen of Argyll virtually disappears from the historical record. Although it has sometimes been argued that he remained in possession of his territories,[2] his power was seriously weakened, and he

[1] *APS*, i, p. 420.
[2] MacDonald, *History of Argyll*, p. 104; MacDonald and MacDonald, *Clan Donald*, ii, p. 70.

was in all probability displaced. The evidence for this view is sketchy but convincing. From his deathbed on Kerrera, Alexander II granted the church of St Bride, in the heart of Lorn (Ewen's territory), to the see of Argyll.[3] The *Icelandic Annals* recorded, under the year 1249, that Dugald, the son of Ruairi, Ewen's cousin and rival, took the kingship in the Hebrides, and this may be more than mere coincidence. It is, in fact, highly likely that Dugald had succeeded a dispossessed or displaced Ewen, and this is also suggested by Ewen's subsequent movements. In 1250, while the king of Man (Harald, the son of Godfrey Dond, the son of Ragnvald) was in Norway answering a summons from King Hakon, Ewen, along with Magnus, the son of King Olaf, undertook an invasion of the Isle of Man. Landing at Ronaldsway, Ewen proclaimed himself king of the Isles, but was eventually driven out. The return of Magnus, Olaf's son, as king of Man in 1252 must have thwarted Ewen's designs upon the kingship of the Isles, and when King Hakon campaigned in Denmark in 1253, both Ewen 'of the Hebrides' and Dugald are on record as among those who accompanied him.[4] Finally, in 1250, a royal bailiff is on record in Argyll, and it may have been about this time that the castle of 'Frechelan' in Loch Awe was either built or taken over by the king.[5] What these fragmentary pieces of evidence cumulatively suggest is that Ewen had been seriously weakened, and quite probably removed entirely from his mainland territories by Alexander's campaign of 1249. With Ewen apparently reduced to a freebooting life in the Hebrides and Scandinavia, the Scottish king had indeed gone a considerable distance toward attaining his objective. As Duncan and Brown have put it:

> the marcher lordship of Argyll had been overthrown, apparently without the striking of a blow, but the isles had not been attacked, and Norwegian sovereignty there was unimpaired. The aims of the Scottish kings were now clear, and they had resorted to arms to achieve them: the total recovery of the isles, and the destruction of the Norse kingdom there.[6]

Ewen's eventual return to a position of power on the western seaboard owed much to political events taking place at the centre of the kingdom, which he seems to have manipulated for his own ends. On 20 September 1255 the Comyn family, which had dominated the minority government of Alexander III and aroused much resentment, was

---

[3] *RMS*, ii, no. 3136.

[4] *ES*, ii, pp. 554, 567–8, 577. Ewen does not seem to have been the only individual interested in Man in the early 1250s: in 1253 King Henry III of England sent letters to Llewelyn ap Gruffydd, the King of Scots, and the King of Norway, commanding them to prevent their men from invading Man during the absence of Magnus: *CDS*, i, no. 1917. Conditions were clearly troubled in the region in the early 1250s.

[5] Duncan and Brown, 'Argyll and the Isles', p. 211.

[6] Ibid.

removed from power in a counter-coup with the aid of King Henry III of England. The ousted nobles were to be permitted to enter King Alexander's favour only when they had atoned to King Henry, or else in the event of invasion by a foreign prince (the latter point illustrates incidentally how strong the feeling of danger from Norway was, since only King Hakon can have been meant by the foreign prince). The very next day after the political revolution, letters patent were issued which took Ewen under the protection of the English king; and further letters patent were issued on 23 September to the effect that, if any complaint was made against Ewen, King Henry III was to mediate.[7] It would appear, from an abstract of a letter dated between 1242 and 1266, entered in the inventory of Scottish records drawn up in 1292, that Ewen owed an annual rent of sixty merks for his lands, which was guaranteed by three of the most powerful of the Scottish magnates: the earls of Fife, Mar, and Strathearn.[8] In 1255, then, Ewen purchased the goodwill of King Alexander, thanks to the help of the English king – which perhaps foreshadows the later alliances between subsequent Lords of the Isles and the English monarchs. The precise reasons behind Ewen's volte-face can only be guessed at. The most likely explanation would seem to be that the vicissitudes of a freebooting life in the Hebrides, and in the service of the Norwegian king, had convinced him of the necessity to come to terms with the king of Scots, in an attempt to regain the comparative wealth of his lordship in Argyll.

In 1260 or 1261 Alexander III assumed personal control of Scottish government, and he quickly acted to raise the Scottish islands question again. That same summer, Scottish ambassadors (an unnamed archdeacon, and a knight named 'Missel') went to Norway. The identity of Missel has not been satisfactorily resolved. Some have argued that his name is a version of Frisel, and that he was Sir Simon Fraser, while others have suggested that it might be a rendering of Malise, the lord of Rossie and son of Earl Gilbert of Strathearn.[9] Whoever Missel was, it appears that he and his colleague made fresh overtures to purchase the Hebrides from Norway outright, but the saga recorded that the Scottish ambassadors dealt 'more with fair words than with good faith, as far as it appeared to the king. And they went away in such a manner that no man knew of it, until they had hoisted their sail.' This surreptitious

---

[7] *CDS*, i, nos. 2014, 2017–18; Duncan and Brown, 'Argyll and the Isles', p. 212; details of 1255 are in Duncan, *Making of the Kingdom*, pp. 560–9.

[8] *APS*, i, p. 115; Cowan, 'Norwegian sunset – Scottish dawn', p. 117. The abstract states that CCCXX merks should be paid, but Duncan thinks that iii was misread as ccc, and that xx means score: thus, 60 rather than 320 merks: Duncan, *Making of the Kingdom*, p. 581, note 31. On the minority of Alexander III in general, see D. E. R. Watt, 'The minority of Alexander III of Scotland', *Trans. Royal Hist. Soc.*, 5th ser., xxi (1971), pp. 1–23; see also the relevant comments of A. Young, 'Noble families and political factions in the reign of Alexander III', in Reid, *Scotland in the Reign of Alexander III*.

[9] Duncan, *Making of the Kingdom*, p. 588, note; Cowan, 'Norwegian sunset – Scottish dawn', p. 117, note 69.

departure angered King Hakon, who had them brought back and 'said
that they should remain in Norway that winter, because they had wished
to depart without leave'.[10] The abrupt departure of the Scottish envoys
without leave from the Norwegian king, and their subsequent enforced
wintering in Norway (where they attended the spectacular coronation of
Hakon's son, Magnus), shows that not only had Alexander III inherited
a legacy of Norwegian hostility from the 1230s and 1240s, but also that
King Hakon was no more willing to cede the Western Isles in the 1260s
than he had been in the 1240s.

In the summer of 1262 word arrived in Norway from the kings of the
Hebrides that disorder was once again prevalent in the Isles. It was
reported that the earl of Ross, and Kiarnak, Makamal's son, with a force
of Scots, 'went out to Skye, and burned a town and churches, and slew
very many men and women'. The saga went on to record how, 'the Scots
had taken the little children, and laid them on their spear-points, and
shook their spears until they brought the children down to their hands;
and so threw them away, dead'.[11] There is a certain macabre irony in the
events of 1262, for the practice of tossing children on spear-points was
known as *gallcerd*, and had originally been associated with the Vikings![12]
The earl of Ross was none other than William, the son of Farquhar
Maccintsacairt. His father had been a consistent supporter of the kings
of Scots throughout the early thirteenth century, beginning with his
suppression of the 1215 MacHeth and MacWilliam uprising, and he had
also played a prominent role in quashing the Galloway uprising in July
1235. The involvement of William suggests that the attack on Skye was
Alexander's response to the failure of the Scottish embassy to Norway
the previous year, and it seems impossible that such a raid could have
been undertaken without the king's assent, even if he did not directly
order it. This in turn suggests that, in the face of the refusal of the
Norwegian king to negotiate, the Scottish king was moving towards
conflict as a means of settling the simmering dispute over the islands. It
is of some consequence that the 1262 campaign was directed against
Skye, which was not under the control of the MacSorleys, but rather fell
within the domain of the Manx kings. Since the Manx kings in turn
ostensibly fell under the authority of the kings of Norway, it is difficult to
see the 1262 campaign as anything other than a direct challenge to
Norwegian authority in the western seaboard. If this line of reasoning is
correct, then the challange certainly succeeded. Other moves also suggest an
increasing Scottish desire to obtain control of the western seaboard: in

[10] *ES*, ii, pp. 601–2.
[11] Ibid., ii, pp. 605–6. Kiarnak is probably the Kermac Macmaghan of *ER*, i, p. 19: he
    was the ancestor of the MacKenzies and Mathesons; see W. Matheson, 'Traditions of
    the MacKenzies', *TGSI*, xxxix–xl (1942–50), p. 196.
[12] See Cowan, 'Norwegian sunset – Scottish dawn', p. 130, note 70.

addition to the raid on Skye, Walter Stewart, Earl of Menteith, had expelled the MacSweens from Knapdale and Arran by 1262.[13] Above all, however, the Skye raid may well have led to the belief held by the messengers to King Hakon that 'the Scottish king intended to lay under himself all the Hebrides'.[14] Greatly concerned by this news, King Hakon called out a levy of both men and stores, 'the most that he thought the land could provide', and ordered the army to meet in Bergen in the early summer.

It has been remarked that few medieval naval expeditions are known in as much detail as King Hakon Hakonsson's expedition to the Western Isles of Scotland in 1263. Indeed, *Hakon's Saga* provides much information about the events of 1263, which culminated in the Battle of Largs, and Gordon Donaldson has suggested that the narrative may have been based on a log book of someone who was present on the campaign.[15] According to the saga, Hakon's aim was to 'avenge the warfare that the Scots had made in his dominions'.[16] It seems unlikely, however, that a full-scale assault upon the Scottish kingdom was intended. It is more likely that the aim of the expedition was a demonstration of muscle, to show that the Isles, which had seemed to be slipping from his grasp, were still the property of the Norwegian crown, and perhaps to ensure a stronger position at the bargaining table, should compromise become necessary.[17] The Scottish king, however, had the advantage of youth and the hard facts of geography on his side: as a leading authority has put it: 'If Hakon was to hold the Isles he must come to Alexander.'[18]

After making the appropriate preparations, including a tour around his kingdom to gather support, Hakon's great fleet set sail from Bergen on 5 or 11 July (two saga manuscripts are at variance here). Hakon's flagship was stated to have been constructed especially for the crossing. It was made entirely of oak, with thirty-seven benches and a dragon's head, gilded all the way to the neck. The numbers of the fleet cannot be determined with accuracy, but the *Icelandic Annals* called it 'so great a host that an equally great army is not known ever to have gone from Norway'. Sturla Thordarsson described its splendour:

> The host of the king
> As it skimmed o'er the main
> Was like unto lightning
> That springs from the sea.[19]

13 Barrow, *Kingship and Unity*, p. 116.
14 *ES*, ii, p. 605.
15 Donaldson, *Northern Commonwealth*, p. 80.
16 *ES*, ii, pp. 606, 609–10.
17 Donaldson, *Northern Commonwealth*, p. 79; E. Linklater, 'The Battle of Largs', in *Orkney Miscellany*, v (1973), p. 38.
18 Cowan, 'Norwegian sunset – Scottish dawn', p. 118.
19 *Hakon's Saga*, p. 344 [this translation is preferred to that in *ES*, ii, p. 613]. On the size of the fleet, see Magnusson, *Hakon the Old*, pp. 4–5.

With a 'gentle, favourable wind', two days' sailing brought the fleet to Shetland, where King Hakon lay in Bressay Sound for two weeks, during which time he imposed a tax upon the inhabitants of Caithness, the northern tip of the Scottish mainland:

> First for life-ransom
> Took from Ness-dwellers
> That wise king of Northland
> A tribute for peace.
> All Scottish subjects
> Shivered in awe
> At sight of that warrior
> Mail-clad 'neath his helm.[20]

One version of the saga also states that Hakon intended to send part of his force to the Moray Firth, to harry there. Although the plan was opposed by many in the army, it may well be that both the tax imposed upon Caithness, and the planned punitive expedition to the Moray Firth, were intended as retribution against the earl of Ross for his role in the 1262 campaign against Skye.

When Hakon arrived in Orkney he was greeted with disappointing news from the Hebrides: word reached him that Ewen of Argyll had 'changed his allegiance, and turned him to the king of Scots'. But the Norwegian king, 'would not believe that, before he had proved it'.[21] It was August when the fleet reached Skye, and the place-name Kyleakin, which means the 'Narrow of Hakon', may preserve a memory of the visit of the Norwegian king. At Skye, Hakon was met by the king of Man, Magnus, as well as Dugald MacRuairi, who, 'begged king Hakon to hasten as much as possible after him'.[22] In the light of both the growing lateness of the campaigning season, and the preparations being made by the Scots to resist an invasion, Dugald's entreaties were well founded. Dugald had been made king of the Hebrides by Hakon in 1249, apparently following Ewen's displacement, and remained steadfast in his Norwegian allegiance. In fact, he had greatly aided the Norwegian cause by foiling a Scottish expedition which was preparing to plunder in the Hebrides in the summer of 1263. Having received word of the assembly of the invasion fleet in Norway, Dugald 'spread the rumour that forty ships were coming west from Norway, and the Scots were deterred by that'.[23]

While the Norwegian fleet was making its slow progress through the Hebrides, and calling on the MacSorleys for their allegiance, King Alexander was busy setting his kingdom on a footing for war. The *Exchequer Rolls*

[20] *Hakon's Saga*, p. 346; *ES*, ii, p. 615.
[21] *Hakon's Saga*, p. 347; *ES*, ii, p. 616, note 3.
[22] Ibid., ii, p. 616, note 12.
[23] Ibid., ii, p. 611.

are an important source for the extensive preparations to meet the Norwegian invasion. One of the most interesting entries reveals that Alexander paid messengers to spy on the movements of the fleet, and it is tempting to suppose that Ewen of Argyll may have played a role in keeping the Scottish king informed of the fleet's movements (though that is undocumented). Other entries reveal that the sheriff of Ayr spent over £60 in building ships and oars, and then employed men to watch over the newly built vessels for twenty-three weeks. The castle at Ayr was also refortified, weapons were deposited within its walls, and it was garrisoned with 120 retainers for three weeks, after the burgesses of Ayr refused to garrison it themselves. The *Rolls* go on to note that, if this misconduct can be proved, the cost of meeting the garrison should fall upon the burgesses; if not, then the sheriff must meet it. At Inverie, on the north shore of Loch Ness, the earl of Buchan, as bailie of the castle, repaired both fortress and drawbridge and had eight soldiers in the garrison for six months. Further preparations were made at Wigtown, Inverness, and Stirling, and hostages were taken from Skye, Kintyre, and Caithness, to ensure the good behaviour of the local nobles in these regions.[24] What these preparations demonstrate is that, despite his intelligence-gathering efforts, Alexander had no clear idea of the ultimate destination of the Norwegian fleet. But the resources mobilised to meet it were formidable, and the construction of ships at Ayr demonstrates just how far the Scottish kings' understanding of the necessities of campaigning on the western seaboard had advanced since the beginning of the century.

From Skye, the Norse fleet sailed south to Kerrera, gathering strength as it did. From Kerrera, a detatchment of fifty ships, commanded by Dugald MacRuairi and Magnus of Man, was sent to harry Kintyre, and five (or fifteen, depending on the manuscript) more were dispatched to Bute before Hakon sailed on to Gigha. There can be little doubt that the first of these detatchments was charged with securing the allegiance of Angus Mór, the son of Donald, the son of Ranald, the Lord of Islay, and Murchaid (either Angus's brother or Murchaid MacSween). The allegiance of this branch of the descendants of Somerled had been wavering ever since the campaigns of Alexander II in the 1220s. Not only had Angus Mór named his eldest son Alexander, after the Scottish king, but, in the 1240s, he had also granted the church of Kilkerran, in Kintyre, to Paisley, 'for the salvation of the soul of my lord Alexander, illustrious king of Scots', indicating a decidedly pro-Scottish leaning.[25] King Alexander seems to have remained sceptical of these MacSorley

---

[24] *ER*, i, pp. 5–6, 14, 18, 22–3. See also Cowan, 'Norwegian sunset – Scottish dawn', pp. 118–19; J. Fergusson, *Alexander the Third* (London, 1937), pp. 101–2; and A. W. Brøgger, *Ancient Emigrants: A History of the Norse Settlements of Scotland* (Oxford, 1929), pp. 172–4, on the Scottish preparations for the invasion.

[25] *Paisley Reg.*, pp. 128–9.

attitudes, however: hostages were taken from Kintyre, including the sons of both Murchaid and Angus, to ensure their loyalty.[26]

In the event, King Alexander had been right to doubt the allegiance of the two chieftains. The saga records how their lands had been ravaged by the Kintyre raiding party:

> Brave warriors of the treasure keeper
> Marched from the South across Cantire;
> The lovers of the sword-storm sated
> On Scotland's soil the birds of Odin,
> Black-clad ravens fiercely swooping
> Upon the corpses of the slain.[27]

Presumably persuaded by this incentive, and probably encouraged by the example of Dugald MacRuairi, who had remained loyal to Norway, Angus and Murchaid finally sent word to King Hakon at Gigha that they were ready to submit:

> And the king said that he would not plunder the headland [Kintyre] if they came into his power on the following day, before mid-day: 'Otherwise I let my men plunder.' The messengers went back. Upon the following morning, Murchaid and Angus came to king Hakon, and submitted their whole case to him, and swore oaths, and gave hostages.[28]

Angus and Murchaid surrendered Islay to Hakon, and Angus received it back from the Norwegian king 'on the same terms as the other chiefs of the Hebrides held their territories of him'. It is also recorded that 'a certain knight' surrendered a castle at the south end of Kintyre – undoubtedly Dunaverty – to Hakon at this time as well.

Among the squadron of ships which had been dispatched to Bute had been one captained by a certain 'Rudri', who 'thought that he had an hereditary right to Bute'. Having earlier caused a 'great dispeace' on Bute and slain many men, he had been outlawed by the king of Scots. Accordingly, he, along with his two brothers, came to King Hakon, probably while the king was at Kerrera, and swore oaths to him. After attacking the castle on Bute and receiving its surrender, Rudri slaughtered nine members of its garrison before crossing to the mainland and 'going far and wide with slaughter and rapine':

> Abodes of false franklins were harried and burnt,
> Hot indeed raged the hall-crushed
> On Scotland's west coast

---

26 *ER*, i, p. 5.
27 *Hakon's Saga*, p. 350; *ES*, ii, p. 620.
28 Ibid., ii, pp. 617–18.

Warriors fell death-doomed in flight
Before the champions of the king ...[29]

It is unfortunate that more is not known of Rudri and his pedigree. If, as seems possible, he was a son of Uspak, then he may have been continuing the activities of his father, who had attacked Bute in 1230, and he may have been exploiting the situation in 1263 to settle private scores.

It is relevant here to discuss the situation of Bute, the evidence for which is very sparse. Bute must have lain in Norse hands in the early twelfth century, for it was included in the diocese of Sodor. What is not clear is whether it was ever held by Somerled's descendants, and, if so, at what point it passed under Scottish control. Working backwards from 1263, when Alexander III's refusal to surrender the island shows that it was clearly in Scottish hands, we come to 1230, when there was a Scots garrison, said to be under the command of a 'certain steward' (probably Walter Stewart, 1204–41), in Rothesay Castle.[30] The efforts – they might almost be called obsessive – first of Uspak, and then of Rudri, to recapture Bute, argue strongly that the island had once fallen within the ambit of the MacSorleys – assuming, of course, that Uspak should be identified as a son of Dugald. The vehemence with which Uspak pressed his claim in 1230 might suggest a recent dispossession; if so, we should probably look to Alexander II's campaign of 1222 which had as its target the Clyde estuary. But as early as 1204, if not before, Alan, son of Walter, the Steward, who died in that year, granted Kingarth in Bute and the parish of the whole island, to Paisley.[31] This suggests that Bute was already in Stewart hands by *c.*1200, and some have argued that this family was established there by Malcolm IV (1153–65), who held them in high esteem.[32] Whatever Rudri's claim on Bute, its capture in 1263 was significant in strategic terms for the Norwegian expeditionary force: with Bute, one of the most important Scottish strongholds in the region, in the hands of an ally, the Norwegians now commanded the Firth of Clyde, the gateway to the heart of the Scottish kingdom.[33]

If the allegiances of the Kintyre and Islay branches of the MacSorleys had returned to the king of Norway, it remained to determine how Ewen of Argyll would react to the Norse fleet which had recently arrived at his front doorstep. This question was resolved while King Hakon still lay at Kerrera before moving south to Gigha. Hakon demanded that Ewen accompany him on his expedition, but Ewen refused: 'he said that

---

[29] *Hakon's Saga*, p. 351; *ES*, ii, pp. 621–2.

[30] Ibid., ii, 475–8. But the saga says the 'certain steward' was killed; Walter Stewart, the lord of Rothesay, has presumably been conflated with the actual garrison commander.

[31] *Paisley Reg.*, p. 15.

[32] Duncan and Brown, 'Argyll and the Isles', p. 203; Duncan, *Making of the Kingdom*, p. 136.

[33] Duncan and Brown, 'Argyll and the Isles', p. 203, note 5; Cowan, 'Norwegian sunset – Scottish dawn', p. 121; Magnusson, *Hakon the Old*, pp. 6–7.

he had sworn an oath of the Scottish king, and held larger dominions of him than of the king of Norway. He bade king Hakon dispose of the dominion that he had given him.' Ewen was thus repeating the tactics he had used on Alexander II in 1249. Hakon, however, detained Ewen, in an attempt to 'soften his loyalty to himself' (apparently unsuccessfully), until the fleet reached Holy Island in Arran. Hakon then set him free, 'and bade him go in peace, wherever he wished; and gave him many good gifts', with the understanding that Ewen would act as an envoy between the two kings, in an attempt to secure peace.[34]

At about the same time that Hakon had released Ewen, the first messengers of the Scottish king – Dominican friars – had arrived on the scene in an effort to settle terms of peace. An apparently cordial series of discussions looked promising, but achieved nothing, possibly because the Norwegians thought the Scots were dealing faithlessly, and also because Alexander III would not concede to Norwegian claims on Bute, Arran and the Cumbraes, even though 'about the rest [of the islands] there was little conflict between the claims of the kings'. With the summer drawing on, and the weather worsening, Hakon withdrew the offer of peace, and replaced it with a final option: serious negotiation or battle. The saga tells how 'King Hakon sent a message to the Scottish king, to the effect that they must either meet, with their whole armies, and discuss further the terms of peace; or else they must fight. The Scottish king was not disposed to fighting with king Hakon.'

All peace talks were accordingly broken off, and Hakon sent forty (or sixty – the manuscripts are at variance again) ships up Loch Long, commanded by Dugald, Dugald's brother Alan, Magnus of Man, Angus, and Murchaid. The choice of these men to lead the foray into Lennox is interesting, and perhaps it was designed as a test of their fidelity to Hakon. On the other hand, the ships of the Hebrideans may have been lighter than those of the Norwegians, and thus easier to portage at Arrochar and into Loch Lomond, the ultimate objective of the expedition. The banks and islands of the Loch were pillaged:

> Those soldiers so flight-shy
> Of dart-storms bold wielder,
> Drew boats over dry land
> For many a length;
> Those warriors undaunted
> They wasted with war-gales,
> The islands thick peopled
> On Lomond's broad loch.[35]

According to the saga, Alan went 'far across Scotland, and slew many men', perhaps even penetrating as far as Stirling Castle, since an item in

---

[34] *ES*, ii, pp. 617, 622, and note 13.
[35] *Hakon's Saga*, p. 355; *ES*, ii, p. 626.

the *Exchequer Rolls* provides a sum paid for lookouts 'at the time the king of Norway was in the area'.[36] Hakon's motive in sending this detachment of ships into Loch Lomond to harry Lennox has long puzzled historians. But the expedition makes perfect sense when placed within the larger context of Stewart expansion on the west coast of Scotland, particularly during the time of Walter the Steward, who in 1263 was sheriff of Ayr. The struggle against Stewart power, begun by Somerled a century earlier, was clearly still in progress, and 'there can be little doubt that Dugald, Alan, Angus and Murchaid knew exactly what they were doing when they carried their torches east of Loch Lomond'.[37]

The events of 30 September to 3 October are generally well known, although the outcome of the so-called 'Battle of Largs' was not decisive. On the night of 30 September/1 October, an autumnal gale drove a Norwegian merchant ship and several longships ashore on the coast at Largs, and the saga relates that eight anchors were required to prevent a similar fate from befalling the king's ship. When the Scots saw that some of the Norwegian ships had been blown ashore, they gathered their forces, went down to the beach, and engaged the Norwegians from a distance with arrows, though the saga states that the Norse defended themselves successfully:

> The Scots attacked them sometimes, but constantly from a distance; a few men fell there but many were wounded. Then king Hakon sent ashore a force from some boats, because the storm lessened somewhat ... As soon as the king's men came to land, the Scots fled.

The following morning the king himself came ashore with many men, and successfully recovered the beached merchant vessel. As this recovery was taking place, the Norwegians noted that a large Scottish force had mustered, and they supposed that the size of the army meant the king of Scots himself was present. At this point a group of Norwegians led by one Ogmund Crow-Dance had occupied what the saga-writer calls 'a certain mound' on the shore (likely to have been a prominent spur of land on the shoreline opposite the north end of the Isle of Great Cumbrae). They were attacked by the Scots, and one of the fiercest battles of the day raged. To ensure that they were not completely cut off, the Norse on the mound attempted to make their way down to the shore, and it was then that the Scots attacked. The saga relates that the withdrawal of the Norwegians began successfully, but that the steep slope of the mound quickly caused confusion to set in: some of the Norse apparently panicked and broke ranks, fleeing to the boats. According to the saga, there were many casualties: 'There was a hard battle there; and also a very unequal one, because there were ten Scots to one Norwegian.' One of the Norwegian casualties was Hakon of

[36] *ER*, i, p. 24; Cowan, 'Norwegian sunset – Scottish dawn', p. 121.
[37] Ibid., pp. 121–2.

Steinn, the 'guards-man' of King Hakon. Despite the disorderly retreat and the carnage of the ensuing skirmish, the Norwegians were able to regroup, and subsequently attacked the Scots, who had, in their turn, taken up position on the mound. As the Scots were driven from the mound, the Norse were apparently able to cover the distance to their boats and sail out to the remainder of the army. This activity concluded the hostilities of the second day. The following morning the Norse were able to come ashore and collect their dead, which Hakon had taken to a nearby church, possibly the chapel of St Vey on the lesser Cumbrae, and then the fleet set sail for Lamlash.[38]

Despite many statements to the contrary, this was neither a great victory nor a total defeat, but rather a 'series of disorderly skirmishes', which decided nothing, and, despite the reports of later Scottish chroniclers, modern historians have concluded that there were probably relatively few casualties.[39] For the Norwegians, Largs represented a series of successful rearguard actions to recover their vessels which had been beached in the storm. It was the Scots who elevated the skirmishes at Largs into a great victory. John of Fordun, for instance, recounted the storm which blew the Norse ashore, and continued: 'Then the king's army came against them, and swept down many, both nobles and serfs.'[40] Perhaps the continuation of the *Chronicle of Man* comes closest to assessing the true outcome of the action at Largs, when it states that 'Hakon, king of Norway, came to regions of Scotland; but effecting nothing, he returned to the Orkneys.'[41]

Following the fighting at Largs, King Hakon lay a few nights at Lamlash, before making a leisurely progress back to Gigha, and then to Kerrera, where messengers communicated back and forth between him and Ewen, without any result. At the calf of Mull, Dugald MacRuairi, Alan, Rudri and Murchaid were rewarded for their services, and the fleet split up. By the end of October, Hakon was back in the Orkneys, where, in a scene movingly depicted in the saga, he fell ill and died on the night of 15–16 December, as first the Bible, and then the sagas of his predecessors, were read to him; he was buried in the church of St Magnus. His significance in the history of both medieval Scandinavia, and Scotland, is well appreciated by historians:

> The culmination of the Middle Ages in Norway is embodied in the figure of Haakon Haakonsson. The ripe summer of Norwegian medieval civilization, and the first rich colours of its autumn, are

---

38 On the battle itself, see *ES*, ii, pp. 625–34; Fergusson, *Alexander the Third*, pp. 102–8; Linklater, 'Battle of Largs', pp. 37–47; and Donaldson, *Northern Commonwealth*, chap. 8.

39 Fergusson, *Alexander the Third*, p. 107; Magnusson, *Hakon the Old*, pp. 9–10.

40 *Chron. Fordun*, i, pp. 299–300; ii, p. 295.

41 *ES*, ii, p. 608.

reflected in the personality of the king who sailed with that mighty armada to his death in the west.[42]

Before the splitting of the fleet at the calf of Mull, Hakon had forfeited Ewen of his lands, and had awarded them instead to Dugald, who had been his loyal servant throughout the campaign.[43] Rudri received Bute, and Murchaid received Arran, while Angus had already been installed in Islay. But these divisions were essentially meaningless, and with them the 'last rays of the Norwegian sunset bathed the MacSorleys in their fading light'.[44] Despite the bold claim of Sturla that, 'in this expedition, king Hakon had won back again all the dominions that king Magnus Bareleg had acquired and won from Scotland in the south', the campaign had been a failure and a disappointment. But it had not been won or lost at Largs. It had begun late, and therefore already under a handicap; and Alexander's patience in prolonging the negotiations with Hakon allowed him to gather a larger force, while, at the same time, forcing the Norwegians to remain in an exposed anchorage until the autumnal storms arrived. Moreover, Alexander's refusal to fight a sea battle with Hakon forced the king of Norway's hand, since he could not afford to fight a battle on land. Finally, and perhaps most significantly, the divided allegiances of the MacSorleys, and especially the reluctance of Ewen of Argyll to commit himself fully to one side or the other, meant that Hakon lacked precious support for his efforts, and ships for his fleet.

Within a few months of the fighting at Largs, Norwegian ambassadors arrived at the Scottish court; they were poorly received and the saga says that the Scots threatened to kill or imprison them because of the devastation the Norwegians had caused to 'more than a third of Scotland'. Later embassies were better treated, and eventually it was agreed that King Magnus should send messengers to Scotland the next summer to discuss peace terms. Meanwhile, more aggressive follow-up measures were taken by the Scots during 1264 and 1265 to ensure the submission of the western seaboard. In 1264, Alexander III assembled a fleet with which to invade the Isle of Man, but news of this caused a flurry of diplomatic activity between the two kingdoms, with the result that King Magnus of Man met Alexander at Dumfries, swore oaths to him, did homage, and surrendered hostages. In return for the king of Scots' protection against any Norwegian retribution, the king of Man had to provide ten warships for the Scottish fleet: five twenty-four-oared and five twelve-oared galleys.[45] Presumably these conditions satisfied the Scottish king, for, either later in 1264 or in the following year, he wrote

42 Brøgger, *Ancient Emigrants*, p. 177.
43 According to a variant of the saga, Dugald's son, Alan, may also have received a share of Ewen's lands: *ES*, ii, p. 635, note 7.
44 Cowan, 'Norwegian sunset – Scottish dawn', p. 122.
45 *Chron. Bower*, v, 347–9.

to the bishop of Sodor promising that he would not go against Man for the time being.[46] When King Magnus died in 1265, Alexander III assumed sovereignty over Man and appointed bailiffs to oversee its affairs for him, thus ending an epoch in the history of the Hebrides and the Irish Sea.[47] The Manx kingship was now extinct, and Man belonged to the Scots, despite an abortive attempt to recover it by Godfrey, the illegitimate son of the last Manx king, in 1275.[48]

In the summer of 1264, the MacSorleys were also the target of royal harrying tactics. According to Fordun, a Scots force, led by the earls of Buchan and Mar and by Alan Durward,

> went to the Western Isles of Scotland, where they slew those traitors who had, the year before, encouraged the king of Norway to bring up in Scotland. Some of these they put to flight; and, having hanged some of the chiefs, they brought with them thence exceeding great plunder.[49]

Hakon's Saga corroborates this expedition to the Western Isles: 'that summer, the Scots went out to the Hebrides with an army; and then Angus in Islay submitted to the Scots, and many of those that had followed king Hakon when he was in the Hebrides'. The slaughter of the chieftains, however, appears to have taken place only in Fordun's imagination. It was probably this expedition for which the earl of Mar received £30 13s 6d to support 200 soldiers taken with him to the Isles by command of the king.[50] Another campaign in the north saw heavy fines taken from Ross and Caithness, probably in retribution for the payments those regions had made to Hakon in 1263.[51] These actions were clearly partially successful in persuading the MacSorleys that their future lay with Scotland. But while Angus of Islay had already submitted to the force sent to the Western Isles, and surrendered his son Alexander as a hostage at Ayr,[52] Dugald remained loyal to Norway.

It remains to determine the attitude of Ewen of Argyll to the momentous events taking place on the western seaboard between 1249 and 1266. In assessing the dilemma of divided allegiances that Ewen faced, there are three key episodes to consider: his negotiations with Alexander II in 1249, his restoration to his Scottish lands in 1255, and his involvement in the events of 1263. On the surface of it, we can trace a lineal progression from a purely Norwegian to a purely Scottish allegiance. In 1249, Ewen refused to give in to Alexander II's demands; in 1263, he refused

[46] *APS*, i, 112; *RRS: Handlist Alexander III*, no. 235, dates the document to 1264–5.
[47] *ES*, ii, p. 657; hostages recorded in *ER*, i, p. 17.
[48] *ES*, ii, pp. 672–3. See below, chap. 5, for further discussion.
[49] *Chron. Fordun*, i, pp. 300–1; ii, pp. 296; see also the saga in *ES*, ii, pp. 648–9.
[50] *ER*, i, p. 11.
[51] Ibid., i, p. 20.
[52] Ibid., i, p. 5.

to join Hakon IV. His restoration in 1255 is generally seen as representing Ewen's acceptance of a purely Scottish allegiance; G. W. S. Barrow has regarded him as 'the first [of the MacSorleys] to trim his sails to the wind of change'.[53] E. W. Robertson, writing in the nineteenth century, was even more eloquent in his assessment of his behaviour:

> Twice in situations of difficulty and danger had the Lord of Argyle proved his steadfast adherence to the path of good faith and honour, and in an age in which the obligations of an oath were but too often lightly esteemed, no brighter example can be found of truthful and unswerving fidelity to his plighted word.[54]

But had Ewen really gone over to a Scottish allegiance in 1255, and remained 'steadfast to the path of good faith and honour', or is the situation more complex than that?

Such an assessment, while having much to recommend it, ignores one key issue: that of historical perspective. Up until the middle of the thirteenth century, divided allegiances had been a non-issue – or at best an infrequent one – for the Hebridean rulers, as neither Scotland nor Norway had been in a position to demand obedience. It is easy, with hindsight, to regard the events of the thirteenth century in the western seaboard as inexorable, as the MacSorleys were sucked into the vortex of Scottish politics. But, for the descendants of Somerled, one of the lessons of history was surely that it was possible to weather the storm of Scottish and Norwegian imperialistic ambitions and retain their independence. No king of Norway had personally visited the Isles between 1098 and 1263, for example; and Scottish pressure in the 1220s and 1240s was sporadic at best – William I had left the West well enough alone, and the minority of Alexander III precipitated a hiatus in Scottish interest between 1249 and 1260. Thus, although the territorial ambitions of both Scotland and Norway in the Western Isles form a prominent theme of the mid-thirteenth century, it is well to remember that the creeping tendrils of imperialism were felt only sporadically.

It may well be that Ewen's actions reveal, rather than an impending sense of which way the winds of change were blowing, a canny sense of playing one side off against the other, in the hope that the storm would blow over, that the *status quo* would be restored, and that the MacSorleys would retain their independence – just as had happened so often in the recent past. Thus, in the account of the 1249 exchange between Ewen and Alexander II, Ewen's insistence that it was possible to serve two masters, and then his request for a truce in order to go to Norway and resign his lands, smacks of pitting one side against the other, or at the very least, delaying tactics. And while it is tempting to suppose that the 1255 settlement brought Ewen firmly into the fold of the Scottish flock,

---

[53] Barrow, *Kingship and Unity*, p. 116.
[54] Robertson, *Scotland under her Early Kings*, ii, p. 86; see also p. 44.

his actions in 1263 seem oddly aloof if this were so. While it is true that Ewen refused to join Hakon's expedition (even after he was detained), which must be seen as a major factor in the Norwegian defeat because of the resources he could have provided, neither did he actively support the Scottish side, at least so far as the evidence goes. At best he provided intelligence on the movement of the Norwegian fleet. Yet again, there is a sense of sitting back and waiting for events to unfold before him, and of making the most of whatever situation presented itself. The outcome of the expedition was far from certain, and a Norwegian victory might well have allowed him to retain some standing in the West. In short, the grasping realities of opportunism were never far from Hebridean politics: we need look no further than Somerled's acceptance of the invitation to come to Man in 1156, or to how Ewen himself benefited from the untimely demise of the Manx king in 1248.

It seems clear that Ewen was firmly committed to the Scottish cause only after 1266, a fact reinforced by the marriage of his son to a daughter of Sir John Comyn, and his daughter, Mary, to Malise, the fifth earl of Strathearn in c.1268.[55] The marriage of Mary is particularly instructive, because she had previously been wedded to Magnus, the king of Man, continuing the traditions of matrimony between the Manx dynasty and the house of Somerled that had existed since the middle of the twelfth century.[56] This new marriage alliance with a prominent family of the eastern nobility, which had exhibited a long-term commitment to the Scottish monarchs, demonstrates how the winds of change were sweeping over the rulers of the West, in the wake of the events of 1263–6.

On the other hand, Dugald MacRuairi, Ewen's cousin and rival, had no intention of submitting to Scottish royal authority, and appears primarily as a freebooter in the Hebrides and the Irish Sea, both before and after the events of the 1260s. In 1258, Irish Annals record that a great fleet, led by Dugald, sailed from the Hebrides to Ireland, and plundered a merchant ship of all its goods on the western side of the island, at Connemara. When the English sheriff of Connacht put to sea with a fleet to pursue the raiders, he cornered them on an 'island in the sea' but was defeated and killed. 'And afterwards', the annal goes on to relate, 'Somerled's son [Dugald] returned to his own country, with joy and profit from triumphant victory.'[57] The following year, 1259, Dugald's daughter married Aed O Conchobair, king of Connacht, reinforcing these Hebridean and Irish Sea connections and providing a stark contrast to Ewen of Argyll (who had wed his daughter to the earl of Strathearn). Once again, it is the marriage alliances made by these Hebridean chieftains which best illuminate their allegiances.

55 Paul, *Scots Peerage*, viii, p. 246. Ewen appeared as a witness to one of the earl's charters at Crieff, in c.1268: *Inchaffray Chs.*, no. 68.
56 *Chron. Bower*, v, p. 345; see also Duncan, *Making of the Kingdom*, pp. 582–3.
57 *ES*, ii, pp. 594–5; see also *Ann. Four Masters*, iii, pp. 368–70.

Indeed, Dugald steadfastly adhered to the Norwegian cause. As we have already seen, he had been in competition with Ewen for kingship in the Hebrides from the 1240s, had been awarded that kingship in 1249, and had supported King Hakon consistently in the 1263 campaign, for which he was duly rewarded with Ewen's forfeited lordship, however temporarily. The saga of Hakon's son, Magnus, records how, after 1263, Dugald was active in opposing the newly won Scottish influence in the North and West. In the autumn of 1264, Dugald attacked those Scots who had invaded Caithness, and 'had killed many of them, and had taken the great treasure that they were carrying with him. He slew there the law-man of the Scots.' In the summer of 1265, he again appears in conflict with the Scots, this time in the Hebrides and the Irish Sea, rather than the far North. The saga narrates how the Scottish forces engaged in a naval battle with Dugald, but that he 'defended himself in ships, and they took no hold of him'.[58] His death, in 1268, was recorded by Irish annalists, who continued to regard him as 'king of the Hebrides and Argyll'.[59] Dugald's son, Eric, followed in his father's footsteps and preferred a Norwegian to a Scottish allegiance: he is recorded as having been sent to the Hebrides with an eighteen-benched ship in 1264.[60]

Dugald and his son, however, remained oblivious to the the winds of change blowing in the West, and so represented something of an anomaly among the MacSorleys. Norwegian authority in the Isles, seldom strong and never consistent, had been steadily waning from the time of Alexander II's expeditions in 1221/2 and 1249, and the events of the years 1263–5 further accelerated its decline. Three years and four embassies after the series of skirmishes at Largs, peace was finally concluded between the two realms in 1266. The *Chronicle of Melrose* presents the negotiations leading up to this treaty as having been accomplished largely by Reginald of Roxburgh, a monk of Melrose Abbey, who achieved a solution which had eluded others for two years:

> In the year of the Lord 1265, during the reign of Alexander III, king of the Scots, sir Reginald of Roxburgh, a monk of Melrose, a man of glorious eloquence and super-excellent resourcefulness, set out for Norway; being sent by the same king to acquire the land of Man (which was formerly called a *regio*), along with the small islands that lie about the broad district of the Scots. And when he arrived there, he was very honourably received by the king ... And thus an agreement was made between the two aforesaid kings. And this is the annual sum of the agreement: that every year in perpetuity the king of Scotland shall give to the king of Norway a hundred pounds

[58] *ES*, ii, pp. 648–9.
[59] Ibid., ii, p. 660.
[60] Ibid., ii, p. 647–8.

of sterlings ... And for greater security, King Alexander has paid in advance to the king of Norway four thousand marks ...[61]

In a skilful analysis of the events leading up to the signing of the treaty, Richard Lustig has cast grave doubt upon both the involvement of Reginald of Roxburgh (the *Chronicle of Melrose* is the only source which mentions his pre-eminent role), and the value of the chronicle itself on this matter. By comparing the terms of the treaty, as related by the chronicle, to those contained in the actual document itself, and by a careful examination of the envoys who journeyed back and forth between the two kingdoms in the years 1264–6, he has shown that the document mentioned in the chronicle must represent a draft agreement, or proposal, which was subsequently altered during further negotiations in Scotland.[62]

The Treaty of Perth, concluded at Perth on 2 July 1266, provided the 'settlement and final agreement for terminating the disagreements, complaints, losses, damage and disputes concerning the isles of Man and the Sudreys and of the rights thereof', between King Magnus IV of Norway and Alexander III of Scotland. It outlined the terms of the settlement:

> The said lord Magnus, King of Norway ... granted, resigned and quit-claimed ... for himself and his heirs forever, Man with the rest of the Sudreys and all other islands on the west and south of the great sea, with all right which he and his progenitors had of old therein or he and his heirs shall have in future ... to be held, had and possessed by the said lord Alexander III, King of Scots ...[63]

According to the treaty, the islands ceded to Scotland would become subject to the laws and customs of Scotland, but the security of their inhabitants was guaranteed, and:

> if they should wish to remain in the said islands under the lordship of the said lord king of Scots, they may remain in his lordship freely and in peace, but if they wish to retire they may do so, with their goods, lawfully, freely and in full peace.

This also meant that the inhabitants of the Isles were not to be punished for the 'misdeeds or injuries and damage which they have committed hitherto while they adhered to the said king of Norway'. In addition to these provisions, shipwrecked sailors were to be able to gather their ships and goods for sale, and were not to be deprived of them. For the cession of the Isles, the king of Scots was to pay the king of Norway 4,000 merks over four years (that is, in 1267, 1268, 1269 and 1270,

---

[61] Ibid., ii, pp. 653–4; Anderson's translation has been modified, based on *Chron. Melrose*, p. 196.

[62] R. Lustig, 'The Treaty of Perth: a re-examination', *SHR*, lviii (1979), pp. 35–57.

[63] *APS*, i, p. 420; trans. from Donaldson, *Scot. Hist. Docs.*, pp. 34–5.

although the second payment was not made until 1269, and the final one was made in 1282), in addition to 100 merks a year in perpetuity.[64]

The Treaty of Perth represents a landmark in the history of the western seaboard, in a way that the fighting at Largs does not, because it finally resolved the nearly two-centuries old territorial dispute between Scotland and Norway over the Western Isles. Unlike the agreement made between Edgar and Magnus Barelegs in 1098, which referred to 'all the islands off the west coast which were separated by water navigable by a ship with rudder set', the Treaty of Perth made it clear that the Western Isles and Man belonged to the Scottish king. But Orkney and Shetland, which were of much greater importance to the Norwegian crown, were carefully excluded from the agreement, and remained the possessions of Norway until the mid-fifteenth century.[65] Thus, as long as the terms of the treaty were observed, there could be no further arguments over boundaries. Another advantage of the treaty was that it was 'an amicable settlement between two equals, voluntarily entered into by both sides'. There was neither implication of military defeat nor loss of face for the Norwegian monarchy, which had 'reached an honourable compromise and received substantial financial compensation in return'.[66] For the king of Scots, there was no implication of homage: the Isles were ceded without any indication of vassalage on the part of the Scottish king. The Treaty of Perth, then, successfully ended two centuries of disagreement over the Western Isles, and ushered in a period of friendly relations between Scotland and Norway.

Indeed, one of the most significant aspects of the Treaty of Perth was a warming in Scoto-Norwegian relations. Through the first half of the thirteenth century, relations between the Scottish and English royal families had been close and carefully cultivated: Alexander II married a sister of Henry III in 1221, while Alexander III married his daughter in 1251. But, after 1266, Scoto-Norwegian relations took a new turn and improved considerably, while Anglo-Scottish relations deteriorated in the late 1280s and 1290s. When King Eric of Norway sought the daughter of Alexander III as a bride in 1281, his offer was accepted by the Scottish king, in spite of the reservations expressed by the girl and her friends, and despite the fact that, as one chronicler put it, 'she could have been allied much more easily and suitably elsewhere'. The same chronicle goes on to state how, following their union in Bergen in August 1281, the new Norwegian queen, in a fashion reminiscent of another Queen Margaret, 'bore herself so graciously toward the king and people that she changed [his] manners for the better; taught him the idiom of France, and of England; and raised him to a more

---

64 Ibid., pp. 34–6. On the treaty, see Duncan, *Making of the Kingdom*, pp. 580–2; and Lustig, 'Treaty of Perth', *passim*.

65 Detailed in Nicholson, *Later Middle Ages*, chap. 14.

66 Lustig, 'Treaty of Perth', pp. 52–3; cf. MacDonald, *History of Argyll*, p. 111.

honourable level in regard to clothes and food'.[67] After her death in 1283, only a year and a half after the marriage, Eric took another Scottish bride: Isabella, the daughter of Robert Bruce, Earl of Carrick, and sister of the future Robert I, King of Scots.[68]

The Norwegian connection also featured prominently in the events that followed the untimely death of Alexander III in 1286. By the time the king had fallen from the cliffs near Kinghorn, he had outlived his first wife, his two sons, and his daughter, Margaret. That left his granddaughter, also named Margaret, the offspring of Eric of Norway and Alexander's daughter, as the acknowledged heir to the throne, for in 1284, following the death of his son, Alexander had secured her recognition as his heir, should he fail to produce another son. But, by October 1290, news reached Scotland that the young girl had died in Orkney, en route to her new kingdom, and the question of the succession was re-opened. In the so-called Great Cause of 1291–2, adjudicated by Edward I of England, one of the thirteen claimants to the Scottish kingship was none other than Eric of Norway. Eric's representatives probably argued that if his daughter, the maid of Norway, was the rightful queen of Scotland, then he, as her father, was the rightful heir, but the claim was only advanced half-heartedly and later withdrawn.[69] Nevertheless, it is significant that, only two decades after the confrontation at Largs, marriage alliances between Scotland and Norway had permitted the King of Norway to register a claim on the Scottish kingship.

From a wider perspective, the treaty of 1266 represented a profound shift in the balance of power in Britain. This can be seen in different ways, depending on the breadth of perspective employed. As the preceding chapters have helped to demonstrate, there were many kings in North Britain in the twelfth and thirteenth centuries apart from the kings of Scots. Indeed, Britain itself, before the second half of the thirteenth century, was a land of multiple kings. Apart from the two major monarchies of England and Scotland, there were the Welsh princes, Irish kings, Manx kings, and kings of the Isles, all of whom claimed, with legitimacy, regal distinction. But, by the twelfth century, the peripheral monarchies were coming under increasing pressure from the English and Scottish kings, who strove to suppress them, or at the very least downgrade their status. When the kings of Scots annexed the Western Isles in 1266, they also, by definition, successfully suppressed

---

[67] *ES*, ii, p. 680.

[68] Ibid., ii, p. 683, note 1.

[69] On these events, see Barrow, *Robert Bruce*, pp. 39–43, 65–6; Nicholson, *Later Middle Ages*, pp. 41–3; Donaldson, *Northern Commonwealth*, p. 100; K. Helle, 'Norwegian foreign policy and the Maid of Norway', *SHR*, lxix (1990); and, for Eric's claim and withdrawal, *Edward I and the Throne of Scotland, 1290–1296: An Edition of the Record Sources for the Great Cause*, ed. E. L. G. Stones and G. G. Simpson (Oxford, 1978), ii, pp. 154–7, 229, 232–3, 240–2.

the sea-kings of that region: that is, the Manx kings and the kings of the Isles. The descendants of Somerled, who had until that time ruled as *rí Innse Gall* or *rí Airer Goidel*, became instead 'barons of the realm of Scotland', as a document of the later thirteenth century put it. As Robin Frame has so aptly phrased it: 'around 1270 the day of multiple kingship in northern Britain seemed to be done. The weight of the house of Canmore was irresistible ...'[70]

Moreover, despite what has just been said about multiple kingship, the majority of the British Isles before 1266 may be said to have fallen under three spheres of influence: those of England, Scotland, and Norway; the latter technically controlled the western seaboard of Scotland and the Isle of Man. When Norway relinquished its claims to the Western Isles and Man in 1266, this represented a major alteration to the *status quo*. Now effective Scottish royal authority reached into the western seaboard, and Scotland had taken control of Man, which was fairly close to England itself and was strategically important for English operations in Ireland; moreover, the Scottish monarchs added contingents of Islesmen to the combined forces of the kingdom. These events have been regarded as representing the first major change in the balance of power in Britain since the reign of Henry II, which had witnessed the resignation by Malcolm IV of the three northern counties to the English king in 1157 and the beginning of the English conquest in Ireland in 1170.[71] Whether our perspective is purely Scottish, or is expanded to include the rest of Britain, the agreement between Scotland and Norway in 1266 had far-reaching implications for everything from Scoto-Norwegian relations to the nature of kingship in Britain.

The 1098 agreement between Magnus Barelegs and King Edgar of Scotland, which ceded to Norway all the islands in the west of Scotland around which a ship could be sailed with its rudder set, had ushered in a period of over a century during which the Hebrides were relatively free from both Norwegian and Scottish royal authority. While the kings of Norway were occupied with civil strife, the kings of Scots were often involved in conflict with their powerful neighbour to the south. The result was a lengthy period, extending throughout the twelfth century and into the thirteenth, when rulers of mixed Scoto-Norse origin plied the seas, largely unaffected by either Scottish or Norwegian demands on their allegiance. Indeed, Somerled and his immediate descendants enjoyed divided allegiances (when such distinctions mattered at all) with little difficulty. The problem for these Hebridean rulers became apparent in the thirteenth century, when the two Alexanders of Scotland and Hakon IV of Norway took a renewed interest in the Western Isles,

---

[70] Frame, *Political Development of the British Isles*, p. 104. The English conquest of Wales, in the late 1270s and 1280s, might be seen as the parallel of the Scottish expansion into the Hebrides, though the comparison should not be pressed too far.

[71] Barrow, *Robert Bruce*, pp. 10–11.

placing these rulers and their respective realms on a collision course. With both monarchies intent on the consolidation of their power within the region, the Hebridean chieftains quickly found themselves caught between the conflicting Norwegian and Scottish aspirations in the Western Isles. From the 1220s, therefore, the juggling of allegiances required of the MacSorleys became impossible to sustain, as the examples of Ewen of Argyll and Dugald MacRuairi attest. By 1263–6, the MacSorleys had been forced to resolve their dilemma of divided allegiances by choosing to serve one side or the other. For reasons largely dictated by political geography, most chose Scotland, although Dugald MacRuairi and his son remained steadfast in their Norwegian allegiance.

The events of the thirteenth century on the western seaboard also highlight both the tradition of Scottish medieval historiography and an intriguing paradox that exists within this tradition. Three of the most important themes in the history of western Europe in the central Middle Ages are the growth and expansion of centralised monarchies, the territorial consolidation of kingdoms, and the expansion of central Europe into the periphery.[72] Scotland certainly shared in all these themes, and it might even be said that the first two led inexorably to the third, as the powerful new Scottish monarchy of David I and his successors set about consolidating the frontiers of their kingdom, ultimately resulting in the annexation of the Western Isles. This annexation, the so-called 'winning of the West',[73] is generally regarded in the Scottish historiographical tradition as a laudable event, which at once opened the West to the influences of eastern Scotland, and completed the development of the feudal kingdom through the extension of royal authority into the last of the untamed outer or peripheral zones.

However, what is clear is that the Scottish historiographical tradition is closely associated with the centralising monarchy of the twelfth and thirteenth century – a view that, as we have seen, is certainly understandable, given the nature of the sparse historical source materials at our disposal. There is thus relatively little room in these accounts, both medieval and modern, for the Hebridean rulers and their plight, as they were crushed between the upper and lower millstones of Scottish and Norwegian royal authority from the 1220s onward. So much is not surprising. Yet it is a curious phenomenon that the same historiographical tradition that applauds the Scottish annexation of the periphery, and the extinction of other regal traditions within these

---

[72] See R. Bartlett, *The Making of Europe: Conquest, Colonization and Cultural Change, 950–1350* (London, 1993), where the phenomenon is described as the 'Europeanization of Europe'.

[73] Barrow, *Kingship and Unity*, chap. 6.

regions, also praises the resistance of the Scottish kings to the attempts at domination by Henry III and Edward I. The roots of this paradox are easily explained, but 'if it is often protested that History is the version of the conqueror, then the conquered are still too often ignored'.[74] Hence the value of a study of the Scottish periphery in the Middle Ages; not only does it provide a viable alternative to the traditional historiography, but it also reveals some intriguing paradoxes within that tradition.

Ultimately, it cannot be said that the Scottish successes of 1263–6 owed everything to Scottish initiative on the one hand, and to poor Norwegian fortune on the other. Additional, external factors, were also at work. One of the most important was the political situation in England. This proved fortuitous for the winning of the West by the Scots, since the English civil war of 1264–5 had handcuffed Henry III, and had prevented him from intervening in the affairs of the Scottish kingdom. That he would have attempted to do so is demonstrated by the fact that, in 1263, he wrote to Alexander III, urging him not to run the risks attached to his proposed expedition to the West – although his real motivation was probably an attempt to discourage the Scots from annexing Man, at a time when Henry was in no position to stop it.[75] Henry's letter therefore serves as a reminder that the Scots would almost certainly never have succeeded in obtaining the Isle of Man, had it not been for the political situation in England; the strategic importance of Man to the English kings was too great, and was shown when, in 1290, Edward I assumed control of the island.

The basic facts of geography, and lines of communication, also dictated that success in the thirteenth century would lie with the king of Scots, and that, from the 1230s onwards, King Hakon was going against the odds in his efforts to maintain a Norwegian hold on the Isles. Argyll and the Isles are connected by the sea, and, as the two Alexanders found out – much to their consternation – in the 1220s, 1240s, and 1260s, campaigns against the mainland territories of the MacSorleys became inseparable from campaigns against the Western Isles. Even more importantly, however,

> the Western Isles were too far from Norway to be effectively policed, both physically and socially and culturally; their only ties with Norway in the thirteenth century were those imposed by power-politics, and the bonds were being inexorably loosened. Even if Hakon's last expedition west-over-sea had been more successful, it would only have been a temporary success.[76]

---

[74] Cowan, 'Norwegian sunset – Scottish dawn', pp. 104–5.
[75] F. M. Powicke, *The Thirteenth Century, 1216–1307* (2nd edn, Oxford, 1962), pp. 589–92; see also Duncan, *Making of the Kingdom*, p. 577.
[76] Magnusson, *Hakon the Old*, p. 23.

Alexander III's reign, then, seemed to extinguish the old order in the West: Norwegian authority in the Isles had been eliminated; the Manx kingship was extinct; the control of Man had passed to Scotland; and the descendants of Somerled – the MacDougalls, MacDonalds, and others – had been forced to resolve their dilemma of divided allegiances and were, for the most part, drawn into the larger community of the realm of Scotland, which was centred on the royal court itself. In the next chapter we shall explore in more detail the process whereby the MacSorleys were transformed from kings into barons.

CHAPTER FIVE

From Kings to Barons: Autonomy and Assimilation, 1264–1293

Alexander of Argyll, Angus the son of Donald, Alan the son of Ruairi, barons of the realm of Scotland ... [1284, *Acts of the Parliaments of Scotland*].[1]

If the century between the death of Somerled in 1164 and the Treaty of Perth in 1266 is a dark one in the history of the western seaboard by virtue of a dearth of source material, then the years from the Treaty of Perth to the first parliament of John Balliol in 1293 are obscure because they can all too easily be regarded as anti-climactic. It is true that the sources are no more abundant between 1266 and 1293 than they are for the preceding two centuries, but since the so-called 'winning of the West' in 1266 is usually viewed in terms of the history of the Scottish kingdom itself, the question of what happened in the western seaboard after its cession is of secondary importance. It is, of course, true to say that the West became more subject to Scottish influences, but this is to oversimplify what was a long and drawn out process. Above all, it is necessary to bear in mind that the integration of the western seaboard after 1263–6 is only intelligible when regarded as the final phase in a lengthy sequence of events dating back some forty years. The process whereby Scottish royal authority was extended into the western seaboard had begun as early as the 1220s, when Alexander II campaigned once or twice and .subdued the Clyde estuary; and Alexander died on the island of Kerrera in 1249 leading another expedition against Ewen of Argyll. Scottish influence in the region was powerful enough that, by 1263, the divided allegiances of the MacSorleys, which had been pursued successfully for nearly a century, began to falter in the face of Norwegian aggression and Scottish expansion. Most of the MacSorleys had to be bribed or black-mailed by King Hakon in 1263 before they would come into a Norwegian allegiance, and by 1268 even the opportunistic Ewen himself had been forced to acknowledge the new *status quo* in the West. If we are concerned only with a political and administrative framework, then it is true that the three decades between 1263 and 1293 saw the western seaboard become an integral part of the Scottish kingdom, the last marginal region to be so incorporated (except for the Northern Isles,

[1] *APS*, i, p. 424.

which were not ceded until 1468–9). Thus, in 1293, the former kingdom of the Isles was divided into sheriffdoms – the administrative units characteristic of the medieval kingdom – while the Isle of Man had fallen under the rule of Scottish bailies. But to consider only political landmarks is to consider only part of the picture: if social and cultural markers are also explored then it becomes clear that the Hebridean chieftains were accommodating themselves to the social and cultural fashions of the day even before the events of 1263–6 overtook them, although there can be no doubt that the settlement of 1266 greatly accelerated the process of acculturation. This chapter, then, asks what happened once the West was won? How were the western seaboard and its rulers integrated into the Scottish kingdom, both politically and, perhaps more importantly, socially? Answering this question will also permit an examination of the society of the West in what must be regarded as a crucial period, namely the thirteenth century. It was the effective integration of the western seaboard into the rest of the Scottish kingdom in the twenty-seven years between the Treaty of Perth and the first parliament of John Balliol that ensured that Argyll and the Hebrides would play a crucial role in the ensuing Wars of Independence.

One of the conditions of the Treaty of Perth was that the supporters of King Hakon were not to be punished, or in any way forfeited of their inheritances in the western lands. The treaty stated:

> for the misdeeds or injuries and damage which they have committed hitherto while they adhered to the said king of Norway they [shall] be no wise punished or molested in their heritages in those islands but stand peacefully therein under the lordship of the king of Scots as other free men and lieges of the said lord king who are known to enjoy the most free justice ...[2]

These conditions were evidently observed, and the division of territory among the MacSorleys from 1266 to 1293 seems to have been little different than the situation in 1249 at the death of Alexander II. The only difference was that, in the years following the Treaty of Perth, the old generation of MacSorleys faded from the scene, and a new generation entered the limelight. The MacDougall lords of Argyll claimed descent from Dugald, the son of Somerled. For two decades from the late 1240s to the late 1260s, they were represented by Ewen, the son of Duncan, the son of Dugald. Although Ewen had figured prominently in the events of the 1240s and the 1260s, little more is heard of him after 1263. He last appears *c.*1268, when he attested a charter of the earl of Strathearn at Crieff, probably at about the same time that his daughter was married to the earl in an alliance that reflects the changing orientation of the western chieftains.[3] He is not heard from again, and

[2] Ibid., i, p. 420; Donaldson, *Scot. Hist. Docs.*, p. 35.
[3] *Inchaffray Chrs.*, no. 96.

must have died sometime between 1268 and 1275, when his son appeared on the scene as a fully grown man. English annals record that, in 1275, Alexander of Argyll was one of the leaders of a Scottish expedition against the Isle of Man in that year, while in the same year the Scottish king petitioned the English king for the release of Alexander's men, vessels and goods, which had been impounded at Bristol.[4] Alexander MacDougall and his son, John, played a prominent role in the politics of the western seaboard for the next thirty years, and were especially prominent as opponents of Robert Bruce in the Scottish civil conflicts of the early fourteenth century. Ewen, Alexander, and John are all styled 'de Ergadia' or some variation ('of Argyll') in the documents from this period. As Lords of Argyll they were in possession of vast insular and mainland territories that included Lorn, Benderloch, Lismore, northern Jura, Mull, the Treshnish Isles, and Coll and Tiree, but the Wars of Independence profoundly altered the balance of power in the West, and the holdings of the MacDougalls were greatly diminished.

The MacDonald lords of Islay claimed descent from Donald, the son of Ranald, the son of Somerled. Donald was probably dead by 1263, by which date his son, Angus Mór, had become an important figure in Hebridean politics. Like his father, Angus is a shadowy figure, predatory and warlike, but also displaying the piety characteristic of the age. Sometime between 1241 and 1249, following in the footsteps of his father and grandfather, he acted as a benefactor of the monastery at Paisley, and the naming of his eldest son Alexander, after the Scottish king, is indicative of the impact of mainstream Scottish society on the West in the mid-thirteenth century. But Angus's predatory side is revealed by a document of 1256, in which the English king ordered his bailies and faithful men of Ireland not to allow Angus or other Scottish malefactors, whose names would be provided by the king of Scots, to be received in Ireland.[5] It is likely that during the troubled minority of Alexander III and the unstable political situation in England which handcuffed the English king after 1258, Angus and the other chieftains in the West engaged in freebooting activity in the Irish Sea; certainly in 1258 Angus's cousin, Dugald MacRuairi, was plundering in and around Ireland. In fact, it may well be that these activities were related to the first stages of the Gaelic resurgence in Ireland; some historians have suggested that Angus entered into a mutual bond with Brian O Neill, king of the Cenél nEogain, whose famous rising began in the early 1250s.[6] Angus's activities in the Irish Sea are corroborated by an undated Gaelic praise poem in his honour, which probably belongs to the middle of the thirteenth century and which implies piratical activity on the Irish coasts. The author boasts:

4 *SAEC*, pp. 382–3; *CDS*, ii, nos. 55, 63.
5 *Foedera*, i, pt. 2, p.11.
6 Duffy, 'Bruce brothers', pp. 68–9.

You have come round Ireland ... rare is the strand whence you
have not taken cattle: graceful long ships are sailed by you ... The
host of Islay has been with you beside Aran, to test their shooting as
far as Loch Con; that fair host of Islay takes cattle from smooth
Innse Modh.[7]

If Angus's activities in the Irish Sea had been designed to undermine
Scottish expansion in the Hebrides, it seems that by 1263 he had returned to
a Scottish allegiance, for his submission to Hakon in that year was
reluctant and had to be won by blackmail; it was not a 'matter of policy,'
as has sometimes been suggested.[8] His allegiance, however, was doubtful
enough; a document, probably dateable to between 1263 and 1266,
provided for his forfeiture if he rose against the king. It may have been
intended to prevent his vacillating between Norway and Scotland,
Hakon and Alexander.[9] Like the other MacSorleys, however, he did not
seem to suffer for his role in the Norwegian incursion, and in 1284 he
was among those Scottish magnates who were present at a council at
Scone. In February of 1293 he was listed as one of the primary landholders
in Argyll, but he disappears from the record shortly thereafter, and his
death is to be placed between 1293 and 1296. Although Angus Mór is often
simply referred to as 'the son of Donald,' his sons, Alexander Óg and
Angus Óg, were commonly referred to as *de Yla*, 'of Islay.' The
MacDonald holdings at the death of Alexander III comprised Kintyre,
Islay, southern Jura, and probably Colonsay and Oronsay, but one of
the major themes of the early fourteenth century is the aggrandisement
of MacDonald territory at the expense of the MacDougalls.

Of the three MacSorley kindreds, the MacRuairis are the least well
documented, but it is clear that, like their cousins, they too were major
players in the Western Isles, particularly in the troubled decade of the
1290s, and in the early fourteenth century. In the early 1260s they were
represented by Dugald MacRuairi, the freebooter who plundered in
Connemara and who was noteworthy for preferring a Norwegian to a
Scottish allegiance in the wake of the events of 1263–6. His son, Erik,
campaigned against the Scots in the West in 1264, but Dugald drops out
of sight after 1266, and for nearly twenty years little is heard of this
branch of the MacSorley kindred. When they emerge back into the light
of the historical record, they are represented by Alan, the brother of
Dugald. He was, along with Alexander of Argyll, a leader of the 1275
expedition to Man and, like both Alexander and Angus, the son of
Donald, he appeared at a 1284 council at Scone. He had two sons,

---

[7] 'An address to Aonghus of Islay', in O. Bergin, *Irish Bardic Poetry: Texts and translations,
together with an introductory lecture* (Dublin, 1970), no. 45, pp. 169–74, 291–4, stanzas
20–5 [adaptations by the author].

[8] MacDonald and MacDonald, *Clan Donald*, i, p. 81.

[9] *APS*, i, p. 112. Professor Duncan has helped greatly with the interpretation of this
rather curious document.

Ruairi and Lachlan, and a daughter, Christiana, and this kindred was prominent in the events of the 1290s and the subsequent Anglo-Scottish conflicts, often appearing as freebooters but eventually siding with the Bruce cause. As Lords of Garmoran the MacRuairis held Moidart, Arisaig, Morar, Knoydart, probably Rhum and Eigg, and possibly Barra, the Uists, and Harris; and, like the MacDonalds, the MacRuairis benefited from the downturn in the fortunes of the MacDougalls in the early fourteenth century.[10]

The Treaty of Perth, although it had ceded the Western Isles to Scotland, had not made any provision for their integration into the kingdom, and it remained for the Lords of Argyll and the Isles to become part of the community of the Scottish realm. While the process of integration had been ongoing (albeit sporadically), from the 1220s, and while it gained momentum with the cession of the West in 1266, this was certainly not an automatic or instantaneous process. It was the decades between 1266 and 1293 that witnessed the political integration of the western seaboard, as the region was slowly brought under centralised control and royal authority was extended westward.

According to the treaty, Man and the Isles 'shall be subject to the laws and customs of the realm of Scotland and be judged and dealt with according to them henceforth'.[11] The best evidence for the extension of Scottish law and custom to the West comes from the first parliament of John Balliol in February of 1293, whereby three new sheriffdoms were carved out of the former kingdom of the Isles.[12] In the north, William, Earl of Ross, the grandson of Farquhar Maccintsacairt, was awarded the sheriffdom of Skye. This encompassed the seaboard north of Ardnamurchan, and the isles of Skye, Lewis, Uist, Barra, Eigg and Rhum; parts of it, at least, seem to have been taken over from the Manx kingdom. In the central region, Alexander of Argyll was appointed sheriff of Lorn. His authority extended from Ardnamurchan to Knapdale, and included Morvern, Lorn, Glenorchy, Craignish, Glassary and Knapdale. Finally, in the south, the sheriffdom of Kintyre comprised the rest of Argyll, including not only Cowal and Kintyre but also the island of Bute; this region was placed in the hands of James the Steward, head of the great Stewart family. This division of Argyll and the Isles into three sheriffdoms by an Act of Parliament represents the first time that royal authority was firmly established in the western seaboard, and is indicative of 'a steady consolidation of royal power in the West in the years between 1266 and 1293'.[13]

---

10 For the division of territories among the MacSorleys, see Duncan and Brown, 'Argyll and the Isles', pp. 204–5; and Gregory, *History of the Western Highlands and Isles of Scotland*, pp. 18–19, 22.

11 Donaldson, *Scot. Hist. Docs.*, p. 35.

12 *APS*, i, p. 447.

13 Duncan and Brown, 'Argyll and the Isles', p. 217.

The scheme of sheriffdoms laid down in 1293 seems to have been the
final stage in an evolving royal policy which, because the terms of the
Treaty of Perth prohibited the forfeiture of the lords of the western
seaboard, instead made use of their most prominent number as agents
of royal authority. It is, unfortunately, difficult to say much about the
nature of this consolidation, or about the means by which it was pushed
forward between 1266 and 1293, because of a dearth of documentation.
Some glimpses, however, are afforded by charters incorporated into
later law collections which pertain to the West during this crucial period.
These documents (printed and discussed by Duncan and Brown)
constitute virtually the only evidence for the process whereby royal
authority was consolidated in the West during the decades following the
Treaty of Perth.

Both documents concern Alexander of Argyll, the son of Ewen. The
first, addressed to the men of Argyll, Kintyre, and 'Laudonia' (that is
Lodoux, Lewis), orders them to help 'A. of Argyll,' to whom the king had
committed custody of the region, protect, defend, and collect royal
debts. It has been dated, on the basis of its mentioning the various 'parts'
of the West and not the sheriffdoms of 1293, to the period between 1264
and 1293 (but not 1286–92). The second document empowers 'A. de
E. sheriff of L.' (Alexander of Argyll, sheriff of Lorn) to take into the
king's peace landholders willing to receive lands at farm in that
sheriffdom and to ensure their protection; it has been interpreted as
representing the forcible feudalisation of the region since the Scottish
kings had no lands of their own in Argyll.[14] Because of its reference to
Alexander as sheriff, this writ must belong to the period after the
administrative reforms of 1293, but it cannot be much later than 1296,
since Alexander of Argyll fell out of favour with Edward I after that date
and was actually incarcerated for a brief period in 1296–7.[15]

What these documents reveal is the gradual evolution of a solution to
the problem of the administration of royal authority – Scottish law and
custom, as the Treaty of Perth put it – in the western seaboard. The first
document shows a prominent landowner in the region, Alexander of
Argyll, being given what has been described as a wide-ranging
'wardenship' or 'lieutenancy' extending over nearly all of the West.
Indeed, it is remarkable that the three 'parts' of the western lands
named in the document – Kintyre, Argyll, and Lewis – correspond to the
three sheriffdoms created in 1293. It seems clear that not only was
Alexander of Argyll the king's chief representative in the West during
most of the twenty-seven years between the Treaty of Perth and the
parliament of 1293, but also that his authority was wide ranging.
Although it is sometimes asserted that the earl of Ross must have

14 Barrow, *Robert Bruce*, pp. 55–6.
15 Duncan and Brown, 'Argyll and the Isles', appendices V, VI, and the discussion on
    p. 217.

enjoyed a similar lieutenancy over Lewis, Skye, and the adjacent mainland before the administrative reforms of 1293,[16] this would seem to contradict the writ of 1264–93; but it is not, perhaps, entirely impossible. Whatever may have been the case, Duncan and Brown have summed it up thus: 'the king was clearly impelled to rely upon his principal supporter in the area to secure the obedience of the landlords of the west whom he was forbidden to oust by the treaty of Perth.'[17]

With the establishment of the sheriffdoms in 1293 a more formalised scheme of control was introduced to the west. The pattern of local government based on sheriffs can be traced to the early twelfth century, to the reigns of Alexander I (1107–24) and David I (1124–53), and although the spread of sheriffdoms was an extended evolutionary process, by about 1292 there were twenty-six to twenty-eight in Scotland. In most cases the sheriff was active as the king's representative and in the king's business at all levels. He held sheriff courts that dealt with both civil and criminal pleas; he held and presided over inquests and assizes; he collected revenues, fines, and forfeitures for the king and handled money and produce; and he called out and led the common host. As the king's representative, the sheriffs were held accountable, and accounted to him with regularity. Thus, the extension of sheriffdoms throughout Scotland was part of the process whereby the kings strengthened their hold on the realm: 'each new sheriffdom represented a stage in the expansion of royal control'.[18] This was true in the West, where it is clear that Alexander of Argyll was the chief instrument of that royal control.

This is illustrated by the second document addressed to Alexander. As sheriff of Lorn he seems to have been empowered to receive oaths of fealty from the landholders in the West, and to confirm them in their holdings. It is significant to note in this context that, only a few months after John Balliol's parliament in February, 1293, Alexander was the recipient of a royal letter which commanded him to cause to be summoned without delay Angus Mór and two other landholders (both apparently MacGregors) in Argyll to do homage to King John. Alexander was reminded that neither he nor those named in the summons were to neglect these instructions.[19] The letter is particularly interesting because it sheds further light on the position of Alexander and the degree to which royal authority had been expanded westward. In the first instance we see Alexander of Argyll acting again in his capacity as sheriff and as the principal representative of the king in Argyll. Moreover, Alexander was to ensure that not only Angus Mór but

[16] Gregory, *History of the Western Highlands*, pp. 22–3.
[17] Duncan and Brown, 'Argyll and the Isles', p. 217.
[18] R. Muir, 'The development of sheriffdoms', in McNeill and Nicholson, *Historical Atlas of Scotland*, p. 30. See also Duncan, *Making of the Kingdom*, pp. 596–8, on sheriffs and sheriffdoms.
[19] *APS*, i, p. 448.

also other landholders in the region obeyed the royal command. It is not known whether Angus obeyed the summons, but it may well be that an undated letter from the barons of Argyll to the king, in which they promise to serve faithfully and to rise against Angus if he does not enter the goodwill of the king, belongs to this period.[20] What seems clear from all of this is that, by 1293, the king commanded the unquestioned loyalty of one of the descendants of Somerled, Alexander of Argyll, and expected another, Angus Mór, to follow suit.

Although the administrative reforms of 1293 represent the most significant extension of royal authority into the West in the latter half of the thirteenth century, there is also a good deal of other evidence pertaining to the integration of the western seaboard into the 'community of the realm of Scotland'. Historians are increasingly recognising the importance of concepts of community in medieval thought and life: 'medieval ideas of custom and law facilitated collective action so that communities of all sorts and sizes were being easily and unselfconsciously formed ... The highest, most honourable, and most perfect of all secular communities was the kingdom.'[21] During the thirteenth century, the abstract concept of a 'Community of the Realm' gradually took hold, first in England and then, later in the century, in Scotland. It is generally agreed that this concept acquired meaning in the reign of Alexander III, although it did not receive its first written expression until 1286. Although there is some debate over whether the community of the realm should be seen as representing 'the totality of lawful subjects who composed the realm',[22] or whether it consisted primarily of the nobility, it received its best expression when the king sought the counsel of his barons. It is through this medium that we can trace the integration of the MacSorleys into the community of the realm, both in their involvement in councils and parliaments and in the internal affairs of the kingdom.

One of the more striking points to emerge from an examination of the western seaboard between 1100 and 1266 is that, before the monumental events of the 1260s, the MacSorleys seldom played a role in Scottish internal affairs. Their activities were confined to the western seaboard, and, when they did appear on the mainland scene, it was usually as enemies of the Scottish kings, as in Somerled's 1164 invasion, or as in the involvement of his grandson Ruairi in northern uprisings in the early thirteenth century. It is a rare thing indeed to find one of Somerled's descendants involved in the internal politics of the Scottish kingdom (as, possibly, in 1175 when Dugald, the son of Somerled, was present at Durham; or as in 1237 when Duncan of Argyll was named in a Scottish letter to the Pope; or, perhaps, as in 1255, when Ewen of

20 Ibid., i, p. 109.
21 Reynolds, *Kingdoms and Communities*, p. 250.
22 Barrow, *Kingship and Unity*, p. 126.

Argyll profited from the troubled minority of Alexander III to regain his territories in the West). But following the Treaty of Perth in 1266 the MacSorleys were integrated into the community of the realm, and came to play a role in Scottish politics alongside other well-established noble families.

Although the evidence is sparse for the MacSorleys in the 1270s and 1280s, two episodes exemplify the extent to which the integration of the descendants of Somerled into the Scottish kingdom had proceeded. In 1275, the Scottish king 'caused more than ninety ships to be collected, with a great army, from Galloway and the islands' in order to contend with an uprising in the Isle of Man. Two of the leaders of this fleet and army were MacSorleys: 'Alexander Fitz John, of Argyle', that is, Alexander, the son of Ewen (whose name was often Anglicised as John), and 'Alan fitz Rother', who is to be identified with Alan, the son of Ruairi, the lord of Garmoran.[23] It seems likely that the two descendants of Somerled would have been responsible for summoning and leading the host from Argyll and the Isles, but, even more importantly, it is quite likely that the fleet of galleys that transported the army was provided by these western chieftains. They may well also have provided fighting men from the Hebrides, or galloglasses. It is also difficult to believe that the extensive knowledge they could provide of the West, and possibly intelligence-gathering operations, did not play a role in their selection as leaders of the expedition.

If conflict between the descendants of Somerled and the Manx kings was nothing new in the Isles, the situation in 1275 represents a novel state of affairs. In the first instance, it stands in marked constrast to the events of 1263, when most of the MacSorleys had gone over, however reluctantly, to a Norwegian allegiance and had, along with the Manx king, taken part in the plundering of the Scottish mainland. It is ironic that, only twelve years later, two MacSorleys figured prominently among the leaders of an army sent to reassert Scottish royal authority in the Isle of Man. Moreover, we see the MacSorleys acting in concert with other Scottish nobles like John de Vesci, John Comyn, and Alan the son of Thomas of Galloway, Earl of Atholl, who were named as the three other commanders of the expedition. As A. A. M. Duncan has so aptly summarised the situation, we see represented in this collection of names 'a small group of fully armed knights, the "common army", footmen or serjeants of Galloway, and the ships of the Islesmen, all bent to the purposes of the king'.[24] Instead of opposing royal authority in the West, the MacSorleys had become agents of its enforcement, and it would be difficult to find a better example of their integration into the mainstream of Scottish society.

The second illustration of the manner in which the MacSorleys were drawn in from the margins of the Scottish kingdom dates from 1284. In

---

[23] *SAEC*, pp. 382–3.
[24] Duncan, *Making of the Kingdom*, p. 582.

January of that year the Lord Alexander, the eldest son of King Alexander III, died after a long illness. The king had already lost his second son and his daughter, Margaret, the queen of Norway, and this crisis prompted a council to be held at Scone. This council acknowledged Margaret, the king's infant granddaughter, the 'Maid of Norway', as 'our lady and right heir of our said lord king of Scotland'.[25] Among the nobles of the realm who were present and gave their grudging assent were three MacSorleys: 'Alex. de Ergadia', 'Anegus filius Douenaldi' and 'Alanus filius Rotherici', that is, Alexander of Argyll, Angus the son of Donald, and Alan the son of Ruairi. This council, or, more accurately, the inclusion of the MacSorleys in it, is of great significance for any assessment of the position of the descendants of Somerled within the late thirteenth-century community of the realm.

In the first instance, it is noteworthy that all three branches of the MacSorleys – the MacDougalls, MacDonalds, and MacRuairis – were present at the council as equal and integral members of the community of the realm, where they rubbed shoulders with other prominent members of the nobility like Alexander Comyn, Earl of Buchan, Patrick, Earl of Dunbar, Malise, Earl of Strathearn, Malcolm, Earl of Lennox, Robert Bruce, Earl of Carrick, Walter, Earl of Menteith, John Balliol, John Comyn, and James Stewart. Although it is true that the three Argyll magnates are named last in the list of thirty-eight nobles who were present, they are the only magnates from the western seaboard so represented and, in any event, their appearance at the end of the list of nobles who attended nicely exemplifies their newly found position within the Scottish kingdom and the community of the realm. Also significant is the inclusion of the MacSorleys as 'barons of the realm of Scotland' by the document. Considering that only thirty years earlier the descendants of Somerled were kings of the Isles, the change in terminology is significant, and reflects just how much the position and status of the MacSorleys had altered, as they were drawn into the nexus of Scottish politics dominated by the core of the kingdom.

If the integration of the Western Isles and its rulers into the kingdom of Scotland in the years following the battle of Largs and the Treaty of Perth proceeded largely without incident, and was generally accepted by the MacSorleys, the same cannot be said of the Isle of Man. There, Scottish authority was clearly resented, and an attempt was made to re-establish a native dynasty. In the wake of the skirmishes at Largs and the Scottish punitive campaigns in the Western Isles in 1264, the Manx king, Magnus, submitted to Alexander III at Dumfries, and acknowledged the Scottish king as his overlord. But Magnus died on 24 November in the following year, and the Treaty of Perth ceded the Isle

[25] *APS*, i, p. 424.

of Man, along with the rest of the Hebrides, to the king of Scots, to be subject to Scottish law and custom. Lordship of the Isle of Man passed to Alexander, the son of Alexander III, who, in a document dating from between 1266 and 1282, was referred to as lord of Man.[26] His lordship can never have been more than titular, however, and in practical terms the government of Man was entrusted to Scottish bailiffs; the first of these, Godfrey mac Mores, has a name suggesting a Hebridean context.[27] Following the standard practice of the day, hostages were taken: the exchequer accounts for the year 1266 include an allowance to the sheriff of Dumfries for the expenses associated with seven hostages from Man.[28]

These Manx hostages must have feared for their lives when, in September of 1275, Godfrey – described as an illegitimate son of Magnus, the king of Man who had died in 1265 – led an uprising against the new Scottish overlords. The rebels 'appointed Godfrey as their prince', seized the strongholds of the island, which had been abandoned by their 'keepers' (presumably a reference to the Scottish bailiffs) and Godfrey then 'disposed of the kingdom at his pleasure'.[29] This action provoked a swift response from Alexander III, who gathered a fleet of ninety ships and landed at Ronaldsway on 7 October. The *Chronicle of Man* and the *Chronicle of Lanercost* state that the king of Scots sent a peace embassy to Godfrey and the Manx, who were already drawn up in battle formation. The embassy was rejected and at dawn on the next day a fierce battle was fought which seems to have turned into a slaughter for the Manxmen:

> the Manxmen, unarmed and naked, could not resist the slingers, ballistaries [crossbowmen], archers and armed men, and fled with Godfrey their king. And the others pursuing them cut down and slew man and beast, as many as they could catch, sparing not for sex or place.[30]

This gives the impression of the victory of a well-armed and co-ordinated host consisting of foot and cavalry over a poorly armed and hastily organised force, but the Lanercost chronicler concluded simply that 'the wretched Manxmen turned their backs, and perished miserably'.[31] According to the *Chronicle of Man*, 537 Manxmen were slain in the battle, and, although the number has the appearance of being reliable it may owe something to poetic conventions: 'Hence a certain rhymester said: '50 ten times, 10 three times, five, and two, fell'.[32] Another source relates that Godfrey escaped the carnage and fled to Wales. This is not impossible,

---

26 *RRS: Handlist Alexander III*, no. 171.
27 *ES*, ii, pp. 653, 657; see also *RRS: Handlist Alexander III*, no. 172.
28 *ER*, i, p. 17.
29 *SAEC*, pp. 382–3.
30 Ibid., p. 383.
31 *ES*, ii, p. 673.
32 Ibid., ii, p. 673, note 1.

since there was a historical connection between the Isle of Man and Wales: in 1193, for instance, a Welsh source records that Rhodri ab Owain subdued Anglesey with the assistance of the son of Godred the king of Man, that is, Ragnvald.[33] Whatever may have been the case, little more is heard of the Isle of Man until 1290, when it was seized from the Scots by Edward I of England. The Manx chronicler had indeed sounded an ominous note when, in the context of the 1275 uprising, he cautioned: 'Beware Manx race of future losses!'[34] Despite the Manx expedition of 1275, however, by the death of Alexander III it appeared that the western seaboard had been subdued and integrated politically into the community of the realm; every indication was that peace would prevail there, as it did elsewhere in the kingdom.

Taken altogether, the evidence from the three decades of the 1270s, 1280s, and early 1290s points not only to the strengthening of Scottish royal authority in the western seaboard, but also to the binding of the MacSorleys to the centre of the Scottish kingdom. The contrast between the position of Ewen of Argyll as undisputed king of the Isles in the 1240s and that of his son as sheriff in 1293 could not be more striking, and neatly encapsulates the transition from sea-kings to barons. Consciously or not, the Hebridean chieftains of the line of Somerled had trimmed their sails to the winds of change, and had moved significantly in from the margins. Just how big that step had been would be seen when the succession crisis of the late 1280s exploded into Scottish civil war and Anglo-Scottish conflict in the 1290s, from which not even the MacSorleys could remain aloof.

The integration of the margins of the Scottish kingdom – not just Argyll and the Isles but also Galloway in the south-west and Moray in the north – is one of the major themes of twelfth- and thirteenth-century Scottish history. Many of the milestones in this process are violent ones: the rebellions in Galloway following the decision of the Scottish king to dismember that province on the death of its lord, Alan, in 1234, or the fighting at Largs in 1263, which paved the way for the political settlement of three years later. It has been noted, perhaps facetiously but with a certain amount of truth, that terminology such as the 'Winning of the West', 'connotes images of palefaces and natives, not to mention a shoot-out at Largs'.[35] Yet as enduring as the theme of conquest has proved – and not just in Scottish history, of course – many historians are increasingly devoting their attention to other, more subtle processes which also shaped interactions between societies and the domination of one society

[33] *SAEC*, pp. 382–3; *Brut y Tywysogyon* (Hergest), pp. 173, 296.
[34] *ES*, ii, p. 673, note 1. On the Isle of Man 1290–1333, see below, chap. 6, pp. 193–9.
[35] Cowan, 'Norwegian sunset – Scottish dawn', p. 105. We should note also that, 'There was even a Marshal Vigleikr on hand who took time out during the expedition to mosey a little in the cave on the west side of Arran's Holy Isle where he scratched out his name in runes.' (ibid.)

by another. In a European context, Robert Bartlett has emphasised not only conquest but also colonisation, accommodation, and acculturation in promoting what he has called the 'Europeanization of Europe'.[36] In a British setting, the work of R. R. Davies has demonstrated how military invasion and conquest may follow a lengthy period of social and economic domination (as in Edward I's conquest of North Wales), or how more subtle means of domination such as overlordship and intermarriage may succeed where other methods fail.[37] Although Davies's work is concerned with relations between England and its Celtic neighbours, there are many parallels to the processes he describes and those whereby the margins of the Scottish kingdom were drawn into the centre, in what might be termed 'internal colonialism'.[38] Recent research on Galloway, for instance, has pointed to the roles of colonisation and accommodation in bringing that region into conformity with the centre of the kingdom even before the events of the 1230s.[39] But recent examinations of Argyll and the Isles, in contrast, continue to stress the military aspects of the process,[40] especially the various expeditions, both Scottish and Norwegian, to subdue the region, which resulted in the battle of Largs in 1263. It may well be asked, then, whether processes such as those just described were at work in the Hebrides both before and after the region was ceded to Scotland in 1266.

We have already had many indications, at various points in our narrative, that the Hebridean chieftains moved within a much broader framework than we might have imagined. In 1175 Dugald, the son of Somerled, was in Durham in the company of a cleric who, to judge by his name, came from an Anglo-Norman background; in 1237, Dugald's son, Duncan, was the only western magnate named in a Scottish document to the pope; and, around 1200, Ranald, the son of Somerled, possessed a double-sided seal with motifs of both the Highland galley and the mounted knight. But it remains to explore in more detail the cultural world within which the magnates of the West moved in the thirteenth century, in an endeavour to understand whether, in social and cultural terms, the West was moving in from the margins before the political settlement imposed by the Treaty of Perth. Moreover, one might ask whether these cultural transformations helped to ease the political transition. There are several areas that can be profitably explored to illuminate this problem, including the patterns of naming

---

[36] Bartlett, *Making of Europe*.
[37] Davies, *Domination and Conquest, passim*.
[38] M. Hechter, *Internal Colonialism: The Celtic Fringe in British National Development, 1536–1966* (London, 1975), discusses internal colonialism in a post-industrial context, but many of the concepts he considers are thought-provoking when applied to the pre-industrial era.
[39] R. Oram, 'A family business? Colonisation and settlement in twelfth- and thirteenth-century Galloway', *SHR*, lxxii (1993).
[40] See, e.g., Cowan, 'Norwegian sunset – Scottish dawn'; and Donaldson, *Northern Commonwealth*.

and matrimony among the west-coast chieftains; the problematic but important issue of West-Highland feudalism; knighthood and its adoption by the western nobles; and the use of charters by these same men. When these issues are explored, it becomes apparent that, by the time the Western Isles were ceded to Scotland, a hybrid society (which fused Gaelic and Anglo-French, feudal, impulses), was either already in existence or well on its way towards formation.

Names and patterns of naming are among the best indicators of cultural change. They were not chosen arbitrarily, and provide important clues to lineage and ancestry. Indeed, in the early Middle Ages, most regions of Europe had localised repertoires of names which make it easy to identify which region or ethnic group is being described.[41] But in the eleventh and twelfth centuries this began to change, sometimes as the result of conquest, sometimes as the result of cultural accommodation, and, 'a circulation of names and saints throughout the system began'.[42] The process is well known for the Scottish kings descended from Duncan I, for example, where the early generations reveal names like Duncan, Donald, and Malcolm, names that are virtually unique to Scotland. But in the fifth generation after Duncan, only two of twelve names in the royal genealogy are Gaelic.[43] Is it possible to detect similar patterns of naming in the western seaboard?

Somerled's own name, as we have seen, was Norse, and at least two of his sons, Olaf and Ranald, bore Scandinavian appellations. The names of others of his offspring – Dugald, Angus, and Gillebrigte – were Gaelic, however. Considering the mixed Gaelic and Norse milieux of the twelfth-century Hebrides this is hardly surprising, and it is also no surprise that in the thirteenth century many more of his descendants appear with Gaelic names: Donald, the son of Ranald; Angus Mór, the son of Donald; Duncan, the son of Dugald; and Ewen, the son of Duncan. Up until the middle of the thirteenth century, then, Gaelic names were predominant among the kindred of Somerled. But, beginning in the middle decades of the thirteenth century, a new generation of MacSorleys appeared on the scene bearing names indicative of a change in cultural orientation. We find that Donald, the son of Ranald, named his second son Alexander,[44] and that both Angus Mór and Ewen named their first-born sons Alexander, probably after King Alexander III, since it is unlikely that either was born before the death of Alexander II in 1249. However, which king these men were named after is of much less importance than the fact that a name associated with the Scottish royal dynasty had been adopted by the

---

[41] See G. Duby, 'Lineage, nobility and knighthood', in *The Chivalrous Society* (London, 1977), pp. 60–3; and also Bartlett, *Making of Europe*, pp. 270–8.

[42] Ibid., p. 271.

[43] See ibid., pp, 274–7; and I. F. Grant and H. Cheape, *Periods in Highland History* (London, 1987), p. 36.

[44] *Paisley Reg.*, p. 127, where Alexander appears as a witness to one of his brother's charters.

ruling families of the western seaboard. Thereafter, there is evidence of both Gaelic-Norse and Scottish influence in the names chosen by these dynasties. Having named their first-born sons after the Scottish king, both Angus Mór and Ewen reverted to Gaelic appellations for subsequent children; Angus Mór's second son was Angus Óg, and Ewen's second son was Duncan.

It cannot be mere coincidence that the name Alexander appears among first-born sons of the dynasties of the West at exactly the same moment that Scottish royal authority was intensifying in the region, and it is therefore reasonable to suppose that the new names emerging in the kindred of Somerled reflect the spread of Scottish influence upon the West, and also a new orientation on the part of the nobles of the region. Just as the Scots of the twelfth century began to name their children William and Henry, after the Norman kings of England, so too did the rulers of the western seaboard partake in 'cultural emulation of a powerful neighbour',[45] by naming their eldest sons Alexander.

Patterns of matrimony, as we have seen, also provide striking illustrations of the world in which the nobles of the Middle Ages moved, and the matrimonial politics of the West in the twelfth century have already been considered.[46] The marriage alliances made by Somerled in the middle of the twelfth century, for example, point to an Irish Sea orientation – Somerled himself had married a daughter of King Olaf of Man, and his sister married Malcolm MacHeth, another Gaelic or Gaelic-Norse figure associated with uprisings against the MacMalcolms. Indeed, the nexus of matrimonial politics in the Irish Sea in the twelfth century was fixed firmly on the Isle of Man: a daughter of Fergus of Galloway married King Olaf of Man, and even Anglo-Normans like the adventurer John de Courcy were keen to bind themselves to the Manx sovereigns, no doubt, at least in part, because of the formidable fleets of galleys which lay at their disposal. It is therefore unfortunate that the matrimonial politics of the West in the first half of the thirteenth century are obscured by the fragmentary nature of the historical sources. But when the sources permit some light to be shed on these questions in the middle decades of that century, the contrast to the patterns that prevailed in the time of Somerled could not be more striking. We have already noted that, about 1268, Ewen of Argyll married his daughter to the earl of Strathearn. This is a particularly significant event because her first husband had been Magnus, the king of Man who died in 1265, and her second marriage reflects the greatly altered political situation after the settlement of 1266. Equally significant is the marriage of Ewen's son, Alexander, to a daughter of John Comyn (the Red), lord of Badenoch, a kinsman of John Balliol and a prominent member of the Scottish nobility; it was this alliance that made the MacDougalls supporters of

---

[45] Bartlett, *Making of Europe*, p. 277.
[46] See also McDonald, 'Matrimonial politics and core-periphery interactions'.

John Balliol and the implacable enemies of Robert Bruce in the Wars of Independence.[47] Donald, the son of Ranald, married a daughter of Walter, the High Steward of Scotland[48] – a not unnatural alliance given the proximity of the great Stewart lordship to the MacDonald territories. Finally, Alan of Garmoran's heiress, Christiana, married a younger son of Donald, Earl of Mar, another prominent eastern Scottish noble.[49] Thus, by the third quarter of the thirteenth century, all three branches of the MacSorleys were actively forming marriage alliances with prominent members of the Scottish nobility, which underlines their inclusion as barons of the realm of Scotland in 1284 and their new-found position within the community of the realm. Indeed, the contrast with the patterns of a century earlier could hardly be more pronounced; the nexus of the matrimonial politics of the West had shifted decisively from the Isle of Man to the Scottish kingdom itself.

Another major theme in the history of the medieval Scottish kingdom is the process whereby it was feudalised in the twelfth and thirteenth centuries. While it may be true that, by the end of the twelfth century, feudalism itself remained 'alien and largely unknown' in the West Highlands,[50] the influences which had prevailed in the southern and eastern regions of the Scottish kingdom, and which had been adopted so readily by native earls in the East, were beginning to spread in concentric rings from these regions, and to be felt in the more remote peripheral or outer zones. Unfortunately, plotting the spread of feudalism into the West Highlands is particularly problematic. This is due in large measure to the scarcity of documents pertaining to the West before the time of King Robert I (1306–29), and the old problem, aptly summarised by G. W. S. Barrow, 'of whether they are scarce because feudalism made little headway or because historical accident has deprived us of documentary evidence for that region'.[51] Another problem that arises is that of the old, sentimental view that Gaelic society in the West was somehow pure and uncorrupted, and that feudalism was a polluting influence that 'advanced into the highlands in the manner of Original Sin raising its ugly head in the Garden of Eden'.[52] Nothing could, in fact, be further from the truth; what little evidence there is suggests that feudalism was eagerly and easily adapted and utilised by the magnates of the West in the thirteenth century, and in many cases we see those same nobles adopting conventions of feudal society like knighthood, the building of castles, and the utilisation of charters to record transfers of land.

[47] *Chron. Wyntoun* (Laing), book viii, chap. vi, l. 1187–9.
[48] Paul, *Scots Peerage*, v, p. 33.
[49] Duncan, *Making of the Kingdom*, p. 582–3.
[50] Dickinson and Duncan, *Scotland from the Earliest Times*, p. 83.
[51] Barrow, *Anglo-Norman Era*, p. 137.
[52] Ibid.

The earliest infeftment for knight service in the West dates from 1240, when King Alexander II granted Gillascop MacGilchrist extensive territories around Loch Awe and Loch Fyne. The lands were held for half a knight's service in the host and a full knight's service in aid, and also for 'Scottish service as the barons and knights on the north side of the Sea of Scotland do it for their lands'.[53] The reference to Scottish service has been regarded as representing the introduction of the customs of Scotia proper into Argyll, for Scottish service was otherwise known as *forinsec* service, service outside or additional to what was due to the lord, often identified as common army service for the defence of Scotia.[54] Although it is true that this grant was made as part of an attempt by King Alexander II to impose royal authority on the western seaboard, we see for the first time a native magnate of the West entering into a feudal relationship. Moreover, 'there are no grounds for believing that as a feudal charter for Argyll in the mid-thirteenth century it was unique, or that between 1240 and 1262 no further feudalization took place in the west'.[55]

A further example of the extension of feudalism into the West Highlands is seen in 1262, when Dugald MacSween granted Skipness and other extensive lands in Knapdale, Kintyre, and Cowal to Walter Stewart, Earl of Menteith. These lands were to be held 'in free barony' (*in libera baronia*) for the service of two-thirds of a knight in the king's army. What is really important here is the use of the term 'in free barony', which described rights of jurisdiction attributed to a baron, especially in the realm of justice.[56] As Barrow explains it:

> while knight service by itself might be merely a matter of military and financial obligations, the possession of a whole or half knight's feu, or in the later period a quarter knight's feu, raised a man to a status of special importance within the realm.[57]

Indeed, the sources fairly abound with references to the 'barons of Argyll': there are examples from 1275, 1296, 1297, 1301 and 1308–9; Gilchrist MacNaughton appeared as a 'baron of the realm' in 1246, as did Alexander of Argyll, Angus Mór MacDonald, and Alan MacRuairi in 1284;[58] and it is interesting that, even though the grant to Gillascop MacGilchrist in 1240 was not described as being 'in free barony', the lands were given with rights typically associated with such grants, *cum furca et fossa*, 'with pit and gallows'. In short, it seems impossible to argue that feudalism made little headway in the West before the end of the

---

53 *HP*, ii, pp. 121–4.
54 Duncan, *Making of the Kingdom*, pp. 378–82.
55 Barrow, *Anglo-Norman Era*, p. 138.
56 Barrow, *Robert Bruce*, p. 292; Barrow, *Anglo-Norman Era*, pp. 135–6.
57 Ibid.
58 *CDS*, ii, no. 55; *Rot. Scot.*, i, p. 32; Stevenson, *Documents*, ii, nos. 445, 610; *CDS*, iii, no. 80; *Inchaffray Chrs.*, no. 73.

thirteenth century, although the state of the sources means that we may never know as much about this subject as we might like.

It is not until the time of Robert I that the evidence for the feudalisation of the West rises above the level of patchiness and allows a more coherent picture to be drawn. By then a military feudal relationship between the Crown and the nobles of the West appears to have been taken for granted, but at the same time it is possible to view the adaptation of feudalism to the unique conditions of the western seaboard. Enough charters survive from Robert I's reign to illustrate that the typical unit of military service in the West, at least among the greatest nobles, was not the knight but rather the Highland birlinn, or galley, of a set number of oars; a galley of twenty-six oars was the most common type of service stipulated. Thus, a charter granted to Ruairi the son of Alan, sometime in the reign of Robert I, gave extensive lands for the service of one twenty-six-oared ship, with men and supplies; Colin the son of Neil Campbell held Lochawe and Ardskeodnish in barony for a ship of forty oars; and Thomas Randolph was granted the Isle of Man for the service of six twenty-six-oared vessels. Many of these grants also stipulate that men and supplies are to accompany the vessel.[59] The heavy service due from the Isle of Man no doubt reflects the formidable fleets that the kings of Man had been able to command in the thirteenth century. Thus, when King Ragnvald assisted his brother-in-law, John de Courcy, in his attempt to win back Ulster in 1205, he is said to have brought with him a fleet of one hundred warships; and when the King of Man submitted to Alexander III and performed homage in 1264, he was bound to provide five twenty-four-oared and five twelve-oared galleys.[60] A. A. M. Duncan, however, has sounded a cautionary note by suggesting that on the western seaboard charters were only sought by the greatest landowners; this perhaps gives the illusion that galley-service was more typical than it actually was, and it is worthwhile bearing in mind that this was the most substantial type of service.[61] Nevertheless, it is certain that none of the chieftains of the western seaboard held their lands as a fief in return for fixed military service before the time of Alexander III, although they were obligated to provide a set number of ships for royal expeditions, as, perhaps, in 1275. It was the achievement of Robert I to bring many of these men into a feudal relationship with the Crown by granting, regranting, or confirming estates as fiefs in return for a fixed number of galleys of so many oars, thereby grafting an older obligation on to the feudal one and creating a blend of old and new in West-Highland feudalism.[62] This in turn demonstrates how feudalism could be adapted better to suit the maritime conditions of the

[59] *RMS*, i, appendix I, nos. 9, 32, 105, 107; *RRS*, v, nos. 46, 239, 366.
[60] *Chron. Bower*, v, pp. 347–9.
[61] *RRS*, v, p. 54; Barrow, *Robert Bruce*, p. 289.
[62] Barrow, *Anglo-Norman Era*, p. 139.

"Dappled sails." The highway of the seas lent unity to the kingdom of the Isles, and contemporary sources abound with references to the galleys that plied the seaways in the middle ages. This fourteenth or fifteenth-century grave slab from Kilmory Knap, Argyll, shows the type of vessel that west highland chieftains used to control the seas. These carvings are probably accurate representations of contemporary vessels; note the sleek lines, high stem and stern posts, oar ports, rigging, mast, furled sail, and stern rudder. *Unless otherwise indicated, photographs are Crown Copyright: Royal Commission on the Ancient and Historical Monuments of Scotland.*

Much altered and expanded in subsequent centuries, Dunvegan Castle on the Isle of Skye has its origins in the thirteenth century. Occupying an irregularly-shaped rock outcropping, it was accessible only from the sea by a sea-gate until 1748: this feature is visible in the centre of the photograph. Dunvegan is notable as the home of the chiefs of the Clan MacLeod and as the longest continually occupied residence in Scotland.

The Ardnamurchan peninsula is home to two exceptional, if poorly documented, strongholds: Mingary and Tioram. Mingary, perched on an isolated rock on the south side of Ardnamurchan at the mouth of Loch Sunart, commands spectacular views of Mull and Morvern. Its massive thirteenth-century curtain walls, hexagonal shape, and isolated location are shown to good effect in this aerial photograph. The castle was much altered in later centuries.

Castle Tioram occupies the summit of a rocky tidal islet jutting from the south shore of Loch Moidart; at high tide, the castle and its islet are entirely cut off from the shore. Mingary and Tioram are closely related in design and are probably contemporary; Tioram certainly and Mingary probably fell within the MacRuari lordship of Garmoran.

Skipness Castle, on the north-east coast of the Kintyre peninsula, guards a strategic conjunction of the seaways. Unlike many castles of the west, it sits on level ground and does not take advantage of natural rock formations. In about 1300 the present castle of enclosure replaced a smaller hall-house and chapel on the site; the massive walls and quadrangular plan are seen to advantage here.

"Tryst of a fleet against Castle Sween." The extensive remains of Castle Sween, perched on a promontory near the mouth of Loch Sween, Knapdale, constitute one of the most important monuments of secular lordship in the west. It was probably built by the eponymous Suibhne, ancestor of the MacSweens, in the twelfth century, and is generally regarded as the earliest surviving stone-built castle on the Scottish mainland. A Gaelic poem recounts the siege of the castle, possibly in 1310, by John MacSween.

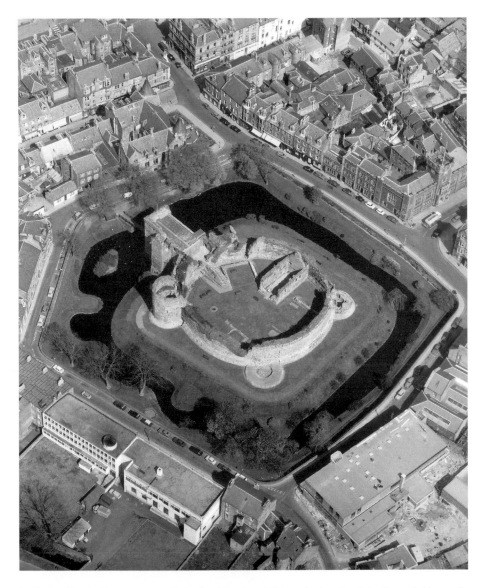

Rothesay Castle. Bute was one of the first islands to fall into the hands of the Scottish kings, who had granted it to the Stewart family by about 1200. Walter the Steward was probably responsible for the construction of Rothesay Castle, the stone curtain wall and moat of which survive. This is almost certainly the castle described in *Hakon's Saga* as being besieged by the Norwegians in 1230. The four round towers were added in the thirteenth century.

At Dunstaffnage, the MacDougall lords of Argyll set out in the mid-thirteenth century to create an up-to-date centre of lordship, with a strong stone-built castle and chapel. Dunstaffnage Castle occupies a strategic site overlooking Loch Etive and a broad stretch of the western seaways. Built by Duncan MacDougall or his son, Ewen, it was the principal MacDougall stronghold and had to be captured by Robert I in his campaign against his implacable foes (1308). Its military features, such as the cylindrical angle-towers, are state-of-the-art, while the elaborate lancet windows in the east wall (visible in centre of the photograph above) bespeak a sophisticated apartment or hall. The nearby chapel (below), even in its ruinous state, is a fine example of Gothic architecture, with beautifully decorated windows. The construction of monuments like these shows how the magnates of the western seaboard were receptive to contemporary European trends.

Iona Abbey, the pre-eminent religious site in the west, was founded by St. Columba *c.*563. Despite the onslaught of the Norsemen at the close of the eighth century, the religious life and symbolic importance of Iona were maintained. It may have been patronised by Queen Margaret, and Somerled attempted to reform the community here in 1164. But it was Somerled's son, Ranald, who refounded the monastery for Benedictines about 1200, and there was much building work undertaken in the thirteenth century. Substantial alterations were made in the fifteenth century.

Probably at the same time as he refounded the monastery on Iona, Ranald also established a nunnery (below) for Augustinian canonesses. Its pink granite ruins are located near the abbey, and are the most substantial of their kind in Scotland. The church, seen here, dates from the thirteenth century. Ranald's sister, Bethag, was the first prioress.

The remains of the chapel of St Blane at Kingarth, Bute, although dating from the late twelfth century, are located on the site of an earlier Christian foundation. *Historic Scotland*. Probably contemporary with the construction of Rothesay Castle, this little chapel has elaborate Romanesque decoration on the chancel arch (below).

Kilmory Knap, Knapdale. The second half of the twelfth century saw much church building in the west, under the patronage of native lords. The chapel at Kilmory Knap contains some fine round-headed windows and may have been patronised by the MacSweens of Knapdale. Kilmory is also noteworthy for its collection of late medieval carved stones (below).See also plate 1.

Teampull Mholuidh, Lewis. There are relatively few chapels of the period that have been identified in Skye and the Outer Hebrides, but one candidate is Teampull Mholuidh (St. Moluag's
church), Europie, Lewis, which might date from the late twelfth or thirteenth century. St. Moluag
was an Irish saint with dedications in Scotland, but there is no evidence for the foundation of the
church here.

St. German's cathedral, Peel, Isle of Man, was constructed in several stages between the twelfth
and fourteenth centuries, but a major enlargement was undertaken by Bishop Simon (1226-48).
It was in his episcopate that the diocese of the Isles emerged as a fully integrated component of
Western Christendom. The cathedral displays Ulster affinities in its architecture, the result of
matrimonial connections between John de Courcy, Lord of Ulster, and the daughter of King
Godfrey. *Manx National Heritage.*

western seaboard, a point which is further illustrated when we come to consider the castles of the region (see Chapter 8).

Regardless of how it was adapted to the maritime culture of the West of Scotland, feudalism was, in origin and in essence, all about knights. According to R. Allen Brown, it originated for:

> the provision, maintenance and training of this particularly expensive and therefore exclusive, type of warrior, with his costly warhorses and equipment, who required from early youth up a lifetime of dedication to horsemanship and the military arts ...[63]

In medieval society the knight came to represent a military elite, and soon thereafter a social elite as well. And, while not all knights were great men, it is certainly true to say that, in England and on the Continent, all great men were becoming knights – a trend which was also followed in Scotland. As we have seen,[64] knighthood had been introduced into Scotland in the twelfth century by its francophile monarchs, and its conventions were also expressed, from an early date, by many members of the native Scottish nobility, especially the earls of Fife, Dunbar, and Strathearn. As Davies has shown, knighthood 'opened the door into an exhilarating international world of aristocratic fellowship and customs' and became an important agent in acculturation and assimilation between peoples in Britain.[65]

This then raises the issue of whether the ideals, manners, and status of knighthood spread to the western seaboard, and were practised by any of the noble families of the region. We certainly need not search far for members of the native Scottish nobility of the Highlands who were influenced by these ideals. Thus Lachlann, the son of Uhtred, the son of Fergus of Galloway, for instance, is better known by the French name of Roland – and he also held the title Constable of Scotland.[66] And it will be recalled that, in 1215, one of the Celtic leaders in the north, Farquhar 'Maccintsacairt', was rewarded with knighthood and later made earl of Ross for his role in quashing an uprising against King Alexander II. The case of Farquhar is particularly interesting, for 'it shows a Celtic leader from the north now on the side of the royal house descended from Malcolm and Margaret; and, because of his services, the Celtic leader is made a feudal knight.'[67]

Given these well-known examples of Gaelic nobles from the northern

---

[63] R. A. Brown, *Castles* (Aylesbury, 1985), p. 7. There is a vast literature on medieval knighthood. A good, recent study of English knighthood is P. Coss, *The Knight in Medieval England, 1000–1400* (Stroud, 1993); David Crouch addresses knighthood in D. Crouch, *Image of Aristocracy in Britain, 1000–1300* (London, 1992). Another important work is that of Duby, *Chivalrous Society*. Although feudalism has been much discussed in a Scottish context, knighthood in Scotland lacks a comprehensive examination.

[64] Chapter 3, pp. 76–7.

[65] Davies, *Domination and Conquest*, p. 51.

[66] *ES*, ii, p. 347, note 2; Stringer, 'Periphery and core in thirteenth-century Scotland'.

[67] Ibid., ii, p. 404; Dickinson and Duncan, *Scotland from the Earliest Times*, p. 74.

and western Highlands adopting the outward trappings, at least, of feudal society, it would hardly be surprising to find the MacSorleys doing the same. Unfortunately, once again the sparse nature of the evidence means that any such examination is bound to be patchy and, to a certain extent, speculative. I have argued elsewhere that the seal of Ranald MacSorley (which has already been considered in Chapter 3), provides strong evidence that, as early as about 1200, ideals of knighthood and chivalry were penetrating the western seaboard, far earlier than has been previously thought.[68] Ranald's seal was double-sided and depicted its owner on one side as a mounted knight with a drawn sword, while on the other was portrayed a Highland galley. Now, the portrayal of Ranald as a knight does not necessarily indicate that he was in fact knighted, and thereby inaugurated into the 'sophisticated, international world of chivalry'; indeed, some Gaelic princes and magnates are known to have portrayed themselves as equestrians without having been dubbed knights.[69] But the use of the equestrian device indicates that Ranald, in common with other Scottish, Welsh, and Manx rulers of the day, was expressing a desire to be a thoroughly modern and up-to-date magnate in a time when the 'Brave New World' of French civilisation was driving all before it. Indeed, given the evident lapping of the waves of feudal influence on the shores of the western seaboard in the thirteenth century, it might have been more unusual if the MacSorleys had remained completely uninfluenced by them, and by the middle of the thirteenth century knighthood seems to have become something of a norm among the ruling class in the West. Sadly, though, the evidence for knighthood being adopted by the MacSorleys is less abundant for Ranald's descendants than it is for the MacDougalls, and it is difficult to say how the trend set by Ranald might have been perpetuated by his descendants. However, in 1293, when Alexander of Argyll was instructed to ensure that Angus the son of Donald performed homage to King John Balliol, the document described Angus as *miles*, that is, a knight,[70] so it would seem that, whether or not Ranald was actually knighted, his grandson, Angus Mór, certainly had been.

The evidence for the adoption of knighthood by the MacDougalls of Argyll is both more abundant and more convincing, and from the time of Ewen until that of his grandson, John, these prominent west-coast nobles were consistently described as knights. Ewen of Argyll is described in both narrative and charter material in a manner that leaves little doubt he had been knighted. Matthew Paris, who narrated Ewen's relations with the Scottish king in 1249, described him as a 'vigorous and very handsome knight'.[71] While this might be attributed to literary

[68] McDonald, 'Images of Hebridean lordship'.
[69] Davies, *Domination and Conquest*, pp. 50–1; quotation on p. 51.
[70] *APS*, i, p. 448.
[71] *SAEC*, p. 360.

convention, there are several reasons for thinking that this is not the case. First, although he spent most of his life at St Albans, Matthew had excellent means of obtaining information, including many informants who were important public figures. This means that he was familiar with the conventions of knighthood, and it is not likely that he would have attributed them to Ewen unless he had, in fact, been knighted. Moreover, there is a very good chance that Matthew Paris had actually met Ewen of Argyll, since both had been in Norway in 1248, and so he should be considered well informed on this issue. Indeed, the journey to Norway opens up the possibility that Matthew Paris had first-hand information on the matter of Ewen's status, and his narrative should not, therefore, be dismissed out of hand.[72] It is certainly corroborated by charter evidence. In a charter of 1240 Ewen granted lands in Lismore to the bishopric of Argyll, in which he referred to himself as *Eugenius miles*, Ewen the knight.[73] This is significant in several respects. In the first instance, the term *miles* was coming in the twelfth century to designate not just a soldier but a knight trained to fight on horseback. Its use was sparing in documents of the eleventh and twelfth centuries, but by the thirteenth century it was beginning to be recognised as a mark of status.[74] Moreover, because its use appears in one of his own charters, it provides us with an insight into how Ewen viewed himself, and how he wished to be portrayed. Finally, in a document from 1255 which details the terms of his restoration, Ewen is described as *dominus* or lord, a term of status which usually, by this time, implied that its holder had been knighted.[75] Taken altogether, then, the evidence in favour of Ewen having been knighted is overwhelming; he therefore appears as a man of two worlds.

Ewen's descendants, Alexander and John, are also described as knights in many contemporary documents. Alexander was called a knight in the Ragman Rolls of 1296 when he swore loyalty to Edward I,[76] and there are numerous references to his son, John, holding similar rank in the later thirteenth and early fourteenth centuries. Thus, a manuscript recording Scottish nobles who swore fealty to Edward I in 1291–2 arranged them in order of status, and one of those mentioned in

---

[72] On Matthew Paris, see Gransden, *Historical Writing in England*, pp. 360–1. It is worth while noting that Matthew included details on heraldry in his text; he also painted armorial shields of English nobles in the margins of his chronicles: ibid, p. 362, and note 47.

[73] *RMS*, ii, no. 3136 = Duncan and Brown, 'Argyll and the Isles', appendix IV.

[74] On the term, see M. Keen, *Chivalry* (New Haven and London, 1984), pp. 27–8; Duby, *Chivalrous Society*, pp. 75–7; J. Bumke, *The Concept of Knighthood in the Middle Ages* (New York, 1982), p. 36; on its use, see D. F. Fleming, '*Milites* as attestors to charters in England, 1101–1300', *Albion*, xxii, (1990), pp. 185–7.

[75] *APS*, i, p. 115. On the interchangability of *miles* and *dominus* by the mid-13th century, see Duby, *Chivalrous Society*, pp. 75–7, and Fleming, '*Milites* as attestors to charters', pp. 187, 191–3.

[76] *CDS*, ii, no. 791 and no. 823 (p. 195).

the ninth category of *armigeri*, young men of knightly class, was John of Argyll. English financial accounts indicate payments in 1314 to 'Sir John of Argyll, knight'; and another similar document of 1313, which records payments to knights attending an English parliament on Scottish affairs, also mentions John.[77] It would seem that by the early fourteenth century knighthood had become something of a norm, at least among the MacDougalls, and again we are struck by how west-coast magnates adapted quickly and easily to the conventions of Scottish society.

The penetration of feudal ideas and practices in the West can be further illustrated in a slightly different fashion by examining a series of charters granted by the MacDonald Lords of Islay to the abbey of Paisley in the late twelfth and the thirteenth century. These charters are preserved in the *Register* of Paisley Abbey, a sixteenth-century compilation, and although they cannot be dated precisely, they can be placed in relative chronological order. Thus we find that, sometime around 1200, Ranald, the son of Somerled, granted eight oxen and two pence for one year from every house in his territory from which smoke issued, and thereafter one penny per year. The grant draws to a conclusion with a terrifying curse. Ranald ordered his friends and people to aid the monks,

> with the certain knowledge that, by St Columba, if any of my heirs does harm to them, he shall have my malediction; or if peradventure any evil should be done unto them or theirs by my people, or by any others whom it is in my power to bring to account, they shall suffer the punishment of death.[78]

The curse of Ranald upon anyone who did injury to the monks of Paisley reminds us of the role that St Columba seems to have played as a formidable and vengeful protector of the Hebrideans, a role that was also illustrated by the dream of Alexander II before his death in 1249. As he lay dying, King Alexander dreamt that three figures appeared to him; that of St Columba bade the king turn back and abort his campaign in the Hebrides. His subsequent death was linked to his refusal to obey the dream-men, and it would seem that St Columba, who always had a reputation as a vengeful and vindictive saint, had claimed another victim. Ranald's curse would certainly have conjured up these terrifying connotations, and so the document provides an interesting glimpse into a society that was moving towards new conventions but still hanging on to some traditional beliefs.

Ranald's son, Donald, repeated his father's grant in similar terms (probably at the same time, since the witnesses to the two charters are identical), and repeated the curse that evil-doers would suffer the pain of

---

[77] 1291–2 document: *Edward I and the Throne of Scotland*, ed Stones and Simpson, ii, p. 367, note 4, and p. 368; 1312–14 documents: *CDS*, iii, nos. 303, 355.

[78] *Paisley Reg.*, p. 125.

death. But later charters by members of the same family are worded more conventionally, without any mention of the curse of St Columba; a charter of Alexander, the son of Angus Mór, was made 'for the welfare of my lord Alexander, illustrious king of Scots'.[79]

It is also informative to consider the witnesses to these charters. Because charters represented formal and legal records of grants of land and rights, they often had appended to them lists of witnesses, men who were present at the ceremony and whose recollection could be called upon, if necessary, should there be subsequent dispute. These lists are of interest to the historian for many reasons, not least because they permit a glimpse of the retainers with which great men surrounded themselves. The men who witnessed the charters of Ranald and Donald are identical and their names, at least, are suggestive of a Hebridean milieu; they bear names like Gillecolm mac Gillemichel, and, in the case of Donald's charter, 'many others of my own men'.[80] But when Angus Mór, the son of Donald, made his grant, the witnesses included men who, to judge by their names, came from a Scottish background, like Gilbert the son of Samuel and William of Strathgryfe; the witnesses to a charter of Alexander, the son of Angus Mór, included both Robert Bruce, the lord of Annandale, and his son, Robert Bruce, Earl of Carrick – grandfather and father respectively of King Robert I.[81] Once again a definite transition is visible between about 1200 and the later thirteenth century: the changing composition of the witness lists to these charters reveals yet another way in which the MacSorleys came in from the margins in the thirteenth century, and by which the balance of old and new in the society of the western seaboard may be judged.

At this point it may be asked what the economy of the western seaboard was like, and whether it was experiencing change at the same rate as the rest of society. It is a difficult question to answer. Contemporary documents are scarce and shed little light on agriculture, trade, and commerce, but the overall impression is that the western seaboard shared in the expansion that characterised the rest of western Europe between about 1050 and 1300.

The French historian Georges Duby has argued in a seminal work on the medieval European economy that the period before about 1100 was dominated by a war economy based on pillage and plunder. The main object of this economy was to obtain gold, silver, and precious stones, and it was characterised by the exchange of gifts between lords and their followers. With the rise of feudalism and the so-called feudal peace of the tenth and eleventh centuries, agriculture became the driving force of

---

[79] Ibid., p. 128.
[80] Ibid., p. 126. Gillecolm mac Gillemichel turns up again as a witness to one of Ewen of Argyll's charters in 1240.
[81] *Paisley Reg.*, pp. 127–9.

the economy and it was only now, in Duby's view, that seigneurial exploitation assumed its dominant role. This mode of production was in turn overshadowed by the rise of cities and the expansion of urban economies in the late twelfth century. Although it may be debated how applicable certain parts of Duby's argument are to the largely pastoral economy of the western Highlands, there can be no doubt that all three stages of his model are in evidence in the economy of the West in our period.[82]

Rulers of the early Middle Ages required gold, silver, and precious gems as 'tangible expressions of their glory', and the chief means of obtaining these items was through nearly continual warfare. It is clear that vestiges of this economy of war and aggression lingered in the western seaboard long after it had disappeared in most of the rest of western Europe, and the Hebridean chieftains must have relied on plunder in order to maintain their followers. Certainly plundering, or piracy as it was known to the authorities in England and Scotland, was a dominant theme in the activities of the Hebridean chiefs as late as the thirteenth century. The best known example is probably that of Ruairi the son of Ranald, who, as late as 1212 and 1214, was pillaging in Derry along with Thomas the son of Roland of Galloway. Irish Annals noted that in 1214 the pair 'plundered Derry completely; and took the treasures of the community of Derry, and of the north of Ireland besides, from inside the church of the abbey'.[83] But perhaps better illustrations still come from the praise-poems written in honour of Ragnvald, the king of Man, and Angus Mór of Islay. Ragnvald is said to have conducted cattle raids on Ireland, and Angus Mór is depicted in a similar light: 'You have come round Ireland', says the poet, 'rare is the strand where you have not taken cattle'. It is perhaps particularly relevant that the author of the praise-poem in honour of Ragnvald speaks of the generous gifts that he had received from the king: 'As I went from your fine house my gifts were not unseemly.' The role of plundering, and especially of cattle and cattle-raiding, is well known in the context of early Irish society, but it is perhaps an open question as to whether these thirteenth-century praise-poems accurately portray the situation or whether they are idealisations representing a conservative literary tradition.[84] But, though we must utilise the praise-poems with caution, there can be no doubt that both Ragnvald and Angus Mór did undertake military expeditions to Ireland. Thus, in 1219 there is a reference to the

---

[82] G. Duby, *The Early Growth of the European Economy: Warriors and Peasants from the Seventh to the Twelfth Century* (London, 1974). Cf. the account of the economy of the earldom of Ulster, in T. E. McNeil, *Anglo-Norman Ulster: The History and Archaeology of an Irish Barony, 1177–1400* (Edinburgh, 1980), esp. chaps. 3, 6.

[83] *ES*, ii, pp. 393, 395.

[84] 'Poem in praise of Raghnall', ed. O Cuiv; 'Address to Aonghus of Islay', in Bergin, *Irish Bardic Poetry*. A useful work is N. Patterson, *Cattle Lords and Clansmen: The Social Structure of Early Ireland* (2nd edn, London, 1994).

excesses committed in Ireland by the Manx king, and in 1256 the king of England ordered his Irish bailiffs to curb the activities of Angus Mór and other Scottish malefactors there.[85] The ancient and time-honoured tradition of plundering to obtain booty seems to have been alive and well and playing an important role in the economy of the western seaboard as late as the thirteenth century.

Our best evidence about the land and produce of the region comes only from the sixteenth century, when Donald Monro, in his *Western Isles* of 1549, often used the terms 'fertile' and 'fruitfull' to describe many of the islands. He noted, to give several examples from many, that Bute and Skye were 'very fertile ground, namely for aits [oats]'; that Islay was 'fertil, fruitfull and full of natural girsing pasture'; and of windswept Tiree, known for centuries as the Granary of the Isles, he observed that, 'Na cuntrie may be mair fertile of corn'. The late twelfth- or early thirteenth-century *Orkneyinga Saga* also commented on the fertility of the land when it commented that 'Kintyre is thought to be more valuable than the best of the Hebridean islands, though not as good as the Isle of Man.' It would, of course, be an exaggeration to portray the Hebrides and Argyll as a land of milk and honey. Compared to the rest of western Europe, the region was lacking in resources. The thirteenth-century *Chronicle of Man* makes a telling comment on this when it remarks of Lewis that it is 'more extensive than the other islands, but thinly peopled, because it is mountainous and rocky, and almost totally unfit for cultivation. The inhabitants live mostly by hunting and fishing.'[86]

By the early fourteenth century it is possible to shed some rather dim light on the produce of the region from contemporary documents. In the accounts for the constable of Tarbert in 1326, frequent mention is made of flour and cheese, and barley and bread are also referred to. In general it appears that wheat was more widely grown in the south of Scotland, while oats and barley predominated north of the Tay. But the Highlands were known throughout the Middle Ages as cattle, hide, and skin producing country, and like contemporary Ireland the mainstays of the economy were cattle and sheep. Thus it is no surprise to find mention of cattle, horses, sheep, pigs and poultry in the accounts for Tarbert, and the thirteenth-century charters of Ranald and his son Donald to Paisley Abbey also mention oxen and cattle. Four centuries later, Donald Monro observed that some of the islands were not well suited to growing crops, and he paid particular attention to cattle and

---

[85] *Foedera*, i, pt. 1, p. 78; i, pt. 2, p. 11.

[86] Munro, *Monro's Western Isles, passim*, but see the editor's comments on these subjects on pp. 5–7 and 129–31; *Orkneyinga Saga* (Pálsson and Edwards), cap. 41; *Chron. Man*, p. 83. The Manx chronicle seems to be conflating Lewis and Harris here under the name of Lewis: the latter is flat and boggy (and the larger of the two), while Harris is mountainous. See also the brief comments of N. Mayhew, 'Alexander III – a silver age? An essay in Scottish medieval economic history', in Reid, *Scotland in the Reign of Alexander III*, p. 57.

sheep, sometimes with the comment that a particular island was 'very gude for scheip'.[87]

As we would expect of a maritime culture, the sea was also exploited. The sea, the lochs, and the rivers of the West provided good fishing, and Monro mentions salmon, herring, white fish, whiting, and haddock, noting where appropriate that many of the islands were 'gude for fisching'. Seals are mentioned as being killed in the Ascrib Isles and on Islay; references to 'murens' being found in the Barra Isles are probably to lampreys or conger eels; and whales were sometimes caught, particularly in Lewis and Uist. John of Fordun also noted this, stating that, 'whales and other sea-monsters abound' on Uist. It is clear, too, that the inhabitants of the Isles, in common with the rest of the peoples of western Europe in the Middle Ages, enjoyed the hunt and the chase. Mull, for example, was said to contain, 'certane woods, mony deiris and fair hunting games', as was Islay and several other of the islands. Hawking was also popular, and many of the islands are noted as containing falcons' nests.[88]

There is even some evidence which pertains to the exploitation of the natural resources of the region, for several thirteenth-century charters refer to mining activity in the Isle of Man. In 1246 King Harald, confirming the grants of his ancestors to Furness Abbey, included 'the use of all kinds of mines which may be found within my kingdom, both beneath the soil and above'. In 1256 King Magnus granted to the bishop of Man and the Isles, among other things, 'all kinds of mines of lead and iron which may be discovered in his land of Man'. The mention of lead is particularly interesting, for in 1292 John Comyn, Earl of Buchan, had permission from Edward I to export lead from the Calf of Man in order to roof eight turrets on his castle of Cruggleton in Galloway – indicating one use to which this valuable resource was put.[89]

The export of lead from the Isle of Man in the thirteenth century in turn raises the question of both internal and long-distance trade and commerce, which was centred in the first instance on the burghs of Tarbert, Dumbarton, and Glasgow. The Exchequer accounts for 1326 sketch a picture of Tarbert as a bustling port, burgh, and castle, with ships frequently arriving and departing. Much activity in the period between 1325 and 1329 was centred on the construction of the castle, and there is mention in the accounts of skilled craftsmen such as masons,

---

[87] *ER*, i, pp. 52–8; *Paisley Reg.*, pp. 125–6; Munro, *Monro's Western Isles, passim.* See also I. F. Grant, *The Economic History of Scotland* (London, 1934), pp. 150–5, where most observations pertain to the 16th century. General background in Duncan, *Making of the Kingdom*, pp. 309–25; and A. Grant, *Independence and Nationhood: Scotland, 1306–1469* (London, 1984), chap. 3.

[88] See note 86; *Chron. Fordun*, i, p. 43; ii, p. 40.

[89] *Monumenta de Insula Manniae*, ed. J. R. Oliver (Manx Soc., 1860–2), ii, pp. 79–80, 89–92; Stevenson, *Documents*, i, no. 266. See J. Steane, *The Archaeology of Medieval England and Wales* (Athens, Georgia, 1984), pp. 223–4 on lead working.

carpenters, plumbers, and roofers. This was a prosperous community. In 1328, when a tenth of incomes was granted to the crown, surviving accounts show receipt of £4 8s 10d from Tarbert over a period of one or two years, which indicates a return of at least £2 4s 5d per year. In comparison, the older and better established towns of Rutherglen, Haddington, and Linlithgow returned between £3 and £3 10s – so Tarbert seems to have been a thriving centre by the end of the first third of the fourteenth century. Other commercial activity in the western seaboard was based on the burgh at Dumbarton, founded in 1222 by Alexander II in the wake of his campaign(s) to subdue the Firth of Clyde region. According to one thirteenth-century charter its trading area extended to the head of Loch Fyne, but this has been seen as an error for Loch Long. Dumbarton was granted the right to hold a fair in 1226, and we can imagine that this would have attracted people from the surrounding countryside and facilitated exchange between merchants from the western seaboard and the rest of Scotland. What is certain is that Dumbarton developed rapidly as a port of communication and commerce with Kintyre and, by way of Tarbert, the rest of Argyll and the West. Finally, there were also commercial contacts between Glasgow and the western seaboard, which ultimately led to conflicts between Glasgow and Dumbarton over access to this new market. Thus, in 1275 the men of Dumbarton were ordered not to trouble the bishop of Glasgow's merchants going to and returning from Argyll with merchandise. The nature of the merchandise that was being traded is not, unfortunately, stated, but all the evidence points to extensive contacts between the West and the rest of Scotland in the late thirteenth century, mirroring the political and social integration of the West that had taken place by that time.[90]

Considering the nature of the contacts between the western seaboard and the rest of the Irish Sea World in our period, it would be unwise to restrict our consideration of commercial activity to the Scottish context alone. There is also good evidence for long-distance trade being undertaken by the MacSorleys. In 1275, for example, we find that some of Alexander of Argyll's men were arrested with their vessel and goods at Bristol on suspicion of piracy; the value of the goods was stated to have been 160 marks but the nature of the merchandise was not mentioned. The fact that the crew of the ship could be suspected of piracy is perhaps a reflection of the role of plunder in the economy of

---

90 Tarbert: *ER*, i, pp. 52–8, 237; Dunbar and Duncan, 'Tarbert Castle', p. 16 (it was of course founded by Robert I). Dumbarton: *RMS*, vii, no. 190; Dunbar and Duncan, 'Tarbert Castle', p. 3. Glasgow: *RRS: Handlist Alexander III*, no. 200. General background to burghs and trade in Barrow, *Kingship and Unity*, chap. 5. Perhaps we ought not to paint too rosy a picture of the Hebridean economy. As Caldwell and Ewart have noted, the Lordship of the Isles never developed any urban economic centres, even at Finlaggan, and there is a remarkable absence of coin finds from the western seaboard between 1100 and 1490: D. H. Caldwell and G. Ewart, 'Finlaggan and the Lordship of the Isles: an archaeological approach', *SHR*, lxxii (1993), pp. 159–60.

the West, but more informative is the fact that we find men and vessels from the western seaboard at Bristol, a major English port. We do not know whether Bristol was the ultimate destination of the Hebridean galley and its crew, but less than twenty years later there is evidence of commercial contacts between the western seaboard and Ireland. In 1292 Edward I granted letters of safe conduct to Alexander of Argyll, Angus the son of Donald, and his son Alexander, in which it was stated that these men frequently sent merchants with goods to Ireland to both buy and sell. Once again we would like to know more about the nature of the goods being traded, but taken together these incidents reveal that long distance trade over the seaways was an important element in the economy of the western seaboard by about 1300.[91]

These commercial contacts with Bristol and Ireland are a reminder that the galleys under the command of the Hebridean chieftains could be used for commerce as well as war, and their construction must have represented an important facet of the economy of the West. There is unfortunately little evidence for this matter before the sixteenth century, but several references to the construction of galleys come from the very end of the thirteenth and the early part of the fourteenth centuries. In a letter to King Edward II in 1309 John of Argyll stated that, 'I keep and build galleys with trusty men to each galley', on Loch Etive or possibly Loch Awe. Even earlier, in 1297, Alexander MacDonald referred to the construction of two huge supergalleys by Lachlan MacRuairi, Alexander of Argyll, and John Comyn beside Comyn's castle in Lochaber. In the later Middle Ages there was a shipyard at Kishorn in Wester Ross, and it is a reasonable conjecture that there must have been many shipyards on the western seaboard, with timber for the galleys coming from Inverness or perhaps even Ireland.[92]

Without question, however, one of the greatest exports of the western seaboard, from at least the late thirteenth century but quite likely much earlier, was its fighting men: the *gallóclaig* or galloglasses. The term means literally 'foreign warrior', and was applied to mercenary troops of mixed Gaelic and Norse extraction from Argyll and the Western Isles, employed by the Gaelic Irish in their struggle against the English. Although the galloglasses are perhaps better known in an Irish context from the fourteenth to the sixteenth centuries, the first mention of them comes in the late thirteenth. By the fourteenth century many leading families of the western seaboard, including the MacDonalds, MacDougalls, MacRuairis and MacSweens, were involved in supplying galloglasses to the Irish, and some of these families established prominent galloglass dynasties in Ireland.

[91] Bristol: *CDS*, ii, no. 55, 63. Ireland: Stevenson, *Documents*, i, no. 276.
[92] Loch Awe: *CDS*, iii, no. 80; Barrow, *Robert Bruce*, p. 179. Supergalleys at Lochaber: Stevenson, *Documents*, ii, no. 445. Shipyards and timber: MacInnes, 'West Highland sea power', p. 527–8. See chap. 6, pp. 177–8, for John of Argyll's letter.

The *Annals of Connacht* relate how, in 1290, Aed O'Domnaill was deposed by his brother, who assumed the kingship in his place. Aed managed to win back the kingship 'through the power of his mother's kin, the Clann Domnaill, and of many other galloglasses [*galloclaech*]'. This is the first time the galloglasses are mentioned by name in the Irish sources, but the passage indicates that not only were they already a well-established feature on the Irish political scene, but also that the Clan Donald was prominent among their suppliers by this time. Several other references in the Irish sources suggest that foreign warriors from the Hebrides were serving in Ireland from about the middle of the thirteenth century. Thus, in 1267 Murchadh MacSween was captured in Ireland and died in the captivity of the earl of Ulster; since the MacSweens had been displaced in Knapdale by 1262 and were later, as the MacSweeneys, to become a prominent galloglass family in Ireland, it may be that the capture of Murchadh should be associated with early galloglass activity.

But in the thirteenth century, at least, it was the MacSorleys who were the major suppliers of galloglasses to the Irish kings. In 1259 Aed O'Conchobair of Connacht went to Derry to marry the daughter of Dugald MacRuairi, and the Irish Annals state that 'he brought home eight score *oglaoch* (young warriors) with her, together with Ailin MacSomhairle'. The warriors referred to are almost certainly galloglasses, and the 160 fighting men with which Aed returned have been seen as the dowry of Dugald's daughter. Moreover, the association of the warriors with 'Ailin MacSomhairle' (Alan MacRuairi) seems to indicate that he was a captain of galloglasses, and if this is so then by the late thirteenth century all three of the branches descended from Somerled were involved in the business of supplying mercenary troops. It is even possible that the death of 'MacSomhairle, king of Airer-Goidel', in 1247 in the strife between Maurice fitz Gerald and the Cenell Conaill at Ballyshannon, is related to galloglass activity; this is the first, but by no means the last, instance in which a king of the Isles is found in the service of an Irish king.[93]

By about 1300, then, a constant stream of mercenaries was flowing from the Hebrides to Ireland, and they were a prominent feature of the Bruce invasion between 1315 and 1318.[94] But one of the major questions surrounding the rise of the galloglasses is why this should have occurred in the middle of the thirteenth century. One explanation is that the poor economic conditions of the region offered few other outlets.[95] But if this is at least partly true it is not wholly convincing, and the tradition of Hebridean fighting men serving in Ireland is connected to the dynamics of the political situation in Argyll and the Isles, where royal

---

[93] *Ann. Conn.*, pp. 91, 131, 185; *Ann. Loch Cé*, i, pp. 377, 431, 457.
[94] *Ann. Conn.*, p. 249; *Ann. Ulster*, ii, p. 429; *Ann. Loch Cé*, i, p. 595.
[95] Duncan and Brown, 'Argyll and the Isles', p. 216.

authority and feudalism were pressed forward in the thirteenth century
and where the Bruce–Balliol conflicts and the Anglo-Scottish wars of the
late thirteenth and early fourteenth centuries upset the equilibrium of
the descendants of Somerled. The origins of the MacSweens as galloglasses,
for example, is no doubt connected with their expulsion from Knapdale
by 1262 at the hands of the Stewarts, while MacDougall involvement as
galloglasses must have gained impetus from the time of their defeat at
the hands of Robert Bruce in 1309. Still another consideration in the
rise of the galloglasses is the general militarisation taking place in
contemporary Irish society. From the eleventh century Irish kings had
become increasingly ambitious about conquering new territories, and
had sought soldiers wherever they could find them. By the middle of the
thirteenth century the more important Irish kings were actively involved
in checking English expansion, and the galloglasses provided an
important and very effective source of manpower. Finally, it is important
to bear in mind that the rise of the galloglasses owed much to the long-
standing connections between the west of Scotland and Ireland; without
these links, the use of foreign warriors by Gaelic Irish kings from the
middle of the thirteenth century would be inconceivable.[96]

Barrow has suggested that the Hebridean chieftains, 'had not absorbed
the sub-French culture of eastern and southern lands, nor could they
share the Scots culture of east-country gentry, burghers and peas-
antry'.[97] It might be more accurate to state that the ruling order in the
West had not absorbed the sub-French culture that characterised much
of twelfth and thirteenth-century Europe to the same degree as their
counterparts in the eastern and southern regions of Scotland. The
political integration of the West into the Scottish kingdom between 1264
and 1293 was accompanied by an equally profound, though perhaps
more subtle, transformation in society as Gaelic and Gaelic-Norse nobles
adapted themselves to the conventions of Scottish society. The process
did not begin with the cession of the Western Isles to Scotland in 1266,
but it was certainly accelerated in the decades between the Treaty of
Perth and the first parliament of John Balliol, and it is reflected in many
mediums. Thus, the Hebridean chieftains utilised Latin charters; they
adopted patterns of naming and matrimony that reflected a Scottish
influence; they entered into feudal relationships with the Scottish
monarchy; they adopted the status and terminology of knighthood; and
they even engaged in long-distance trade and commerce.

[96] On the galloglasses, see G. A. Hayes-McCoy, *Scots Mercenary Forces in Ireland
(1565–1603)* (Dublin and London, 1937), pp. 4–35; A. McKerral, 'West Highland
mercenaries in Ireland', *SHR*, xxx (1951); J. Lydon, 'The Scottish soldier in medieval
Ireland: the Bruce invasion and the galloglass', in G. G. Simpson (ed.), *The Scottish
Soldier Abroad, 1247–1967* (Edinburgh, 1992); and K. Nicholls, *Gaelic and Gaelicised
Ireland in the Middle Ages* (Dublin, 1972), pp. 87–90.
[97] Barrow, *Kingdom of the Scots*, p. 382.

All of this had the result that a hybrid society emerged in the West, paralleling the rest of the thirteenth century kingdom which has been seen as possessing a 'hybrid kingship, hybrid institutions, hybrid law, a hybrid church, and an increasingly hybrid landowning class'.[98] Indeed, it might be argued that processes whereby the MacSorleys adapted themselves to the new conventions mirrored those whereby the Scottish kingdom itself had been transformed in the twelfth and thirteenth centuries: it was a transition from above, instigated by the Scottish kings in the East and the MacSorleys in the West; it was attained largely through peaceful means, rather than by military conquest; and the balance between old and new in both east and west is certainly striking. Historians have come to regard the Lordship of the Isles in the fourteenth and fifteenth centuries as a hybrid Gaelic-feudal institution, but to do so may under-emphasise the degree to which society in the western seaboard in the thirteenth century was already well on its way towards such hybrid status.

[98] A. Grant, 'Scotland's "Celtic Fringe" in the late Middle Ages: the MacDonald Lords of the Isles and the kingdom of Scotland', in Davies, *British Isles*, p. 119.

CHAPTER SIX

MacDougalls, MacDonalds and MacRuairis in the Wars of Independence, *c*.1293–1329

Yis Ihon off Lorne hattyt ye king
For Ihon Cumyn his emys sak ...

* * *

Angus off Ile yat tyme wes syr
And lord and ledar off Kyntyr,
Ye king rycht weill resawyt he
And wndertuk his man to be ...

[John Barbour, *c*.1375][1]

In the previous chapter we saw how, in the decades between the Treaty of Perth and the first parliament of John Balliol, the western seaboard was brought in from the margins and integrated into the community of the realm of Scotland. A by-product of this integration was that the West would be, almost for the first time, directly affected by events unfolding beyond Drumalban, in the Scottish kingdom itself; and, conversely, that Hebridean chieftains would play a prominent role in the Anglo-Scottish conflicts that characterise the later thirteenth and early fourteenth century in Scottish history:

> the most important political consequence [of the cession of the West to Scotland] was that the Lords of the Isles and their followers now became much more involved in the internal affairs of the kingdom of Scotland. Very soon we find them taking sides in the wars of Independence.[2]

Thus, some of Robert Bruce's most implacable enemies were the MacDougall lords of Argyll, while he received considerable aid from the MacDonalds of Islay and the MacRuairis of Garmoran. The roles of the descendants of Somerled in the Wars of Independence are a further reflection of the new-found place of the western seaboard in the Scottish kingdom; indeed, it might be said that the Scottish civil conflicts and Anglo-Scottish wars of the late thirteenth and early fourteenth centuries

[1] Barbour, *Bruce*, ii, p. 154 (bk. vi, ll. 504–5); ii, p. 69 (bk. iii, ll. 659–62).
[2] Steer and Bannerman, *Late Medieval Monumental Sculpture*, p. 202.

were the crucible in which the integration of the West into the Scottish kingdom was tested.

The dominant theme of Hebridean politics in the later thirteenth and early fourteenth century – from about 1286 to 1329 – is the struggle for dominance between the MacDougalls and the MacDonalds. Traditionally, the two kindreds are regarded as occupying opposing sides in the Scottish civil war and the Anglo-Scottish conflict:

> The tribe of Dugald, son of Somerled, took the side of the Baliols, and the race of Ranald, son of Somerled, the side of Robert Bruce, and all the garrisons from Dingwall in Ross to the Mull of Kintyre were in the possession of MacDugald during that time, while the tribe of Ranald were under the yoke of their enemies.[3]

Other traditions suggest that the MacDonalds themselves were divided in their allegiance to the Bruce cause, but acknowledge that the MacDougalls remained steadfast in their opposition:

> [Angus Óg MacDonald] was always a follower of King Robert Bruce in all his wars ... But Alexander, Angus' brother ... being married to a daughter of Macdougall of Lorn, otherwise called John Baccach, or Lame ... would by no means own King Robert's quarrell [sic], but fought always against him with Macdougall, and likewise with Macdougall against his brother Angus ... For the MacDougalls for a long time fought against the MacDonalds.[4]

The reality is better reflected in the contemporary documents, which become more abundant for the 1290s, and reveal a much more complicated situation than these late sources suggest. By 1296 Angus Mór's son, Alexander Óg, who was a hostage at Ayr for the good behaviour of his father in 1264 or 1266,[5] was in the forefront of events in the western seaboard, although the problem of his allegiances during the turbulent decade of the 1290s has yet to be satisfactorily explained. It is not, however, Alexander Óg, but rather his younger brother, Angus Óg, who is best known for his role in the Anglo-Scottish conflict and who is generally regarded as a consistent supporter of Bruce. His role, too, needs to be clarified, for although he was certainly instrumental in the Bruce cause from about 1306, his early allegiance was not to Bruce but rather, with his brother, to Edward I. The struggle between the Clan Dougall and the Clan Donald is not, therefore, as straightforward as is often suggested, and must be viewed within the context of the dynamics of both the Scottish civil conflict and the Anglo-Scottish wars.

---

[3] *Clanranald Bk.*, p. 157; compare Gregory, *History of the Western Highlands and Isles of Scotland*, p. 24.

[4] Macdonald, *Hist. Macdonalds, HP*, i, pp. 14–15.

[5] *ER*, i, p. 5. The provision for a nurse in these accounts suggests that Alexander was a child in the mid-1260s.

In March 1286, King Alexander III was killed in a night-time riding mishap. Both his son and heir, Alexander, and his daughter, Margaret, the queen of Norway, had predeceased him, and the sole surviving representative of the ancient Scottish royal line was his infant grand-daughter, Margaret, 'the Maid of Norway'. She had been acknowledged as Alexander's heir at a council in 1284, and by the summer of 1290 her marriage to the heir of Edward I of England had been negotiated and had received the consent of the Scottish nobles in the treaty of Birgham, which obtained safeguards for Scottish independence. But these plans were nullified when, in September 1290, the little girl died at Kirkwall, Orkney, *en route* to Scotland, turning a simple accident on a stormy night in 1286 into a dynastic tragedy and a succession crisis that would shatter the relatively peaceful conditions of the thirteenth century.

Even before the death of the Maid of Norway in 1290, storm clouds were brewing on the horizon. Within a few weeks of Alexander III's fatal accident, Margaret's claim was probably challenged in parliament by Robert Bruce 'the Competitor', the aged lord of Annandale and grandfather of the future Robert I, who advanced his own claim as a descendant of King David I; soon afterwards John Balliol, the Lord of Galloway, another descendant of David I, appears to have arrived to contest the Bruce claim and advance his own. For two years Scotland teetered on the brink of civil war; and it is hardly surprising that, following the death of the Maid of Norway in 1290, with war between Bruce and Balliol and their supporters threatening, Edward I of England was invited to arbitrate in the dispute. Although Edward's motives concerning the Scottish succession have often been the subject of considerable debate, he was a logical choice as an experienced ruler and arbitrator, and by June 1291 he had secured his recognition as overlord of Scotland by the various competitors and their promise that they would abide by his decision. With these preliminaries out of the way, the first session of the drawn-out lawsuit known as the 'Great Cause' on the Scottish succession got underway in August 1291. It began with the determination of the composition of the court, which was to consist of 104 auditors: twenty-four were nominated by Edward, forty by two of the competitors, Balliol and his kinsman, John Comyn, and forty more by Robert Bruce. After several lengthy recesses and long and convoluted legal discussions, Edward finally delivered a judgement in favour of Balliol in mid-November 1292. King John was inaugurated at Scone on 30 November, and finally, on 26 December, he did homage to Edward I at Newcastle; more ominously, he was made to repudiate the terms of the Treaty of Birgham and all of the other safeguards of Scottish liberty.

John Balliol's kingship lasted scarcely four years. His position had been made increasingly difficult by demands that he appear in person at parliament in England to answer for his own court's decisions; in effect, appeals were now permitted to go directly from Scotland to England, which undermined the authority and independence of the Scottish king. This had been explicitly prohibited by the treaty of Birgham: 'If not designed deliberately to make the new king's position intolerable, there can be no doubt that the English measures were meant to demonstrate that a Scottish ruler was now no more than one of the king of England's feudal barons ...'[6] The last straw was a demand that King John and many of his nobles should provide feudal military service for King Edward in his war with Philip IV of France. In 1295, control of the Scottish government was taken out of King John's hands, and in early 1296, the Scots ratified a treaty with France. These actions clearly implied war between Scotland and England.

The war began in March 1296, when the Scots army, led by John Comyn, Balliol's kinsman, mustered and attacked Carlisle; Edward I responded by attacking and sacking Berwick at the end of March, massacring many of its inhabitants. A month later, on 27 April 1296, the Scottish army was overwhelmed at Dunbar, and many Scottish nobles hastened to submit to Edward. On 2 July, John Balliol was forced to append his seal to a document admitting his wrongdoing, and to surrender his kingdom and people into the hands of Edward I. He was then ceremonially stripped of his royal attire, and left Scotland, never to return. Edward made a triumphant progress through Scotland, as far north as Elgin, during the summer of 1296, in the course of which he collected the fealty of many Scottish nobles. At the end of August more submissions were made in a Parliament at Berwick, and, before departing for the south, the English king appointed governors to rule Scotland on his behalf.[7]

How did these turbulent events affect the MacSorleys, and what roles did they play in them? It is certainly possible, in the years between 1286 and 1296, to discern a polarisation in the allegiances of the two main kindreds descended from Somerled, the MacDougalls and the MacDonalds. In 1286, Angus Mór, the son of Donald, and his eldest son, Alexander Óg, were members of the 'Turnberry Band', along with the Bruces, James Stewart, and two Scottish earls. The context of the document is, admittedly, not easy to discern. Although its wording reflects a Bruce claim to the kingship, it is perhaps more significant that its members agreed to support the earl of Ulster, Richard de Burgh, and Thomas de Clare, against their Irish adversaries. The Turnberry Band is, indeed, often seen in the light of affairs in Ireland, where de Burgh and de Clare had been campaigning against the Irish in Connacht in both 1285

---

[6] Barrow, *Kingship and Unity*, p. 162.
[7] On these events in general, see Nicholson, *Later Middle Ages*, chaps. 2–3; Barrow, *Robert Bruce*, chaps. 1–5; A. A. M. Duncan, 'The community of the realm of Scotland and Robert Bruce: a review', *SHR*, xlv (1966); and A. A. M. Duncan, *The Nation of Scots and the Declaration of Arbroath* (Historical Association, 1970).

and 1286; since Robert Bruce the Competitor was a nephew by marriage to Thomas de Clare, it has been suggested that the Anglo-Irish lords were in fact enlisting support in Scotland for an Irish expedition. However, it is important to bear in mind that Bruce was unlikely to become involved in Ireland without reciprocation, and it has been suggested that he was seeking Irish troops for an anticipated contest with Balliol.[8]

Whatever the context, the inclusion in the agreement of Angus Mór, one of the most powerful magnates of the western seaboard, was natural. His activities in an Irish sphere have already been noted in the previous chapter, and it is not unreasonable to suppose that he may have been responsible for supplying galleys and Hebridean fighting men (*gallóclaig*) for enterprises in Ireland, or that Hebridean troops may have been sought by Robert Bruce.[9] Moreover, an alliance between the Bruces and the Clan Donald made sense in geopolitical terms, too. With their chief castle at Turnberry on the Ayrshire coast, the Bruces were, in a sense, west-coast magnates themselves, and their power base lay in close proximity to the lords of Islay. But there is more to it than simple facts of geography, and it has been argued that the Bruces were well integrated into Gaelic society.[10] In this context it is surely significant to note that Robert Bruce the lord of Annandale and Robert Bruce his son appear as witnesses to a charter of Alexander of the Isles to Paisley Abbey, sometime before the death of King Alexander in 1286.[11] In his analysis of Bruce's followers, G. W. S. Barrow has pointed out that many were, in fact, neighbouring lords like the Souleses, Lindsays, and Biggars, and Angus Mór and his son should probably also be seen as falling into this category as well.[12]

If it is not surprising to find the MacDonalds adhering to the Bruce cause, it is even more natural to find the Clan Dougall of Argyll supporting the Balliols, although here the motivation is certainly more straightforward. The adherence of the MacDougalls to Balliol was based upon ties of kinship, for Alexander of Argyll, the son of Ewen, was married to a daughter of John Comyn 'the Red'. Since the Comyns were, in turn, allied to the Balliols through marriage – John Balliol's sister had married John Comyn – it was natural for Alexander to support the Balliol cause, along with his kinsmen, the Comyns. This connection is nicely reflected in the choice of Alexander of Argyll as one of the forty auditors chosen by Balliol in August 1291 to adjudicate in

---

8 Stevenson, *Documents*, i, no. 12. See Powicke, *Thirteenth Century*, p. 598, and note; Barrow, *Robert Bruce*, pp. 25–6; Nicholson, *Later Middle Ages*, pp. 28–9; and A. A. M. Duncan, 'The Scots' invasion of Ireland, 1315', in Davies, *British Isles*, p. 101.
9 See McKerral, 'West Highland mercenaries'.
10 Duffy, 'Bruce brothers', pp. 72–4, with examples.
11 *Paisley Reg.*, p. 129.
12 Barrow, *Robert Bruce*, p. 50.

the Great Cause; it has been noted that many of Balliol's most important auditors were related to him by blood.[13]

It is difficult to know how the kindred of Somerled reacted to the decision in favour of Balliol's claim to the Scottish kingship in November 1292, for the evidence is patchy. But it is certainly noteworthy that, at John Balliol's first parliament in February, 1293, Alexander of Argyll was, as we have seen, appointed sheriff of Lorn and became the king's representative in a large part of the western seaboard. Although it might be tempting to regard this appointment as a reward for his support, it is important to recall that Alexander had also held a wide-ranging lieutenancy in the West during the reign of King Alexander III, which should caution against such a view. Alexander of Argyll's position probably depended more upon his status as a prominent landholder in the region than upon his adherence to the Balliol cause, although it certainly must have owed something to his allegiance and service to the Scottish king. At the same time, it is noteworthy that Angus Mór, the head of the Clan Donald, absented himself from the parliament of February 1293. Moreover, a few weeks later, as we have seen, Alexander of Argyll was ordered in his capacity as sheriff to summon Angus Mór and several other landholders of the West to perform homage. It is, once again, tempting to speculate that the MacDonalds were following the lead of the Bruces, for in November 1292, Robert Bruce Earl of Carrick, son of the Competitor, refused to do homage to Balliol, tried to transfer the earldom to his son (the future king),[14] and went to Norway. But however we interpret the Clan Donald's attitude to Balliol's accession, the way that the MacDonalds and the MacDougalls adhered to opposite sides during the period of the Guardianship, the Great Cause, and Balliol's kingship does neatly mirror the wider division of the Scottish nobility during these troubled years.

As we have seen, it was the question of Scottish appeals to King Edward I which caused part of the crisis in the authority of John Balliol's kingship. It is noteworthy that, of six Scottish appellants to Edward, no fewer than three were of Hebridean or Manx origin; and the most important of these was none other than Alexander of the Isles, the eldest son of Angus Mór. The appeal of Alexander to the English king, or, more accurately, the dispute that underlay it, provides the key to understanding the dynamics of the politics of the later 1290s in the western seaboard.

The roots of the dispute and subsequent appeal lie in a marriage alliance between the Clan Donald and the Clan Dougall. Sometime

---

[13] Stones and Simpson, *Edward I and the Throne of Scotland*, ii, p. 220; E. M. Barron, *The Scottish War of Independence: A Critical Study* (London, 1914), pp. 110–11.

[14] The transfer was blocked by King John, who insisted that Carrick be taken into royal hands; the younger Robert Bruce can only have gained the earldom after doing homage to Balliol and paying his relief. See *APS*, i, p. 447. I am grateful to Dr Grant for this point.

before 1292, Alexander of the Isles married Juliana, either a sister or, less probably, a daughter, of Alexander of Argyll. This marriage seems to have sparked a dispute between the two kindreds, and in 1292 the two Alexanders referred a territorial dispute to King John, although neither the identity of the lands nor the outcome is known. Then, in 1295, Alexander of the Isles appealed to Edward I. In his complaint, it was alleged that John Balliol had occupied part of Lismore and was refusing to hand it over to Alexander and his wife.[15] Since Alexander was joined in his complaint by Juliana, Lismore has been seen as representing her dowry; the fact that it was occupied by Balliol means that the earlier judgement had gone against the family of the Isles.

The decade of the worst Anglo-Scottish warfare, between 1296 and 1306, was also marked by extreme unrest in the western seaboard, and the impression left by the surviving documentation is that Edward I had very little control over the affairs of the West. Alexander of Argyll had, like most of the Scottish nobles, sworn loyalty to Edward I in the summer of 1296 at Elgin, and his name also appears in the so-called Ragman Rolls from the parliament at Berwick in late August.[16] But despite this, he seems to have been distrusted by Edward,[17] possibly because of his kinship to the Comyns and Balliols, or possibly because of the ongoing dispute between him and his MacDonald namesake. Whatever the case, we enter a period of some five years, between late summer 1296, and June 1301, when the MacDougalls were clearly out of favour with Edward. Thus, on 10 September, 1296, Alexander, Earl of Menteith, the son of Earl Walter, who had displaced the MacSweens of Knapdale in 1262, was granted a commission to take possession of the 'castles, fortresses, islands and all the lands' belonging to Alexander of Argyll and his son, John, who, it was said, 'have not yet come into our peace'.[18]

It would appear that Edward's wishes were successfully executed, for we next hear of Alexander as a prisoner at Berwick Castle. Edward I authorised his release in May 1297, and in that same month Alexander's son, John, was named among those magnates invited to accompany Edward I on a military campaign in Flanders.[19] The invitation to John to accompany Edward, coming so close on the heels of his father's release from incarceration, has all the appearance of the son serving as a hostage for the good behaviour of the father. But to judge by subsequent references it is unlikely that John accompanied the expedition; this is perhaps just as well, since almost immediately upon his release Alexander was the prime mover of unrest in the western seaboard again.

[15] *Rot. Scot.*, i, p. 21.
[16] *CDS*, ii, nos. 791, 823.
[17] MacDonald, *History of Argyll*, p. 123.
[18] *Rot. Scot.*, i, p. 31.
[19] Ibid., p. 40; Stevenson, *Documents*, ii, no. 429; *CDS*, ii, no. 884.

It seems clear that Alexander of Argyll and his son, John, were pursuing an aggressive policy of expansion in the 1290s that both fed on the lawlessness in the western seaboard and added to it. Two reports, written by Alexander of Islay to King Edward I in the summer of 1297, claim that Alexander of Argyll had been active in the West, plundering and devastating MacDonald lands after his release from incarceration in May. Alexander of Islay complained that, having come to the king's peace at Elgin (in the summer of 1296) and then having been released from captivity (May 1297), Alexander MacDougall had laid waste the writer's lands, 'and the men living in the same lands were killed, and fires were set, and many other evils were done'. At the conclusion of the letter, Alexander begged Edward to instruct the nobles of Argyll and Ross to aid him in keeping the peace; perhaps he was either holding or aspiring to hold the lieutenancy previously enjoyed by his MacDougall namesake.[20] According to a second letter, Alexander of Argyll was also guilty of providing refuge to other enemies of Edward in the West. He complained that the lord of Argyll had given refuge to his kinsman Lachlan MacRuairi after he escaped from custody, and that Alexander had aided him in fitting out massive war galleys. The letter concluded with a reminder to the English king that none of the money Alexander of Islay had been promised for his service had yet been received.[21]

But the Clan Donald was not the only kindred to feel the thrust of MacDougall expansion in the 1290s. Sometime around 1296, John of Argyll defeated the Campbells and killed their leader, Colin Mór, in an encounter at the String of Lorn, a stretch of territory between Loch Avich and Loch Scamadale. The seventeenth-century *Genealogie of the Campbells* relates how Colin Campbell was also known as 'Coline na Sreinge' that is, of the String,

> because in a fight with mcCoul [MacDougall] of Lorn in the mountain betwixt Lochow and Lorn called the String after he had put the mcCouls [MacDougalls] to flight throw his eager persuing the chase and forcing a pass called the a-dhearg that is to say the red foord he was unfortunately killed and a heap of stones ... stands near that place as a monument of it to this day.[22]

It may be as a result of this victory over the Campbells that we find Alexander of Argyll in control of revenues of the Campbell lands of Lochawe and Ardskeodnish in 1304–5;[23] certainly the evidence points to the fortunes of the Campbells taking a downturn at this time. So, too, apparently, did those of the long-suffering MacSweens; in 1301 we find

---

20 Stevenson, *Documents*, ii, no. 444.
21 Ibid., ii, no. 445.
22 *HP*, ii, pp. 84–5. A variant of the manuscript names John of Argyll as the leader of the MacDougalls who defeated Colin.
23 *CDS*, ii, no. 1646 (p. 439).

John MacSween making a complaint to the English king that John of Argyll had entered his lands with an armed band and, in co-operation with Sir John Menteith, was preventing him from inhabiting them. This may explain why John MacSween was in the service of the English in 1301; no doubt John hoped that faithful service would advance his cause and see him re-established in Knapdale. But if that was the case, he was to be disappointed, for in 1310 he and his brothers won a grant from the English king of the whole land of Knapdale – provided that they could recover it from the hands of their enemies. The Gaelic poem that recounts the 'tryst of a fleet against Castle Sween' probably refers to their attempt to regain Knapdale, but the MacSweens were never successful in pursuing their claim, and ended up as galloglasses in Ireland.[24]

Alexander of Islay, and his younger brother, Angus Óg, were, in contrast to their MacDougall kinsmen, the ready, willing, and apparently able agents of Edward I between early 1296 and at least 1301. As early as April, 1296, Alexander of Islay was appointed as Edward's bailiff, and in this capacity he was ordered to seize Kintyre, which had been escheated by John Balliol, and to give possession of it to Malcolm 'le fiz Lengleys'.[25] The identity of this Malcolm, whose surname is given as 'le fiz Lengleys', 'son of the Englishman', or sometimes as simply 'le Engleys', 'the Englishman', remains unknown; it has been suggested that, because his claim was to part of Kintyre, he might have been a member of the MacSween family, ousted from Knapdale in 1262 by the earl of Menteith, or else that he might be the same individual as Malcolm MacCulian who appears holding lands in Kintyre in 1306.[26]

A letter of Alexander to Edward I, from the summer of 1296, requested clarification of the king's earlier instructions. Kintyre, said Alexander, had many tenants-in-chief, and they should not be impleaded except by lawful inquest. Alexander stated that he had already taken possession of the lands of the Stewart in Kintyre and was poised to take his castle (Dunaverty), but he requested further instructions.[27] Edward's reply to his bailiff is, unfortunately, not known, but in September 1296 Edward awarded Alexander £100 worth of lands as a reward for the 'good service' that he had shown in the past and would continue to show in the future.[28] It is interesting to note that in several of these documents from 1296 Alexander is referred to as 'our beloved' by Edward I, which, although formulaic, clearly demonstrates the favour in which he was held, just as the incarceration of Alexander of Argyll in

24 Stevenson, *Documents*, ii, no. 616; *Rot. Scot.*, i, p. 90; *Book of Dean of Lismore*, pp. 7–13, and notes on pp. 257–9.
25 *Rot. Scot.*, i, p. 22; *CDS*, ii, no. 853.
26 Barrow, *Robert Bruce*, p. 58.
27 *CDS*, v, no. 152; full document and discussion in Dunbar and Duncan, 'Tarbert Castle', pp. 3–5, and appendix, p. 16.
28 Stevenson, *Documents*, i, no. 390.

the same period illustrates how far out of favour that branch of the descendants of Somerled had fallen.

It is also at this time that Alexander's younger (and more famous) brother, Angus Óg, appears on the scene. Like his brother, he was active in the cause of the English king. In 1297 he acted in concert with his brother against the predatory activities of the MacRuairis, his kinsmen, and in 1301 he lent considerable assistance to naval operations against the MacDougalls. In a letter to Edward I from that same year, Angus Óg asked whether Alexander of Argyll had submitted, and, if he had not, Angus requested instructions so that he could assist Hugh Bisset in destroying Alexander, along with Edward's other enemies in the West; in this letter Angus refers to himself as Edward's 'humble and faithful servant'.[29] Another letter of 1301, this time by Hugh Bisset, stated that Angus Óg had been active, along with John MacSween, in naval activities against the MacDougalls in the vicinity of Bute and Kintyre.[30]

In striving to understand the relations between the two Alexanders in the years from 1295 to about 1300, the dispute over Lismore, which had been simmering since at least 1292, and which was an open sore between the two kindreds, is crucial. In the first instance, this dispute ensured that the Clan Donald and the Clan Dougall were polarised to opposite sides of the Scottish civil conflict: 'the successful pursuit of his [Alexander of Islay's] claim would have been wholly dependent on his own efforts. In these circumstances, Alexander would have been eager to act as Edward's agent against the Macdougalls.'[31] But even more importantly, the activities of the MacDonalds and MacDougalls, and especially the destruction of 1297, is only intelligible when seen as an extension of this conflict. Indeed, it is tempting to view the west-coast warfare of 1297–1301 as nothing more or less than a continuation of the dispute that had apparently begun in 1292 and which flourished in the environment of relaxed royal authority in the West brought about by the Scottish civil war and foreign conflict with England. Certainly patriotism seems to have had little to do with the allegiances of the MacDonalds and MacDougalls in the 1290s; the former were simply using Edward I to help them attain their goal and, presumably, obtain their lands on Lismore; and, if kinship with the Comyn–Balliol faction was a motivating factor in the actions of the MacDougalls, then the fury of their attacks on the MacDonalds and others in 1297 looks very much like the settling of old scores.

The situation between 1301 and 1306 in the West is relatively clear for the MacDougalls, but much less so for the MacDonalds. It was, in all probability, the naval activities of the MacDonalds and others referred to above that eventually forced Alexander and John of Argyll to submit to

29 Ibid., i, no. 615.
30 Ibid., i, no. 614.
31 W. D. Lamont, 'Alexander of Islay, son of Angus Mór', *SHR*, lx (1981), p. 163.

the authority of the English king. In June 1301, Edward I empowered the Admiral and Captain of the Cinque Ports to receive Alexander of Argyll, his sons John and Duncan, and other members of the family into the king's peace.[32] The submission of the MacDougalls had certainly been made good by 1304, in which year Edward I wrote to John of Argyll to excuse him from coming to Parliament at St Andrews by reason of his illness; the English king added that 'we have great confidence in you and your loyalty', and further urged John to remain active in keeping the peace in his territory.[33] For his part, Alexander also appears to have entered the king's peace. As we have seen, in 1304–5 he rendered account for some Campbell lands in Argyll, and in September 1305, when Edward I appointed John of Brittany as his lieutenant in Scotland, Alexander of Argyll was among those named to his advisory council.[34] From about 1304–5, then, the MacDougalls became adherents of the English king; it was a position that was to be buttressed by the murder of their kinsman, John Comyn, by Robert Bruce in 1306.

In contrast to the MacDougalls, there is a dearth of evidence for the MacDonalds between 1301 and 1306; indeed, both Alexander and Angus Óg vanish from the record during these years. The major difficulty is determining when Alexander passed from the scene and was replaced by his brother, Angus Óg. Generations of historians have puzzled over the fate of Alexander MacDonald, and his activity, or lack of it, between 1297 and 1308. Some have argued, on the basis of the chronicle of John of Fordun (who was himself very confused at this point) that he was captured in Galloway by Edward Bruce in 1308; while others have suggested, not very convincingly, that Alexander was less influential with the MacDonald clansmen and was eventually displaced by his brother, Angus Óg.[35] These explanations are unsatisfactory, and to answer the question of what happened to Alexander MacDonald we must look to contemporary Irish annals.

The *Annals of Ulster* record, under the year 1299, that:

Alexander MacDomnaill, the person who was the best for hospitality and excellence that was in Ireland and in Scotland, was killed, together with a countless number of his own people that were slaughtered around him, by Alexander MacDubghaill.[36]

---

[32] Stevenson, *Documents*, ii, no. 610.

[33] Ibid., ii, no. 637.

[34] Palgrave, *Docs. Hist. Scot.*, i, no. 145.

[35] MacDonald and MacDonald, *Clan Donald*, i, p. 88; MacDonald, *History of Argyll*, pp. 126–7.

[36] *Ann. Ulster*, ii, p. 393. Although it seems most likely to me that the Alexander MacDomnaill killed in 1299 was the brother of Angus Óg, this identification is not conclusive, and a great deal of uncertainty surrounds the MacDonald genealogy at this point. Seán Duffy has regarded the Alexander who perished in 1299 not as Alexander Óg, the son of Angus Mór, but rather as Angus Mór's brother of the same name, while David Sellar is inclined to the view that it was Alexander Óg who was

This contemporary account has often been overlooked by historians, but it provides the most straightforward account of Alexander's fate. He was not on the scene between 1301 and 1308 because he was dead, and his demise at the hands of Alexander MacDougall must surely be seen as the final act in the ongoing dispute over Lismore that had been simmering since 1292, and which was played out in the West with particular violence in the chaotic years 1296–7. The death of Alexander of the Isles by his kinsman and namesake in 1299 goes far towards explaining the intensive naval activities of the MacDonalds, Bissets, and MacSweens in 1301 to subdue Alexander of Argyll. Moreover, there is other contemporary evidence to support the view that Alexander had passed from the scene by 1301. It may be no coincidence that, in his letter to Edward I in 1301, Angus Óg styles himself 'de Yle', the designation reserved for the head of the kindred; moreover, it is apparent from the content of the letters that he had taken over the campaign against the MacDougalls from his brother. Although it was his brother who had defeated the MacRuairis in 1297 and taken them into custody, it was Angus who was holding them and who was negotiating with Edward on their behalf in 1301.[37] It is also noteworthy that John Barbour makes no mention of Alexander in his epic poem, *The Bruce*, and this seems to suggest that he was unaware of the existence of Alexander.[38] Taken altogether, then, the evidence seems overwhelmingly to indicate Alexander's having been removed from the scene by 1301.

On 10 February 1306, Robert Bruce killed his rival, John Comyn, in the Greyfriars' church at Dumfries. The underlying motivation behind the meeting of the two men, as well as the circumstances of the murder, remain problematic, but the event, followed by Bruce's inauguration at Scone on 25 March, changed the complexion of the whole conflict, and added a new dimension as well. Bruce's murder of John Comyn, and his seizure of the throne, made the Comyns and their kinsmen his bitter foes, and from 1306 there was civil war between the Balliol–Comyn and Bruce factions in addition to the war between England and Scotland. As one authority has put it, 'To Robert I's Scottish enemies, English overlordship was a lesser evil than Bruce kingship, and so the Balliol–Comyn faction, hitherto prominent upholders of Scottish independence, allied with the English.'[39] Accordingly, if the murder of Comyn and the installation of Bruce as king signalled a revolution in Scotland, it also produced a revolution in the politics of the western

killed. S. Duffy, 'The "Continuation" of Nicholas Trevet: a new source for the Bruce invasion', *Proceedings of the Royal Irish Academy*, xci (1991), pp. 311–12; compare W. D. H. Sellar, 'MacDonald and MacRuari pedigrees in MS 1467', *West Highland Notes and Queries*, xxviii (1986), p. 7.

[37] Stevenson, *Documents*, ii, no. 615.
[38] Lamont, 'Alexander of Islay', p. 164.
[39] Grant, *Independence and Nationhood*, p. 4.

Highlands. So long as Balliol had been king, the MacDonalds had been pro-English and the MacDougalls had upheld the Scottish cause. But the events of 1306 swept the magnates of the western seaboard along in their train. Alexander and John MacDougall, kinsmen of Comyn and Balliol, were thrown into the English camp by the murder of John Comyn, and remained Bruce's implacable foes until their deaths. Barbour tells us several times, emphatically, that the enmity of John MacDougall toward Robert Bruce was based upon the former's kinship to the murdered Comyn:

> Yis Ihon off Lorne hattyt ye king
> For Ihon Cumyn his emys sak,
> Micht he hym oyer sla or tak
> He wald nocht prys his liff a stra
> Sa yat he wengeance of him mycht ta.[40]

The MacDougall desire for vengeance upon the king was not long in coming. Within three months of his inauguration at Scone, Bruce was a fugitive. On 19 June he had been defeated by the English at Methven, near Perth, and many of his supporters were captured and felt the vengeful wrath of Edward I. Following the defeat at Methven, Bruce and his remaining supporters fled west to Drumalban, the mountainous region that divides Perthshire from Argyll, hoping to find refuge in the remoteness of the West Highlands.[41] At the head of Strathfillan, at Dalry (Dail Righ) near Tyndrum, Bruce found his route blocked by the men of Lorn, probably led by John MacDougall, who inflicted a second defeat on the fugitive king. The chronology of the events of the summer of 1306, including the date of the so-called battle of Dalry, is problematic.[42] The fourteenth-century chronicler, John of Fordun, placed Bruce's defeat at Dalry in August 1306, but this may be too late. It seems more likely, based on the evidence of subsequent movements by the English, that the encounter between John of Argyll and Robert Bruce must have taken place in July, either the 13th or the 30th.[43] Whatever may have been the case, the impact of this second defeat, coming within about a month of that at Methven, was profound. From this point, Bruce and his men took to the mountains as fugitives and ceased to form an organised fighting force.[44] Moreover, the dual defeats at Dalry and Methven paved the way for the subsequent capture and imprisonment or execution of many of Bruce's followers, including his wife and daughter and his brother, Neil. Thus, the MacDougalls had played a prominent role in

40 Barbour, *Bruce*, ii, p. 154 (bk. vi, ll. 504–8; see also bk. iii, ll. 1–5 (p. 46).
41 Barrow, *Robert Bruce*, p. 160.
42 Professor Duncan has pointed out that there was an encounter between Robert and the English, at Loch Tay, following Methven: A. A. M. Duncan, 'The War of the Scots, 1306–23', *Trans Royal Hist. Soc.*, 6th ser., ii (1992), p. 138.
43 *Chron. Fordun*, i, p. 342; ii, p. 334–5; Barrow, *Robert Bruce*, p. 160–1.
44 Ibid.

the opening stages of the Scottish civil conflict. They dealt Bruce and his cause a crippling blow, which ultimately forced the king to flee from Scotland in the closing months of 1306.

But if the murder of John Comyn had earned Bruce the enmity of the Comyns, Balliols, and their allies, including the MacDougalls, then it also ensured that other families were his supporters. We have seen that Angus Óg, the brother of Alexander and the son of Angus Mór, seems to have succeeded his brother as lord of Islay around 1299, following the death of Alexander at the hands of his MacDougall namesake in that same year. Angus was still active in 1301 in the service of the English king against the renegade MacDougalls, but from then until 1306 he disappears from the scene. When he re-emerges in the pages of Barbour's *Bruce*, it is as a supporter of Robert Bruce. When and why did Angus Óg shift allegiances? And how accurate is Barbour on the role of Angus?

Writers from at least the nineteenth century until the present day have been prone to explain Angus's shift into the Bruce faction on so-called noble grounds, or else, at the very least, as representing the 'traditional' Bruce–MacDonald alliance that stretched back to the Turnberry Band of 1286.[45] But, as we have seen, there was no traditional alliance between the MacDonalds and the Bruces: both Alexander and Angus Óg had acted as Edward I's agents in the West for the suppression of the patriots.[46]

Rather than searching for traditional alliances and hereditary friendships to explain the shift in the MacDonald position, it is probably better to explore the issue in terms of Hebridean politics of the late thirteenth and early fourteenth centuries. As we have seen, the dispute over Lismore had thrown the MacDonalds behind Edward I in 1296, no doubt because they hoped that loyal service would work to their advantage and help them to advance their claim. That Angus Óg continued to serve Edward after the death of his brother in 1299 should come as no surprise; Angus was still operating against his enemies, the MacDougalls, and no doubt regarded service with the English king as the most effective manner in which to pursue his feud. It is hard to believe that Angus Óg would not both have taken up the pursuit of his brother's claim to Lismore, and have sought a degree of vengeance for his death, but so much is speculation. It seems certain, however, that from 1299 until about 1301 the interests of the English king and the lord of Islay coincided, namely the taming of the MacDougalls. But the events of 1304–6 must have put an end to this partnership between the English king and the lord of Islay.

By 1304–5 the MacDougalls, pressed by the MacDonalds and other agents of Edward, entered the peace of the English king. By early 1306

---

45 MacDonald and MacDonald, *Clan Donald*, i, p. 93; MacDonald, *Clan Donald*, p. 58.
46 Lamont, 'Alexander of Islay', p. 161.

their kinsman, John Comyn, was dead, and they had become the foes of Bruce. The submission of the MacDougalls meant, in turn, that Angus would have lost his use for the English king, that there could be little hope of settling old scores, and, indeed, that the claim to Lismore might even have become something of an embarrassment.[47] But, more than anything, it was the killing of Comyn by Bruce that must have detached Angus Óg from the cause of the English king: it meant that the Comyns, Balliols, and their allies were pushed firmly into the English camp, and, since the MacDougalls and the MacDonalds had been at odds for over a decade, it would have been natural for Angus Óg to go over to the Bruce cause to pursue his feud. So, while it might be going too far to say that Angus Óg returned to his family's traditional allegiance in 1306, or that the MacDonalds were the hereditary friends of the Bruces, it would also be true to say that the 1286 Turnberry Band must have paved the way for Angus's entry into the Bruce camp, and the two families were certainly not unknown to one another. Once again, then, it seems that the major determinant in the allegiances of the Hebridean chieftains was the simmering dispute of the 1290s, and once again Hebridean politics and the larger canvas of the Bruce–Balliol struggle and the Anglo-Scottish civil war were closely intertwined. However, if Angus Óg had been motivated by simple opportunism to join Bruce's cause in 1306, then it would also be true to say that he rose above it, and he was to prove an important supporter for the remainder of his life.

When Angus Óg appears on the scene after the silence of 1301–6, it is in the pages of Barbour's *Bruce*. This epic poem, dating from the 1370s, describes the careers of Robert Bruce and his devoted follower and lieutenant, James Douglas. Although it is often vague in its chronology and is sometimes inaccurate in details, it is also an important source for the Wars of Independence because it is fuller and presents a much more vivid picture than other sources.[48] Barbour describes how, after the defeat at Dalry, Robert Bruce and his men took to the mountains. Bruce then resolved to go to Kintyre, which was accomplished by way of the Lennox, with assistance from the earl of Lennox and Neil Campbell, who was sent ahead to prepare the way for the party. Bruce and his followers crossed Loch Lomond, took to the sea and sailed past Bute, and eventually arrived at Dunaverty, a sea-girt fortress at the southern extremity of Kintyre. It is at this point that Angus Óg enters the narrative:

> Anguss off Ile yat tyme wes syr
> And lord and ledar off Kyntyr,
> Ye king rycht weill resawyt he
> And wndertuk his man to be,

---

47 Ibid., p. 163.
48 See Webster, *Scotland from the Eleventh Century*, p. 43; and, now, A. A. M. Duncan's edition of Barbour's *Bruce* (Edinburgh, 1997).

> And him and his on mony wys
> He abandownyt till his serwice,
> And for mar sekyrnes, gaiff him syne
> Hys castell off Donavardyne
> To duell yarin, at his liking.
> Full gretumly thankyt him ye king
> And resawyt his seruice.[49]

We have seen that there were compelling reasons for Angus Óg to have gone over to the Bruce cause by 1306, and it is perhaps even more difficult to see why Bruce would settle on going to Kintyre unless he could be assured of assistance from its lord. But there are problems in accepting Barbour at face value here, and this may be one point in the narrative where the details are either erroneous or confused. The major difficulty lies in determining who was in possession of Dunaverty in 1306. The issue is complicated by the fact that Edward I had granted part of Kintyre, likely including Dunaverty, to Malcolm le fiz Lengleys, otherwise identified as Malcolm MacCulian, without due process, in 1296.[50] A document of March 1306, relating the movements of Robert Bruce, suggests that the king obtained possession of Dunaverty from Malcolm MacCulian in exchange for another castle, and had it stocked with supplies, along with Loch Doon in his own earldom of Carrick.[51] It is difficult to reconcile the contemporary documentary evidence and the narrative of Barber from some seventy years after the event, and if Bruce had been in possession of Dunaverty in 1306 this would certainly explain his decision to make his way to Kintyre in the summer of that year, following the double defeats of Methven and Dalry. But, whatever may have been the case, our knowledge of the situation in Kintyre in 1306 is certainly incomplete, and whether Angus Óg was in possession of Dunaverty as Barber suggests, or whether it was already held by Robert Bruce, there is good evidence to suggest that at that date Angus Óg was a Bruce supporter.

Barbour tells us that Bruce stayed at Dunaverty for only three days, and in this he is probably correct, for by 22 September the stronghold was under siege by the English. But by then Robert Bruce had eluded his pursuers, slipping away to Rathlin. It is interesting to note that, on 25 September, Edward wrote to Sir John Menteith, the commander of the siege, saying that he understood the inhabitants of Kintyre were not aiding the besiegers of Dunaverty by providing supplies, and that they

---

49 Barbour, *Bruce*, ii, p. 69 (bk. iii, ll. 659–69). Duncan has suggested that Barbour's narrative of the events of Dunaverty and Rathlin relate to one episode that occurred in Islay: Duncan, 'Scots' invasion of Ireland', p. 102, and note 13.

50 *Rot. Scot.*, i, pp. 22–3; Barrow, *Robert Bruce*, pp. 148–9.

51 *Anglo-Scottish Relations, 1174–1328: Some Selected Documents*, ed. E. L. G. Stones (2nd edn, Oxford, 1970), no. 34.

should be instructed to perform their duty.[52] This seems to suggest that the inhabitants of Kintyre were loyal to Angus Óg and Robert Bruce.[53]

Where Robert Bruce sojourned for the remaining months of 1306 and early 1307 is one of the larger unsolved mysteries surrounding his life (although not one of the most important), and it is unlikely to be conclusively resolved on the basis of the surviving evidence. The problem is, however, relevant in the present context. Since Bruce's sister, Isabella, was the queen of Norway, it has been argued that he took refuge in the Orkney Islands, at that time still under Norwegian control, while another view holds that he sheltered in Ulster and in the Hebrides.[54] But these apparently disparate opinions are not mutually exclusive, and Ranald Nicholson has argued that 'the truth is probably that Bruce visited all of these places: the whole western seaboard from Ulster to Orkney was linked by rapid sea communication, and, for various reasons, he had cause to traverse the whole of it'.[55] It thus seems certain that, at some point during his self-imposed exile, Bruce was in the Hebrides. According to Fordun, he received considerable aid from Christiana of the Isles, that is the daughter and sole legitimate child of Alan MacRuairi, lord of Garmoran; she was related to Bruce by marriage and was probably instrumental in aiding him during these troubled months.[56] Certainly by late January 1307 the English believed Bruce to be in the Clyde estuary, and they dispatched ships to intercept him there.[57] But it was too late. By February he had managed to escape the tightening English net and slipped back into his earldom of Carrick. So, just as the MacDougalls had been instrumental in turning the newly inaugurated king into a fugitive in the summer of 1306, so, too, had other west-coast kindreds been instrumental in assisting his cause. As Colin MacDonald put it,

> It was fortunate, indeed, for Bruce that he had at this dangerous moment such devoted and trustworthy supporters as the MacDonalds, the MacRuaris and the Campbells, for if they had been overawed by Edward's threats, had wavered and had deserted 'Bruce he would have been captured by the English forces and fallen a victim to Edward's pitiless vengeance.[58]

In 1307 the tide began to turn in favour of King Robert. Early in that year he had returned to his own earldom of Carrick, from where he launched 'one of the most remarkable military achievements in British

---

52 *CDS*, ii, no. 1834.
53 MacDonald, *History of Argyll*, p. 130.
54 Barron, *Scottish War of Independence*, pp. 248–59; Barrow, *Robert Bruce*, pp. 168–9.
55 Nicholson, *Later Middle Ages*, p. 74.
56 *Chron. Fordun*, i, p. 343; ii, p. 335; Barrow, *Robert Bruce*, p. 170.
57 *CDS*, ii, no. 1888.
58 MacDonald, *History of Argyll*, p. 131.

history'.[59] In May he routed the English at Loudon Hill, and then, on 7 July, Edward I died, 'an event from which King Robert's cause could draw immeasurable encouragement'.[60] The initiative in the struggle thus passed to Bruce, but for several years his chief opponents were not the English but rather the Comyn–Balliol faction rooted in Galloway, the North-East, and Argyll. In late 1307 Bruce concluded a truce with the earl of Ross, which secured Ross, Sutherland, and Caithness in the far North; in May 1308 the Comyns were decisively defeated at the battle of Inverurie, and the North-East was subdued by the 'herschip' (harrowing) of Buchan; and in June 1308 James Douglas brought Galloway under Bruce's control.[61] It is interesting to note that John of Argyll was among those endeavouring to apprehend Robert Bruce in 1307: in July of that year he was given money and supplies for twenty-two men at arms and 800 foot soldiers to guard the town of Ayr and its environs.[62]

These successes against his domestic foes form the backdrop to Robert Bruce's conquest of Argyll, by which the power of the MacDougalls was shattered and the way cleared for further campaigns against the English. According to Fordun:

> The same year [1308], within a week after the Assumption of the blessed Virgin Mary [15–23 August], the king overcame the men of Argyll, in the middle of Argyll, and subdued the whole land unto himself. Their leader, named Alexander of Argyll, fled to Dunstafinch [Dunstaffnage] castle, where he was, for some time, besieged by the king. On giving up the castle to the king, he refused to do him homage. So a safe conduct was given to him, and to all who wished to withdraw with him; and he fled to England ...[63]

Walter Bower, a fifteenth-century chronicler, incorporated Fordun's narrative but added some lines from an earlier verse chronicle which has important independent value for Robert Bruce:

> If you add a thousand, three hundred and five and three,
> in the week when the feast of the Assumption of our Lady is held,
> King Robert had conquered the people of Argyll.
> This people, reared in arrogant words and deeds,
> obeyed the king's commands whether willingly or not.[64]

[59] Grant, *Independence and Nationhood*, p. 6.
[60] Nicholson, *Later Middle Ages*, pp. 76–7.
[61] Ibid., 76–9.
[62] *CDS*, ii, no. 1957. It was probably at this time that Bruce had another encounter with John of Argyll. Barbour relates (bk. vi, ll. 475–594) the story of how the king was pursued relentlessly by John of Argyll's bloodhound near Cumnock in Ayr, and adds that John had with him at that time 800 men (bk. vi, ll. 483). It is striking that Barbour's number should tally so exactly with that given in the English document.
[63] *Chron. Fordun*, i, p. 345; ii, p. 338.
[64] *Chron. Bower*, vi, p. 345.

By far the most detailed account of the conquest of Argyll, however, comes from Barbour's narrative in *The Bruce* – though it does not assign a set of dates to the events that it relates. Barbour described these key events in the subjugation of Argyll: first, the so-called battle of the pass of Brander between the men of Alexander and John of Argyll and Robert Bruce; second, the siege of Dunstaffnage Castle; third, the submission of Alexander and the escape of John.[65] Barbour provides no details on the route taken by Bruce and his army, but we know from the letter written by John of Argyll to the English king in early 1309 (discussed below) that the Scottish king utilised both naval and land forces in his campaign; the naval forces were no doubt provided by his Hebridean allies, including the MacDonalds and MacRuairis. The land approach most probably taken was through Campbell territory around Loch Awe, turning westwards near the modern village of Dalmally. The actual location of the conflict is also contentious. Traditionally, it has been placed at the pass of Brander, where the steep slopes of Ben Cruachan fall down towards the River Awe, and it often goes by the appellation of the battle of the pass of Brander. Barbour, however, never refers to it as such, nor do any of the other sources just mentioned. This is how Barbour describes the location:

> ... sa strayt and so narow was
> Yat twasum samyn mycht nocht rid
> In sum place off ye hillis sid.
> Ye nethyr halff was peralous
> For a schor crag hey and hydwous,
> Raucht to ye se doun fra ye pas,
> On athyr halff ye montane was
> Swa combrows hey and stay
> Yat it was hard to pas yat way.[66]

Barbour states that the hillside descended into the sea; therefore Loch Etive seems a more likely candidate than the River Awe, for Loch Etive is a sea-loch leading into the open sea, whereas Loch Awe is a freshwater loch surrounded by land. Moreover, Barbour also relates that John of Argyll watched the fighting from his galley on the sea. This too would support a location on the slopes of Ben Cruachan above Loch Etive rather than above the River Awe, for it was impossible to sail ships from Loch Awe to Loch Etive, and there is no evidence of a tarbert between them. This means that if the battle had taken place at Brander and John was in his galley on Loch Etive, he could not have witnessed the conflict as Barbour relates. Other evidence also points to this conclusion. If John had stationed his galleys on Loch Awe there could have been no

---

[65] Barbour, *Bruce*, ii, pp. 239–44.
[66] Ibid., ii, pp. 239–40 (bk. x, ll. 18–26).

possibility of retreat or escape to open waters if Bruce's forces were victorious; and, moreover, Loch Awe was really a Campbell loch: the Campbells took their titular designation from it and their principal stronghold was at Innis Chonnel.[67] It seems, then, that we should dispense with the nomenclature of the battle of the pass of Brander, and replace it with the battle of Ben Cruachan.

According to Barbour, John of Argyll concealed his men along the hillside in order to roll boulders down on Bruce's forces as they advanced along the narrow path. But his plans were foiled when the king dispatched a force of lightly armed men, possibly Highlanders, under the command of James Douglas to get further up the slope and surprise the Argyllsmen. This stratagem worked, and, as the Argyllsmen attacked, Douglas's troops rushed down and dislodged the attackers, sending them into a panicked flight:

> And als apon ye toyer party
> Come Iames of Dowglas & his rout
> And schot apon yaim with a schout,
> And woundyt yaim with arowis fast,
> & with yar suerdis at ye last
> Yai ruschyt amang yaim hardely ...[68]

Pressed by Bruce's men, the forces of John of Argyll fled to a bridge, probably over the River Awe, hoping to destroy it behind them, but the bridge was captured and Bruce's forces pursued the Argyllsmen to Dunstaffnage Castle, which was then besieged:

> Ye king yat stoute wes stark & bauld
> Till Dunstaffynch rycht sturdely
> A sege set and besyly
> Assaylit ye castell it to get ...[69]

Barbour says that Dunstaffnage fell after a short siege, but it may be that he is compressing the narrative at this point. In the wake of this siege Alexander was said by Barbour to have submitted to the king, while John escaped in his ships.

Further light is shed upon the campaign by an undated letter of John of Argyll to King Edward II:

I have received your last letter [dated, or received?] on March 11th, for whose contents I express my deep gratitude to your majesty. When it arrived I was confined to my bed with illness, and have

---

67 MacDonald, *History of Argyll*, pp. 134–6; Professor Duncan, who is preparing a new edition of Barbour, informs me that Barbour is meticulous about distinguishing between fresh and salt water; hence, his references to the sea must here mean Loch Etive.

68 Barbour, *Bruce*, ii, p. 241 (bk. x, ll. 67–72.

69 Ibid., ii, p.243 (bk. x, ll. 112–15).

been for six months past. Robert Bruce approached these parts by land and sea with 10,000 men, they say, or 15,000. I have no more than 800 men, 500 in my own pay whom I keep continually to guard the borders of my territory. The barons of Argyll give me no aid. Yet Bruce asked for a truce, which I granted him for a short space, and I have got a similar truce until you send me help. I have heard, my lord, that when Bruce came he was boasting and claiming that I had come to his peace, in order to inflate his own reputation so that others would rise more readily in his support. May God forbid this; I certainly do not wish it, and if you hear this from others you are not to believe it; for I shall always be ready to carry out your orders with all my power, wherever and whenever you wish. I have three castles to keep as well as a loch twenty-four miles long, on which I keep and build galleys with trusty men to each galley. I am not sure of my neighbours in any direction. As soon as you or your army come, then, if my health permits, I shall not be found wanting where lands, ships or anything else is concerned, but will come to your service. But if sickness should prevent me I will send my son to serve you with my forces.[70]

Finally, there is important evidence provided by the whereabouts of Alexander and John of Argyll in 1309 and 1310. In March 1309 Alexander was present at Robert I's St Andrews parliament.[71] In December of that same year both he and John were in Ireland, where they are also recorded in April 1310. In the summer of 1310 they were in England.[72] This evidence points inescapably to the conclusion that the final fall of the MacDougalls had taken place by late 1309, a conclusion that is supported by the fact that Robert Bruce issued a charter from Dunstaffnage on 20 October of that year.[73]

The major difficulty is determining the sequence of events that led up to the flight of the MacDougalls from Scotland in late 1309. It is pretty well universally agreed that there were two campaigns against Argyll, but their nature and dates remain contentious.[74] I propose a new interpretation which links the date given in the verse chronicle used by Bower with the events described by Barbour, and which ties Fordun's account to the events of 1309 rather than 1308. That is to say, I suggest the battle of Ben Cruachan was followed by the temporary submission of Alexander of Argyll and by a truce with John in 1308, while a second campaign in the late summer of 1309 finally succeeded in taking

---

[70] trans. Barrow, *Robert Bruce*, p. 179; calendared in *CDS*, iii, no. 80.

[71] *APS*, i, p. 459.

[72] Professor Duncan has communicated to me information from PRO, E101/235/9 which places Alexander and John in Ireland in December 1309; see *CDS*, iii, no. 132 and no. 95 (misdated to 1309) for their whereabouts in 1310.

[73] *RRS*, v, no. 10.

[74] Compare, e.g., the views of Barrow (*Robert Bruce*, pp. 179–80), Nicholson (*Later Middle Ages*, pp. 79–80), and McDiarmid (Barbour, *Bruce*, i, pp. 85–6).

Dunstaffnage by October and in forcing the MacDougalls out of Scotland by the end of the year.

To begin with, the accounts of Barbour and Fordun differ considerably in their general sequence of events. Fordun relates Robert Bruce's subjugation of Argyll, the siege of Dunstaffnage, the refusal of Alexander to submit, and his flight to England, all in the year 1308. Barbour, on the other hand, says that Alexander submitted after the battle of Ben Cruachan and a siege of Dunstaffnage, while John escaped by sea. The verse chronicle used by Bower makes no mention of Alexander or his fate, but dates the subjugation of Argyll firmly to 1308.

If we apply the date in the verse chronicle preserved by Bower, and used by Fordun, to the narrative of Barbour we can place the battle of Ben Cruachan in August 1308, which the itineraries of Robert Bruce and James Douglas might just permit. This defeat for the men of Argyll seems to have resulted in the temporary submission of Alexander, which would explain his presence at the St Andrews Parliament in March 1309; Barrow is surely right in his assessment that, 'it would be extraordinary if he had come to Bruce's peace before there had been any serious Argyll campaign'.[75] John of Argyll, however, did not submit; perhaps he agreed to a truce, and his letter to the king of England should therefore be regarded as belonging to early 1309.[76] There are two advantages to placing the letter here rather than in early 1308.[77] First, if it were written in 1308, before the submission of Alexander, it is difficult to explain why John, and not Alexander, was its author. But if Alexander was either a captive or a hostage when it was written, its attribution to John is much easier to explain. Second, if it belongs to 1309 the letter can be regarded as describing the campaign of August 1308, one which can be securely dated and about which there is little question. If the letter is held to belong to early 1308 then a suitably early campaign must be found for it to refer to; and while it is not beyond the realms of possibility that Robert might have campaigned against Argyll early in 1308, there is no real evidence for it. While the objection that the tone of the letter would seem to preclude its predating the battle of Ben Cruachan is a valid one,[78] given the aim of the letter – men and money for John – it is perhaps less than surprising that he understated the events of 1308. The final subjugation of Argyll would then belong to 1309.

The charter evidence strongly suggests a sea attack on Dunstaffnage between August and October. In early August 1309 King Robert was at Loch Broom in the north, probably collecting men and ships; by 20 October he was at Dunstaffnage; by early November the king was back at

---

[75] Barrow, *Robert Bruce*, p. 180.
[76] As is suggested by Barron, *Scottish War of Independence*, p. 335; MacDonald, *History of Argyll*, p. 134.
[77] As does Barrow: *Robert Bruce*, p. 179.
[78] Ibid., p. 180.

St Andrews; and by December the MacDougalls had fled from Scotland altogether.[79] The exact date on which Dunstaffnage fell is not known, but Robert's return to St Andrews would seem to suggest a date around 25 October. The August date given by Fordun is probably therefore too early for the final subjugation, but he had taken this date from the poetic account that Bower quoted, and had tied it to the wrong siege and outcome; neither are in the poem. Fordun must have obtained his information on these events from another source: they seem to belong to October 1309, and are therefore our only account of events at that point. Clearly, then, Alexander of Argyll's submission of late 1308 was only temporary, and sometime before the late summer of 1309 he must have been back at Dunstaffnage, where his final expulsion was recorded by Fordun. Whether or not this sequence of events is accepted, it is certain that Alexander and John had been defeated and cleared out of Scotland by October 1309, and that they had fled to Ireland by the end of the year. The power of the MacDougalls had finally been broken.[80]

Whether we are considering the regional situation on the western seaboard or the larger canvas of the Wars of Independence as a whole, it is clear that the importance of the Argyll campaign cannot be understated. It destroyed Alexander and John MacDougall, who now joined their kinsmen, the Comyns, as refugees at the English court, and although, as we shall see, John remained a peripheral figure in the West (as commander of the English fleet), the period of MacDougall dominance was over. Their fortunes took a sudden and prolonged downswing, while the star of their kinsmen and rivals, the MacDonalds, moved into a long ascendant. In the larger context, the Argyll campaign was also significant. By March 1309, when Bruce held his parliament at St Andrews, Alexander of Argyll was a prisoner or a hostage, and John of Argyll was at least temporarily out of the picture. The tables had been completely turned in the Bruce–Balliol civil conflict: 'the Balliol–Comyn faction was defeated and leaderless, while Robert I controlled most of Scotland north of the Forth and much of the south-west'.[81] Having won the upper hand in the domestic contest by late 1309, Bruce was free to establish his rule throughout the whole of Scotland by capturing those strongholds that remained in English hands.

The fate of the father and son, Alexander and John MacDougall, can be found in contemporary documents, mostly English in provenance. They were never again prominent in Scotland, and appear largely as pensioners of the English king, although John was active in the service

[79] *RRS*, v, nos. 9–11.
[80] I am particularly grateful to Professor Duncan, who has brought his expertise on the reign of Robert I to bear on this problem, and has discussed it at length with me. The views expressed here are entirely my own, of course.
[81] Grant, *Independence and Nationhood*, p. 6.

of Edward II until his death in 1317. Alexander of Argyll was probably already an old man by the time of the Argyll campaigns of 1308 and 1309. Even before this, in October 1307, his son, John, had been appointed sheriff of 'Argyll and Inchegall and guardian of these parts against the enemy'.[82] Since Alexander had been sheriff of Lorn since the administrative reform of 1293, the appointment of his son in his stead suggests that he was getting too old to do the job effectively. He also seems to have been infirm, for we find that in July 1310 one Nicholas of Corewenne, described as the physician of Alexander of Argyll, had a payment of 100 marks.[83] Between 1309 and 1311 he seems to have been in residence at Carlisle, where he was staying at the king's expense, and he was still alive on 1 April 1310, when the treasurer of Ireland was commanded to pay £100 for the sustenance of his men in Ireland, and officials in York were instructed to pay him and his son 50 marks each for their own sustenance.[84] But he was dead by 18 January 1311, when the king commanded the treasurer of Ireland to pay his son John a further £100 for the support of those troops of his father's that had now fallen under John's command.[85]

John of Argyll outlived his father by only seven years, but 'in the years between his defeat and his death he did all he could to advance English interests and to injure Scotland'[86] – or, probably more accurately, to injure the Bruce cause. Barbour has John of Argyll being captured by Robert I around 1315, held briefly at Dumbarton, and then imprisoned at Lochleven, where he died.[87] Such an account is not sustainable, and the contemporary documentary evidence tells a different story. A long trail of payments and letters permits us to glimpse John as an expatriate in the service of the English king. Between 1309 and 1311 he was staying at Newcastle, at the expense of the English king, and in April 1310 he was given £100 for the sustenance of his men in Ireland.[88] In July and August 1310 he was empowered to receive into the king's peace his enemies from the Isles, and then in July 1311, Edward II awarded 'our noble and beloved' John of Argyll the title of 'Admiral and Captain of our Fleet of Ships' ('Admirallum et Capitaneum Flotae nostrae Navium'), and gave him authority to use the fleet on the coast of Argyll and the Isles and other parts of Scotland in order to pursue and to restrain the king's enemies and rebels.[89] In his capacity as Admiral, a number of English ports were ordered to provide him with ships in the summer of 1311, but several complained that the notice was too short,

---

82 *CDS*, iii, no. 18.
83 Ibid., iii, no. 157.
84 Ibid., iii, no. 566 (b) and (d).
85 Ibid., iii, no. 191.
86 MacDonald, *History of Argyll*, p. 138.
87 Barbour, *Bruce*, iii, p. 111 (bk. xv, ll. 303–15).
88 *CDS*, v, nos. 566 (b) and (d); iii, nos. 132, 191.
89 *Rot. Scot.*, i, pp. 90, 93, 99.

and John seems to have been unable to accomplish much in his new capacity.[90] Slightly earlier, in March, King Edward had granted John a manor in Yorkshire and the fruits of a Templar church 'in aid of his support', until further arrangements could be made for his benefit; he also received other payments in 1312 and 1313.[91] In January 1315 King Edward, 'compassionating the losses and sufferings of John of Argyll, now dwelling in Ireland, at the hands of the Scottish rebels', commanded the treasurer of Ireland to 'make provision for the decent sustenance of him and his family there'.[92] John seems to have remained in Ireland until 1316, from where he actively continued his efforts in the English cause.[93] By February 1315, after years of campaigning on behalf of Edward against the Scottish rebels, he won a minor victory when he expelled the Scots from the Isle of Man (see below), and the English king ordered the Irish treasurer to make good John's losses and provide further support for his men. Later in the same month John captured twenty-three Scottish rebels on the 'sea-coast of Scotland' and the English king ordered them moved from the Isle of Man to Dublin.[94] His efforts continued into late 1315, for in September he was in Dublin, impatiently awaiting the arrival of the navy of the Cinque Ports, and demanding wages for his men. Later in the month he requested that he be allowed to keep six vessels with which to 'harass the Scots' over the winter months.[95] Our final glimpse of John MacDougall, the implacable foe of Robert I, comes in May 1316 when, having returned from Ireland to London, and being described as 'impotent in body', he was granted 200 marks yearly by the king 'for the support of himself and his family'. English wardrobe accounts reveal that he died on pilgrimage to Canterbury in September 1317.[96]

The defeat of the last of the Comyn–Balliol faction by late 1309 paved the way for the establishment of Bruce's rule throughout Scotland between 1310 and 1314. The dominant theme of these years was the capture of the strongholds in the south of Scotland held by the English and their allies, a feat accomplished largely through guerrilla warfare and unorthodox tactics. By the spring of 1314 only five strongholds

[90] *CDS*, iii, nos. 216–17; v, nos. 559–60, 563. More payments for his support were also made in the early summer of 1311: ibid., v, no. 562 (c), (d), (e).

[91] Ibid., iii, nos. 250, 303, 320.

[92] Ibid., iii, no. 415. John had gone to Ireland in March 1314 on the king's affairs: ibid., iii, no. 355.

[93] *Rot. Scot.*, i, pp. 122, 132.

[94] *CDS*, iii, nos. 420–1.

[95] Ibid., iii, nos. 447, 450.

[96] Ibid., iii, nos. 490, 912; T. Stapleton, 'A brief summary of the Wardrobe Accounts of the 10th, 11th, and 14th years of Edward II', *Archaeologia*, xxvi (1836), p. 341. John of Argyll's career as Admiral of the Western Seas is also considered in W. S. Reid, 'Sea-power in the Anglo-Scottish War, 1296–1328', *Mariner's Mirror*, xlvi (1960), which contains much of value on fleets and naval activities in the West during the period under consideration.

remained in English hands, including Stirling, which, by an arrangement between Edward Bruce and the commander of the garrison of the castle, was due to surrender if not relieved by midsummer. This was a challenge that Edward II could not ignore, and he invaded Scotland with a massive force of cavalry and infantry with which to relieve Stirling Castle. The resulting conflict at Bannockburn, on 23–24 June 1314, saw the English routed in what has been called 'a complete victory for Robert's army, and the greatest humiliation of English arms since the loss of Normandy over a century earlier'.[97]

The story of Bannockburn has been told repeatedly, and the multitude of works on this topic, including Barrow's masterly study, means that it is not necessary to reiterate the details here. The battle was a complicated affair that occupied two days; a preliminary engagement in the afternoon of 23 June lifted the morale of the Scots, and in the morning of 24 June the Scots bore down on the English, who had spent an uncomfortable night in a marshy position. After hard fighting the English rear ranks began to flee across the Bannock Burn and a general panic ensued; Edward II was chased to Dunbar where he set sail for England, and with his flight the Scots had won the day.

In the events of 23–24 June 1314 Argyll and the Isles had a considerable role to play. There are two aspects to consider here: first, the composition of the Scottish army; and second, the role of Angus Óg. The Scottish forces were grouped into four battalions or brigades; three were commanded by trusted kinsmen and friends of the king and the fourth was headed by Robert Bruce himself. Barbour gives us the composition only of the king's brigade, which we are told comprised: 'Ye men of Carryk halely / And off Argile & of Kentyr / And off ye ilis quharof wes syr / Angus of Ile ...'[98] Barbour relates that the king's contingent was held back and committed to the battle at a decisive point; the Highlanders and Islesmen rushed headlong toward the enemy and,

> Yai faucht as yai war in a rage,
> For quhen ye Scottis ynkirly
> Saw yar fayis sa sturdely
> Stand in-to battail yaim agayn
> With all yar mycht and all yar mayn
> Yai layid on as men out of wit,
> And quhar yai with full strak mycht hyt
> Yar mycht na armur stynt yar strak.
> Yai to-fruschyt yat yai mycht our-tak
> And with axys sic duschys gave
> Yat yai helmys and hedis clave ...[99]

[97] Grant, *Independence and Nationhood*, pp. 9–10.
[98] Barbour, *Bruce*, iii, p. 14 (bk. xi, ll. 340–4).
[99] Ibid., iii, p. 55 (bk. xiii, ll. 138–48).

For Barbour this was the climax of the engagement; all four Scottish brigades were engaged, and 'for the English, the battle was now past saving'.[100] If the men of Argyll and the Isles had played a key role in the battle of Bannockburn, what of their leader, Angus Óg MacDonald? John Barbour seems to imply that Angus Óg was present at the head of the contingent from the West, and certainly by the seventeenth century his presence at Bannockburn had passed into MacDonald tradition.[101] Barrow certainly has no doubts that Angus Óg had been a participant in the events of 23–24 June, and if, as has been argued, Angus Óg had been a supporter of Bruce since the dark days of 1306–7, it is difficult to see how he could not have been present in 1314.

Five months after the battle of Bannockburn a parliament at Cambuskenneth enacted that those who had died in battle against the king or who had not come into his peace, 'are to be disinherited forever of lands and tenements and all other status within the realm of Scotland. And they are to be held as foes of the king and kingdom.'[102] The estates of those who suffered forfeiture were used to reward Bruce's supporters, and Angus Óg was one of those who so benefited. If his motives for joining Bruce had originally been dictated by enmity for the MacDougalls, it is also safe to say that his conduct rose above simple opportunism. He had played a key role in the troubled times of 1306–7 and had provided men and quite likely a personal presence at Bannockburn in 1314. Thus, 'rewarding Angus Og and his family and strengthening their position was an obvious and straightforward step'.[103]

It is unfortunate that few complete charters of Robert I to Angus Óg and his family survive; the grants must be either inferred or are known only from the list of lost charters in Appendix II of the *Register of the Great Seal of Scotland*. The dates of these grants are, unfortunately, not known, but they are unlikely to have been made before the Cambuskenneth Parliament in late 1314. It seems certain that Angus Óg was confirmed in Islay and the other MacDonald territories, including parts of Kintyre, although no charters to this effect survive, and other men were also rewarded with lands in Kintyre. But Robert I did grant Lochaber and the adjacent lands of Morvern and Ardnamurchan, to Angus Óg, along with Duror and Glencoe. And Alexander of Islay, possibly Angus Óg's son and successor, was the recipient of a grant of Mull and Tiree, formerly MacDougall possessions.[104] Thus, one of Bruce's earliest and staunchest supporters was suitably rewarded, and became one of the most powerful men in the West, if not the most powerful. But Angus Óg's power throughout his territories was not

---

100 Barrow, *Robert Bruce*, p. 228.
101 Barbour, *Bruce*, iii, p. 14 (bk. xi, ll. 342–3); Macdonald, *Hist. Macdonalds, HP*, i, p. 16.
102 *APS*, i, p. 464; translated in Nicholson, *Later Middle Ages*, p. 92, with commentary.
103 Barrow, *Robert Bruce*, p. 291.
104 *RMS*, i, appendix II, pp. 512, 553; Barrow, *Robert Bruce*, p. 291. For other landholders in Kintyre, see *RMS*, i, appendix I, no. 105; appendix II, pp. 533, 551.

totally contiguous, and key strongholds remained in the hands of the king or his other supporters. Dunstaffnage Castle, for example, was placed in the keeping of one of the Campbells, while the king himself retained Dunaverty Castle and significantly rebuilt Tarbert Castle in mid-Argyll.[105] Indeed, it has been suggested that too much can, in fact, be made of the grants to Angus Óg MacDonald by Robert I. Many lands that he might have received had been granted to the Stewarts, the earls of Ross, the Campbells and Thomas Randolph. Some of these men received far more territory than did the MacDonalds, and one historian has seen Bruce's policy as representing the creation of a 'family hegemony' throughout the West.[106]

John Barbour relates how, shortly after the departure of Edward Bruce for Ireland in 1315, King Robert sailed to subdue the Western Isles. In a gesture that no doubt appealed to the sense of tradition and prophecy of the Hebridean chieftains, he had himself borne across the isthmus between Knapdale and Kintyre from East Loch Tarbert to West Loch Tarbert in a galley with the sails hoisted:

> And quhen yai yat in ye Ilis war
> Hard tell how ye gud king had yar
> Gert his schippis with saillis ga
> Owt-our betuix ye Tarbartis twa
> Yai war abaysit sa uterly,
> For yai wyst throw auld prophecy
> Yat he yat suld ger schippis sua
> Betuix yai seis with saillis ga
> Suld wyne ye Ilis sua till hand
> Yat nane with strenth suld him withstand.[107]

The 'auld prophecy' alluded to by Barbour might very well be nothing more than a twist in the tale, or a distant memory, of the nearly identical feat attributed to Magnus Barelegs in 1098, by which the Norwegian king laid claim to Kintyre.[108] While we may question the letter of the account, we should not doubt its spirit, and it reveals much about Robert I's policies in the West.

Above all, it demonstrates how, as a king who had strong links with the western Gaidhaeltachd, Robert I understood the political significance of the Western Highlands. The feat at Tarbert in 1315 is doubtless connected with the Bruce invasion of Ireland in that year, and with an understanding that the resources of the West were crucial to this

---

105 Ibid., i, appendix II, p. 534; MacDonald, *History of Argyll*, p. 144; Dunbar and Duncan, 'Tarbert Castle', p. 14.
106 Grant, 'Scotland's "Celtic Fringe"', p. 123.
107 Barbour, *Bruce*, iii, p. 111 (bk. xv, ll. 291–300).
108 Duffy, 'Bruce brothers', p. 71.

undertaking. Indeed, the western seaboard had provided men and resources on a consistent basis from the early days of Bruce's struggle. In 1306–7 he had received aid from Angus Óg MacDonald and Christiana MacRuairi; in 1308 men of the Isles had participated in the invasion of Galloway; in 1314 Islesmen had fought at Bannockburn. We do not know whether Edward Bruce took Islesmen with him to Ireland in 1315, but King Robert did so in 1317, and both a MacDonald and a MacRuairi leader fell with Edward Bruce in 1318. The fleets of galleys commanded by the western chieftains were also crucial to Bruce's cause. Hebridean galleys had menaced the Isle of Man in 1310 and 1313, and had no doubt sustained the Bruce invasion of Ireland in 1315. As Barrow has put it, King Robert knew the West from experience, and 'he succeeded with the chiefs doubtless because he understood them and possessed the gifts which they admired'.[109]

Following the conquest of Argyll in 1309, King Robert succeeded in taming the Highlands, thus continuing the policy of his predecessors Alexander III and John Balliol. By the end of his reign, if not before, Robert I had transformed the political situation in the Western Highlands. In the far North, Skye and Wester Ross were held by the earls of Ross, first William, a former enemy but from 1308 a Bruce supporter, and then his son Hugh; while Garmoran had been converted into a fief held by the MacRuairis for ship-service. Argyll, most of which had been held by the MacDougalls, was parcelled out as fiefs to King Robert's supporters, including Angus Óg MacDonald and the Campbells, propelling the latter into the foremost ranks of the Scottish nobility.[110] The administration of the region, too, was extended and developed. Between 1315 and 1325 the sheriffdom of Argyll was created, carved out of the sheriffdom of Perth, and possibly representing a part implementation of the scheme laid down by John Balliol in 1293. And, finally, between about 1320 and 1330 a bustling new burgh, port, and castle were established at Tarbert. In doing so, King Robert 'surely had in mind the need to bind the whole of the western seaboard to the rest of the kingdom by ties of trade, by a shared prosperity, as well as by a strong fortress and by the sheriff's wand and summons'.[111]

In the years after Bannockburn, little more is heard of Angus Óg, and the date of his death, like that of many of his predecessors, is uncertain. MacDonald tradition of the seventeenth century put his demise around 1300, which is impossible; while more recent tradition asserts that he died closer to the time of King Robert I in 1329. In fact, the evidence of the MacDonald succession, though itself murky, suggests that Angus Óg passed from the scene between 1314 and 1318. Irish Annals record the

---

[109] Barrow, *Robert Bruce*, p. 291.
[110] Ibid., pp. 291–2.
[111] Dunbar and Duncan, 'Tarbert Castle', p. 16.

death of Alexander MacDonald, *rí Airer Goidel*, at Dundalk in 1318, along with the chief of the MacRuairis. The identity of this Alexander has not been established beyond all doubt, but he may have been the son and successor of Angus Óg as chief of the Clan Donald (as evidenced by his title of *rí Airer Goidel*) and the recipient of a grant of Mull and Tiree by Robert I. If this interpretation is correct, then Angus Óg must have been dead by 1318.[112] A grave-slab in the Iona museum with an inscription that reads, 'Here lies the body of Angusius, son of Lord Angusius MacDonald of Islay,' is sometimes thought to belong to Angus Óg, but it has been shown that this cannot be the case and that the individual referred to must be a son of a later Lord of the Isles.[113]

It is surely more than a little disappointing that the career of Angus Óg did not evoke more notice by contemporaries. What evidence there is, some of it circumstantial, admittedly, points to his having been a supporter of Robert Bruce from 1306, probably pushed into his camp by enmity toward the MacDougalls and the revolution brought about by the events of early 1306 which swung the MacDougalls into Edward's train. No doubt the survival of the lost charters from the reign of Robert I would throw further illumination on the career and allegiances of Angus, but there must be a certain irony in the fact that the most extensive documentation pertaining to him comes from early in his career, when he supported the English king against the MacDougall leaders, Alexander and John. Perhaps all that can be said is that, if Angus Óg served Robert Bruce as faithfully as he did Edward I in the 1290s, his rewards were well deserved.

The situation after the deaths of the MacDonald and MacRuairi chiefs at Dundalk is not clear. In 1336 John, the son of Angus Óg, styled himself *dominus Insularum* (Lord of the Isles), and it may be he who is on record as *ballivus* of Islay a decade earlier. But since John did not die until 1387, he must have been a young man, if not a minor, in 1318, and it is possible that he did not immediately succeed his probable brother, Alexander. We may therefore have to account for a Ruairi, or Roderick, called 'de Ile' and seemingly of the Clan Donald, who was forfeited in 1325: he was perhaps another son of Angus Óg, or else of Alexander Óg. It is true that the genealogies make no allowance for Alexander and Ruairi, although this might result from their evidently short tenure of the chieftainship, and it is also true that Ruairi is an unusual Clan Donald forename for this period. Some mention must also be made of the problematic and mysterious Donald of Islay, who appears in several documents of the late thirteenth and early fourteenth centuries. He has

---

112 *Clanranald Bk.*, p. 159; *History of the MacDonalds*, p. 17; *Ann. Inisf.*, p. 429. It should be noted that the text of the *Annals of Inisfallen* is corrupt at this point, and the entry breaks off tantalisingly in the middle of Alexander's name, which the editor supplies as 'MacDomnaill'.

113 Steer and Bannerman, *Late Medieval Monumental Sculpture*, p. 110.

been regarded variously as another son of Angus Mór and an elder brother of Angus Óg; as a grandson of Angus Mór and a son of Alexander Óg; or else as a son of Alexander, the brother of Angus Mór. The first two interpretations gain no support from the genealogies, while the traditional pedigrees do contain a reference to a nephew of Angus Mór called Donald. W. D. Lamont has argued that 'the existence of Donald of Islay is so problematical that it must not be assumed', but while his exact place in the genealogies and the date of his *floruit* may remain opaque, his existence cannot seriously be called into question.

The evidence, then, patchy though it is, suggests a period of upheaval in the MacDonald succession between 1318 and at least 1325, and it may be that this was accompanied by internal rivalry which permitted a brief period of MacRuairi dominance in the West in the 1320s.[114]

It is not until the 1330s that the situation in the West becomes clearer. By then the major player was certainly John MacDonald, the son of Angus Óg, but the death of Robert I had brought about major changes in the political situation which reverberated throughout the western seaboard as well. In 1332 the Bruce–Balliol contest and Anglo-Scottish conflict were rekindled when King John Balliol's son, Edward, and others of the so-called 'disinherited', who had been forfeited of their Scottish lands in the wake of Bannockburn, were not discouraged from pursuing the claims in Scotland by King Edward III of England. In 1332 Balliol and his followers routed the Scots at Dupplin, and Balliol was crowned at Scone, but he was driven out later that same year. In 1333 Balliol re-established himself with English help at the battle of Halidon Hill, and David II, Robert I's young son and successor, fled to France for safety, where he remained until 1341. It has been said that many of the Scottish nobles displayed a 'fickle loyalty'[115] through the renewed strife of the early 1330s, but one noteworthy figure who remained aloof was John MacDonald. In 1335 the earl of Moray, acting as regent, had negotiated with John at Tarbert in an attempt to secure his loyalty to the nationalist cause, but during the next year, on 12 September 1336, an indenture was drawn up between Edward Balliol and John whereby Edward confirmed John in his lands in exchange for support.[116] But despite his pro-Balliol leanings, John's power and prestige suffered remarkably little in the wake of David II's return from France in 1341.

114 *Acts of the Lords of the Isles*, no. 3; *ER*, i, pp. 52, 196–8; *RMS*, i, appendix II, no. 699. See the discussion of the problem, and the somewhat different views presented, in Steer and Bannerman, *Late Medieval Monumental Sculpture*, pp. 202–3; Grant, 'Scotland's "Celtic Fringe"', p. 137, note 41; *Acts of the Lords of the Isles*, pp. 279–83, 286; Lamont, 'Alexander of Islay', pp. 160–8; and Duffy, '"Continuation" of Nicholas Trevet', pp. 311–12. On Donald of Islay, see Barrow, *Robert Bruce*, pp. 163, 360, note 124; and Lamont, 'Alexander of Islay', pp. 165–7, for a full discussion, and references to the relevant documents; see also Duffy, '"Continuation" of Nicholas Trevet', pp. 311–12; and Sellar, 'MacDonald and MacRuari pedigrees', note 24.
115 Nicholson, *Later Middle Ages*, p. 142.
116 *Acts of the Lords of the Isles*, no. 1.

In 1343 a concord was drawn up between John and David II, whereby the Lord of the Isles was confirmed in possession of his territories. It is difficult to know how to interpret John's actions, especially given his father's apparently steadfast adherence to the Robert I's cause. It seems likely that John was uncommitted to either side, instead keeping on good terms with both the English and Scottish governments in an attempt further to consolidate his power.[117] But it may just be that his policy was related to the heritage of the kingdom of the Isles, and that John was aspiring to virtual independence within his sphere of influence. An alliance with a Balliol king who had benefited from John's support might have been preferable to one with a Bruce king whose father had largely tamed the west Highland chieftains; perhaps, as Colin MacDonald suggested, anything was preferable to 'the firm control of a near-at-hand Scottish king whose power could be brought to bear much more easily on recalcitrant or disloyal subjects'.[118]

Although the dominant themes of the period the Wars of Independence in the West are the struggle between the MacDougalls and the MacDonalds, and the roles of these two kindreds in the Scottish civil war and the Anglo-Scottish conflict, it remains to consider other West-Highland families and their role in the affairs of the period.

The MacRuairis might well be called the lost kindred of Somerled, partly because their history is less well documented and generally less well known than their kinsmen the MacDougalls and MacDonalds, but also because they left no famous surname or clan descended from them. However, they, too appear as prominent figures in the western seaboard, often in the background, flitting in and out of the light of historical documentation. Alan MacRuairi, one of the three Hebridean chieftains who was present at the council at Scone in 1284, had passed from the scene by 1296. His sole lawful child was his daughter, Christiana, who married Duncan, the son of Donald, Earl of Mar, and was therefore related to Robert Bruce by marriage since Duncan's sister, Isabel, was Bruce's first wife.[119] Known as either Christiana of Mar or Christiana of the Isles, she was the lady of Moidart, Knoydart, Arisaig, Eigg and Rhum, and possibly Barra, the Uists, and Harris, and it was she who, as we have seen, aided Robert Bruce in the dark days of 1306–7, when the king fled Scotland and sheltered in the western seaboard.[120]

117 Nicholson, *Later Middle Ages*, p. 154.

118 MacDonald, *History of Argyll*, p. 154. General background in Grant, *Independence and Nationhood*, pp. 16–22; and in Nicholson, *Later Middle Ages*, pp. 142–3, 154–5; see also Steer and Bannerman, *Late Medieval Monumental Sculpture*, appendix II, pp. 203–4; and *Acts of the Lords of the Isles*, Introduction.

119 Ibid., genealogical table II.

120 Professor Duncan has kindly brought to my attention, too late for detailed discussion here, an apparently unpublished and little-known charter of Christiana MacRuairi, now in the Royal Faculty of Procurators, Glasgow. Most likely dating from the 1320s, it grants to Arthur Campbell, the son of Arthur Campbell, the lands of Moidart,

But if Christiana MacRuairi was a consistent supporter of Robert Bruce, the attitude of her half-brothers, Lachlan (who appears in contemporary documents as Roland) and Ruairi (Latinised as Roderick) was more ambiguous and opportunistic.[121] They have been likened to 'Highland rovers', and it has been suggested that they inherited the piratical tendencies of the Vikings; modern scholars have tended to share this view, regarding Lachlan, at any rate, as a 'sinister figure', and a 'buccaneering predator' who played 'solely for his own hand'.[122] Although they had ostensibly submitted to Edward in 1296, within a year we find Lachlan and Ruairi causing trouble in the western sea-board. Along with Alexander of Argyll, their names figured prominently in the reports that Alexander of the Isles sent to King Edward in 1297. It was reported that Lachlan and Ruairi, 'plundered the greater part of the king's land of Skye and Lewis, and killed the men in the same lands, and set fires, and violently oppressed the women, and burned up the ships in the service of the king'.[123] Eventually, however, the two brothers were apprehended by their MacDonald kinsman. Lachlan soon escaped this custody and sought refuge in Lochaber with Alexander MacDougall and his Comyn kinsmen, where it was reported they were outfitting massive war galleys. In 1299 Lachlan allied himself with Alexander Comyn, the brother of John Comyn, and was reported to be ravaging the North; in 1306 we find him at Ebchester in County Durham where he petitioned the English king to have the lands of Sir Patrick Graham. The last mention of him comes in 1308, in a letter of the earl of Ross to King Edward II. The earl reported that he had assigned lands in the Isles to Lachlan, but that he was not answering for their revenues. The earl therefore asked the king whether he would command Lachlan to do so, and the letter ends with the apt observation that 'Lachlan is such a high and mighty lord, he will not answer to anyone except under great force or through fear of you.'[124] Lachlan then disappears from the record; the earl of Ross had surely taken the measure of the man. His brother, Ruairi, seems to have submitted to the English king, perhaps around 1301, and although the duration of his custody is not known, in 1301 his sons were in the power of Angus Óg, who held himself responsible for their loyalty and recommended them to the English

Arisaig, and Morar, the islands of Eigg and Rhum, and the island called *insula sicca*, i.e. Eilean Tioram, for the service of one twenty-oared galley. I intend to publish this significant document, and a commentary, elsewhere.

121 Many recent accounts of the MacRuairis include a third son of Alan named Ranald. But David Sellar has shown that 'the Ranald who appears in recent MacDonald histories as a brother of Ruari and Lachlan MacRuari is a *doppleganger* for Lachlan; the name "Roland", which appears on the record, truly an equivalent for "Lachlan", has been amended to "Ranald"': Sellar, 'MacDonald and MacRuari pedigrees', p. 5.

122 MacDonald and MacDonald, *Clan Donald*, i, p. 87; Barrow, *Robert Bruce*, p. 290.

123 Stevenson, *Documents*, ii, no. 444.

124 *CDS*, iv, p. 400; translation adapted from Barrow, *Kingdom of the Scots*, p. 382.

king.[125] It is likely that, following the demise of his brother, Ruairi stepped into his shoes, but he was a supporter of Robert Bruce and was rewarded by that king, for some time during his reign Christiana, perhaps at the instigation of the crown, made over to him extensive MacRuairi lands in the West, for which he owed the service of one twenty-six oared vessel to the king. He was probably the 'MacRuaidhri king of Innsi Gall' whose death at Dundalk was recorded by Irish Annals in 1318.[126] It may well be that the death of Angus Óg had allowed the Clan Ruairi to come to the fore in the western seaboard, however briefly, and the extensive territories made over to Ruairi by his half-sister serve as a reminder that the MacRuairis, too, were a potent force to be reckoned with in the western seas.[127]

While it is true that one of the essential qualifications for Hebridean lordship between 1164 and the early fourteenth century was descent from the mighty Somerled, other families also emerged in this period as prominent landholders in the West. We have already encountered the MacSweens and the MacNaughtons, for example, and by the thirteenth century many others, such as the MacKinnons, MacLachlans, MacLeans, MacLeods, and MacQuarries emerge into the light of historical documentation.[128] But perhaps the greatest success story in the western seaboard, apart from the kindred of Somerled, belongs to the Campbells, and no history of the western seaboard in the central Middle Ages can omit some mention of this important family.

The precise origin of the Campbells remains something of a mystery. Their ancestry is described in various genealogies as Norman, Gaelic, or British, and although a Gaelic origin is perhaps favoured, convincing arguments for British roots in the Lennox, where the early associations of the family seem to lie, have also been put forward. The family was descended from Duncan MacDuibhne, a chieftain of Loch Awe who flourished in the early thirteenth century but for whom there is no contemporary evidence; he is known from a fourteenth-century Campbell charter and the family was originally known as O'Duibhne. We are on firmer ground with Gillespic Campbell, probably Duncan's son, who is on the record in 1263 and 1266 and who is the earliest member of the family to appear in contemporary documents. Barrow has stated that the Campbells were certainly not landless adventurers in origin, and David Sellar has argued that they were, by the third quarter of the thirteenth century, already holding tracts of land in Argyll and

---

[125] Stevenson, *Documents*, ii, no. 615.
[126] *RMS*, i, appendix I, no. 9; *Ann. Loch Cé*, i, p. 595.
[127] On the MacRuairis in general, see Barrow, *Robert Bruce*, p. 290; Barrow, *Kingdom of the Scots*, pp. 380–2; and MacDonald and MacDonald, *Clan Donald*, ii, chap. 1. Despite the early date of publication, there is much of value in W. C. MacKenzie, *History of the Outer Hebrides* (Paisley, 1903), including a substantial amount on the MacRuairis.
[128] I. Moncreiffe, *The Highland Clans* (London, 1967), *passim*.

Clackmannanshire, and possibly in Dumbartonshire and Ayrshire, and that they were allied by marriage to the earls of Carrick, making them territorial lords of some standing.[129]

Whatever the origins and early status of this family, there can be little doubt that their rise to greatness dates from the time of the Wars of Independence when, perhaps because of their close links with Ayrshire, where Bruce interests were strong, they were consistent supporters of the Bruce cause. Gillespic's son, Colin Mór, appears on record about 1281, and he played a prominent role in Scottish affairs for the next fifteen years. A landholder around Loch Awe, he was an auditor for Robert Bruce the Competitor in 1291, along with Mr Neil Campbell, evidently a kinsman, and, as we have seen, he was slain by Alexander of Argyll in the MacDougall aggrandisement that accompanied the turmoil of the second half of the 1290s. He was succeeded in the headship of the family by his son, Neil, who was the bailie of the crown lands of Lochawe and Ardskeodnish to which he may have had an hereditary claim. These lands were confirmed to his son, Colin, in 1315, for the service of a galley of forty oars.[130] Neil Campbell was one of Bruce's ardent supporters and most trusted councillors until his death in 1315. His second wife was Mary, the sister of Robert Bruce, and he has been described as 'one of that small band of noblemen without whose help in 1306 and 1307 Robert Bruce would hardly have survived'.[131]

From about 1290 the name Campbell begins to proliferate in contemporary documents, and these kinsmen also shared in the rise of the family's fortunes. There are on record Donald, Dugald, Duncan, and Arthur Campbell, and although these are sometimes regarded as the brothers of Neil, Sellar will only admit Dugald and perhaps Donald to that relationship. Also on record are a Thomas Campbell and Mr Neil Campbell. By the middle of the reign of Robert Bruce, these men had acquired considerable holdings in the West, consisting largely of forfeited MacDougall lands, including Lorn, Benderloch, and lands in Kintyre. Thus, Donald Campbell was awarded part of Benderloch for the service of a twenty-six oared ship; Dugald received the island of Torsa and other lands in Argyll; and Arthur Campbell received the constableship of Dunstaffnage with its associated lands, and other territory in Lorn.[132] Although their rise to dominance in the south-western Highlands belongs to the fifteenth and sixteenth centuries, the star of the Campbells was in the ascendant in the thirteenth and early fourteenth centuries, when they were, 'well on their way to becoming the great dominant power on the Argyllshire mainland, and most of the

[129] Barrow, *Robert Bruce*, p. 289; W. D. H. Sellar, 'The earliest Campbells – Norman, Briton or Gael?', *Scot. Stud.*, xvii (1973).
[130] *RRS*, v, no. 46.
[131] Barrow, *Robert Bruce*, p. 289.
[132] *RRS*, v, no. 366; *RMS*, i, appendix II, pp. 534–5, 551.

advance had been achieved at the expense of the Macdougalls of Lorne'.[133]

It remains to consider developments in the Isle of Man in the troubled years between 1286 and 1333. Apart from the abortive uprising of 1275 and the appointment of bailiffs to govern on behalf of the Scottish king, little is known of Man in the period of Scottish overlordship between 1266 and 1286 or 1290. However, the Isle of Man occupied a central place in the naval struggles that characterise the Irish Sea World in the late thirteenth and early fourteenth centuries, representing an important if often overlooked subtheme in the Wars of Independence.[134]

On 4 June 1290 Edward I placed the Isle of Man in the charge of Walter de Huntercombe and took the Manx community into his protection, but he had already been in possession of the island since at least February.[135] Later that same year the inhabitants of the Isle of Man wrote to Edward, stating that, for protection and defence, they had willingly subjected themselves to his power.[136] The letter refers to Man as 'lately desolate and full of wretchedness', so perhaps the Scottish administration had broken down in the wake of the death of Alexander III and the advent of the Guardianship. While it is curious that this petition came after the seizure of the island by Edward and not before, it may well be that the change in overlordship was not unwelcome to the Manx, who, if the uprising of 1275 provides any indication, were chafing under Scottish rule. It may even be that, by welcoming the English, the inhabitants of Man hoped to play off one side against the other and regain some measure of independence, but if that was the case they were destined only to see their island become a bone of contention between England and Scotland for the next four decades.

That Manx politics of the late 1280s and early 1290s were connected with Scottish and English affairs is hinted at by the involvement of the earl of Ulster. Edward's letter of 4 June stated that the Isle of Man had been handed over to him by Richard de Burgh, Earl of Ulster. Presumably, then, sometime between the death of Alexander III in March 1286

---

133 Barrow, *Kingdom of the Scots*, p. 380. In addition to the works cited in this dicussion, see also MacDonald, *History of Argyll*, pp. 142–3, and *passim*; Moncreiffe, *Highland Clans*, pp. 108–16; and A. McKerral, *The Clan Campbell* (Edinburgh and London, 1953).

134 See Reid, 'Sea-power in the Anglo-Scottish War'; and, now, C. McNamee, *The Wars of the Bruces: Scotland, England and Ireland, 1306–1328* (East Linton, 1997).

135 Stevenson, *Documents*, i, no. 103; see also E. B. Fryde *et al.* (eds.), *Handbook of British Chronology* (3rd edn, London, 1986), p. 64, with references. The period is discussed in some detail in A. W. Moore, *A History of the Isle of Man* (1900; repr. Manx National Heritage, 1992), i, pp. 181–94; A. W. Moore, 'The connexion between Scotland and Man', *SHR*, iii (1906); and in the notes to *Chron. Man*, pp. 233–4. These works will be superseded by the important forthcoming S. Duffy (ed.), *A New History of the Isle of Man*, vol. III: *The Medieval Period, 1000–1405* (Liverpool University Press, forthcoming).

136 *Foedera*, i, pt. iii, p. 74. Many of the sources relating to this period are printed and translated in *Monumenta de Insula Manniae*, ii, but the dates assigned to the documents in this work must be treated with caution.

and the first indications of English control four years later, de Burgh had taken control of Man and installed bailiffs to run the island on his behalf. In the light of the history of contacts between Man and Ulster this is hardly surprising, and it fits in well enough with the ongoing English policy of exploiting turbulence in the Irish Sea world for their own ends. But the involvement of de Burgh might also reflect the spilling over of Bruce–Balliol tensions into the Irish Sea. When the 1275 uprising in Man was suppressed by the Scots, it was largely a Galloway affair, undertaken with the backing of the Comyns and MacDougalls. Seán Duffy has suggested that, because of the long-standing enmity between them, it is possible that the rulers of Carrick opposed this Galloway enterprise with the backing of their Stewart and MacDonald allies, the very people who appear in the Turnberry Band of 1286.[137]

Whatever might have been the case, the seizure of Man by the English in 1290 has been regarded as sinister, for Edward had effectively taken control of an island belonging to Scotland without the consent of the Guardians of that kingdom; indeed it was in his hands even before the death of Margaret, the Maid of Norway, in September. Whether Edward entertained plans for the subjugation of Scotland in 1290 is contentious, but the strategic importance of Man to both sides cannot be denied, and there seems little doubt that the Scottish presence in Man, only a few miles from the English coast, made the English profoundly uncomfortable. Henry III had attempted to dissuade Alexander III from undertaking a campaign to the Isles in 1263, and the Scots would almost certainly never have acquired Man in 1266 had it not been for the political situation in England. It is hardly surprising, then, to find Edward I taking advantage of the opportunity to seize Man in 1290. In 1307 he would claim that the examination of documents revealed that Man had been held by his ancestors, the kings of England, 'and that we have, in like manner, been seized of the same'. According to Edward's argument, Man had been granted to Alexander III and later to John Balliol by the English kings – an interesting interpretation of Manx history which conveniently ignored both the Scandinavian dynasty of Man and the Treaty of Perth of 1266 which ceded it to Scotland, but which might reveal much about Edward's attitude towards the relations between England and Scotland.[138] Whether Edward's actions should be regarded as sinister or not, they certainly represented, 'a surprising intervention in the affairs of another realm'.[139]

Between 1293 and 1296 there followed a brief interlude of Scottish suzerainty. In January 1293, after the decision by Edward in favour of

---

[137] See S. Duffy, 'Ireland and the Irish Sea Region, 1014–1318' (Dublin University, Ph.D. thesis, 1993), pp. 163–5; I am grateful to Dr Duffy for providing me with a photocopy of relevant parts of his thesis, and for permission to cite it.

[138] *Foedera*, i, pt. 4, p. 75; *Monumenta de Insula Manniae*, ii, pp. 139–40.

[139] M. Prestwich, *Edward I* (London, 1988), p. 362.

John Balliol in the Great Cause and his subsequent inauguration at Scone, Walter of Huntercombe was ordered to give over possession of Man to Balliol.[140] We have seen how the kingship of John Balliol partly foundered and failed over the issue of appeals to England from Scotland, and we have also noted that of six Scottish appellants to Edward, three were from a Hebridean or Irish Sea context. One of these appellants was Manx. In June 1293 the Lady Affrica, described as 'kinswoman and heiress' of King Magnus of Man (d. 1265), appealed to Edward I over her ancestral claim to the Isle of Man, and the English king ordered Balliol to appear before him to answer the appeal.[141] It seems likely that Affrica saw the death of Alexander III and the establishment of a new regime as an opportunity to press her claim, which must have seemed hopeless under Scottish overlordship, and her appeal might support the contention that the Manx hoped to play English and Scots off against one another. But Affrica's petition ultimately seems to have amounted to nothing, and in 1305 she resigned her claim to Simon Montagu, a minor Somerset baron who was just possibly also her husband, and who was in charge of a fleet operating in the Western Isles and Irish Sea.[142]

Following the deposition of John Balliol in 1296, the Isle of Man reverted to the English king. By April 1298 it was in the possession of Anthony Bek, Bishop of Durham, and it seems to have remained in his charge until his death in 1311.[143] By then, however, the storm clouds were on the horizon.

Robert I, familiar with the western seaboard and the Irish Sea world, would have been quick to recognise the strategic importance of Man; as long as the English controlled it the south-western approaches of Scotland were vulnerable, and it was the headquarters of the fleet responsible for protecting traffic between Ireland and the English coasts. It was therefore natural that Bruce and the Scots would endeavour to wrest Man from the English, and between 1310 and 1318 considerable efforts were expended by the Scots in pursuit of this aim. Indeed, by 1320, Scottish sea-power was threatening to dominate the Irish Sea.[144]

In late 1310 the English king addressed a letter to his sheriffs, bailiffs, and faithful subjects in the counties of Cheshire, Lancashire, Cumberland and Westmorland. He stated that he had learned from 'certain persons' that:

Robert Bruce, our enemy and traitor, is striving with all his power, and purposes to despatch all his navy during the present winter,

---

140 *Foedera*, i, pt. 3, p. 116.
141 *Rot. Scot.*, i, p. 18.
142 *Monumenta de Insula Manniae*, pp. 137–8; Duffy, '"Continuation" of Nicholas Trevet', pp. 305–6.
143 Fryde *et al.*, *Handbook of British Chronology*, p. 65.
144 Reid, 'Sea-power in the Anglo-Scottish War', p. 19.

from outward Islands, to our Island of Man, for the purpose of destroying it, and of establishing there a retreat for him and his accomplices, our enemies and rebels; and likewise to seize upon all victuals and other necessities ... and for the supply of his navy, which, if permitted, would plainly tend to our damage, and to the disgrace and dishonour of our whole kingdom ...[145]

Several points in the letter demand our attention. In the first place, who were the 'certain persons' from whom the English king had acquired this information? We can reasonably speculate that John of Argyll was among their number, and was probably the king's most important informer. He had been in exile in England and Ireland since 1309, and was serving the English king in Ireland in 1310 and 1311; in the latter year he was made Admiral of the western seas, perhaps as a counter-measure to Bruce's reported naval activities. Given his Hebridean background (which must have provided him with many contacts, even in exile), his knowledge of the western seaboard, and his faithful service to the English king, it is easy to imagine John providing crucial intelligence to the English about the activities of King Robert in the western seaboard. Second, we should note the mention that Bruce's navy was dispatched from 'outward Islands'. No doubt many of the galleys in this fleet were supplied by his MacDonald and MacRuairi allies, and only four years earlier, in 1306–7, Christiana MacRuairi had helped king Robert escape into the vastness of the western seaboard, while in 1308 the force that invaded Galloway with Edward Bruce was said to have come from the 'outer isles'. Finally, the observation that the Scottish king hoped to establish a retreat in Man for himself and his allies is interesting, and it might provide some hint that Bruce hoped to use the island as a staging point for his invasion of Ireland. Certainly the Scottish king was well aware of the strategic importance of Man and the necessity to control the western seaways. Indeed, control of Man was a vital pre-requisite for the invasion of Ireland in 1315 and, like that expedition, action against the English in Man would have constituted the opening of a second front by the Scots.[146]

It is probably in connection with Bruce's activities in 1310 that the English king wrote to the bailiffs of Bristol and other towns and commanded them to, 'despatch in all haste to the Isle of Man the navy which we have required of you', to go against the Scots and, 'to molest them in every way you can devise'.[147] And it is almost certainly in connection with Bruce's fleet, and with the activities of the Scottish sea-captain

---

[145] *Rot. Scot.*, i, p. 96; *Monumenta de Insula Manniae*, ii, pp. 149–51.

[146] There is a vast literature on the Bruce invasion of Ireland. See, among others, Duffy, 'Bruce.brothers'; Duncan, 'Scots' invasion of Ireland'; R. Frame, 'The Bruces in Ireland', *Irish Historical Studies*, xix (1974); and Duffy, '"Continuation" of Nicholas Trevet'.

[147] *Rot. Scot.*, i, p. 92; *Monumenta de Insula Manniae*, ii, pp. 145–7.

Thomas Dun, that Edward wrote to all his bailiffs and faithful subjects in England in late 1310, commanding them to arrest without delay 'many malefactors of the Isle of Man, who, adhering to the party of Robert Bruce our enemy and betrayer, have effected much damage upon us and our faithful subjects in England'.[148] Similar letters were addressed to bailiffs in Ireland and in Wales; the extent of Scottish naval activity is revealed by the fact that the Scots sailed into Holyhead and captured an English ship in 1315.[149] The letter also seems to suggest that Bruce and the Scots had adherents in the Isle of Man; perhaps they were acting as a fifth column to create dissent there, but whatever the case, they were certainly causing the English king a good deal of anxiety.

By 1310 the domestic situation in England was worsening as opposition to Edward II crystallised. The ensuing political instability spilled over into the Isle of Man, creating a confusing and unstable situation. Edward II may have granted the island to Piers Gaveston shortly after his accession, but by 1310 it was once again under the control of Anthony Bek and administered by his steward, Gilbert Makaskyl.[150] It probably remained in Bek's hands until his death in March 1311, and in May of that year it was granted to Sir Henry Beaumont, one of the king's cousins. His tenure was brief because he aroused the suspicions of the king's opponents, the Ordainers, and later that same year the grant was revoked and Gilbert Makaskyl and Robert de Leiburn received custody. Henry de Beaumont was restored and deprived yet again in 1312, and then, some time before April 1313, the Isle of Man was seized by Simon Montagu.[151]

The English vacillations in Man provided an opportunity for Robert I and the Scots. On 18 May 1313, Robert landed at Ramsay with a large fleet, and a few days later, on 21 May, laid siege to Rushen Castle. It was defended by Dungal MacDouall, but fell on 12 June.[152] Dungal MacDouall of Galloway was an inveterate opponent of the king. It is not clear in what capacity he was holding the castle, but he had surrendered Dumfries Castle to Robert in February 1313 and was allowed to go free; he evidently crossed to the Isle of Man and took command of Rushen. It must have been satisfying for Robert to accept Dungal's second surrender within the space of six months, but he was once again set free and became a veteran in the service of the English king.[153]

The situation in Man between 1313 and 1318 is difficult to ascertain. The sources are patchy, contradictory, and inconclusive, but they suggest

[148] *Rot. Scot.*, i, p. 96.
[149] Nicholson, *Later Middle Ages*, p. 94.
[150] *CDS*, iii, no. 481.
[151] *Chron. Lanercost* (Maxwell), p. 184, relates the grant to Piers Gaveston, but other sources would place it in 1311; documents in *Monumenta de Insula Manniae*, ii, pp. 143–61; see also *Chron. Man*, pp. 233–4; for seizure by Simon Montagu, see *CDS*, iii, no. 307.
[152] *Chron. Man*, p. 111.
[153] On Dungal's career, see Barrow, *Robert Bruce*, pp. 192–3, and *passim*.

that, despite Bruce's conquest of 1313, neither side was in firm control and the domination of the island teetered precariously back and forth for several years, punctuated perhaps with intermittent conflicts. An English safe-conduct to go there in September 1314 may or may not indicate that the island was in English hands, and a petition of Duncan Mackoury from 1314 or 1316 seems to indicate ongoing conflict.[154] By February 1315 the English king had received news that John of Argyll had expelled the Scots from Man; this had probably occurred in late 1314 or January 1315. Later that same year John was at Dublin, anxiously awaiting the arrival of a fleet with which to harass the Scots over the winter. But the advantage that this gave to the English never seems to have been pressed, possibly because John was infirm. In 1316 King Robert made a prospective grant of the lordship of Man to Thomas Randolph, Earl of Moray, and in the summer of 1317 Randolph was preparing to menace both Man and Anglesey with a fleet.[155] Edward II seems to have held the island in the summer of 1317, although a document of July described the 'hostile attacks of our enemies and rebels the Scots' [156] – probably a reference to the activities of Thomas Randolph in the region. Man was subsequently granted to John de Athy in 1318, but in 1322 Thomas Randolph gave a safe-conduct to go there and in 1324 another grant of the island was made to the earl of Moray by Robert Bruce. It would thus appear that in 1318 Man was still in the hands of the English, but by 1322 it had passed to the Scots; perhaps the Anglo-Scottish truce of 1319 had seen its custody returned to the Scots.[157] Whatever may have been the case, Man was formally acknowledged to be under Scottish control by the English king and parliament in 1328, and it remained so until 1333 when, in the renewed Anglo-Scottish conflicts engendered by the death of Robert I in 1329, the island was seized by Edward III and granted to William Montagu.[158]

Consideration of the history of the Isle of Man between 1290 and 1333 brings our story full circle. At the turn of the eleventh century, the Isle of Man was a prize sought by Irish, Norse, and Hebridean factions. In the middle of the twelfth century Somerled added it to his extensive insular kingdom (however briefly), and a hundred years after his demise it passed to the Scots, probably against the wishes of the English kings, who could do nothing to prevent its annexation at that time. The strategic importance of the Isle of Man no doubt prompted Edward I's seizure of the island in 1290, but this in turn sparked off a new round of struggles for hegemony. The English needed the Isle of Man as a naval

154 *CDS*, iii, nos. 391, 521. Duncan was a follower of John of Argyll who should possibly be identified with Duncan MacRuairi: see Sellar, 'MacDonald and MacRuari pedigrees', p. 4, and note 6.
155 *RRS*, v, no. 101; *CDS*, iii, no. 562.
156 *Monumenta de Insula Manniae*, pp. 169–70.
157 Moore, 'Connexion between Scotland and Man', 406–7.
158 Stones, *Anglo-Scottish Relations*, p. 167; *Monumenta de Insula Manniae*, ii, pp. 180–2.

base for their activities against the Scots, and to control the western seaways to Ireland; the Scots needed it to protect their vulnerable flank, and as a prelude to their invasion of Ireland. And so the situation in the Irish Sea in 1300 was little different than it had been two centuries earlier. The players had changed and the stakes were higher, but the playing field and the rules remained the same: whoever aimed to control the western seaways would first need to control the Isle of Man.

CHAPTER SEVEN

The Western Seaboard meets Western Christendom: The Church and Monasticism, c.1100–1300

Within this Ile thair was an Abbay of Monks and ane Monasterie of Nunnis with ane paroche kirk, with sundrie ather chapells dotit of auld be the kings of Scotland and be the Clan-Donald [Donald Monro, 1549].[1]

Scarba ... where there is a chapel of the Blessed Virgin, at which many miracles are performed [John of Fordun, c.1385].[2]

One of the major themes of the centuries between about 1050 and 1300 is the widening of the bounds of Latin Christendom, the area that acknowledged the authority of the pope and celebrated the Latin liturgy. Developments in the eleventh century launched the papacy into the spiritual leadership of western Christendom and greatly enhanced its prestige, and the rise and development of papal law courts, legates, and councils, with an increase in papal correspondence, meant that the authority of the papacy became greater and its decisions more enforceable. But the expansion of western Christendom manifested itself in other ways, too. The international reformed religious orders enjoyed tremendous popularity between 1100 and 1300, and spread like wildfire across western Europe. There was a multiplication of dioceses (the areas that fell under the jurisdiction of a bishop), as new bishoprics were created. At the grass-roots level, the parochial system continued to develop and expand, and popular devotion was even affected as the cults of the universal saints eclipsed those of the local saints which predominated in the early middle ages. In short, 'from around 1050 Rome ... created a new institutional and cultural uniformity in the western church'.[3]

It is worth while asking how these developments affected the western seaboard, on the geographic fringes of western Europe. Did it share in

[1] Munro, *Monro's Western Isles*, pp. 62–3.
[2] *Chron. Fordun*, i, p. 43; ii, p. 39.
[3] Bartlett, *Making of Europe*, p. 250.

these trends or remain aloof? Considering the turbulence and warfare that seem to characterise the twelfth and thirteenth centuries in the Western Isles, not to mention the freebooting activities of some of Somerled's descendants and the Manx kings, we could be forgiven for losing sight of the fact that this was a Christian society. Yet, the roots of Christianity in the West were ancient, and in common with other kings, princes, and nobles of western Europe, the Hebridean chieftains shared in the patronage of churches, the foundation of monasteries, the creation of a new bishopric, and the construction of chapels and churches. If we seek to understand fully these sea-kings, we must also explore their roles as patrons and benefactors of the Church. It is no exaggeration to say that between 1100 and 1300 the religious life of the western seaboard was profoundly altered as the kingdom of the Isles was engulfed by the same trends as were sweeping through the rest of western Europe.

Exploring religious life in Argyll and the Isles in this period is not an easy task. The major difficulty that hampers our knowledge of secular politics is even more accentuated for the ecclesiastical sphere: the lack of source material. The fame of religious sites like Iona, both today and in the past, obscures the fact that remarkably little is known about their history and development. As a striking example of this, none of the names of the abbots of Iona between 1203 and 1320 is known! The monastic and diocesan registers, collections of documents recording grants of lands and privileges to abbots and bishops, that are so crucial to our understanding of church patronage, are not extant for Iona, Saddell, Ardchattan or Oronsay, nor for the dioceses of Argyll or the Isles. Only the register of Paisley Abbey, a sixteenth-century compilation, has come down to us, and although it sheds much light on the Church in the West, its survival also serves to highlight how much has been lost. The library of Iona, referred to several times in the later medieval period, was probably destroyed in the turmoil of the Reformation; and the strife in the Isle of Man in the fourteenth century probably contributed to the loss of ecclesiastical documents relating to the diocese of the Isles. The evidence from the chronicles and annals, both Scottish and Irish, is sparse for this period. Some papal documents pertaining to the region survive, as do a few charters for Iona and Saddell, buried in later confirmations and legal documents. In the absence of written sources, the archaeological and architectural evidence is instructive, but remains problematic where questions of dating are concerned. In short, our knowledge of the Church in the western seaboard must be gleaned from scattered fragments of evidence.

Christianity in the western seaboard, as in the rest of the Scottish kingdom itself, was ancient by the time of Somerled MacGillebrigte. Argyll and the Isles had been closely linked with Ireland, the Isle of

Man, Wales, and other regions even further abroad during the so-called 'Age of the Saints' from the sixth to the eighth centuries, when saints like Columba (d. 597), Moluag (d. c.592), Donnan of Eigg (d. 617), and Maelrubha (d. 722) – all of whom travelled largely by sea[4] – established important monastic centres on Iona, Lismore, Eigg, and at Applecross. Place-names containing the Gaelic element *kil* (Gaelic *cille*, church or churchyard), which are abundant in the western seaboard and seem to date from before AD 800, help to reveal the legacy of these early saints, about whom little is known (with the exception of Columba) from the literary sources. Thus, we find commemorations of Adomnán (abbot of Iona, d. 704) at Killeonan near Campbeltown in Kintyre; Angus (d. 535) at Killanaish in Knapdale; Barre (d. c.610) at Kilbarr in Barra; Cainnech (d. c.600) at Kilchenich in Tiree and Kilchenzie in Kintyre, Coil, and South Uist; Ciaran (d. c.549) at Kilchieran in Islay; Donnan at Kildonnan on Eigg, South Uist, Skye, Bernera in north-west Lewis, and at Eilean Donan and Loch Broom on the mainland; Moluag (d. c.592) at Kilmaluag on Lismore; St Columba (d. 597) in numerous dedications of Cill Chaluim Chille; and Maelrubha (d. 722) at Applecross, Clachan Ma-Ruibhe on Loch Carron, and Eilean Ma-Ruibhe on Loch Maree, which is itself named after him. Other place-names are also indicative of the Christian legacy in the West, including Appin (Argyll), derived from the Irish *apdaine*, the jurisdiction of an *ab* or abbot; Dysart (Argyll), from the Irish *diseart*, the cell of a hermit; or Elie (Iona), from the Irish *ealadh*, a landing place that received corpses destined for burial at a hallowed cemetery. And, although the evidence of the physical remains is largely silent for the early period of Christianity in the Isles, enough traces survive in the archaeological record to bear out the literary and toponymic evidence. The remains of an early Christian monastery, including a double beehive cell, are to be found at Eileach an Naoimh in the Garvellachs; some traces of the early medieval *vallum* or earthwork bank survive at Iona; and the most remarkable achievements of the period are surely the great free-standing crosses of Kildalton in Islay, and Iona, dating from the eighth or ninth centuries.[5]

Nowhere was the legacy of Christianity in the West more pronounced than on Iona. This tiny island lies about a mile off the south-west tip of the Isle of Mull, separated from it by the Sound of Iona. The Northumbrian scholar and monk, Bede, called it *Hii insula*, and Columba's biographer, Adomnán, referred to it as *Ioua insula*. Adomnán used the adjectival form, so that in the nominative the name of the island would have been *I* or *Io*, similar to Bede's *Hii*, where the *h* is silent. In the Middle Ages it was usually called *Icolmkill* or *I*, and the modern English

4 See J. Marsden, *Sea-Road of the Saints: Celtic Holy Men in the Hebrides* (Edinburgh, 1995).
5 W. F. H. Nicolaisen, *Scottish Place Names* (1976; repr. London, 1986), pp. 142–4; Smyth, *Warlords and Holy Men*, pp. 107–10; Bowen, *Saints, Seaways and Settlements*, pp. 73–4, 99–104; Barrow, *Kingship and Unity*, p. 64; RCAHMS, *Argyll, passim*.

form, Iona, is derived from a misreading of the form *Ioua*, where the *u* and *n* can be difficult to distinguish in some medieval scripts.[6]

The rise of Iona to prominence belongs to the sixth century, when, in about 563, St Columba made the island his home and established a Christian community there which became a place of world-wide fame and pilgrimage, even to the present day. The story of Iona under Columba and his successors as abbots is well known and need not be recounted here.[7] Following his death in 597 the island was renowned as a centre of culture and pilgrimage, even though the succession to the abbacy was not always without incident. Then, in the late eighth century, when Iona was at the height of its prestige, it felt the first attacks of the Vikings. The earliest on record occurred in 794; in 795 Rathlin and Skye were plundered; in 798 the Hebrides and Ulster suffered; and in 802 Iona was raided and burned again. In 806, the Vikings returned and killed 68 members of the monastic community. This prompted the migration of most of the monks to Kells in Ireland, an inland site and one that would be safe from the ravages of the Northmen. The precious relics of St Columba soon followed: in 849 and 878 some relics were transferred to Kells; and in 849 others were taken to Dunkeld by Kenneth MacAlpin. It was a drastic step, and one that symbolised the troubled times of the Christian community on Iona.

But, despite the depredations of the Vikings and the migration of most of the monks to Kells, Iona was not completely abandoned and a small community of monks seems to have remained. In 825 the monk Blathmac was tortured to make him reveal the hiding place of monastic treasure; the story of his martyrdom was recorded as far away as Reichenau in Germany. Scattered references in Norse and Irish sources indicate that Iona endured the hardships of the first years of Viking raiding, and that the island enjoyed something of a revival by the middle of the tenth century. In 980 Olaf Cuaran, the Scandinavian king of Dublin, went on pilgrimage to Iona and died there, possibly having entered the monastic community. On Christmas Eve 986 the monastery was plundered again, with the abbot and fifteen monks being killed; and in about 1007 a Viking coffin washed ashore on 'the Holy Island, in the Hebrides' where the abbot's servants found it and desecrated it. The lector of Kells was drowned, and priceless relics of St Patrick and St Columba were lost *en route* from Ireland to Scotland (possibly to Iona), in 1034, and in 1098 Magnus Barelegs stopped at Iona as he plundered his way south through the Hebrides to reassert Norwegian authority in

---

[6] MacQuarrie and MacArthur, *Iona Through the Ages*, p. 4. See also *OPS*, ii, pt. 1, p. 284.
[7] The major source for Columba and Iona in his time is, of course, the biography written by Adomnán: *Life of Columba*, ed. A. O. and M. O. Anderson (Edinburgh, 1961). See also Smyth, *Warlords and Holy Men*, chaps. 3, 4; MacQuarrie and MacArthur, *Iona Through the Ages*, pp. 3–11; M. Herbert, *Iona, Kells and Derry: The History and Historiography of the Monastic Familia of Columba* (Oxford, 1988); and B. T. Hudson, 'Kings and Church in early Scotland', *SHR*, lxxiii (1994), pp. 158–9.

the Isles. His saga relates how he was overtaken by the urge to open the church of St Columba, but that he did not go in, ordering instead that the door be locked and entry prohibited.[8]

Finally, in the last quarter of the eleventh century, Margaret, the wife of Malcolm Canmore, is said by the twelfth-century chronicler Orderic Vitalis to have 'rebuilt the monastery of Iona ... which had been destroyed in the time of wars, and by great age. And she gave the monks fitting revenues for the work of the Lord, and restored it.'[9] Elaborate claims have sometimes been made for Margaret's involvement at Iona on the basis of this statement, but her contemporary biographer, Turgot, who discussed her patronage of Dunfermline and St Andrews, had nothing to say of Iona, and no architectural remains survive on the island from that period.[10] It is of course true that Iona remained within the ambit of the Scottish kings until 1098,[11] and so it is not inconceivable that the monastery was patronised by Queen Margaret. But if she endowed Iona in any fashion, Orderic seems to have been the only chronicler to have taken note of it; and, if the community there was thriving in the mid-twelfth century, it may have had little or nothing to do with Margaret's patronage, which appears dubious at best.

There is good evidence that Iona was home, at least in the twelfth century but almost certainly earlier, to a community of Culdees. In 1164 the *Annals of Ulster* named several members of the monastic community, including Augustine, *sacart mor* (arch priest), Dubshidhe, *fer leginn* (lector), Mac Gille-Dubhe, *disertach* (hermit), and Mac Forcellaich, head of the Culdee community.[12] The name Culdee or *céli dé* means servant or companion of God, and the Culdees originated in eighth-century Ireland as a reform movement. There, they were often associated with monasteries, where they formed a separate community, and in Scotland they appear as secular clerics, anchorites, or living according to a monastic rule. Culdee houses are documented at many locations in Scotland. At Iona there seems to have been a monastic community with a group of Culdees alongside it, a situation very much reminiscent of that in, Ireland where the Culdees were often associated with a larger community who respected them but did not share their devotions.[13]

---

8 References from *ES*, *passim*.
9 *SAEC*, p. 116.
10 See the cautious comments of A. J. Wilson, *St Margaret Queen of Scotland* (Edinburgh, 1993), p. 68.
11 See Hudson, 'Kings and Church in early Scotland', p. 159.
12 *Ann. Ulster*, ii, pp. 144–7; also in *ES*, ii, pp. 253–4.
13 On the Culdees or *Céli Dé*, see P. O'Dwyer, *Céli Dé: Spiritual Reform in Ireland, 750–900* (Dublin, 1981); P. O'Dwyer, 'Celtic monks and the Culdee reform', in J. P. MacKey (ed.), *An Introduction to Celtic Christianity* (Edinburgh, 1989); I. B. Cowan, 'The post Columban Church', *Scottish Church History Soc. Records*, xviii, no. 4 (1974); I. B. Cowan and D. E. Easson, *Medieval Religious Houses: Scotland* (2nd edn, London, 1976), pp. 46–54; H. Zimmer, *The Celtic Church in Britain and Ireland* (London, 1902); and W. Reeves, *The Culdees of the British Isles* (Dublin, 1864).

Thus, despite the onslaught of the Northmen at the close of the eighth century, the religious life and the symbolic importance of Iona was maintained between 800 and the middle of the twelfth century. A small monastic community, perhaps with a complement of Culdees, seems to have continued its devotions and even enjoyed a resurgence in the middle of the tenth century. Whether or not Queen Margaret was a patron of Iona, we find a flourishing community there in the middle of the twelfth century, but by then the political situation had been greatly altered as the Isles fell under the dominion of Somerled MacGillebrigte.

Despite his apparent propensity for warfare, Somerled, like most princes of his age, also took an interest in the welfare of the Church. Although there is little evidence on which to judge his role as a benefactor, he appears to have exhibited at least the conventional piety expected from one of his status, and it is hardly surprising that much of his attention was reserved for Iona, the ancient ecclesiastical centre located at the very heart of his island kingdom. The *Annals of Ulster* record how, in 1164:

> dignitaries of the community of Iona ... came to meet Columcille's successor, Flaithbertach Ua-Brolchain, [asking him] to take the abbacy of Iona, by counsel of Somerled, and the men of Argyll and of the Hebrides. But Patrick's successor, and the king of Ireland, Ua-Lochlaind, and the nobles of Cenel-Eogain, restrained him.[14]

It is difficult to know how to interpret these events. They may have represented an attempt to reform the Church on Iona in accordance with ecclesiastical reforms taking place in contemporary Ireland, Scotland, and Wales. Irish and Scottish kings and Welsh princes were involved in church reform in this period, and several of the important reforming councils in Ireland in the twelfth century had been held under the auspices of regional kings.[15] But it is notable that Somerled specifically invited Flaithbertach Ua-Brolchain, a northern Irish bishop and one who led an attempt to reform the Irish Columban churches, 'in line with, or in opposition to, the organisation of the new orders imported from abroad'.[16] It is just possible that in turning to northern Ireland, and to Flaithbertach Ua-Brolchain in particular, Somerled was making a deliberately conservative gesture which drew upon the revived Celtic Christianity in Northern Ireland, and which was the ecclesiastical equivalent of his rebellions against the kings of Scots. This hypothesis might be supported by the fact that Somerled's actions prompted King

---

[14] *ES*, ii, pp. 253–4.

[15] See B. T. Hudson, 'Gaelic princes and Gregorian reform', in B. T. Hudson and V. Ziegler (eds.), *Crossed Paths. Methodological Approaches to the Celtic Aspect of the European Middle Ages* (Lanham, N.Y., and London, 1991).

[16] See Byrne, 'Trembling sod'; and F. X. Martin, 'Diarmait Mac Murchada and the coming of the Anglo-Normans': both in Cosgrove, *Medieval Ireland*, pp. 38, 54–5.

William to deprive Iona of churches which it possessed in Galloway, granting them instead to Holyrood Abbey; the whole episode is puzzling, but is suggestive of strong undercurrents of tension between the mainland and Iona about this time.[17]

But Somerled's attempted reform at Iona represents not the dawning of a new age in Christianity in the western seaboard; it is rather the twilight of an old one. It has been said that the middle of the twelfth century marks the transition from the ancient to the medieval world at Iona.[18] With some modification of dates this general comment may be applied to the whole of the western seaboard. The twelfth century witnessed the weakening, if not the total dissolution, of old links with Ireland, and the rise of new connections that brought the western seaboard firmly into the fold of western Christendom. Whether we consider the organisation and patronage of the Church, the growth of the reformed religious orders, or even the establishment of parishes and popular religion, it is clear that by about 1200 the west-coast region was conforming more and more closely with the unity imposed by the Church of Rome, and was beginning to assume its place as an integral part of Latin Christendom.

The establishment of territorial dioceses was of central importance if the western seaboard was to become a fully integrated component of western Christendom. In a territorial diocesan system, bishoprics were concretely defined: 'each required an individual incumbent, who usually possessed a cathedral church. Both bishop and diocese had names.'[19] Indeed, Latin Christendom was in effect a cellular body in which the individual components were the dioceses. Both the Irish and the Scottish churches were undergoing restructuring along territorial diocesan lines in the course of the twelfth century, and it is hardly surprising to find the same thing happening in the western seaboard.

The diocese of Sodor or the Isles first appears in the historical record in about the year 1079. A list of bishops appended to the *Chronicle of Man* states that 'Roolwer was the first bishop before the time when Godred Crovan began to reign', and adds that he was buried at the church

---

17 *RRS*, ii, no. 141. Something must surely be said of Iona as the 'traditional' burial place of Scottish kings. Although this is asserted with such frequency as to give the impression of being well-established fact, modern scholarship is highly sceptical. Hudson has noted that information on kingly burials at Iona does not appear in the sources until the 13th century, and contemporary records such as the *Scottish Chronicle*, the *Duan Albanach*, and the *Prophecy of Berchán*, do not mention Iona as a royal burial place (although the *Prophecy* does name the place of burial of some kings). It has, accordingly, been suggested that the later medieval sources were deliberately striving to give Iona prestige as a royal cemetery, and this in turn has been linked to the efforts of the descendants of Somerled to re-establish Iona as the premier monastery of the region: Hudson, 'Kings and Church in early Scotland', p. 159. The supposed kingly burials are, therefore, probably only fiction, but Iona was certainly the burial place of later Lords of the Isles and members of leading west Highland families: Dunbar and Fisher, *Iona*, p. 12.

18 Steer and Bannerman, *Late Medieval Monumental Sculpture*, p. 13.

19 Bartlett, *Making of Europe*, p. 5.

of St Maughold in Man. Although Roolwer, about whom nothing else is known, is the first of the bishops named in the chronicle, it is certain that he was not the first bishop in the Isles. The chronicle goes on to note that, 'there were, indeed, many bishops from the time of blessed Patrick, who is said to have been the first to preach the Catholic faith to the Manxmen, but it is sufficient to have begun the account of the bishops from Roolwer'. This is because the chronicler claimed to be 'entirely ignorant of who or what were the bishops before Roolwer's time; for we neither find any written documents on the subject, nor have we any certain accounts handed down by our elders'.[20] Modern scholarship labours under much the same constraints some seven centuries later; and although the names of some of the early bishops in the Isles are known, their relation to Roolwer and his place among them remains uncertain.

The titles of the twelfth-century bishops included Skye, Man, the Isles, Sudreys, and Sodor. They recognised the metropolitan status of York until 1153, when they were placed under the authority of Nidaros/ Trondheim in Norway. It is significant that the first bishop to appear in the Icelandic Annals was Reginald (*c*.1170), which means that he was probably the first bishop to have recognised the metropolitan status of Trondheim as opposed to York. Despite the status of Trondheim, however, some bishops continued to seek consecration at York or, occasionally, Dublin, as late as the early thirteenth century. Thus, in 1219 the bishop of the Isles was sent to Dublin to seek consecration, while in 1244 Pope Innocent IV noted that sometimes the archbishop of York and sometimes the archbishop of Trondheim had been in the habit of consecrating the bishops of the Isles. Certainly the far-flung nature of the diocese will have posed considerable problems: as Innocent IV noted in 1244, 'the church of Nidaros is very remote from the church of Man and separated from it by a dangerous sea'.[21] A century later, in 1349, the rights of Trondheim were reduced when the pope excused the bishop of the Isles from making a personal visit to Trondheim to profess his obedience.

The right to elect the bishops of Sodor was granted to the monks of Furness Abbey in Cumbria by King Olaf in 1134. In his charter he stated that 'I have committed and forever granted to the church of the blessed Mary of Furness on account of the proximity of the place, and for the excellent life of the inhabitants, the honour of the said episcopal election.' At the same time, writing to the Archbishop of York, King Olaf provided that the new bishop should be chosen from among the monks

---

20 *Chron. Man*, pp. 112–15.
21 Cited in A. Ashley, *The Church in the Isle of Man* (York, 1958), pp. 14–15. See also Watt, *Fasti*, pp. 197–9; and I. B. Cowan, 'The medieval Church in Argyll and the Isles', *Scottish Church History Soc. Records*, xx, pt. 1 (1978), p. 15.

of Furness and should seek consecration from York's hands; these electoral rights were confirmed by Olaf's successors.[22]

In his charter to Furness, Olaf stated that the new bishopric was being erected so that 'the Christian religion in my kingdom shall be preserved entire under its own bishop, rather than rendered desolate under strangers, and as it were mercenaries, who seek their own and not the Lord's advantage'.[23] We do not know what circumstances prompted Olaf's clerk to make this remark. However, his comments point to a time when this had been the case, and since bishops of Iona, Kingarth, Man and Skye are known from the seventh to eleventh centuries,[24] it is possible that Olaf was erecting Man and the Isles into a single diocese along territorial lines, effectively substituting a territorial diocesan organisation for an earlier monastic and tribal one. A papal bull, purporting to date from 1231 but in fact a forgery of the fourteenth or fifteenth century, reveals the extent to which the diocese of the Isles formed a cell within the larger body of western Christendom. The document is addressed to Simon, bishop of Sodor, and mentions the cathedral church of the diocese, at Peel on the Isle of Man; it states that the bishop should have the third part of the tithes from the churches in the Isles; and it gives a comprehensive list of some twenty islands that constituted the diocese. We would be hard put to find a better example of how thoroughly the diocesan organisation of the western seaboard had been brought into conformity with the rest of western Europe.[25]

Although the early bishops of the diocese are known to have borne several titles, they seem to have been normally associated with the Isle of Man. Bishop Simon (1226–48), an Argyll man and one of the most important of the early bishops, was said by the *Chronicle of Man* to have began the construction of the cathedral of St German at Peel on the west coast.[26] This was a site of some significance, already occupied by two churches: St Patrick's, the ruins of which still survive and date to the eleventh or twelfth century; and the parish church of St German on the spot occupied by the cathedral.[27] In fact, the construction of St German's occurred in three phases: the first and second in the twelfth and thirteenth centuries, and the final stage after the destruction caused by the Anglo-Scottish struggle for control of Man in the fourteenth century.

22 *Monumenta de Insula Manniae*, ii, pp. 1–6, 13–14, 17–18. Furness was a Savignac house, founded by Stephen, Count of Blois, and future king of England (1135–54) in 1123 at Tulketh. It moved to Furness in 1127 and, in common with the Savignac order, merged with the Cistercians in 1147.
23 *Monumenta de Insula Manniae*, ii, pp. 1–2.
24 Fryde *et al.*, *Handbook of British Chronology*, pp. 313, 315–16, 322; see also D. E. R. Watt, 'Bishops in the Isles before 1203: bibliography and biographical lists', *Innes Rev.*, xlv (1994).
25 Poole, 'Scottish islands in the diocese of Sodor', pp. 258–63; see also Megaw, 'Norseman and native in the Kingdom of the Isles', pp. 29–34.
26 *Chron. Man*, pp. 100, 116–117.
27 R. H. Kinvig, *A History of the Isle of Man* (3rd edn, Liverpool, 1975), p. 79.

It was the second stage of building, begun by Bishop Reginald, which was completed by Bishop Simon, who was buried in the new, enlarged, presbytery of the cathedral. It has been noted that the cathedral's architecture has more in common with Anglo-Norman Ulster than with the west Highlands of Scotland, possibly because of matrimonial connections between John de Courcy, Lord of Ulster, and Affrica, the daughter of King Godfrey and the sister of King Ragnvald, who was the founder of Grey Abbey in County Down, and who may also have been a patron of the cathedral building at Peel.[28]

The administration of the far-flung diocese must have posed some unique practical difficulties. The first known date for an archdeacon of Man is between 1188 and 1190, while the first appearance of an archdeacon of Sodor is 1320. It has been suggested that administrative duties must have been divided between Man and the Sudreys, and in the thirteenth century officials bearing the title of Man and Sodor appear respectively in 1219 and between 1235 and 1244; but, since these dates do not overlap, such a division must remain speculative. More conclusive is the evidence for a separatist trend in the Scottish part of the diocese even before the split engendered by the Great Schism in 1378, following which the diocese was claimed by rival bishops adhering to rival popes at Rome and Avignon. Between 1326 and 1331 the 'canons of Snizort and the clergy of Skye' elected Cormac as bishop, and in 1331 their proctors were in Bergen seeking his confirmation, which suggests that the election was taken seriously by Trondheim. The outcome of the claim is not known, but it sheds some faint light on the ecclesiastical situation in the Isles. A bishop of Skye is on record in the eleventh century, and it is possible that the community at Snizort had a continuous existence dating back from the fourteenth century to that time or even earlier. In this context it is perhaps noteworthy that there are substantial remains of an early medieval church on the island in the river Snizort at Skeaboast bridge. After the split in the diocese engendered by the Great Schism in 1378, Snizort was home to the Scottish bishop of Sodor and a community of clergy, but even with the bishop located there, administrative problems still persisted. In 1433 Bishop Angus of the Isles petitioned the pope for the removal of the cathedral church from Snizort to some other place within the diocese.[29]

As we would expect, the most prominent patrons of the new bishopric from its inception to the demise of the kingdom of the Isles in 1265 were

---

[28] J. G. Dunbar, 'The medieval architecture of the Scottish Highlands', in MacLean, *Middle Ages in the Highlands*, p. 42; R. A. Curphey, 'Peel Castle summer excursion: June 1979', *Proceedings of the Isle of Man Natural History and Antiquarian Soc.*, ix (1980–2), pp. 64–6.

[29] Cowan and Easson, *Medieval Religious Houses: Scotland*, p. 209; Watt, *Fasti*, p. 207. Material on Snizort is gathered in A. Nicolson, *History of Skye: A Record of the Families, the Social Conditions and the Literature of the Island*, ed. A. Macleod (Glasgow, 1930, 2nd rev. edn, 1994), appendix 4.

the kings of Man descended from Godred Crovan. It was King Olaf who had been responsible for setting the see upon a territorial footing, and his charter was confirmed by his successors Godfrey in 1154 and Ragnvald between 1188 and 1190; it received its first papal confirmation in 1194 or 1195. Royal patronage of the see could sometimes lead to disputes between the kings and the monks of Furness. Such a dispute took place as early as 1151 or 1152, and another occurred in the early thirteenth century. Bishop Reginald (1217–26) was a kinsman of King Ragnvald and was not elected by the monks of Furness; he had probably been nominated by the king and elected by a chapter of the clergy of the diocese. His rival, Nicholas (c.1217–25), had apparently been elected by the monks of Furness, and had been consecrated in an unprecedented situation at Dublin. But he failed to obtain recognition from King Ragnvald, and sought and received a papal mandate instructing the king to show him favour in 1219. In 1224 Pope Honorius wrote to the archbishop of York saying that Nicholas, the bishop of Man and the islands, had long been in exile from his see, and giving the archbishop authority to accept his resignation; it is therefore unlikely that he ever actually took up residence as bishop.[30]

As kings of the Isles, the descendants of Somerled of Argyll may also have acted, on occasion, as patrons of the diocese of Sodor. Bishop Cristin (c.1170), was an Argyll man, and it has been suggested that he was elected by the monks of Furness under pressure from the sons of Somerled.[31] It is curious that the descendants of Somerled do not appear as more active patrons of the diocese, but since they were, about this time, involved in the creation of the diocese of Argyll, much of their effort must have been reserved for the patronage of this see.

When the Treaty of Perth ceded the Western Isles and Man to Alexander III, King of Scots, in 1266, it carried with it the patronage of the see, and not long afterwards, in 1275, we find King Alexander disputing the right of the monks of Furness to elect a bishop. The choice of the monks had fallen upon Gilbert, the abbot of Rushen, but his election was contested by King Alexander, who instead presented Mark, a Galloway man, to the archbishop of Trondheim for consecration. His bid was successful and Mark was consecrated in 1275 or 1276.[32]

But the political situation in the Irish Sea was a rapidly changing one, and by the time of Gilbert's death the Isle of Man had passed into English hands, having been seized by Edward I in 1290. The next bishop, Alan (1305–21), was also from Galloway, but he was probably the man whom Anthony Bek (Bishop of Durham and Lord of Man until his death in 1311), imposed against the wishes of the monks of Furness. With Scottish control of the Isle of Man (at least intermittently), between

[30] *ES*, ii, p. 427; *Chron. Man*, pp. 84, 116; Watt, *Fasti*, p. 200.
[31] Ibid., p. 199.
[32] *SAEC*, pp. 381–2.

1313 and 1333 came a revival of Scottish patronage. In December 1324 King Robert I reserved patronage of the see for himself, and the next bishop after Alan was Bernard, the abbot of Arbroath, who was consecrated in 1328 and died in 1331.[33]

If the diocese of the Isles was a twelfth-century reconstitution on a territorial basis of an earlier form or forms of organisation, then the diocese of Argyll was an entirely new creation, the origins of which are perhaps less opaque, but which still present problems of their own. According to Walter Bower, John the Scot, Bishop of Dunkeld, sent his chaplain, Harald, to Rome to secure the division of the diocese, because he was unfamiliar with the language of its western half which encompassed Argyll.[34] The date of inception of this new bishopric, usually given as around 1200 on the basis of Bower, can be framed more precisely by John's episcopate at Dunkeld, between 1183 and 1203, and by the mention of the diocese of Argyll in the *Liber censuum*, produced by the papal chancery between April 1192 and March 1193.[35] It has been suggested that the date of the creation of the diocese may be further defined by its mention in a list drawn up by Albinus, Cardinal Bishop of Albano, usually dated May 1189. But recent study has established that this text belongs most probably to the period after March 1192, and that the earliest mention of the diocese is therefore that of the *Liber censuum* in 1192 or 1193.[36] The date of the creation of this new bishopric must therefore lie between 1183 and 1193, but there is a further complication: the see of Argyll is not mentioned in the famous papal bull *Cum universi* of March 1192, which freed nine Scottish sees from subjection to York. Given the absence of the see in the papal bull, and its inclusion in the *Liber censuum*, it could be that the creation of the diocese of Argyll lies between March 1192 and March 1193. This assumes, of course, that the absence of the new bishopric from *Cum universi* is attributable to the fact that this document was based upon an up-to-date list of Scottish bishoprics. But it has been shown that later reissues of the bull, which omit mention of the see of Argyll, were clearly copied from obsolete lists, and it is possible that *Cum universi* was itself based on an older compilation. The circumstances under which an earlier list might have been obtained are murky, but it has been suggested that a now-lost bull of Pope Lucius III, confirming liberties for the Scottish Church, perhaps in 1182, might have contained a list of sees which composed that Church.

---

[33] *Chron. Man*, p. 118; Watt, *Fasti*, pp. 201–2.

[34] *Chron. Bower*, iii, pp. 387–9, and notes on p. 479; implied in Alexander Myln, *Vitae Dunkeldensis Ecclesiae Episcoporum*, ed. C. Innes (Bannatyne Club, 1831), p. 8.

[35] *Le Liber Censuum de L'Eglise Romaine*, ed. P. Fabre (Paris, 1889), i, pp. 230–2.

[36] See Duncan, *Making of the Kingdom*, pp. 275–6, and *Scotia Pontifica: Papal Letters to Scotland before the Pontificate of Innocent III*, ed. R. Somerville (Oxford, 1982), appendix III.

If this were the case, then Argyll would not have been included, and this hypothetical list could have formed the basis for *Cum universi* a decade later.[37]

If the date of the creation of the diocese was between 1183 and 1193, what were the circumstances of its inception? Modern historians are almost universal in expressing dissatisfaction with the explanation provided by Walter Bower. As one expert has put it: 'it is dubious whether any medieval bishop would willingly divide his diocese with the subsequent loss of revenue, and if Gaelic was an obstacle this would also be true for the remaining part of Dunkeld'.[38] It seems more likely that the see of Argyll was in fact a creation of either Ranald or Dugald, the sons of Somerled. It is possible that they were eager to create a see where they could act as patrons, in a similar fashion as the earls of Strathearn at Dunblane or, more appropriately, like the kings of Man at the newly reconstituted diocese of the Isles. Indeed, the political situation in the Isles may have had something to do with the erection of the new diocese. The Manx king, Ragnvald, was a dominant figure in the West in the later twelfth century, and it is possible that the resurgence of the Scandinavian dynasty in Man under this potent ruler forced the descendants of Somerled to find another outlet for their patronage of the Church. Another possibility is that the initiative for the creation of the new diocese came from King William I (1165–1214), perhaps acting jointly with the son or sons of Somerled: 'about 1181–3 the king, faced with accepting a bishop of Dunkeld whom he disliked, permitted the lord or lords of Argyll to procure the creation of the diocese by the pope'. Certainly Bishop John struggled to reverse the decision after 1183, and A. A. M. Duncan has suggested that, if the see was *sub judice*, this might explain its omission from *Cum universi*.[39]

The suggestion that the creation of the bishopric of Argyll was the work of the descendants of Somerled is reinforced by the location of the cathedral of the diocese. From at least 1225 and most likely from the inception of the see, the cathedral was located on the island of Lismore in Loch Linnhe, in the very heart of MacDougall territory. The view that the seat of the bishop was for a while at Muckairn, on the south side of Loch Etive, is based solely upon the interpretation of the place-name Killespeckerrill as 'the church of bishop Harald' and is dubious at best. The choice of site is significant: the church at Lismore had, according to tradition, been founded by St Moluag (d. 592), and abbots of Lismore are known from the seventh century, so it is possible that there had been

[37] Somerville, *Scotia Pontifica*, appendix III.
[38] Cowan, 'Medieval Church in Argyll and the Isles', p. 21. See also D. E. R. Watt (ed.), *Ecclesia Scoticana* (*Series Episcoporum Ecclesiae Catholicae Occidentalis Ab Initio Usque Ad Annum MCXCVIII*, ed. O. Engels and S. Weinfurter, series VI, tomus I; Stuttgart, 1991), pp. 11–13.
[39] Duncan, *Making of the Kingdom*, p. 276.

a Christian community in continuous existence from the seventh to the twelfth centuries.[40]

Whatever the circumstances of its creation, the early history of the bishopric is dominated by vacancies, and only two bishops are known to have held it before 1250. The first was Harald. Bower says that he was the chaplain of Bishop John of Dunkeld, and was consecrated at the inception of the see, but he does not appear on the record until the late 1220s; and if Bower is correct this would make his episcopate a very long one indeed. In fact, since Bower elsewhere confuses John with his namesake, who was later bishop of Dunkeld from 1211 to 1214, and since Harald did not die until about 1230, it has been suggested that Harald was in fact the chaplain of the second Bishop John. Sometime after his death the see was given into the care of Simon, Bishop of Sodor, as custodian, and he held it in this capacity until 1236, when the bishop of Moray was ordered to conduct an election and fill the vacancy. William, the bishop of Moray's chancellor, was subsequently elected and consecrated in 1240, but he was drowned in 1241 and another lengthy vacancy ensued.[41]

These evidently disturbed conditions in the diocese may well have some bearing on the political events of 1249, when Alexander II invaded Argyll to confront its lord, Ewen, recently returned from Norway where the title king of the Isles had been bestowed upon him. The see of Argyll had been vacant for at least seven years in late 1248, when the bishops of Glasgow and Dunblane were ordered to arrange an election; for at least some of the vacancy the see had been in the care of Clement, Bishop of Dunblane. The vacancy in the see is a condition which must in some way be connected with the MacDougall lords of Argyll, as patrons of the see, and it is possible that Ewen was interfering in the diocese, perhaps, we might hypothesise, appropriating its revenues for himself? His role as a patron of the see is certainly not in doubt, for in 1240 he granted territory amounting to fourteen pennylands in Lismore to the bishop. This hypothesis is strengthened by the fact that, in early 1249, papal approval was given for a plan to transfer the cathedral to a new site on the mainland to be chosen by the two bishops of Glasgow and Dunkeld, with part of the cost being met by the king. The gift of Alexander II on his deathbed at Kerrera of the church of Kilbride (near Oban) to the bishop of Argyll might indicate that this was to be the new site, and the proposed transferral of the cathedral from Lismore to the mainland suggests a challenge to Ewen of Argyll as patron of the see. Thus, ecclesiastical affairs may have played a role in the events of 1249, and if there is no doubt that the primary cause of the king's hostility towards

---

40 I. Carmichael, *Lismore in Alba* (Perth, n.d.), p. 90; cf. Cowan and Easson, *Medieval Religious Houses: Scotland*, p. 210; see also Watt, *Ecclesia Scoticana*, pp. 11–13.

41 Duncan, *Making of the Kingdom*, 276; Watt, *Ecclesia Scoticana*, p. 13; Duncan and Brown, 'Argyll and the Isles', p. 209; Watt, *Fasti*, p. 26.

the lord of Argyll was the latter's assumption of the title king of the Isles, 'when the Scottish fleet sailed into Kerrera sound it was not only to attack the lordship of Ewen but also to restore the see of Argyll'.[42]

If one of the characteristics of Latin Christendom in the eleventh to the thirteenth centuries was the establishment of territorial dioceses and the creation of new sees, then it is pretty clear that the western seaboard was sharing in the general expansion of western Christendom during this period. It is of course true that these areas were not newly converted in the twelfth century, but the reconstitution of the bishopric of the Isles in 1134 with a single incumbent, cathedral church, and a well-defined territory, brought the Church in the Isles into line with the rest of western Christendom, a development paralleled in contemporary Ireland and Scotland. Still another distinguishing characteristic of western Christendom in the high Middle Ages was the close connections forged between Rome, the seat of the reformed papacy, and the provincial churches, by means of papal letters and directives, papal legates, and councils and synods.[43]

Throughout the course of the twelfth and thirteenth centuries there is a considerable amount of surviving correspondence between Rome and the Western Isles, which underlines the degree to which this region became a member of the universal Church. The trend is most pronounced for Iona and the Isle of Man. Thus, shortly after its refoundation in *c.*1200 as a Benedictine monastery by Ranald the son of Somerled, Iona was taken under papal protection by a bull of Pope Innocent III and its independence safeguarded. Later in the century, further steps were taken to ensure Iona's independence. In 1247 Pope Innocent IV granted the abbot of Iona the privilege of wearing the mitre and ring in the absence of a bishop or papal legate, and excused him from attending provincial chapters of Benedictine houses in Scotland. And in 1289 Nicholas IV confirmed that the abbey was to be free of the jurisdiction of the bishop of the Isles and directly subject to the Roman church, a mandate that was perhaps engendered by threats of a visitation from the bishop of the Isles.[44]

The Isle of Man was also not unknown to the papacy. In 1186 Pope Urban III issued a bull protecting Furness Abbey and its lands, includ-

---

42 Duncan and Brown, 'Argyll and the Isles', p. 210. On Ewen's patronage: *RMS*, ii, no. 3136, where the date of 1251 needs to be corrected to 1240: see Duncan and Brown, 'Argyll and the Isles', appendix 4. Correspondence of 1248–9: *Vetera Monumenta Hibernorum et Scotorum Historiam Illustrantia*, ed. A. Theiner (Rome, 1864; repr. Osnabruck, 1969), nos. 139–40.

43 See C. Morris, *The Papal Monarchy: The Western Church from 1050 to 1250* (Oxford, 1989), pp. 55–6; and Bartlett, *Making of Europe*, pp. 243–50.

44 *Calendar of Entries in the Papal Registers relating to Great Britain and Ireland: Papal Letters*, ed. W. H. Bliss *et al.* (London, 1893–), i, pp. 231, 504; see also A. MacQuarrie, 'Kings, lords and abbots: power and patronage at the medieval monastery of Iona', *TGSI*, liv (1984–6), pp. 358–9.

ing those on the Isle of Man. But closer connections came in the thirteenth century. In 1219 King Ragnvald resigned Man to the papacy, to be held as a papal fief:

> Be it known to your Holiness, that we, in order that we may be partakers of the blessings which belong to the Roman church, at the admonition and exhortation of our beloved father, lord Pandulph, Bishop elect of Norwich, our chamberlain and your Legate, have given and offered to him by name, and to the Roman church, and to you, and your Catholic successors, our Island of Man, which belongs to us by hereditary right, and for which we are bound to make suit to no man, and henceforward we and our heirs will forever hold in fee the said Island from the Roman church, and will perform homage and fealty for the same, and in recognition of lordship, in the name of tribute, we and our heirs will forever pay annually to the Roman church, twelve marks sterling ...[45]

In 1223 Ragnvald was the recipient of a letter from the pope exhorting him to ensure that the churches of his land be endowed with sufficient land to support their priests.[46]

The submission of Ragnvald to the papacy was accomplished through the medium of Pandulph, the papal legate (1218–20). The practice of sending out papal legates, or of using bishops as legates to perform the necessary business of the papacy in the provincial churches, to settle disputes, hold councils, pass judgements, or refer more serious matters to Rome, had grown from the second half of the eleventh century. Given the integration of the western seaboard into the framework of western Christendom in the course of the twelfth century, and the close contacts with Rome that existed by the early thirteenth century, it is hardly surprising to find papal legates active in the Isles by the late twelfth century. Indeed, it might well have been the contribution of these legates to help forge closer connections between Man and the Hebrides and Rome. In 1176, the legate Vivian, cardinal priest of St Stephen in Monte Coelio, arrived in Scotland, and later that year he travelled to Ireland before returning to hold a council in Edinburgh in 1177. But the *Chronicle of Man* noted his presence in the Isles: it stated that he came to the Isle of Man where he caused King Godfrey 'to be united in lawful marriage with his wife'. The English chronicler, Roger of Howden, noted that Vivian visited Scotland, Ireland, and the Isles, and added that he was also supposed to visit Norway.[47] It would be informative to have more information on Vivian's activities in the Isles. However, considering the accusation made against Godfrey's father, King Olaf, that he was in the habit of keeping concubines, it might be

---

[45] *Monumenta de Insula Manniae*, ii, pp. 53–5.
[46] Ibid., ii, pp. 62–3, misdated to 1220 by the editor when the text clearly states the year 1223.
[47] *ES*, ii, pp. 296–7; *Chron. Man*, pp. 76–7, 128–9; *SAEC*, pp. 266–7.

that Vivian's supervision of the marriage of Godfrey was intended to enforce the stricter rules surrounding marriage that were prevalent from the mid eleventh century. Other legates with jurisdiction in the Isles in the twelfth century are also known. In 1178 Peter of St Agatha was in Britain to summon the churchmen of Scotland, Galloway, Ireland and the Isle of Man to Rome for the Lateran Council which was to be held in 1179.[48] In 1180 the legate Alexius was in Scotland to help resolve the disputed election to the diocese of St Andrews, but the chronicle attributed to Benedict of Peterborough noted that his legatine authority extended not only to Scotland but also to the adjacent Isles and Ireland.[49] If Pope Gregory VII had boasted 'how great is the authority of this see [Rome]', by the beginning of the thirteenth century it encompassed even the most marginal bounds of western Christendom. The western seaboard acknowledged the authority of the papacy and displayed the same reverence for the see of Peter that helped to define western Christendom itself.

Although not untouched by monasticism, the western seaboard appears to have remained unaffected by the predominant trends in western European monastic life in the early Middle Ages. For five centuries, from the middle of the sixth to the end of the eleventh centuries, most organised religious life in most of western Europe was based upon St Benedict's *Rule for Monks*. By about 1100, however, the church reform movement and the changing social conditions in Europe had contributed to the ending of the Benedictine monopoly on organised religious life (though Benedictine monasticism did, of course, continue), and to the rise of new, international, religious orders. Among these new orders the most prominent and ultimately the most successful were the Augustinian canons, who made a break with the past by adopting as their patron not Benedict but Augustine, and the Cistercians, who thought themselves the only true followers of St Benedict's *Rule*. Because these orders served quite different needs – the Augustinians serving the world and the Cistercians fleeing from it – by about 1150 they had succeeded in making themselves the most popular of the new religious orders that had put down roots throughout most of western Christendom.[50]

The introduction of the Benedictine monks and the reformed religious orders to both Ireland and Scotland, where they were previously unknown, was a development of the twelfth century. In Scotland, Queen Margaret had established a house of Benedictine monks at Dunfermline after about 1070, but its continued existence through the

[48] Ibid., p. 270.
[49] Ibid.
[50] On these religious orders, a good introduction is Lawrence, *Medieval Monasticism*; see also the relevant chapters of R. W. Southern, *Western Society and the Church in the Middle Ages* (Harmondsworth, 1970).

turbulent years of anti-foreign reaction that followed her death and that of her husband is difficult to verify until its patronage was taken over by David I in the 1120s. It was not until the twelfth century that the reformed religious orders made their way into Scotland, under the patronage of the descendants of Malcolm and Margaret, Anglo-Norman newcomers, and native Scottish magnates alike. The first Augustinian community in Scotland was founded at Scone in about 1115–20, by Alexander I; others followed at Holyrood, Jedburgh, St Andrews, Cambuskenneth, Inchcolm, and Inchaffray. The first Cistercian monastery in Scotland was Melrose, founded by David I in 1136. This order eventually had eleven houses in Scotland, including Dundrennan, Newbattle, Coupar Angus, Glenluce, Saddell, and Sweetheart. In Ireland, there were no Benedictine monasteries before 1111, and although two, Cashel and Ross Carbery, are recorded before 1148, the number remained small because of the popularity of the new religious orders. The contribution of St Malachy of Armagh to the reorganisation of monastic life in Ireland was outstanding. First abbot of Bangor, then bishop of Connor and Down, and finally archbishop of Armagh, he resigned in 1137 to become bishop of Down and died in 1148. In 1127 Savignac monks were brought to Erenagh in his diocese of Down, probably with his sanction; by 1137 there were communities of Augustinian canons at Cork, Armagh, Cong, and Bangor; and in 1142 the first Cistercian monastery in Ireland was founded at Mellifont. Thereafter these new orders flourished under both Irish and, after 1172, Anglo-Norman patronage.[51]

Even as Somerled was attempting to turn back the clock with his overture to Flaithbertach Ua-Brolchain, the tide of the new religious orders was rising in the western seaboard under the patronage of the Manx kings. The *Chronicle of Man* states that, in 1134, 'King Olaf gave to Ivo, Abbot of Furness, a piece of his land in Man, to establish a monastery at a place called Rushen.' The 'abbey of Man' is mentioned in a papal document of 1154, and the community is said to have relocated to Douglas in 1192 before moving back to Rushen four years later. The abbey church was dedicated in 1257 by Bishop Richard of Sodor.[52] Furness was a Savignac house (the Savignacs were an austere order which adhered strictly to the *Rule* of St Benedict), and since this order

---

51 For Britain in general, see J. Burton, *Monastic and Religious Orders in Britain, 1000–1300* (Cambridge, 1994). On Scotland, see Barrow, *Kingship and Unity*, chap. 4; Barrow, *Kingdom of the Scots*, chaps. 5, 6; on Ireland, see J. Watt, *The Church in Medieval Ireland* (Dublin, 1972), p. 46; and J. Watt, *The Church and the Two Nations in Medieval Ireland* (Cambridge, 1970).

52 *Chron. Man*, pp. 62–3, 80–1, 108–9; W. de Gray Birch, 'On the date of foundation ascribed to the Cistercian abbeys of Great Britain', *Journal of the British Archaeological Association*, xxvi (1870), p. 358; Cowan and Easson, *Medieval Religious Houses: Scotland*, p. 237. W. C. Cubbon, 'History of Rushen Abbey, Ballasalla, Isle of Man – 1134 AD', *Proceedings of the Isle of Man Natural History and Antiquarian Soc.*, iv (1932–42), is rather dated.

merged with the Cistercians in 1147, it would seem that Rushen became Cistercian at this date also, if indeed it had not been so from the beginning, as is sometimes suggested.

The evidence for other religious houses on the Isle of Man is sparse. The Manx chronicle states that King Godfrey granted the land of Mirescoge to the abbot of Rievaulx in 1176, and that a monastery, evidently Cistercian, was planted there. But it was short-lived, and 'in the process of time the land and the monks were made over to the abbey of St Mary of Rushen'.[53] There was also a convent of Cistercian nuns at Douglas, probably founded by King Ragnvald; it was in existence by 1313 when King Robert Bruce stayed there in the course of his expedition to conquer Man.[54]

As a founder of a house of Savignac monks, King Olaf was in select company in the British Isles in the 1130s. Through the 1120s and the 1130s, the patronage of first the Savignacs and then the Cistercians was largely the prerogative of powerful nobles like Stephen of Blois, later king of England, or King Henry I, and it was not until the second half of the twelfth century that patronage of these orders spread to the knightly order of society. The popularity of the Savignacs in the 1120s and 1130s no doubt helps to explain why Olaf turned to them for his foundation at Rushen; moreover, Furness Abbey and its daughter, Calder, were in close proximity to the shores of the Irish Sea. In an age when family and political connections also counted for much in choosing a religious order to patronise, Olaf's connections with the English court must also be seen as significant. The *Chronicle of Man* states that during the troubled years following the death of Godred Crovan, Olaf resided at the court of Henry I of England (1100–35). It is notable that Henry and his wife Matilda were patrons of the new religious orders, and although Olaf's residence at their court would have predated the introduction of the Savignacs and the Cistercians into England, there can be no doubt that such connections were influential in determining his choice.[55]

In the history of the western seaboard it is not, however, the Manx kings who appear as the pre-eminent monastic patrons. That distinction was reserved for the descendants of Somerled, and among their number none was a better friend of the monks than Ranald, the son of Somerled. Although Somerled had attempted the revival of the religious community on Iona, it appears to have been Ranald who was responsible for the establishment of the Benedictine monastery on Iona. This was the MacDonald tradition of the seventeenth century and it is supported by the chronology of the foundation, which was in place by 1203. There is also little question that this was a Benedictine monastery, since the grant

---

[53] *Chron. Man*, pp. 76–7; Cowan and Easson, *Medieval Religious Houses: Scotland*, p. 237.

[54] *Chron. Man*, pp. 110–11; Cowan and Easson, *Medieval Religious Houses: Scotland*, p. 238.

[55] See B. D. Hill, *English Cistercian Monasteries and their Patrons in the Twelfth Century* (Chicago, 1968), p. 31, for the influences that might act on the founder of a monastery.

of papal protection to Iona in 1203 and a papal mandate of 1443–4 referred to the Benedictine monastery on the island of Iona. The date of the foundation is suggested by the papal protection granted by Innocent III in December of 1203, as well as by the fact that the monastery was overrun in 1204 by angry Irish churchmen who claimed that it had been established 'in violation of the rights of the community of Iona' and 'mustered and destroyed' it accordingly. This bizarre episode suggests that Ranald's new foundation was not met with the greatest enthusiasm by the existing clergy. But the Benedictines must have returned quickly after 1204, or else remained on Iona, because in 1247 the pope granted the abbot the use of the mitre and ring and other privileges.[56]

In attempting to answer the question of why Ranald turned to the Benedictines over the more popular reformed religious orders on Iona, it is probably best to venture across the sea to Ireland, where Benedictine monasticism was enjoying a resurgence in the same period. From 1172 onwards many new religious foundations were made by both Anglo-Norman and Irish lords, including twelve Benedictine monasteries.[57] It is interesting to note that several of these were founded by John de Courcy, the lord of Ulster, who, like Somerled, was related by marriage to the kings of Man.[58] In addition, the occurrence of certain architectural features in the abbey church itself indicates that Irish masons were employed during the thirteenth-century phases of building there.[59] An Irish connection therefore probably lay behind Ranald's Benedictine foundation on Iona, although we have already noted another connection between the MacSorleys and Benedictine monasticism, for Ranald's brother, Dugald, appeared in the *Liber Vitae* as a benefactor of the monks of Durham Cathedral. While the hypothesis of at least one scholar who suggested that it was Dugald rather than Ranald who founded the community on Iona must be rejected,[60] this does at least indicate another link between the Somerled's descendants and Benedictine monasticism.

Saddell Abbey is located in a glen on the east side of the Kintyre peninsula, eight miles north of Campbeltown. It was largely demolished in the 1770s, and all that remain are sparse, overgrown fragments, representing the presbytery, north transept, and part of the south claustral range. Yet despite its fractured appearance, Saddell is impor-

---

56 Document of 1203: *Diplom. Norv.*, vii, no. 4. Events of 1204: *ES*, ii, p. 363. Papal mandate of 1443/44: *HP*, p. 86. See also MacQuarrie and MacArthur, *Iona Through the Ages*, p. 14; and R. A. McDonald, 'Scoto-Norse kings and the reformed religious orders: patterns of monastic patronage in twelfth-century Galloway and Argyll', *Albion*, xxvii (1995).

57 A. Gwynn and R. N. Hadcock, *Medieval Religious Houses: Ireland* (London, 1970), pp. 5, 102–9.

58 On John de Courcy's religious foundations in Ireland, see G. H. Orpen, *Ireland Under the Normans* (Oxford, 1911–20), ii, pp. 20–2.

59 Dunbar and Fisher, *Iona*, p. 17; RCAHMS, *Argyll*, iv, no. 4.

60 W. D. Lamont, *Ancient and Medieval Sculptured Stones of Islay* (Edinburgh and London, 1968), p. 25; W. D. Lamont, *The Early History of Islay* (Dundee, 1966), p. 20.

tant because it was the only house of Cistercian monks to be founded in the west Highlands. It is also safe to say that it is among the most poorly documented religious houses of Scotland, and accordingly nearly every aspect of its history remains problematic. Although Saddell is traditionally associated with Somerled, the links to Ranald are much stronger and better documented, and there are good reasons to believe that he, and not Somerled, was responsible for its foundation.

The only good piece of evidence to support the tradition that Somerled was the founder is a list of Cistercian houses, in a French hand, of the thirteenth century. Under the year 1160 the house of 'Sconedale' was mentioned, possibly – though by no means certainly – a reference to Saddell.[61] This association was upheld by a number of later writers, including A. and A. MacDonald, but some more recent scholars, apparently unable to make up their minds, settle for a compromise and make Somerled and Ranald co-founders.[62] It must be admitted that the thirteenth-century list is the closest source to the foundation. Yet it is consistently contradicted by other reliable sources that suggest Ranald was in fact the founder. Documents from the abbey itself were confirmed by Pope Clement VII in 1398 and by King James IV in 1498 and 1508, and several of these confirmations described Ranald as the founder.[63] This association is further supported by the seventeenth-century MacDonald tradition embodied in the *Book of Clanranald*.[64] It should be noted that this early MacDonald tradition stands in contradiction to that cited by A. and A. MacDonald in 1896, who argued that, since they believed Somerled to have been buried there, he must also have been the founder.[65] There is in fact no convincing evidence that Somerled was buried at Saddell, and this argument cannot be utilised as proof that he was its founder.[66] In short, were it not for the existence of the thirteenth-century Cistercian list it would be easy to dismiss Somerled's claim as 'an unjustified association of the great name Somerled with the foundation and an interesting example of the development of a tradition'.[67]

[61] de Gray Birch, 'Date of foundation of Cistercian abbeys', p. 361; see also *ES*, ii, p. 247.

[62] MacDonald and MacDonald, *Clan Donald*, i, p. 53, 60, 513–14, among others, makes Somerled the founder. M. Barrett, *The Scottish Monasteries of Old* (Edinburgh, 1913), p. 151, and A. McKerral, 'A chronology of the Abbey and Castle of Saddell, Kintyre', *PSAS*, lxxxvi (1951–2), p. 115, make Somerled and Ranald co-founders. J. E. Scott, 'Saddell Abbey', *TGSI*, xlvi (1969–70), who confuses Ranald the son of Somerled with Ragnvald the king of Man, seems to contradict himself. On p. 117 he suggests that Somerled was the founder, while on p. 123 he supposes it was Ranald. This is perhaps a good indication of the confusion surrounding the founder's identity!

[63] *HP*, i, pp. 146–9; *RMS*, ii, no. 3170. See also A. L. Brown, 'The Cistercian Abbey of Saddell, Kintyre', *Innes Review*, xx (1969–70), pp. 130–1.

[64] *Clanranald Bk.*, p. 157.

[65] 'The tradition of the family *has always been* [my italics] that Saddell ... was the last resting place of the great Celtic hero': MacDonald and MacDonald, *Clan Donald*, i, pp. 60, 513–14.

[66] For a full argument against Somerled having been buried at Saddell, see McDonald, 'Death and burial of Somerled', pp. 6–10.

[67] Brown, 'Cistercian Abbey of Saddell', pp. 131–2.

Apart from this, however, there is another reason to suppose that the founder of Saddell should be identified as Ranald and not his father. We have seen how Somerled was markedly hostile to the Anglo-French influence which permeated Scotland following the accession of David I in 1124, and how this hostility expressed itself in the form of uprisings against the Scottish kings in 1153 and 1164. We have also noted how, in 1164, Somerled turned to the conservative Christianity of Northern Ireland in an attempt to revitalise the community of Iona, at a time when the Cistercians were already established in the Isles, at Rushen on Man. Given this, it seems probable that Somerled was unreceptive to the new religious orders which were becoming popular in Scotland in this period, while his son, who was apparently more cosmopolitan, also appears much more receptive to the new impulses of religious life making their way into Scotland in the twelfth century.

Dating Saddell is also a controversial matter. While one version of the thirteenth-century list mentioned above put the date at 1160, at least one recent work has suggested a date as late as 1226,[68] and nearly every decade between has also been proposed. Archaeological excavations and architectural studies support a date consistent with Ranald's being the founder, however. In 1967 a number of Romanesque chevron-and-roll decorations were uncovered in the presbytery, and these fragments have been dated to the late twelfth or early thirteenth century.[69]

The connections which inspired Saddell are critical, since it was the only Cistercian house in the Highlands. For many years it was thought to have been a daughter of Rushen Abbey on the Isle of Man, a tradition which seems not unreasonable in the light of the close connections between Man and the house of Somerled. Recent scholarship, however, has established a link between the Cistercian abbey of Mellifont in Ireland and Saddell, based on a papal bull of Clement VII in 1393 which confirmed the election of Macratius, a monk of Saddell, as abbot. Although the bull is not explicit, the implication is that Saddell was founded from Mellifont because the newly elected abbot of Saddell was expected to receive confirmation from Mellifont. Mellifont was the first Cistercian abbey in Ireland, and it was a thriving community: between 1147 and 1153 it had established seven daughter houses and in 1170 it reportedly housed 300 lay brothers. Given the contacts between Iona and Ireland, and considering Ranald's geographical position as *rí Innse Gall*, we should hardly be surprised if Irish influences lay behind his religious foundations.[70]

Ranald was also the founder of the nunnery on Iona, the pink granite ruins of which still stand four hundred yards south-west of the abbey.

---

68 F. Van Der Meer, *Atlas De l'Ordre Cistercien* (Paris and Brussels, 1965), p. iv, suggested 1226.

69 RCAHMS, *Argyll*, i, no. 296.

70 Connection between Saddell and Mellifont: Brown, 'Cistercian Abbey of Saddell', pp. 130–1. On Mellifont: C. Conway, *The Story of Mellifont* (Dublin, 1958).

The community here was said by the *Book of Clanranald* to have been of black, or Benedictine, nuns. This tradition can no longer be accepted, however, for a papal mandate of 1422 stated that the Iona nunnery was home to Augustinian canonesses.[71] Neither the date of this foundation nor the location of its mother house can be determined with any certainty. Architectural evidence shows that the church was erected during the first quarter of the thirteenth century, and it is likely that the canonesses were brought from Ireland. Augustinian nunneries were numerous in Ireland by 1200, and there are Irish parallels in some elements of the nunnery church itself.[72] The first prioress of Reginald's new foundation was his sister, Bethag. The *Book of Clanranald* stated that 'Bethag, daughter of Somerled, was a religious woman and a Black Nun', while the *History of the Macdonalds* said that she was a 'prioress of Icollumkill'.[73] By remarkable good fortune the inscription of her grave was preserved until the nineteenth century: it read 'Behag niin Shorle vic Ilvrid Priorissa' ('Bethag, daughter of Somhairle, son of Gille-Brigde, Prioress').[74] It has even been suggested that Bethag may have been the first owner of the so-called Iona Psalter, now in the National Library of Scotland, which was written and illuminated in Oxford in the thirteenth century and commissioned by an Augustinian canoness with a special interest in Iona saints. As was the case with virtually all Scottish nunneries, this community has little recorded history. It was evidently home to only a few canonesses, and possessed modest endowments of land in and around Mull, including Staoineig on Iona itself.[75]

Although these were the only monastic houses actually founded by Ranald, he and his descendants were also generous benefactors of the Cluniac priory (later the abbey of Paisley), founded by Walter fitz Alan in about 1163. Sometime around 1200, Ranald granted to the monks of Paisley eight oxen and two pence from every house in his domains from which smoke issued, and one penny per year thereafter. His wife, Fonia, also gave to the abbey the teind of all the property which God had given her as well as those things which she had for her use. It is perhaps relevant to note that Gerald of Wales recorded a custom among the Welsh that a donation of one-tenth of all their worldly goods – cattle, sheep, and other livestock – was commonplace, especially when they married, went on a pilgrimage, or made an effort to amend their ways. This was known as the Great Tithe.[76] Perhaps Fonia's grant bears some

71 *Clanranald Bk.*, pp. 157; *HP*, iv, pp. 175–6.
72 RCAHMS, *Argyll*, iv, no. 5; Dunbar and Fisher, *Iona*, pp. 8–10; Gwynn and Hadcock, *Medieval Religious Houses: Ireland*, pp. 5, 307–26.
73 *Clanranald Bk.*, p. 157; Macdonald, *Hist. Macdonalds*, *HP*, i, p. 11.
74 Steer and Bannerman, *Late Medieval Monumental Sculpture*, p. 90; see also Martin Martin, *A Description of the Western Islands of Scotland circa 1695* (1703; repr. Stirling, 1934), pp. 290–1, for the appearance of the slab in 1695.
75 See RCAHMS, *Argyll*, iv, no. 5, and notes.
76 *Paisley Reg.*, p. 125. Gerald of Wales, *Descriptio Kambriae*, in *Opera*, ed. J. S. Brewer *et al.* (Rolls Ser., 1861–91), vi, p. 203. Gerald noted that the custom was to donate the

resemblance to that custom described by Gerald, but whatever the case, we see one of the noble families of the western seaboard enthusiastically embracing the new religious orders.

The connection between Ranald and Paisley Abbey is particularly interesting, both because Paisley lay outside the territory ruled by Somerled and his sons, in the Stewart lordship, and because Somerled's death occurred at nearby Renfrew. It is therefore tempting to suppose that Reginald's generous gifts to Paisley were the result of the monks of Paisley – the nearest religious house – taking care of Somerled's body after his death in battle in 1164.[77] This suggestion is strengthened by the fact that the original place for the house of monks was the 'inch' beside Renfrew and the priory did not move to Paisley until 1169.[78] It is odd, however, that no mention of such a motive for Ranald's endowments is made in his charter, where one would expect to find it when such an opportunity existed. Instead, the gift was made in conventional terms, 'for the welfare of myself, my wife, my heirs and my people'.

There is no question that Ranald was the most active of Somerled's descendants in founding monasteries in the western seaboard. But we cannot allow his achievement to overshadow that of his kinsmen, many of whom were also benefactors of the Church. We have already noted that Ranald's brother, Dugald, was a benefactor of the Benedictine community at Durham in 1175, and had his name entered in the *Liber Vitae* of Durham Cathedral. Dugald's son, Duncan, founded Ardchattan Priory on Loch Etive in 1230 or 1231. This was one of only three monasteries of the Valliscaulian order in north Britain, with Beauly and Pluscarden in Scotland being founded at about the same time. Virtually nothing is known of its history, however, and it is now better known for its gardens and late medieval monumental sculpture than for its original role. Finally, one other religious house comes on to the record in the western seaboard at the very end of our period. John of Fordun recorded the presence of a community of canons-regular on Colonsay, while Walter Bower placed it, correctly, on Oronsay. Oronsay Priory is first mentioned in official documents in 1353, and later records verify that it was a house of canons-regular. But who was its founder? The seventeenth-century *Book of Clanranald* stated that John, the son of Angus Óg and Lord of the Isles, founded the 'monastery of the Holy Cross a long time before his death'. Since there were no other monasteries founded in the western seaboard at this time, the 'monastery of the Holy Cross' must be a reference to Oronsay, although any association with the canons-regular of Holyrood remains unproven. The date of the foundation must lie sometime between 1325, the date at which John probably assumed the headship of the Clan Donald, and 1353, when the

tithe to the church where they had been baptised.
[77] MacDonald and MacDonald, *Clan Donald*, i, p. 522.
[78] *Paisley Reg.*, p. 249; Cowan and Easson, *Medieval Religious Houses: Scotland*, p. 65.

community appears on the record for the first time. Since John died in 1387, this would seem to substantiate the claim in the clan history that the abbey was erected 'a long time before his death'.[79]

This is not the place for a detailed consideration of the diverse motives that might lead to the founding of a monastery or the decision to patronise a community of monks, canons, or nuns. But it is important to determine how the motives of Ranald and his kindred related to the larger medieval context. As elsewhere in Europe, care of the eternal soul and fear of damnation were important impulses acting on monastic patrons, and, as the terms of the grants made by Ranald and his descendants to Paisley show, were very much in the forefront in the western seaboard, too. However, such religious impulses were also tempered by, and entwined with, more worldly considerations, for monastic patrons both expected and received more than just spiritual benefits for their actions. Nunneries, for instance, provided an honourable refuge for widowed or unmarried members of aristocratic families; abbeys always provided hospitality for their benefactors; and some orders, like the Cistercians, were notable developers of land, while others, like the Augustinians, made themselves useful as chaplains or scribes. In the present context it may be significant that the first prioress of Iona was Ranald's sister, Bethag; similarly, the fact that Ranald and his descendants issued Latin documents means it is not beyond the realms of possibility that monks were employed as scribes. Finally, the foundation of monasteries for the reformed religious orders was closely tied to the notion that a backward and run-down church was indicative of a backward kingdom. We know that in the western seaboard in the twelfth century there was at least one old-fashioned community, at Iona, and there may well have been others, like St Maugholds on the Isle of Man. But these communities were increasingly seen as old-fashioned and obsolete, since they lacked the discipline and rule that contemporaries demanded, and in physical terms their monastic enclosures were much less impressive than the new stone-built abbeys and priories. Indeed, the foundation of monasteries for the reformed religious orders has sometimes been seen as an attempt to introduce 'civilising' influences into the marginal regions of Britain by their rulers. This is certainly how contemporaries regarded the process. Here is how Walter Daniel, an admittedly contemptuous observer, described the nature of the local recruits to Dundrennan, founded in 1142 by Fergus, Lord of Galloway:

Some men of those parts are turned into monks of a sort, if they have been formed into a religious house, though under the counsel

[79] *Chron. Fordun*, i, p. 43; iv, p. 39; *Chron. Bower*, i, pp. 14–15; *Clanranald Bk.*, p. 160; *Cal. Papal Letters*, iii, p. 490; Cowan and Easson, *Medieval Religious Houses: Scotland*, p. 94; Steer and Bannerman, *Late Medieval Monumental Sculpture*, appendix III, p. 215.

and guidance of others; scarce any have the assiduity to reach per-
fection of themselves, for they are by nature dull and brutal and so
always inclined to carnal pleasures. Rievaulx made a plantation in
this savagery, which now, by the help of God ... bears much fruit.[80]

It remains to consider the development of the parochial system in the
western seaboard, a crucial but problematic topic. On the one hand the
creation of a system of parishes in Scotland has been hailed as, 'the
greatest work of transformation for the church and people accomplished
between the time of Saint Margaret and the middle of the thirteenth
century'.[81] On the other hand the origins and development of the parish
system are clouded in obscurity for Scotland as a whole, and the
problem is accentuated in the western seaboard by the lack of documentation. Many churches in Argyll and the Isles do not appear on the
record until the mid-sixteenth century, and the comment frequently
encountered in the relevant volume of the *Origines Parochiales Scotiae*,
that 'the early history of this church is unknown', is all too typical.[82]
Nevertheless, by utilising what evidence does exist and by using the
development of the parochial system in Scotland as a parallel, it is possible to
say something about the evolution of parishes in the western seaboard.
    The work of Ian Cowan was instrumental in revealing the origins and
evolution of the parochial system in Scotland. Before the twelfth
century, parishes in Scotland, as in England before the Norman
Conquest, seem to have been large districts served by clergy resident at
central churches, called *monasteria* or minsters. This organisation was
gradually undermined as new churches were founded within the bounds
of the minster territory by kings, bishops, or local landholders who
appointed a resident priest and assumed the patronage of the church.
These developments eroded the need for a community of priests, and
witnessed the decline of the status of the minsters, which frequently
became parish churches. The earliest recorded erection of a proprietary
church is that of Ednam in Roxburghshire by Thor Longus about 1105.
The process, however, was piecemeal and haphazard until the time of
David I (1124–53). An assize of that king made compulsory the exaction
of tithes from the lands served by a church, thereby defining the parish
as a legal and territorial unit, but the extension of the parochial system
seems to have continued into the late thirteenth century. One major
theme in the history of the parishes of medieval Scotland is that of
appropriation. Although the tithes of the Church were intended to
maintain a priest in every parish, this was not their sole purpose. From
the inception of the parish system these revenues were also regarded as

---

[80] Walter Daniel, *Vita Ailredi Abbatis Rievall'*, ed. F. M. Powicke (London, 1950), p. 45.
[81] Barrow, *Kingship and Unity*, p. 72.
[82] *OPS*, ii, pt. 1, p. 11, referring to Kilkivan.

a means of endowing other ecclesiastical institutions besides the parish, and in the later twelfth century the religious houses were the principal recipients of churches.[83]

In Argyll and the Isles, as in the rest of Scotland, the creation of parishes was an extended evolutionary process. The early administration of the Church seems to have been based on minsters, and several possible minster sites have been identified in the western seaboard. Snizort in Skye, with its pendicles of Kilmalovok in Raasay and Kilmory in Waternish, is a strong candidate for a mother church with its associated‚chapels which served all or most of the island. This community may well have existed into the fourteenth century when, as we have already noted, the clergy of Snizort elected a bishop of the Isles. Another potential minster within the western seaboard is Rothesay in Bute, described in 1407 as the 'abbacie' of Rothesay. This has been interpreted as evidence of the existence of an early church which may have served the whole island, or else to land in Rothesay which belonged to another religious institution in the vicinity. Such an institution existed at Kingarth in the seventh and eighth centuries, but its continued existence into the high Middle Ages cannot be verified.[84]

It is not until the thirteenth century that there is evidence for the creation of parishes in the western seaboard, and even then the documentation is patchy. In the early thirteenth century Alan, the son of Walter the Steward, granted to the monks of Paisley Abbey the church of Kingarth in Bute, 'with all its chapels and the whole parish [*parochia*] of the same island'. Now, it is tempting to regard this as the erection of a parish based on an earlier church, but one difficulty is that the term *parochia* did not immediately take on its present connotation of an area under the jurisdiction of a baptismal church. In the twelfth century it could apply to a wider area of jurisdiction, but by the thirteenth century its use in the narrow sense had become commonplace. This reference would therefore seem to indicate that Bute was erected into a parish with its parish church at Kingarth. If so, this would be the earliest documented parish in the western seaboard, and it is interesting that it should occur in an area where feudal colonisation was extensive, namely the Stewart lordship. This might serve to reinforce the connection between the extension of feudalism and the erection of parish churches that has been noted as a characteristic of the evolution of the parochial system in Scotland.[85]

---

[83] I. B. Cowan, 'The development of the parochial system in medieval Scotland', *SHR*, xl (1961); I. B. Cowan, 'Appropriation of parish churches', in McNeill and Nicholson, *Historical Atlas of Scotland*, pp. 37–8; M. Morgan, 'The organization of the Scottish Church in the twelfth century', *Trans. Royal Hist. Soc.*, 4th ser., xxix (1947).

[84] Cowan, 'Medieval Church in Argyll and the Isles', p. 25.

[85] On Kingarth: *Paisley Reg.*, p. 15; *OPS*, ii, pt. 1, pp. 210–11. On the term *parochia*, see Cowan, 'Development of the parochial system', pp. 43–4. On the Stewart lordship, see Barrow, *Anglo-Norman Era*, pp. 64–70.

By the middle of the thirteenth century there is evidence for a number of parishes in existence in the western seaboard. Churches and chapels recorded by about 1250 include Kilkerran, Kilmarow, Killean, and Kilcalmonell in Kintyre; St Charmaig and Kilmory in Knapdale; Kilfinan, Kilmadan, Inverchaolan, Dunoon, and Kilmun in Cowal; Kilninver in Lorn; Kilbride in Kerrera; and Arisaig in Morvern. Churches and chapels on record in the later thirteenth and fourteenth century, to about 1390, include Kilbride and Kilmore in Arran; Inchkenneth, Mull; Kilchrenan and Inishail in Lorn; Kilmalie in Lochaber; Kilbarr on Barra; Kilpeter on South Uist; and Kilmuir and the Chapel of the Holy Trinity on North Uist.[86] The documentary evidence for thirteenth and fourteenth-century churches is corroborated by the architectural evidence, and the remains of many churches and chapels in the West can be dated with some confidence to the thirteenth century (see Chapter 8). Many other parishes are only recorded in the middle of the sixteenth century; for example, none of the parishes on Skye is documented in the Middle Ages, and their first mention comes in Donald Monro's *Western Isles* of 1549. This does not mean that they did not exist at an earlier period; it only means that the historian cannot speak with confidence of their existence then. What we can say is that it would appear that the development of parishes was well underway in the western seaboard by the end of the thirteenth century, spurred on no doubt by the cession of the Western Isles to Scotland in 1266, and the extension of Scottish influences into the region from the middle of the thirteenth century.

It is striking, and it may be no coincidence, that many of the earliest churches and chapels on record in the West were located in Kintyre, Knapdale, and Cowal. These were areas in close proximity to the sprawling Stewart lordship which, by the end of the thirteenth century, dominated the Firth of Clyde and south Argyll. In the middle of the thirteenth century the Stewarts had gained ascendancy over Cowal and had become the patrons of the Lamonts, its leading native family, and by 1262 Walter Stewart of Menteith had obtained part of Knapdale and Cowal from Dugald MacSween.[87] It may therefore be conjectured that the feudalisation of these regions, or their proximity to the Stewart lordship, helped to promote the development of the parochial system, and therefore accounts for the dense concentration of thirteenth-century churches and chapels in Kintyre, Knapdale, and Cowal.

It is also striking that several, at least, of these thirteenth-century churches are associated with lay landholders, and it may be that they represent proprietary churches which appear on the record only as they were appropriated by other ecclesiastical organisations, in this case, Paisley Abbey. Two cases are particularly noteworthy, and in each the

[86] *OPS*, ii, pt. 1, *passim*.
[87] Barrow, *Anglo-Norman Era*, pp. 64–70, esp. p. 68.

landholders were prominent members of the native nobility. In 1247 Pope Innocent IV confirmed a grant by Dugald MacSween of a penny-land to the rector of the church of Kilcalmonell in Kintyre, and in the charter Dugald is referred to as 'lay patron' (*laicus patronus*) of the church. Fourteen years later, in 1261, Dugald granted Paisley Abbey the right of patronage of Kilcalmonell, along with the chapel of St Columba at Skipness, after the death of the rector of the church. In the second case, Duncan the son of Ferchar, and Lauman the son of Malcolm, granted to Paisley sometime between 1230 and 1246 the church of Kilfinan, a pennyland of Kilmore on Lochgilp with the chapel of St Mary, and three-and-a-half pennylands which they and their ancestors held at Kilmun, along with the right of patronage pertaining to the church at Kilmun.[88] These grants would seem to suggest that there was a strong proprietary nature to the churches in the western seaboard in the middle of the thirteenth century, as indeed there had been in Scotland generally in the twelfth.[89]

If there is little evidence for the evolution and early history of the parochial system in Argyll and the Isles, it is clear that, as elsewhere, parochial revenues were also utilised to endow other religious institutions, particularly the monasteries. Cowan's work has shown to just what extent the western seaboard conformed to the larger Scottish pattern in this respect, although the exact date at which churches were appropriated is often unknown. By the end of the Middle Ages many of the churches in Argyll and the Isles had been appropriated to various religious institutions. Thus, the abbey at Iona held thirteen churches in the diocese of the Isles, including four of five on Mull, and three in Argyll, while the nunnery on Iona held two churches, and the priory on Oronsay also held two. In the diocese of the Isles, however, many churches remained unappropriated, due in large measure to their remoteness from appropriating institutions. These included four in Lewis, one in Harris, two in the Uists, one in each of Barra, Eigg, and Gigha, six or seven in Skye, and three in Islay. In the diocese of Argyll a similar situation prevailed. There were eight unappropriated churches in Morvern, a circumstance which owed much to remoteness from a potential appropriating institution. The bishop of Argyll held six churches; the priory of Ardchattan held six; Paisley Abbey held three; and Saddell fared particularly poorly in this respect, apparently having only one church which it subsequently lost.

The strength and nature of popular religion is an area which is difficult to gauge, not just for the Western Isles but for all of Scotland in general. One of the most important manifestations of medieval popular religion was the cult of the saints. The saints were regarded as intercessors

[88] *Paisley Reg.*, pp. 123, 120, 132.
[89] Ibid., p. 135.

between God and humankind – once human, by virtue of their sanctity they had become members of the kingdom of Heaven, where they could intercede on behalf of the faithful who invoked their assistance. In the early Middle Ages, the cults of saints tended to be very localised. There was no formal process for canonisation, and saints were chosen by popular devotion. We have already noted how church dedications in the western seaboard containing the Gaelic element *kil* reflect the saints that were popular in the Hebrides in the early Middle Ages. They are traditional saints with Irish connections: Columba, Moluag, Maelrubha, or Barr. We can also glimpse the popularity of these saints in certain personal names. Hence, we find individuals bearing names like Gille-adomnán (servant of St Adomnán), Somerled's grandfather; Gillebrigte (servant of St Bride), Somerled's father; Gillecolm (servant of St Columba), who appears as a witness to a charter in 1240; and Gillemoluac (servant of St Moluag), who appears, most appropriately, as dean of Lismore in 1240.[90]

Without question the most popular and important of the Hebridean saints was Columba. Not surprisingly, the attention of scholars has been directed towards the cult of St Columba between the time of his death in 597 and the removal of his relics to Dunkeld and Ireland in 849 in the wake of the Viking attacks on Iona. We hear little about the cult of St Columba in the eleventh, twelfth, and thirteenth centuries, yet even six hundred years after his death it seems that Columba was far from forgotten in the western seaboard. As late as the turn of the thirteenth century his name could still be invoked as a protector of the Hebrideans. We have already noted how, in a grant to Paisley Abbey, Ranald, the son of Somerled, invoked the curse of St Columba on anyone who did harm to the monks.[91]

Ranald's charter, in Latin, to the Cluniac monks of Paisley itself represents a nice blend of old and new. But as late as about 1200, even in the midst of the ecclesiastical reorganisation that we have been noting, St Columba was not forgotten. It is interesting to note, though, that subsequent grants by Ranald's descendants were more conventionally worded, and dropped the curse altogether. Ranald's son, Donald, repeated his father's grant in similar terms, including the curse, but his son, Angus Mór, makes no mention of Columba in his own grant to Paisley sometime later. It would be instructive to be able to date the charters more closely, but if we can judge by the terms of these grants, the importance of St Columba was perhaps waning by the lifetime of Angus Mór in the thirteenth century.

Yet even as late as the middle of the thirteenth century St Columba was not forgotten, and he figured prominently in the events of 1249.

[90] *Clanranald Bk.*, p. 155; *RMS*, ii, no. 3136.
[91] *Paisley Reg.*, p. 125. See chap. 5, above, p. 148.

The saga of King Hakon related how, as he lay with his fleet at Kerrera, King Alexander II had a dream in which three men appeared to him:

> The third was by far the largest in figure, and the most frowning, of them all ... He spoke to the king and asked whether he intended to go plundering to the Hebrides. He thought he answered that that was certain. The dream man bade him turn back, and said to him that they would not hear of anything else.[92]

When the king refused to call off his expedition, he fell ill and died. The saga then went on to reveal the identity of the dream men: they were St Olaf, St Magnus, and St Columba, and it was St Columba that had ordered the Scottish king to turn back.

A similar type of story appears in the *Chronicle of Man*, which relates a miracle performed by St Maughold or Machutus. Little is known of this mysterious saint, but there was apparently a monastic community dedicated to him at St Maugholds in the north-eastern tip of the Isle of Man, which seems to have flourished between the seventh and the eleventh centuries.[93] The Manx chronicle relates how, when Somerled invaded Man and plundered the island in 1158, one of the leaders of his army, a man named Gilcolum, wanted to drive off the cattle grazing outside the precincts of the church and cemetery of St Maughold. Somerled, who is, interestingly enough, portrayed in a favourable light by the chronicler, refused to violate the sanctuary, but finally granted permission for Gilcolum and his men to do as they wished. The results were predictable. The community of St Maughold appealed to the saint, who appeared in a dream to Gilcolum, staff in hand, and, asking what he had done to Gilcolum to prompt his intentions, drove the staff into his heart:

> The unfortunate man uttered a fearful shriek, which awoke all who were sleeping in the surrounding tents. Again the saint transfixed him, again he shrieked. A third time the saint repeated the blow, a third time the man shrieked. His sons and followers, alarmed by the screams, hastened to him, inquiring what had happened. Scarcely able to move his tongue, he answered with a groan: 'St Maughold has been here, and, thrice transfixing me with his staff, has killed me.'

The dying man's pleas to the saint for forgiveness were ignored and he died 'in great torture and agony'.[94]

It has been noted that in the turbulent political conditions of the early Middle Ages saints often assumed the role of protector of their monastic

---

[92] *ES*, ii, pp. 556–7.
[93] Kinvig, *History of the Isle of Man* (3rd edn), p. 48; Cowan and Easson, *Medieval Religious Houses: Scotland*, appendix I, makes no mention of such a community, however.
[94] *Chron. Man*, pp. 71–5.

families and territories. Some of the miracles attributed to St Columba in his *Life* by Adomnán have a distinctly vengeful flavour to them, and even as late as the twelfth century another prominent northern saint, Cuthbert, could act as a 'fierce and powerful protector of his own people and goods'.[95] In the often troubled conditions of the Irish Sea world and the Hebrides in the twelfth and thirteenth centuries, it must have been important not only for the monasteries but also for the Hebrideans and Manx to possess supernatural protectors like St Columba and St Maughold. The question that St Maughold asked of Gilcolum – 'In what have I injured thee or thine, that thou art now about to plunder my place?' – must have been frequently repeated in the course of our period, for as late as 1214 we find Ruairi the son of Ranald plundering the monastery at Derry! Were such supernatural defenders effective? They were perhaps at least as effective as anything else. The *Chronicle of Man* states that once St Maughold struck down Gilcolum, 'such a great fear seized upon Somerled and his army, that, as soon as the ships were floated by the rising tide, the fleet left the port, and returned home as quickly as possible'.[96] And the saga of King Hakon suggests that it was the intervention of St Columba that caused the death of Alexander II at Kerrera in 1249. However the modern reader may be inclined to look askance at such supernatural intervention, it was very real to medieval people, and in the western seaboard as elsewhere in western Europe the saints were regarded as important protectors of their territories and people.

However little is known of saints like Maughold, it seems that the veneration of traditional saints, who acted in traditional roles, was widespread in the Western Isles in the twelfth century and even in the thirteenth. Yet this was also the time when important changes in the cult of the saints were beginning to manifest themselves across western Europe, and it remains to be determined whether these changes extended to the western seaboard. The rise of the papal monarchy and its influence across western Christendom had profound implications for the cult of the saints. Not only did the papacy assume control of the process of canonisation, but the rise of the universal saints meant that the local cults so characteristic of the early Middle Ages were either eclipsed or replaced. Without question the most popular of these universal saints was the Virgin Mary, whose cult reached its zenith in the thirteenth century, but apostolic saints like Peter and John were also popular, as was the cult of Christ and the Holy Trinity. In the course of the twelfth and thirteenth centuries the cult of these saints swept across western Europe and transformed the face of popular devotion.

Dedications to the Virgin Mary were as popular in Scotland as

---

[95] Ward, *Miracles and the Medieval Mind*, p. 61. On this phenomenon, see also P. Geary, *Furta Sacra: Thefts of Relics in the Central Middle Ages* (rev. edn, Princeton, 1990).

[96] *Chron. Man*, pp. 74–5.

elsewhere in western Europe: 'north and south, east and west, on the mainland and among the islands, there are traces of ancient sanctuaries bearing her name'.[97] In the Western Isles there are dedications to her in Kintyre, Knapdale, Argyll, Arran, Bute, Mull, Iona, Scarba, Rhum, Skye, the Uists, and Lewis, but the major difficulty is in ascertaining those dedications that originate in our period. As we noted in connection with the development of the parochial system, it is not uncommon for the first mention of a church to occur only in the Reformation. Contemporary dedications to the Virgin Mary in the western seaboard before about 1350 or 1400 are known at several sites, however, including Kilmarrow (Kintyre); Kilmory (Knapdale); Kilmore (east of Lochnell); Rothesay (Bute); Kilmorie (Arran); and Kilmuir (North Uist). The Benedictine abbey and the Augustinian nunnery on Iona were both dedicated to Mary, as were the Cistercian abbeys of Saddell and Rushen (like all Cistercian houses). And John of Fordun noted in his list of the Scottish islands that on Scarba there was 'a chapel of the Blessed Virgin, at which many miracles are performed'. It would seem, then, that the cult of the Virgin was as popular in the western seaboard as it was elsewhere in western Christendom, and it is possible that this popularity was due in part to the influence of the reformed religious orders, especially the Cistercians, with their emphasis on the Marian cult. But Mary was not alone among the universal saints represented in the western seaboard. Other dedications that appear on the historical record during our period are those of St John at Killean (Kintyre); St Peter at Kilpeter (South Uist); and the Holy Trinity at Teampull na Trianaide (North Uist). Of course, these dedications must be set beside traditional ones, such as those to St Bride, which continued to appear in our period, and which reveal a blend of old and new in the popular devotion of the inhabitants of the western seaboard.[98]

Once again the *Chronicle of Man* provides a neat illustration of the strength of popular devotion in the western seaboard. This thirteenth-century chronicle contains two miracle stories. One, which we have already noted, relates to St Maughold and took place in the mid-twelfth century. The other took place about a hundred years later, and relates to a miracle of the Virgin Mary. According to the chronicle, there was an aged chieftain named Donald who, to escape persecution by Harald, the son of Godfrey Dond (1249–50), fled to the abbey of St Mary at Rushen. He was only lured from this sanctuary by promises of safe conduct by the king, who, after a while, reneged on his promise and imprisoned Donald. Kept under heavy guard night and day, Donald prayed to Mary to intercede for him with God so that he might escape from his incarceration. His plea did not go unanswered. One day when the

---

[97] J. M. MacKinlay, *Ancient Church Dedications in Scotland: Scriptural Dedications* (Edinburgh, 1910), p. 70.

[98] *OPS*, ii, pt. 1, *passim*. See also MacKinlay, *passim*.

guards were inattentive, the chains that bound him miraculously fell off Donald's legs and he was able to escape. 'The prisoner,' states the chronicler, 'thus liberated by the divine favour, came ... to the monastery of St Mary of Rushen, thanking the Almighty, and his most compassionate mother for his freedom.'[99]

On the one hand, then, consideration of the Church and monasticism in the western seaboard indicates that the region participated fully in the phenomenon of the expansion of western Christendom, including the creation and definition of territorial dioceses, the spread of the international religious orders, the evolution of the parochial system, and the spread of the universal saints. The Manx kings and the descendants of Somerled were generous benefactors of the Church and appear as conventional and up-to-date in their piety. Yet, on the other hand, a consideration of popular devotion suggests a lingering strand of conservatism, as saints like Columba were invoked as late as the turn of the thirteenth century and as sites like Iona and Lismore retained their importance as ecclesiastical centres. It would seem that, if the society of the western seaboard in the thirteenth century was striking a balance between old and new, the same could be said of religion. St Mary might have made a strong impression upon the Hebrideans by the thirteenth century, but they had not forgotten St Columba.

[99] *Chron. Man*, pp. 102–5.

CHAPTER EIGHT

A Golden Age? The Monuments of the Western Seaboard

Mull, where are two castles, Doundowarde (Duart), and Dounarwyse (Aros) ...

Out at sea, at a distance of four miles from Mull, is Carneborg, an exceeding strong castle ...

Hycolumbkil, or Iona, where there are two monasteries, one of monks and the other of nuns ...   [John of Fordun, c.1385].[1]

It would appear from much of the foregoing narrative that the history of the western seaboard in the twelfth and thirteenth centuries consisted of nothing but incessant conflict, as the descendants of Somerled engaged in internecine strife, and as Hebridean, Scottish, Manx, Norwegian, and English elements struggled for supremacy in the Isles. Yet, although the chronicles and annals for this period in Hebridean history are indeed full of discord, we must be cautious before concluding from these jejune accounts that the West in the twelfth and thirteenth centuries was perpetually racked by raiding, warfare, and turbulence. Medieval chroniclers did not make it their business to take notice of the daily rhythms of life, and our sources are almost certainly deceptive and unrepresentative of life in the western seaboard in the central Middle Ages. This deficiency stems in part from the provenance of the major historical sources: both Scottish and Norwegian accounts tended to notice the MacSorleys only when they impinged on the consciousness of royal authority in those realms, and that usually meant whenever disorder was rampant. The sources are disappointingly silent about the years in between conflicts, and the charter and other documentary evidence is too meagre to be of much help before the fourteenth century. But it is quite likely that, under the strong lordship of a Ranald, Duncan, or Ewen, the West was largely peaceful and was certainly prosperous. This is where the evidence provided by the physical remains becomes vitally important. 'It is the greatest error,' wrote Eileen Power, 'to suppose that history must needs be something written down; for it may just as well be something built up, and churches, houses, bridges or amphitheatres can tell their story as plainly as print to those who have

---

[1] *Chron. Fordun*, i, pp. 43–4; ii, pp. 39–40.

eyes to read.'[2] Indeed, if the evidence provided by the monuments is considered, it can be argued that the Western Isles were experiencing something of an age of silver, if not quite of gold, in the thirteenth century.[3] Moreover, if it is sometimes tempting to view the Gaelic-Norse rulers of the Hebrides as little more than backward and barbarous warlords, then a study of the monuments they erected goes a long way toward discrediting such an interpretation. Although they ruled on the periphery of the Scottish kingdom, and, indeed, on the very margins of western Europe itself, these Hebridean chieftains demonstrated little reluctance to embrace the most up-to-date and contemporary trends in both military and ecclesiastical architecture.

There can be few visitors to the western seaboard of Scotland who have failed to be struck by the remarkable group of secular and ecclesiastical monuments that dot the landscape, often occupying stunning positions overlooking bays, lochs, and commanding stretches of the western seas. These monuments, frequently noted and discussed by early travellers to the region like Donald Monro, Martin Martin, Thomas Pennant, and Samuel Johnson and James Boswell, are well catalogued and have been exhaustively described. The standard was set by MacGibbon and Ross, who treated the region thoroughly in their massive multi-volume *Castellated and Domestic Architecture of Scotland* and *Ecclesiastical Architecture of Scotland*.[4] In this century, the Royal Commission on the Ancient and Historical Monuments of Scotland [RCAHMS] has catalogued many of the physical remains of Scotland's heritage. The survey is complete for Argyll and the Isles, with inventories of the Outer Hebrides and Skye being published in 1928, of Kintyre in 1971, and of the medieval and later monuments of mid-Argyll and Cowal as recently as 1992.[5] Finally, the excellent series *Exploring Scotland's Heritage*, produced by the RCAHMS and the HMSO, provides an admirably readable synthesis of scholarly information. What follows can be no more than a brief overview of the more significant physical remains, but it is important to set these impressive monuments within their cultural context in an attempt to understand their place within the society of the West.

Castles

The western seaboard of Scotland is home to what one scholar has called 'the most remarkable collection of thirteenth-century lords' strongholds

---

[2] E. Power, *Medieval People* (10th edn, London, 1963), p. 155.

[3] Cowan, 'Norwegian sunset – Scottish dawn', pp. 124–5.

[4] D. MacGibbon and T. Ross, *The Castellated and Domestic Architecture of Scotland* (Edinburgh, 1887–92); D. MacGibbon and T. Ross, *The Ecclesiastical Architecture of Scotland* (Edinburgh, 1896–7).

[5] For an admirable account of the Argyll survey, see Dawson, 'Argyll: the enduring heartland'.

to be found in any single region of Britain'.[6] As a group, the stone castles of the western seaboard are of significance to historians and archaeologists because they often survive as extensive ruins, due in large measure to the fact that Robert I's policy of demolishing strongholds does not appear to have been implemented in the West, where the castles were utilised against his implacable enemies, the MacDougalls.

Many of these structures appear to be – in their earliest stages of construction – roughly contemporary with one another, but they are all very poorly documented; indeed, the history of many of them remains a virtual blank right through the medieval era, and dating is generally dependent upon typology and architectural details, at best a tricky and relative business. The comment of MacGibbon and Ross that 'the history of [Castle Sween] is almost a blank' is, indeed, sadly typical of most of the fortifications in question.[7] In form these castles generally consist of massive curtain walls, usually constructed upon rocky outcrops which determine their irregular plan. They are almost all accessible directly from the sea and control substantial stretches of the western seaways and strategic routes of communication; their position and certain aspects of their construction thus reinforce the maritime culture of the western seaboard in the Middle Ages. Although they are sometimes associated with the extension of royal authority in the area in the course of the thirteenth century (and some, at least, were constructed as a result of royal initiative), current scholarly opinion connects most of these remarkable monuments with the ruling families of western Scotland: the MacDougalls, MacDonalds, MacRuairis, and others.[8]

North of the point of Ardnamurchan, there are important early stone castles on Barra and Skye. Kisimul Castle, 'the gem of the outer

---

[6] Barrow, *Kingship and Unity*, pp. 112–13.

[7] MacGibbon and Ross, *Castellated and Domestic Architecture*, iii, p. 63. Note also the comments of Cruden, *Scottish Castle* (London, 1963), p. 12: 'a sense of frustration consequently attends the analysis of many of our finest monuments. Their history will never be known, for in the long run the written record is the last word; all else is supposition.'

[8] In addition to those works just cited in the text, see J. G. Dunbar, *The Architecture of Scotland* (London, 1966); C. J. Tabraham, *Scottish Castles and Fortifications* (Edinburgh, 1986); Dunbar, 'Medieval architecture of the Scottish Highlands', pp. 38–70. There is much of value in Miket and Roberts, *Mediaeval Castles of Skye and Lochalsh*, and J. Gifford, *Highland and Islands* (London, 1992). A popular but still useful guide is M. Lindsay, *The Castles of Scotland* (London, 1986), which does, not however, list all of the castles discussed here. On specific castles, see W. D. Simpson, 'Castle Sween', *TGAS*, new ser., xv, pt. 1 (1960), pp. 3–14; W. D. Simpson, 'Skipness Castle', *TGAS*, new ser., xv, pt. 3 (1966), pp. 87–109; W. D. Simpson, 'Castle Tioram, Moidart, Inverness-shire; and Mingary Castle, Ardnamurchan, Argyllshire', *TGAS*, new ser., xiii (1954), pp. 70–90; Dunbar and Duncan, 'Tarbert Castle', pp. 1–17; H. B. Millar, 'The Castle of Fraoch Eilean, Loch Awe, Argyll', *TGAS*, new ser., xv, pt. 3 (1966), pp. 111–28; W. D. Simpson, 'The architectural history of Rothesay Castle', *TGAS*, new ser., ix, pt. 3 (1937–40), pp. 152–83; J. G. Dunbar, 'Kisimul Castle, Isle of Barra', *Glasgow Archaeological Journal*, v (1978), pp. 25–43; W. D. Simpson and J. G. Dunbar, *Dunstaffnage Castle* (rev. edn, Edinburgh, 1990); and W. D. Simpson, *Dunstaffnage Castle and the Stone of Destiny* (Edinburgh, 1958).

Hebrides',[9] crowns a small offshore islet in Castlebay on the south coast of Barra; at high tide, the castle seems to rise right from the surface of the water. It is a remarkably complete castle of enclosure, consisting of curtain walls surrounding an irregularly shaped courtyard, the overall plan being dictated by the outline of the rocky platform upon which it is built. The walls rise to their full height, but the main feature of the castle is the square, three-storey, great tower on the south-east side. Various dates for Kisimul Castle have been suggested, ranging from the eleventh to the early fifteenth centuries. John of Fordun did not mention a castle on Barra in his list of island fortresses, and the earliest documentary reference to Kisimul comes from the mid-sixteenth century. So, while there is at least the possibility that this stronghold dates from the thirteenth century, the matter must remain contentious. But whether it belongs to our period or to a later era, there can be little doubt that Kisimul represents one of the finest monuments of the outer Hebrides.

The Isle of Skye contains many spectacular and picturesque castle ruins, most of which date from the later medieval period. But Dunvegan Castle, notable as the home of the chiefs of the Clan MacLeod and the longest continually occupied residence in Scotland, dates in part from the thirteenth century. Indeed, the very name, Dun Bhegan, points to an ancient origin, for it means the fort of Began, which is a Scandinavian personal name. Situated in the north-western extremity of the island, Dunvegan occupies the irregularly shaped summit of a basalt out-cropping, some fifteen metres above the shore of Loch Dunvegan. It is separated from the landward mass by a ditch, and the best approach is from the north-western side where the land falls gently away; indeed, until 1748, the only access to the castle was from a sea-gate on this side. The only visible remains of the thirteenth century are the curtain walls, sea-gate, and ditch. The curtain walls, which originally encircled the entire summit of the rocky crag upon which the castle now sits, are two metres thick and rose to a height of three metres. In the fourteenth century a tower was added on the north-east side of the curtain walls, and the whole structure was much altered in subsequent centuries, particularly the mid-nineteenth, to give it its present appearance.

On the peninsula of Ardnamurchan itself, two strongholds deserve to be singled out for particular mention, Mingary and Tioram. Mingary Castle perches on an isolated rock on the south side of Ardnamurchan at the mouth of Loch Sunart, and commands spectacular views over Mull and Morvern. MacGibbon and Ross admirably described its situation:

Occupying, with its irregular outline, the whole of the top of an isolated rock from 20 to 30 feet [six to nine metres] high, this fortress guards the entrance from the open sea, both to the Sound of Mull and to Loch Sunart, while it is so placed as to command a view

[9] Moncreiffe, *Highland Clans*, p. 82.

down the greater part of the Sound ... Mingarry [*sic*] thus possessed the gateway to the southern division of the islands.[10]

Like its companion castles, Mingary has a massive curtain wall of thirteenth-century date, hexagonal in shape, which encloses a courtyard, although there are few thirteenth-century architectural details to be seen because of later modifications and additions. The curtain walls rise directly above the sea from the rocks on the seaward side, while the castle is cut off on the landward side by a dry ditch. The walls which rise from this rocky platform are up to twelve metres in height on the landward side, and there is a gate on the seaward side which is probably of later medieval or sixteenth-century date.

Closely related in both design and date to Mingary is Castle Tioram, which stands at the extreme point of a tongue of land jutting from the southern shore of Loch Moidart. This very complete castle occupies the entire summit of a rocky outcrop, which is cut off entirely from the shore at high tide. Roughly pentagonal in shape, the walls of Tioram are up to two-and-a-half metres thick and twelve metres high; at the seaward side they pose a sheer obstacle rising eighteen metres from the water. As with the other castles in question, these curtain walls represent the primary work of the structure, but there is a massive tower of somewhat later date, and other additions were made up to 1600. It is clear that Mingary and Tioram are closely related and are probably contemporary, although it has been suggested that Mingary is much more strategically located than is Tioram. Tioram (certainly) and Mingary (probably) fell within the MacRuairi lordship of Garmoran.[11]

Lorn contained more medieval castles than any other region of Argyll. Castle Fraoch Eilean sits on one of a group of islands at the north end of Loch Awe, about two miles from the head of the loch and half a mile from the western shore, near the entrance to the pass of Brander. It displays remains of four different periods of building, but the earliest datable works are twelfth- or thirteenth-century. These consist of an oblong stone hall-house measuring approximately twenty-two by thirteen metres, probably originally of two storeys, which closely resembles the oldest work at Castle Sween; this was later enclosed by a stone curtain wall. This castle is recorded in a charter of 1267 by Alexander III to Gilchrist MacNaughton, who was granted 'custody of our castle and island of Frechelan, so that they should cause the said castle to be built at our expense and repaired as often as necessary, and

---

10 MacGibbon and Ross, *Castellated and Domestic Architecture*, iii, p. 42.
11 Christiana MacRuairi's charter in the Royal Faculty of Procurators at Glasgow (see above, p. 189, note 120) listed *insula sicca*, that is, *eilean Tioram*, among her possessions. This may be the earliest reference to the castle, although it is not specifically mentioned. Tioram may also be the *Insual Tyreym* mentioned by Fordun in his list of Scottish islands: *Chron. Fordun*, i, p. 44; ii, p. 40.

should keep it safely for our use'.[12] Although the charter is open to several interpretations and is not completely beyond suspicion, such a grant would have been in keeping with the consolidation of royal power in the West following the Treaty of Perth in 1266.[13] Also on Loch Awe, Innis Chonnell Castle occupies a small island close to the south-east shore of the loch. It is square in plan with a forecourt but no keep, and represents several building stages. The earliest surviving work may, like Fraoch Eilean, represent a hall-house, probably of thirteenth-century date; it is first mentioned in the early fourteenth century, and is associated with the Campbells of Loch Awe. On Lismore, ruinous Achadun Castle, consisting of a great square enclosure, was the thirteenth-century stronghold of the bishops of Argyll, while Castle Coeffin, which commands an extensive prospect of Loch Linnhe and the Sound of Mull, consists of a ruined oblong hall-house of possible thirteenth-century date. It may have been erected by one of the MacDougalls of Lorn, within whose lordship Lismore occupied an important place.

Without question, however, one of the most impressive castles of the western seaboard, if not in all of Scotland, is Dunstaffnage. It occupies a strategic site overlooking Loch Etive, and enjoys a commanding view across Ardmucknish Bay. Located near the point of a low-lying peninsula, the castle itself rises from an irregularly shaped rocky platform. The name Dunstaffnage is partly Celtic and partly Norse, meaning the dun or fort of the Staff Ness, the promontory of the Staff. It is not certain how the castle obtained this name, although it may be that it occupies the site of the Dál Riatan fort known as Dun Monaidh. The present structure was erected in the second quarter of the thirteenth century by either Duncan of Argyll or his son Ewen, and it was the principal stronghold of the lords of Argyll, as evidenced by its crucial role in the campaign to subdue Argyll by Robert I in 1309. Although much added to in successive centuries, most of the original MacDougall stronghold still stands, consisting of a roughly quadrangular curtain wall, two-and-a-half to three metres thick, rising eighteen metres above the general ground level and ten metres above the courtyard level, with cylindrical angle-towers. The curtain wall has a parapet walk, and arrow slits form a prominent feature in the south-west and south-east walls. The courtyard once housed domestic ranges on the east and north-east walls, with extra accommodation provided in the two main angle towers. Nearby there are the ruins of a small chapel of contemporary date with the castle.

Four miles south-south-west of Dunstaffnage stands Dunollie Castle, perched at the summit of a rock promontory at the north end of Oban

[12] *HP*, i, p. 107.
[13] Millar, 'Castle of Fraoch Eilean', pp. 119–20, argues for the veracity of the charter, but compare RCAHMS, *Argyll*, ii, no. 290.

bay, with a commanding prospect of Kerrera, Lismore, and the Sound of Kerrera and Mull. The site is known to have been fortified in Dál Riatan times, and the surviving remains represent a fifteenth- or sixteenth-century tower-house with enclosing walls. Although this castle is undocumented in the thirteenth century, it is possible, although contentious, that this, too, was an important site within the MacDougall lordship.[14]

The Isle of Mull and the adjacent mainland of Morvern are home to a remarkable group of strategically situated castles that effectively control the Sound of Mull. Duart Castle stands on the east coast of Mull, commanding the intersection of the Sound of Mull, Loch Linnhe, and the Firth of Lorn. As first laid out it consisted of a simple castle of enclosure built on a rectangular plan, although little of this structure is visible today. The most prominent feature at Duart is the tower-house or keep, probably of fourteenth-century date, but like many of the other castles of the West, Duart has been extensively restored. The shattered remains of Aros Castle stand on top of a rocky platform on a promontory at the mouth of the Aros river, overlooking Salen Bay on the east coast of Mull. The site is of considerable importance, as it 'is near the centre of the Sound [of Mull] where it bends, so that the fortress commands a clear view both up and down the channel'.[15] Although very fragmentary in nature, the surviving remains consist of a hall-house and bailey with a ditch and bank, probably of thirteenth-century origin. Finally, there is Ardtornish Castle in Morvern, which occupies the tip of a promontory projecting into the Sound of Mull just over a mile southeast of the mouth of Loch Aline. The major remains represent, as at Aros, a hall-house which has been dated on stylistic evidence to the thirteenth century. As a group these three castles, Duart, Aros, and Ardtornish, are particularly significant because they are all within sight of each other, and command the eastern section of the Sound of Mull.

Another strategically and spectacularly located castle is Cairnburgh, in the Treshnish Isles. It occupies two adjacent isles, Cairn na Burgh More and Cairn na Burgh Beg, at the north-eastern end of the Treshnish chain of islands, about three miles south-west of Treshnish point, Mull. The site is of great strategic significance because it commands the most important sea-lane into the Inner Hebrides, but it is isolated and there is no safe anchorage. The main part of the castle is on Cairn na Burgh More, and although it is recorded as early as 1249, when it was one of four castles held by Ewen of Argyll of the Norwegian king, the surviving buildings are of fifteenth- to seventeenth-century date.[16]

Kintyre and mid-Argyll are also home to some impressive monuments of secular lordship. The most notable of these is Skipness Castle, situated

---

[14] RCAHMS, *Argyll*, ii, no. 286; Ritchie and Harman, *Argyll and the Western Isles*, no. 23.
[15] MacGibbon and Ross, *Castellated and Domestic Architecture*, iii, p. 125.
[16] RCAHMS, *Argyll*, iii, no. 335.

in a strategic location at the north-eastern point of Kintyre. It guards the confluence of Loch Fyne, Kilbrannan Sound and the Sound of Bute, and it possesses extensive views of Arran, the Kintyre coast, and the channel between Arran and Bute. Unlike many of the castles of the western seaboard, it does not take advantage of any natural rock formations to strengthen its position, but sits instead on level ground some 250 yards from the sea. In plan it is a great quadrangular curtain wall of red sandstone some two to two-and-a-half metres thick and ten metres high, enclosing a courtyard, the maximum dimensions of which are approximately thirty-four by twenty metres. There is a hall-house in the north-eastern corner, a square tower in the western wall, and another square tower in the south-eastern corner. The earliest traceable work at Skipness appears to have consisted of a two- or three-storey oblong hall-house, approximately seventeen by eleven metres in dimension, in the north-eastern corner, and it is probably this structure which is referred to as the 'castle of Skipness' ('castrum ... de Schepehinche') in a document of 1261. At a later date, perhaps around 1300, massive stone curtain walls were erected to replace the palisaded defences that must have accompanied the hall-house, transforming the earlier structure into a castle of enclosure. In 1261 Skipness Castle, along with the nearby chapel of St Columba, was in the possession of Dugald, son of Suibhne, probably being held on behalf of the MacDonald chiefs of Kintyre.[17] The same Dugald may have been the builder of the first castle at Lochranza on Arran, just across Kilbrannan Sound from Skipness, giving the MacSweens a firm grip on the region. Like many of the other castles under discussion here, Lochranza appears to the modern observer as a late medieval tower-house, but it was in fact a later medieval adaptation of an existing structure which was similar in plan to the early castle at Skipness. If Lochranza was indeed built by Dugald MacSween, then this family had a secure hold on Kilbrannan Sound.

Tarbert Castle, located five miles north of Skipness, is strategically located overlooking Tarbert Harbour, and guards a vital portage between the Clyde estuary and the western seaboard. Its ruinous remains comprise three distinct units: a small, square, inner bailey which occupies the summit of a rocky knoll; an extensive outer bailey with curtain wall and towers; and a tower-house of fifteenth- or sixteenth-century date added on to the walls of the outer bailey. The earliest work is that of the inner bailey, dated by careful comparative study to the middle of the thirteenth century, but the castle was substantially expanded in the later years of Robert I, between about 1325 and 1329.[18] It is possible – indeed, very likely – that the initial construction of this castle was undertaken in the years following Alexander II's campaign in 1221 and/or 1222, and that it therefore represents the intrusion of royal

17 *Paisley Reg.*, pp. 120–1.
18 Dunbar and Duncan, 'Tarbert Castle'.

authority in the West rather than a fortress constructed by the chieftains of the western seaboard.

No account of the castles of the western seaboard would be complete without mention of the magnificent Castle Sween, one of the most important monuments of secular lordship in the whole of Scotland, albeit one of the most poorly documented. It is, in the words of MacGibbon and Ross, 'A remote fortress which stands on a promontory near the mouth of Loch Swin [*sic*], a long and picturesque arm of the sea, on the west side of Knapdale'.[19] In its majestic setting, this is one of the great castles of Scotland to date from the twelfth or thirteenth century. The chief feature of Castle Sween is a quadrangular curtain wall, two metres thick and twelve metres high, which encloses a courtyard about twenty-one by fifteen metres. Against the two corners of the north side have been added two later towers, one round and one square, the former probably of sixteenth-century date, the latter of thirteenth-century date. The mostly featureless curtain walls are unbroken by windows or arrow-slits, and there are two entrances, one in the south wall and the other a sea-gate on the west. The quadrangular plan and simple typology of Castle Sween have given rise to considerable debate about its date and whether it should be regarded as a castle of enclosure or a keep, but there seems little doubt that it was in existence by the late twelfth century, and that it probably represents the earliest surviving stone-built castle walls in Scotland, at least on the mainland. It was quite probably constructed by the eponymous Suibhne, ancestor of the MacSweens, or his son, Dugald.[20]

Bute was one of the first islands of the western seaboard to fall into the hands of the Scottish kings, who granted it to the Stewart family, possibly as early as the reign of Malcolm IV (1153–65) but almost certainly by *c.*1200. It was probably Walter the Steward (1204–41) who constructed the castle of Rothesay on Bute which Fordun later admired as 'fair and impregnable'. Unlike many of the other castles of the western seaboard, it is situated in an area of no obvious defensive potential, although Rothesay Bay, an important anchorage, is nearby and proximity to the harbour was a consideration in the choice of site. However, unlike those castles whose plan was dictated by local topography such as rock outcroppings or island sites, Rothesay's builders were free to work unhindered by such restrictions. Accordingly, Rothesay Castle consists of an almost circular curtain wall of stone some ten metres high, two-and-a-half metres thick, and forty metres in diameter. As with other castles of similar design, the courtyard would have housed domestic buildings, probably constructed of wood. The date of the earliest stone castle here may be as early as the third quarter of the twelfth century, with the four great round towers, now largely demol-

---

[19] MacGibbon and Ross, *Castellated and Domestic Architecture*, iii, p. 58.
[20] Tabraham, *Scottish Castles and Fortifications*, pp. 41–2.

ished, being added later, possibly in the third quarter of the thirteenth century. Rothesay is almost certainly the unnamed castle in Bute that was besieged by Uspak and his Norsemen and Hebrideans in 1230. *Hakon's Saga* describes the siege in great detail and relates that the attackers hewed at the soft stone of the castle walls with axes; the tactic was successful, and when the walls collapsed, the castle fell to the Norse. There is no doubt that the castle we see today represents essentially that stormed in 1230,[21] and Rothesay is one of the best-preserved castles dating from the twelfth and early thirteenth centuries to be found anywhere in Scotland.

Churches, chapels, and monasteries

Although these castles may be the most spectacular of the monuments constructed by the rulers of the western seaboard, their achievements in erecting monuments to the glory of God should not be underestimated, even though the ravages of time and man have been less kind to these structures, leaving 'bare ruined choirs' scattered across much of the West. The twelfth and thirteenth centuries saw a tremendous burst of ecclesiastical building in Argyll and the Isles, and there are dozens of small chapels and parish churches dotting the landscape which attest to the zeal of the rulers of these regions and their dependants in providing for their souls.

The parochial churches and chapels of the west coast are particularly numerous in Kintyre, Cowal, Mid-Argyll, Mull, and North Argyll. These structures have been described as 'simple oblong buildings of unicameral plan having a minimum of architectural elaboration',[22] although several display rich decoration characteristic of the thirteenth century. They are almost certainly to be associated with the origins of the parochial system in Argyll and the Isles, and, although tiny and largely simple in construction, they attest to a thriving religious life in the West in our period. On Bute, the chapel of St Blane at Kingarth, itself situated on the site of an early Christian foundation, consists of a nave and small chancel, but there is an elaborate chevron-patterned decoration in the Romanesque style on the chancel arch. The work seems to date from *c.*1170 to 1200, and it has been suggested that the chapel dates from the period of the Stewart lordship and is contemporary with Rothesay Castle.[23] The second half of the twelfth century also saw much church building in Argyll, under the patronage of native lords. Especially

---

21 Cruden, *Scottish Castle*, p. 34. On Rothesay, see also Tabraham, *Scottish Castles and Fortifications*, pp. 40–1; Ritchie and Harman, *Argyll and the Western Isles*, no. 32; and *ES*, ii, pp. 475–6, for the 1230 siege.

22 RCAHMS, *Argyll*, i, p. 22.

23 Ritchie and Harman, *Argyll and the Western Isles*, no. 51; Dunbar, 'Medieval architecture of the Scottish Highlands', p. 40; W. Galloway, 'Notice of the chapel dedicated to St Blane at Kingarth in Bute', *Archaeologia Scotica*, v (1890), pp. 317–35.

noteworthy is a group of Kintyre parish churches and chapels such as Kilchenzie, Kilcousland, Kilkivan, and Killean, which are simple, rectangular structures with little or no elaborate decoration. Killean, however, is notable for a twelfth-century nave and a thirteenth-century chancel, which has the remains of a decorated window; it was patronised by Ruairi, the son of Ranald, in about 1222, and was granted to the bishop of Argyll in 1243.[24] In Knapdale there are similar structures at Keils and Kilmory Knap; the latter is of particular interest because of the fine twin round-headed windows in the east wall.[25] Also in Knapdale, the island of Eilean Mor at the mouth of Loch Sween provided an ideal setting for an early Christian sanctuary, and it is hardly surprising that a small rectangular medieval chapel should have been erected on the site in the twelfth or early thirteenth century. These churches were probably patronised by the MacSween lords of Knapdale. Other churches of twelfth- or thirteenth-century date and simple design in the Isles south of Ardnamurchan include those of Pennygowan, Inchkenneth and Kilvickeon (Mull), Kildalton (Islay); and the old parish church on Gigha; while fragments of carved stone suggest the existence of a twelfth- or thirteenth-century structure at Soroby on Tiree. There are relatively few churches of the period that have been identified on Skye and the Outer Hebrides, but Kilmaluag (Raasay), Teampull na Trinaid (North Uist), and Teampull Mholuidh (Europie, Lewis) all seem to be of later twelfth- or thirteenth-century date.[26]

The chapels at Skipness and Dunstaffnage represent the zenith of ecclesiastical architecture in the west of Scotland, Iona excepted. Kilbrannan chapel at Skipness is situated almost 400 yards from the castle, near Skipness Bay, and it was probably built in the late thirteenth or early fourteenth century to replace the earlier chapel of St Columba which was incorporated into Skipness Castle during its second stage of rebuilding. Although roofless, it is in a good state of preservation, and consists of a single-chambered structure measuring approximately twenty-five by eight metres. The nave and chancel each have four lancet windows, and the east window, divided into two by a central mullion, is a particularly fine feature. The chapel at Dunstaffnage stands about 150 yards south-west of the castle, and its architectural details point to a date contemporary with the construction of the castle, sometime in the middle of the thirteenth century. Like Kilbrannan, it consists of a single-chambered rectangular building, measuring about twenty by six metres. The chancel has elaborate windows in the north, south, and east walls, and there is some splendid decoration on the jambs, mouldings, and

---

24 RCAHMS, *Argyll*, i, nos. 280–1, 286–7; see also Dunbar, 'Medieval architecture of the Scottish Highlands', p. 40. A chapel is also documented at Kilkerran in the 13th century, though nothing remains today: see *OPS*, ii, pt. 1, pp. 12–13.

25 MacGibbon and Ross, *Ecclesiastical Architecture*, i, pp. 84–6.

26 Dunbar, 'Medieval architecture of the Scottish Highlands', pp. 41–2; see also the relevant *Inventories* by the RCAHMS.

arch-heads of the windows;[27] indeed, this is one of the masterpieces of Gothic architecture anywhere in Scotland.

By about 1200, however, the architectural centre of gravity in the western seaboard was the tiny island of Iona, where it would remain throughout the rest of the Middle Ages. Without question the leading ecclesiastical monument in the Western Isles is the Benedictine abbey refounded by Ranald, the son of Somerled, in about 1200. This stands within the area once occupied by the Celtic monastery of St Columba (founded *c*.563), and Ranald's Benedictine church was probably built on the site of its early medieval predecessor. Although there are few written records, architectural details suggest that the initial construction took place between about 1200 and 1220, with further work commencing in about 1220 and again in 1270, while the fifteenth century saw a final burst of rebuilding before the Reformation. The first church consisted of a short choir without aisles, transepts with small chapels, and a nave with aisles at the east side only. The north transept is the only part of this early church to survive reasonably intact, and it reveals much of what Ranald's church must have looked like with its late Romanesque windows and arches. There is also late twelfth- or thirteenth-century work in the north and west walls, but these were remodelled in the fifteenth century, and most of the choir and the crossing also date from this period. In the second phase of construction the eastern arm of the church was enlarged considerably, and it was only now that a cloister and the associated monastic outbuildings were begun. An ambitious project to enlarge the south transept did not proceed beyond the level of the foundations, and there seems to have been little further construction until the middle of the fifteenth century when the choir was rebuilt. The whole structure fell into ruin from the seventeenth century, and it was extensively restored earlier this century.[28]

About a quarter of a mile south-west of the abbey on Iona stand the picturesque pink granite ruins of an Augustinian nunnery. This was also founded by Ranald, probably at about the same time as the nearby abbey was refounded, and its first prioress was Ranald's sister, Bethag or Beatrice. The nunnery remains are the most substantial of their kind in Scotland; it has been called 'one of the best-preserved examples in the British Isles of the smaller medieval nunnery'.[29] The church is the most interesting and substantial part of the ruin, and dates from the early part of the thirteenth century. It is small, of simple, rectangular design, about twenty by twelve metres, and consists of a nave and choir with a north aisle extending along both. It is executed in the same architectural style

27 RCAHMS, *Argyll*, i, no. 277 (Kilbrannan); iv, no. 243 (Dunstaffnage); see also Simpson and Dunbar, *Dunstaffnage Castle*.

28 See the excellent guidebook to the site by Dunbar and Fisher, *Iona*; and the detailed description of the site in RCAHMS, *Argyll*, iv, no. 4. There is also much of value in R. Fawcett, *Scottish Abbeys and Priories* (London, 1994).

29 Dunbar and Fisher, *Iona*, p. 8.

as the abbey, but had a vaulted choir and north choir-chapel, a rare feature in the Highlands. The masonry is notable for its good quality, and the church is richly decorated with sculptured capitals and dog-tooth ornament. The claustral buildings on the south side of the church date from the later medieval period.[30]

Iona also possesses two other ecclesiastical monuments from the period of the central Middle Ages which are easily overlooked by the modern visitor: St Oran's chapel and St Ronan's church. St Ronan's, which stands just to the north of the ruins of the nunnery, served as the parish church for the island. It is of simple rectangular plan, measuring only about eleven and a half by five metres, and dates from the late twelfth or early thirteenth century; in 1923 it was restored as a museum for carved stones and it has recently seen further restoration work undertaken. St Oran's chapel takes its dedication from Oran (Odhran), a cousin of St Columba. It stands in the ancient burial ground located a short distance to the south-west of the abbey, and part of the medieval paved street that led to the abbey from the Reilig Odhráin burial ground can be seen nearby. St Oran's is the oldest surviving building on the island, probably dating from the mid- to late twelfth century, and may have been erected by the pre-Benedictine ecclesiastical community of Iona. It is rectangular in plan, and measures only nine by five metres internally, but it has an elaborately decorated doorway in the west wall, with carved capitals and a semi-circular arch decorated with bird- or animal-head and chevron ornament. It has been suggested that St Oran's chapel was erected to serve as a family mortuary chapel by either Somerled or his son Ranald, and it was certainly used as a burial-place by the later MacDonald Lords of the Isles. An elaborate tomb-recess in the south wall may belong to John, the fourth and last Lord of the Isles (1449–93, d. 1502), or to his son, Angus Óg.[31]

In comparison with the splendid medieval monuments of Iona, the remains of the religious houses at Saddell in Kintyre and Ardchattan in Lorn may well seem disappointing, but each is nevertheless significant in its own way. Saddell Abbey, the only Cistercian monastery in the west Highlands and Islands, stood near the mouth of Glen Saddell, eight miles north of Campbeltown; while Ardchattan Priory, situated on the north shore of Loch Etive about four miles east of North Connell, at the foot of the Benderloch hills, was one of only three houses of the Valliscaulian order in Scotland. All that can be discerned of the church and conventual buildings at Saddell today are the presbytery and the north transept, as well as part of the south claustral range; the remainder of the buildings are represented by overgrown mounds of debris.

---

[30] Ibid., pp. 8–10; see RCAHMS, *Argyll*, iv, no. 5, for a detailed description; and Dunbar, 'Medieval architecture of the Scottish Highlands', p. 41.

[31] Dunbar and Fisher, *Iona*, p. 10, 12; RCAHMS, *Argyll*, iv, nos. 12, 13; MacGibbon and Ross, *Ecclesiastical Architecture*, i, p. 220–3.

Both the overall layout of the site and some architectural fragments suggest a date in the second half of the twelfth century, but this was never a large or prosperous foundation, and in 1507 it was claimed that there had been no monastic life here within living memory. The remains were extensively quarried in about 1770 to provide building materials for nearby Saddell Castle. Ardchattan Priory is both more complete and contains more original architecture than does Saddell, although it has been much altered over the centuries. A church with associated conventual buildings was erected here soon after the foundation in 1230 or 1231 by Duncan MacDougall. This structure had a small choir and crossing, north and south transepts with chapels, and a nave with a narrow aisle on the north side. In the fifteenth and early sixteenth centuries a new choir was built, and parts of the crossing, north transept, and nave were also rebuilt. All that remains of the thirteenth-century church is the south transept with its two chapels, and some fragments of the nave and crossing.[32] Oronsay Priory, located at the west end of the island of Oronsay, was the only other religious house of the western seaboard. It was founded in the second quarter of the fourteenth century by John, the first MacDonald Lord of the Isles (1336–86), for a community of Augustinian canons. Although some of the buildings may date from the mid-fourteenth century, most of the surviving remains belong to a string of successive building operations between the late fourteenth and sixteenth centuries.[33]

The monuments and society

Perhaps more important than these monuments' physical form and location is what they reveal about the society of the western seaboard. 'The castles of the Hebrides, many of which are standing, and many ruined, were always built upon points of land on the margin of the sea. For the choice of this situation there must have been some general reason, which the change of manners has left in obscurity.' Thus did Dr Johnson ponder the purpose of the castles of the western seaboard, for which he could find no satisfactory explanation. There can be little doubt that the building of stone castles, often on islands, rock promontories, or sea-girt sites, is one of the most important and spectacular achievements of the rulers of the western seaboard in the thirteenth century. Their achievement is made more notable for the fact that these strongholds contrast sharply with the motte-and-bailey enclosures of earth and timber erected across eastern and southern Scotland by the feudal lords of the same period.[34] On the one hand, then, the castles of the western seaboard form an impressive set of monuments. Yet, as one

[32] RCAHMS, *Argyll*, i, no. 296 (Saddell); iv, no. 217 (Ardchattan).
[33] Ibid., v, no. 386.
[34] See P. Yeoman, *Medieval Scotland* (London, 1995), chap. 6.

authority has stated, it is difficult to avoid regarding them at first sight as enigmas:

> That such formidable fortresses were built on the fringe of a rapidly developing feudal country by men of Celtic origin, at a time when their Norman neighbours to the east were seemingly content, by and large, with castles of timber and clay, is not readily understood.[35]

The castle, best defined as the fortified residence of the lord, in which the residential role is as important as the military, is often seen as the ideal symbol of feudal society.[36] And, while it is true that the first castles appear in Scotland in the twelfth century, they are associated not only with the introduction of Anglo-Norman influences but also with the Norse, who controlled much of the north, including Shetland, Orkney, Caithness, and who had a profound impact on the Hebrides and Argyll as well. The earliest datable new stone castle in Scotland comes not from the realm of the feudal kingdom, but rather from the area under Norse influence. Cubbie Roo's Castle, on the island of Wyre in Orkney, was probably constructed by Kolbein Hruga, a substantial landholder in Orkney and Norway, who, according to the *Orkneyinga Saga*, had 'a fine stone fort ... a really solid stronghold' built around 1150.[37] In its ruinous state today it consists of the base of a tower, about eight metres square, set within a ditched enclosure. It was entered through a doorway at first-floor level. It is not known how many storeys the tower had, although it has been suggested that three would have afforded a good view across Gairsay Sound. Similarly, the stone castle at Old Wick in Caithness was probably erected by Harald Maddadson, Earl of Orkney, or one of his kinsmen, in the mid-twelfth century.[38] The construction of stone castles by Norse nobles and earls in northern Scotland serves as a warning that 'influences other than feudal created an environment encouraging to castles',[39] although it is quite likely that the construction of these structures was influenced, at least in part, by contacts with feudal society. Harald Maddadson, for instance, had married the daughter of Earl Duncan of Fife, whose son had built an impressive motte-and-bailey castle in Strathbogie (at what is now Huntly). Whatever may have been the case, the rulers of the western seaboard were well positioned to take advantage of the dual heritage of castle building in Scotland. Moreover, the up-to-date nature of castles like Dunstaffnage also shows how the

---

[35] Tabraham, *Scottish Castles and Fortifications*, p. 43.

[36] See, among others, Brown, *Castles*, pp. 5–10; and R. A. Brown, *Castles From the Air* (Cambridge, 1989), pp. 1–7.

[37] *Orkneyinga Saga* (Pálsson and Edwards), cap. 84. The Scottish kings, however, were no doubt already building in stone at their castles: David I (d. 1153), for instance, at Edinburgh and Roxburgh, as well as at Carlisle.

[38] Tabraham, *Scottish Castles and Fortifications*, p. 32; Gifford, *Highland and Islands*, p. 46–7.

[39] Cruden, *Scottish Castle*, pp. 18–20.

Scoto-Norse chieftains of the Hebrides were ready and able to adopt the castle to their own particular needs. Duncan of Argyll, the probable builder of Dunstaffnage, may not have been of Norman stock, but he appears as pro-Scottish in his leanings and was named in a Scottish document to the Pope in 1237. Whether he should be seen as an 'enthusiastic' baron and vassal of the king is open to debate, but there can be little doubt that 'the Celtic chiefs of the West seem to have grasped the significance of feudalism and adapted it to suit their own needs'.[40] In this respect the testimony of the stones serves to reinforce the evidence provided by the few documents that record infeftments in the West from the thirteenth and early fourteenth centuries, where the service most commonly specified was that of a galley with a certain number of oars.

The siting and design of these castles were, of course, determined by the maritime orientation of the region. It is no coincidence that the castles of the West are characterised by coastal locations, and were built on islands, promontories, peninsulas, and other sea-girt locations that command sweeping stretches of the western seas. The castles of Duart and Dunstaffnage, for example, are situated to control the confluence of the Sound of Mull and the Firth of Lorn as well as the entry to Loch Etive and Loch Linnhe. Mingary, Aros, Ardtornish, and Duart are strategically sited to control entry to the Sound of Mull and are intervisible with one another; indeed, together with Dunollie Castle near Oban, these castles have been seen as part of a unified system of defence. Moreover, despite their location on top of rocky outcroppings, many of these fortifications are situated in close proximity to good harbours, and it is most unusual for any of them to lack a sheltered anchorage nearby (though that is the case at Mingary). Skipness, Dunstaffnage, Duart, Aros, Ardtornish and Dunvegan, for example, all had sweeping anchorages close by the strongholds, ideal for sheltering the galleys which were the instrument of domination on the western seaways. In some instances, the only access to the castle was from a sea-gate. Dunvegan is notable in this regard, but many other castles of the West possessed sea-gates in addition to an entrance from the landward side. All these features point to the castles of the western seaboard as being an integral component of the maritime culture of the region, and demonstrate how the castle, normally used to control stretches of land, was adapted by the Hebridean chieftains to control stretches of sea as well. This connection between the castles and the sea is neatly demonstrated in the fourteenth-century Gaelic poem in the *Book of the Dean of Lismore* which recounts the siege of Castle Sween in about 1310 by John MacSween. 'Tryst of a fleet against Castle Sween', begins the poem, and it goes on to recount the siege of the castle by an Irish-based fleet. What

[40] Tabraham, *Scottish Castles and Fortifications*, p. 43.

the poem illustrates is the integration of these castles into the maritime culture of the western seaboard, a fact which was recognised (if somewhat romantically) as long ago as the eighteenth century by the geographer John MacCulluch:

> Those who see Dunstaffnage Castle by approaching it from the land, will find nothing picturesque or interesting in its appearance: it is a heavy square mass, on a bare and ugly shore. But it is far otherwise from the sea ... On the land side, its aspect is mean; and, as a defence, it appears feeble; but, towards the sea, it carries with it that air of rude strength and romance which leads us back to the ages of Highland and feudal independence.[41]

It is at Dunstaffnage that we can best appreciate another aspect of the nature of these monuments, both secular and ecclesiastical. The castle at Dunstaffnage is of the type known as a castle of enclosure; the chapel, even in its ruinous state, is a fine example of Gothic architecture. Yet, while admiring the sophisticated details of these monuments, it is easy to forget that we are on the margins of not only Scotland and Britain but also of western Europe in general, a long way indeed from the birthplace of both the castle and the style of architecture known as Gothic, in northern France. The western seaboard is a region that is often dismissed as barbarous, backward, turbulent, and far from the mainstream of European culture, yet the evidence of the stones suggests a sophisticated culture that was striving to be thoroughly contemporary.

In order to resolve the paradox posed by the monuments of the western seaboard it is necessary to look beyond their pragmatic roles as fortresses, residences, or places of worship, to their roles and meanings as symbols. The hall and castle were aristocratic buildings. The hall is a much older structure, while the association of the castle with aristocratic power began in northern France in the early eleventh century as the power of magnates came to be centred on castles. But both hall and castle provided the nobility with an opportunity to display their wealth, power, prestige, and, in the case of the castle, to extend their jurisdiction over the surrounding area. The castle was, in short, a symbol of lordship and domination as much as a military (or residential) structure, and by the early twelfth century it had become the major device through which nobles advertised wealth and power. By the late twelfth century every great noble had to have a castle to express his status. As David Crouch has summed it up, 'there was an overt intention by the designers [of castles] to impress contemporaries with their wealth and importance, as much as to build a fortress'.[42] Since, as we have seen, the magnates of the West were displaying the desire to be fully up to date in other respects as

---

[41] Cited in Simpson, *Dunstaffnage Castle and the Stone of Destiny*, pp. 24–5.
[42] Crouch, *Image of Aristocracy*, p. 263; on the hall, see also Yeoman, *Medieval Scotland*, pp. 90–3.

well, it is hardly surprising that they would choose to erect suitable monuments with which to advertise their status.

Aristocratic patronage of the church operated under similar principles. Magnates did not, of course, necessarily found monasteries and endow churches only for worldly gain, and these motives were mingled, consciously or unconsciously, with spiritual concerns. The spiritual benefits of church patronage included the salvation of the soul and burial privileges within the church or monastery, while worldly benefits might embrace certain rights and privileges related to the church. But, as with the construction of castles, the patronage of churches also provided an opportunity to display wealth, prestige, and status. Churches, as Christopher Brooke has observed in an English and Norman context (no less applicable here), were intended to impress with the scale of their architecture in 'an age acutely sensitive to the physical impression created by a church'.[43] If the architecture and design of a twelfth- or thirteenth-century monastery, even a modest-sized one, like Iona, is compared to the dry stone and timber structures of a Celtic monastery, then the impression that such structures could make on contemporaries will become clear. Churches no less than castles, then, were status symbols in the twelfth and thirteenth centuries, and the monuments of the West are therefore advertisements to the wealth and power of the nobles who had them built.

Dunstaffnage was an up-to-date stronghold, built to impress and overawe as well as protect its lord. Its plan, that of a quadrangular curtain wall with projecting but shallow cylindrical angle-towers, was based on the latest contemporary models; indeed, it has been argued that the castle at Dunstaffnage, 'size for size was the equal of its counterparts in northern England and the Welsh Marches'.[44] The elaborate lancet windows in the first-floor level of the east and north walls speak of sophisticated accommodation, and the builders of Dunstaffnage, the MacDougall lords of Argyll, Duncan and his son Ewen, were 'obviously fully conversant with current trends in castle building'.[45] The nearby chapel, called a 'masterpiece in miniature', was also clearly the work of a master of Gothic architecture; it is impressive even in its ruinous condition. Indeed, the chapel at Dunstaffnage has been called, 'worthy in all respects, save that of mere size, to take its place alongside the noblest ecclesiastical monuments of contemporary France or the rest of Britain'.[46] Here, then, were no monuments to a provincial aristocracy, but structures that were up to date and contemporary in every way with major developments in England, Wales, and elsewhere in Europe.

---

[43] C. Brooke, 'Princes and kings as patrons of monasteries', in *Il Monachesimo e la Riforma Ecclesiastica (1049–1122)*, Settimana internazionale di studio, 4, Passo della Mendola, 1968, *Miscellanea del Centro di Studi Medioevali VI* (Milan, 1971), pp. 131–2.

[44] Simpson and Dunbar, *Dunstaffnage Castle*, p. 3.

[45] Tabraham, *Scottish Castles and Fortifications*, p. 42.

[46] Simpson and Dunbar, *Dunstaffnage Castle*, p. 25.

CHAPTER NINE

Conclusion:
In Search of the Kingdom of the Isles

Oh Children of Conn of the Hundred Battles
Now is the time for you to win recognition ...
[Clan Donald's Incitement to Battle at Harlaw, 1411][1]

Fitting uncomfortably between the Viking Age and the Lordship of the Isles, the centuries between about 1100 and 1300 in Scotland's western seaboard teeter on the abyss of obscurity. They are bathed in a perennial historical twilight, at best always in danger of being outshone by the dazzling brilliance of the ages that precede and follow them, at worst in peril of being written off as an epilogue to one era or the prologue to another. Yet, peering out at us from their precarious perch between the Vikings and the Lords of the Isles, the Kings of the Isles are able to transfix us with a stare as piercing as that of the smooth-chinned king from the Lewis chessmen – if only we know where to look.

Although there had been 'kings of the Isles' before 1100, and although the Latin title *dominus Insularum*, adopted by the self-styled Lords of the Isles and first used in 1336, was derived from the Gaelic *rí Innse Gall*, perhaps at no other time did the concept of the kingdom of the Isles possess so much viability in political terms. Somerled held sway over an insular and mainland kingdom that stretched from Man to Skye and from Kintyre to Glenelg. The extent of his lordship is reflected in the composition of the army with which he invaded the mainland in 1164: it included fighting men from Kintyre, Argyll, the Isles, and Dublin. And, even though his extensive kingdom fragmented upon his death, for another century there were still kings in the Isles. It is, of course, easy to lose sight of this. Seen against the larger backdrop of the British Isles, dominated by the amazing success stories of the English and Scottish monarchies, the kingdom of the Isles may seem a poor, backward cousin whose history is dull or even unimportant by comparison. But it could be said that the kingdom of the Isles represents a lost kingdom in the history of medieval Britain.

A kingdom needs a king. The history of the western seaboard between 1100 and 1300 was dominated by vigorous sea-kings descended from

[1] Cited in C. Proctor, *Ceannas Nan Gaidheal: The Headship of the Gael* (Armadale, 1985), p. 16.

the mighty Somerled of Argyll (d. 1164) and the equally formidable Godred Crovan (d. 1095). For a hundred years between the demise of Somerled and the death of the last Manx ruler in 1265, one of the major themes in the western seaboard was the struggle for hegemony between these two kindreds, which, though often violent, assumed a definite equilibrium. These sea-kings are compelling, spirited figures. They lived hard and died harder. Their praises were sung by Gaelic bards, and their formidable fleets of galleys inspired awe and terror in enemies and allies alike. They appear as thoroughly up-to-date rulers on the one hand, embracing contemporary trends in architecture and building magnificent stone castles and chapels like those at Dunstaffnage; yet on the other hand they were ready, willing, and able to undertake old-fashioned plundering expeditions in the Hebrides or the Irish Sea long after the Viking Age had passed. Ranald the son of Somerled, Ragnvald the son of Godfrey, Ewen the son of Duncan, Angus Mór the son of Donald – these were men whose deeds were celebrated the length and breadth of the western seaways and beyond. Somerled's career was recorded in Scottish, Irish, Norse, and Manx sources; both the St Albans chronicler, Matthew Paris, and Sturla Thordarson, the Icelandic author of Hakon's saga, praised Ewen of Argyll; Gaelic bards sung the deeds of Ragnvald of Man and Angus Mór of Islay. Yet, paradoxically, although they were mighty figures in their own day, these sea-kings seldom figure in modern history books. They might be called the lost kings of the medieval British Isles.

It is not hard to see why the kingdom of the Isles and its rulers have all but disappeared from the history of Britain, and why we should have to look so hard to discover them. In the first instance, there is the dearth of information at our disposal. The vicissitudes of the centuries have deprived us of many historical sources. We need only consider the rich and varied information contained in the register of Paisley Abbey to realise what a wealth of material may have once existed at Iona, Lismore, Rushen, or Peel, only to have perished in the turmoil of the Reformation and subsequent ages. Moreover, we must bear in mind that the practice of recording land grants came relatively late to the western seaboard. Yet another difficulty that threatens to overwhelm the kingdom of the Isles is that of historical perspective. Throughout this study we have had to rely upon sources of Norse, Irish, English, and Scottish provenance; there is no indigenous chronicle tradition (setting aside the Manx chronicle, which is not impartial towards the kindred of Somerled) to set beside these sources and to provide us with the perspective of the Hebridean chieftains, their motives or their outlook on the events that unfolded across our period. This is a history written largely from the outside looking in, glimpsed through a glass darkly. Much is bound to remain obscure, distant, and problematic, and hence many of my conclusions will have to remain speculative and tentative.

Modern traditions of historical writing have also been unkind to the kingdom of the Isles. A short-lived political entity on the margins of the superpowers of medieval Britain (indeed, it ultimately fell prey to not one but both of those superpowers), the kingdom of the Isles tends to fall between the cracks of modern historical writing. A loser in the battle to become a nation-state, it is an orphan with no place in national historical writing. Only current trends towards a more holistic British history, which have prompted closer study of the so-called margins, have helped to rescue the kingdom of the Isles from its dim twilight and thrust it into the glare of the historical spotlight.

Still another reason for the relative obscurity of the western seaboard relates to its geographical location on not only the western margin of the Scottish kingdom but also the northern frontier of Europe itself. In one sense the region is, indeed, peripheral and, seemingly, disconnected from developments in Scotland and elsewhere. Yet on another level, this isolation is more illusory than real, created by a land-locked perspective and an inadequate understanding of the maritime culture of the western seaboard. To the inhabitants of the Isles, the seas were a highway. Whether they were taking on goods for trade in Bristol, taking on booty in Connemara, or disgorging fighting men at Renfrew, the galleys at the disposal of the kings of the Isles provided fast and efficient transportation and communication within the ambit of the Irish Sea world, and linked the Hebrides and Man with Wales, Ireland, England, Scotland, the Orkneys and Norway. Whether they were used for commerce or for war, the seaways gave a unity to the western seaboard in our period, and the maritime culture of the region meant that the West could form its own core to the margins defined by the neighbouring shorelands.

It is also all too easy to view the kingdom of the Isles as peripheral in a cultural as well as a geographical sense, and to regard its kings as relics left over from the days of the Vikings, ossified in a sort of heroic-age time warp until they were overwhelmed by the surging tide of Scottish royal authority. It would, of course, be difficult, not to mention foolish, to deny that there were many threads of continuity between the Viking Age that preceded it and the kingdom of the Isles itself. As proof of this we need look no further than Somerled's genealogy, name, or title. And it would be difficult to deny that Somerled's uprisings against the kings of Scots were anything but conservative in nature. But at the same time, we can see the western seaboard as a frontier, where a still largely heroic Scoto-Norse society came into contact with dynamic new forms of culture which ultimately originated in the Frankish kingdom across the Channel. Even in the very next generation after Somerled new cultural impulses are seen at work in the Western Isles.

Like other marginal regions of western Europe in the period between about 1000 and 1300, the western seaboard shared in the major social and cultural trends that were sweeping not just Britain but all of Europe.

By the early thirteenth century, the kings of the Isles were striving to be contemporary, up-to-date rulers, a task at which they succeeded admirably. We find them adapting to feudalism, seeking the status and prestige of knighthood, and building the castles that were a prerequisite for power and status in contemporary society. We find them patronising the church on a lavish scale, founding monasteries for the reformed religious orders, and building the churches and abbeys that declared their status as religious patrons of the first order. Where Gaelic conservatism encountered the brave new world of Frankish society, the result was a dynamic cultural synthesis that produced the sea-girt castles and strongholds of the West, fiefs held in return for galley service, and even seals that depicted galleys on one side and mounted knights on the other.

Yet, while it was born in the twilight of one age, there is also a sense in which the thirteenth century saw the kingdom of the Isles enter its own twilight. Concerned by the disorder in the western seaboard, which had a tendency to spill over Drumalban into the heart of the Scottish kingdom, the kings of Scots from the 1220s onward set their sights on the subjugation of the West. This was an extended process, accelerating from the 1240s and reaching its political culmination in the 1266 Treaty of Perth whereby the western Isles and Man were ceded to Scottish control. The MacSorleys, for the most part, accepted the situation without demur, and the distribution of MacSorley lands before and after the events of the 1260s was little different. By 1293, when a new administrative scheme was drawn up for the West, the integration looked to be complete. The MacSorleys had taken their place alongside other Scottish nobles in the *communitas regni*, the community of the realm, and a new age looked to be dawning.

But scarcely had the sun risen than the Bruce–Balliol conflict and the Anglo-Scottish wars of the late thirteenth and early fourteenth century laid the foundations for the ultimate undoing of the achievements of Alexander III, John Balliol, and Robert I in the West. No sooner had these kings succeeded in taming the Hebridean chieftains and bringing their men and galleys into their service than the conditions of civil strife and foreign war upset the fundamental equilibrium of the upper strata of Hebridean society. The MacDougalls of Argyll, the implacable foes of Robert I, were defeated in 1308–9, and Alexander and John MacDougall spent the rest of their lives in exile in England and Ireland. Although the family was restored to much-diminished lands by King Robert's son and successor, David II, the MacDougalls eventually died out in the senior line. The other MacSorleys fared better because they had thrown their support behind Bruce. Angus Óg MacDonald and Ruairi MacRuairi were confirmed in their lands by Robert I and shared, along with the Campbells and others, in the distribution of forfeited MacDougall territories. But in 1346, the MacRuairis suffered the same fate as their MacDougall kinsmen when the last MacRuairi chief died leaving no heirs save a sister, Amie. Since she was married to John MacDonald, the son and heir of Angus Óg MacDonald, this chance event united the extensive MacRuairi lands of Garmoran, the territories and islands between Ardnamurchan and Skye, and the Uists, with the Clan Donald possessions of Islay, Kintyre, Mull, Coll and Tiree. The result was a virtual recreation of Somerled's vast twelfth-century island and mainland kingdom, with all the Hebrides except Skye, and much of the mainland, from Glenelg to Kintyre, falling into MacDonald hands. From 1336 until 1493, the history of the western seaboard is the history of the Lordship of the Isles, and in one very real sense the Lordship of the Isles is an epilogue to the kingdom of the Isles.

Born in the power vacuum of the Irish Sea world in the late eleventh century, the kingdom of the Isles attained maturity in the twelfth century with the rise of Somerled of Argyll. Reaching its golden years in the thirteenth century, perhaps under the kingship of Ewen of Argyll, a great-grandson of Somerled, it was effectively killed with the cession of the Western Isles to Scotland by the Treaty of Perth in 1266. Its funeral pyre was the Bruce–Balliol conflicts and the Anglo-Scottish wars of the late thirteenth and early fourteenth centuries, but the phoenix that arose from the ashes was nothing less than the MacDonald Lordship of the Isles, which was to play so prominent a role in the history of later medieval Scotland.

Appendix: Genealogical Trees

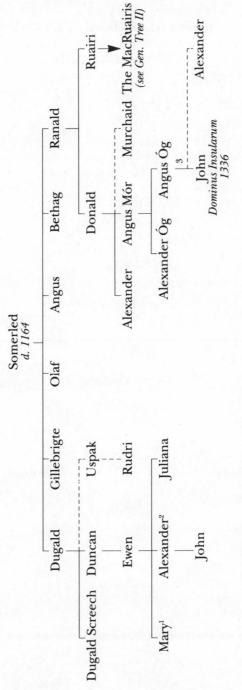

GENEALOGICAL TREE I

THE MACSORLEYS

Somerled
d. 1164

Dugald — Gillebrigte — Olaf — Angus — Bethag — Ranald

Dugald Screech — Duncan — Uspak

Ewen — Rudri

Mary[1] — Alexander[2] — Juliana

John

Donald — Angus Mór — Murchaid — The MacRuairis *(see Gen. Tree II)*

Ruairi

Alexander — Alexander Óg — Angus Óg — Alexander

John
Dominus Insularum
1336

------ broken line indicates probable descent

1. married (i) Magnus King of Man
   (ii) Malise earl of Strathearn

2. married daughter of John Comyn

3. MacDonald succession uncertain at this point

GENEALOGICAL TREE II

THE MACRUAIRIS

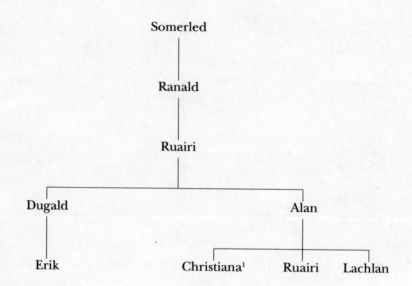

1. Christiana married Duncan of Mar, son of Donald, earl of Mar

GENEALOGICAL TREE III

THE KINGS OF MAN

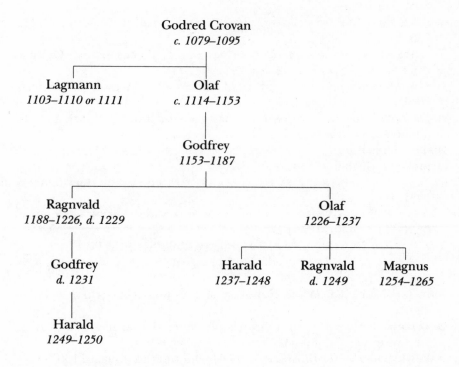

Bibliography

PRIMARY SOURCES

[——], 'An address to Aonghus of Islay', in O. Bergin, *Irish Bardic Poetry: Texts and translations, together with an introductory lecture* (Dublin, 1970).

[——], 'A poem in praise of Raghnall, King of Man', ed. B. O Cuiv, *Eigse*, viii (1956–7).

The Acts of the Lords of the Isles, 1336–1493, ed. J. and R. W. Munro (SHS, 1986).

The Acts of the Parliaments of Scotland, ed. T. Thomson and C. Innes (Edinburgh, 1814–75).

ADOMNÁN, *Life of Columba*, ed. A. O. and M. O. Anderson (Edinburgh, 1961).

Anglo-Scottish Relations, 1174–1328: Some Selected Documents, ed. E. L. G. Stones (2nd edn, Oxford, 1970).

Annála Connacht: the Annals of Connacht, AD 1224–1544, ed. A. M. Freeman (Dublin, 1944; repr. 1970).

The Annals of Inisfallen (MS Rawlinson B 503), ed. S. Mac Airt (Dublin, 1951; repr. 1977).

The Annals of the Kingdom of Ireland by the Four Masters, ed. J. O'Donovan (2nd edn, Dublin, 1856).

The Annals of Loch Cé, ed. W. M. Hennessy (Rolls Ser., 1871).

The Annals of Tigernach, ed. W. Stokes, in *Revue Celtique*, xvi–xviii (1895–7).

Annals of Ulster, ed. W. M. Hennessy and B. McCarthy (Dublin, 1887–1901).

[BARBOUR, JOHN], *Barbour's Bruce*, ed. M. P. McDiarmid and J. A. C. Stevenson (STS, 1980–5).

BARBOUR, JOHN, *The Bruce*, ed. A. A. M. Duncan (Edinburgh, 1997).

The Book of Clanranald, in A. Cameron, *Reliquiae Celticae: Texts, Papers and Studies in Gaelic Literature and Philology*, ed. A. MacBain and J. Kennedy (Inverness, 1894).

BOWER, WALTER, *Scotichronicon*, ed. D. E. R. Watt (Aberdeen, 1987–).

Brut y Tywysogyon or The Chronicle of the Princes: Red Book of Hergest Version, ed. T. Jones (Cardiff, 1955).

Calendar of Documents relating to Scotland, ed. J. Bain *et al.* (Edinburgh, 1881–1986).

Calendar of Entries in the Papal Registers relating to Great Britain and Ireland: Papal Letters, ed. W. H. Bliss *et al.* (London, 1893–).

Charters, Bulls, and Other Documents Relating to the Abbey of Inchaffray, ed. W. A. Lindsay *et al.* (SHS, 1908).

The Charters of the Priory of Beauly with Notices of the Priories of Pluscardine and Ardchattan, ed. E. C. Batten (Grampian Club, 1877).

The Chronicle of Lanercost, 1272–1346, trans. H. Maxwell (Glasgow, 1913).

The Chronicle of Man and the Sudreys, ed. P. A. Munch and Rev. Dr Goss (Manx Soc., 1874).

The Chronicle of Melrose (facsimile edn), ed. A. O. Anderson *et al.* (London, 1936).

DANIEL, WALTER, *Vita Ailredi Abbatis Rievall'*, ed. F. M. Powicke (London, 1950).

Diplomatarium Norvegicum, ed. G. R. Unger and H. J. Huitfeldt (Kristiana, 1849–1919).

Documents Illustrative of the History of Scotland, 1286–1306, ed. J. Stevenson (Edinburgh, 1870).

Documents and Records illustrating the History of Scotland, ed. F. Palgrave (London, 1837).

Early Scottish Charters prior to 1153, ed. A. C. Lawrie (Glasgow, 1905).

Early Sources of Scottish History, 500 to 1286, ed. A. O. Anderson (London, 1922; repr. Stamford, 1990).

Edward I and the Throne of Scotland, 1290–1296: An Edition of the Record Sources for the Great Cause, ed. E. L. G. Stones and G. G. Simpson (Oxford, 1978).

English Historical Documents, vol. I: *c.500–1042*, ed. D. Whitelock (London, 1955).

The Exchequer Rolls of Scotland, ed. J. Stuart *et al.* (Edinburgh, 1878–1908).

Foedera, Conventiones, Litterae et Cuiuscunque Generis Acta Publica, ed. T. Rymer (Record Commission edn, 1816–69).

FORDUN, JOHN OF, *Chronica Gentis Scotorum*, ed. W. F. Skene (Edinburgh, 1871–2).

GERALD OF WALES, *Descriptio Kambriae*, in *Opera*, ed. J. S. Brewer *et al.* (Rolls Ser., 1861–91).

GERALD OF WALES, *The History and Topography of Ireland*, trans. J. J. O'Meara (Harmondsworth, 1951; rev. edn, 1982).

[GERALD OF WALES]: Giraldus Cambrensis, *Expugnatio Hibernica: The Conquest of Ireland*, ed. A. B. Scott and F. X. Martin (Dublin, 1978).

Heimskringla: History of the Kings of Norway, trans. L. M. Hollander (Austin, Texas, 1964).

Highland Papers, ed. J. R. N. Macphail (SHS, 1914–34).

Joannis de Fordun Scotichronicon cum Supplementis et Continuatione Walteri Boweri, ed. W. Goodall (Edinburgh, 1759).

Le Liber Censuum de L'Eglise Romaine, ed. P. Fabre (Paris, 1889).

Liber Vitae Ecclesiae Dunelmensis, ed. J. Stevenson (Surtees Soc., 1841).

Monumenta de Insula Manniae, ed. J. R. Oliver (Manx Soc., 1860–2).

MYLN, ALEXANDER, *Vitae Dunkeldensis Ecclesiae Episcoporum*, ed. C. Innes (Bannatyne Club, 1831).

Orkneyinga Saga: The History of the Earls of Orkney, trans. H. Pálsson and P. Edwards (Harmondsworth, 1978).

Regesta Regum Scottorum, vol. I: *The Acts of Malcolm IV, King of Scots, 1153–1165*, ed. G. W. S. Barrow (Edinburgh, 1960).

Regesta Regum Scottorum, vol. II: *The Acts of William I, King of Scots, 1165–1214*, ed. G. W. S. Barrow (Edinburgh, 1971).

Regesta Regum Scottorum, vol. V: *The Acts of Robert I, King of Scots, 1306–1329*, ed. A. A. M. Duncan (Edinburgh, 1988).

Regesta Regum Scottorum: Handlist of the Acts of Alexander III, The Guardians, John, 1249–1296, comp. G. G. Simpson (Edinburgh, 1960).

Reginaldi monachi Dunelmensis libellus de admirandis beati Cuthberti virtutibus, ed. J. Raine (Surtees Soc., 1835).

Registrum Magni Sigilii Regum Scotorum, ed. J. M. Thomson *et al.* (Edinburgh, 1882–1914).

Registrum Monasterii de Passelet, ed. C. Innes (Maitland Club, 1832).

Rotuli Scotiae in Turri Londinensi et in Domo Capitulari Westmonasteriensi Asservati, ed. D. Macpherson *et al.* (London, 1814–19).

Saga of Magnus Barelegs, in *Heimskringla*, trans. Hollander.

Scotia Pontifica: Papal Letters to Scotland before the Pontificate of Innocent III, ed. R. Somerville (Oxford, 1982).

Scottish Annals from English Chroniclers, 500 to 1286, ed. A. O. Anderson (London, 1908).

A Scottish Chronicle known as the Chronicle of Holyrood, ed. M. O. Anderson (SHS, 1938).

Scottish Historical Documents, ed. G. Donaldson (Edinburgh, 1970).

Scottish Verse from the Book of the Dean of Lismore, ed. W. J. Watson (Scottish Gaelic Texts Soc., 1937).

SIMEON OF DURHAM, *A History of the Church of Durham*, in *The Historical Works of Simeon of Durham*, trans. J. Stevenson (Church Historians of England, 1855; repr. Llanerch, Lampeter, 1988).

SNORRI STURLUSON, *Saga of Olaf Tryggvason*, in *Heimskringla*, trans. Hollander.

STURLA THORDARSSON, *Hakon's Saga*, in *The Saga of Hacon and a Fragment of the Saga of Magnus with appendices*, trans. G. W. Dasent (Rolls Ser., *Icelandic Sagas*, iv, 1894); alternative translation in *ES*, ii.

Tigernach's Continuator, ed. W. Stokes, in *Revue Celtique*, xviii (1898).

Vetera Monumenta Hibernorum et Scotorum Historiam Illustrantia, ed. A. Theiner (Rome, 1864; repr. Osnabruck, 1969).

The Voyage of St Brendan, in *The Age of Bede*, ed. D. H. Farmer (rev. edn, Harmondsworth, 1988).

WYNTOUN, ANDREW, *The Orygnale Cronykil of Scotland*, ed. D. Laing (Edinburgh, 1872–9).

SECONDARY SOURCES

ANDERSON, M. O., *Kings and Kingship in Early Scotland* (Edinburgh, 1973).

ARMIT, I., *The Archaeology of Skye and the Western Isles* (Edinburgh, 1996).

ASHLEY, A., *The Church in the Isle of Man* (York, 1958).

BANNERMAN, J., *Studies in the History of Dalriada* (Edinburgh, 1974).

——, 'The Scots language and the kin-based society', in D. S. Thomson (ed.), *Gaelic and Scots in Harmony: Proceedings of the Second International Conference on the Languages of Scotland* (Glasgow, 1990).

——, 'MacDuff of Fife', in Grant and Stringer, *Medieval Scotland*.

BARRETT, M., *The Scottish Monasteries of Old* (Edinburgh, 1913).

BARRON, E. M., *The Scottish War of Independence: A Critical Study* (London, 1914).

BARROW, G. W. S., *Feudal Britain* (London, 1956).

——, 'The reign of William the Lion, king of Scotland', in J. C. Beckett (ed.), *Historical Studies VII* (London, 1969).

——, *The Kingdom of the Scots* (London, 1973).

——, *The Anglo-Norman Era in Scottish History* (Oxford, 1980).

——, *Kingship and Unity: Scotland, 1000–1306* (London, 1981).

——, 'The sources for the history of the Highlands in the Middle Ages', in MacLean, *Middle Ages in the Highlands*.

——, *Robert Bruce and the Community of the Realm of Scotland* (3rd edn, Edinburgh, 1988).

——, *Scotland and Its Neighbours in the Middle Ages* (London, 1992).

BARTLETT, R., *The Making of Europe: Conquest, Colonization and Cultural Change, 950–1350* (London, 1993).

BOSWELL, JAMES, *The Journal of a Tour to the Hebrides*, ed. P. Levi (Harmondsworth, 1984; with Johnson, *Journey to the Western Islands*).

BOWEN, E. G., *Saints, Seaways and Settlements in the Celtic Lands* (Cardiff, 1977).

BRAY, E., *The Discovery of the Hebrides: Voyagers to the Western Isles, 1745–1883* (London and Glasgow, 1986).

BREEZE, D., and RITCHIE, A., *Invaders of Scotland* (Edinburgh, 1991).

BREMNER, R. L., *The Norsemen in Alban* (Glasgow, 1923).

BRODERICK, G., 'Irish and Welsh strands in the genealogy of Godred Crovan', *Journal of the Manx Museum*, viii (1980).

BRØGGER, A. W., *Ancient Emigrants: A History of the Norse Settlements of Scotland* (Oxford, 1929).

——, and SHETELIG, H., *The Viking Ships: Their Ancestry and Evolution* (new edn, London, 1971).

BROOKE, C., 'Princes and kings as patrons of monasteries', in *Il Monachesimo e la Riforma Ecclesiastica (1049–1122)*, Settimana internazionale di studio, 4, Passo della Mendola, 1968, *Miscellanea del Centro di Studi Medioevali VI* (Milan, 1971).

BROOKE, D., 'Gall-Gaidhil and Galloway', in Oram and Stell, *Galloway*.

——, *Wild Men and Holy Places: St Ninian, Whithorn, and the Medieval Realm of Galloway* (Edinburgh, 1994).

BROWN, A. L., 'The Cistercian Abbey of Saddell, Kintyre', *Innes Review*, xx (1969–70).

BROWN, E. A. R., 'The tyranny of a construct: feudalism and the historians of medieval Europe', *American Historical Review*, lxxix (1974).

BROWN, R. A., *The Normans and the Norman Conquest* (London, 1969).

——, *Castles* (Aylesbury, 1985).

——, *Castles From the Air* (Cambridge, 1989).

BUCHANAN, GEORGE, *The History of Scotland*, trans. J. Aikman (Glasgow, 1827).

BUMKE, J., *The Concept of Knighthood in the Middle Ages* (New York, 1982).

BURTON, J., *Monastic and Religious Orders in Britain, 1000–1300* (Cambridge, 1994).

BYRNE, F. J., 'The trembling sod: Ireland in 1169,' in Cosgrove, *Medieval Ireland*.

CALDWELL, D. H., and EWART, G., 'Finlaggan and the Lordship of the Isles: an archaeological approach', *SHR*, lxxii (1993).

CAMPBELL, M., *Argyll: The Enduring Heartland* (London, 1977).

CANDON, A., 'Muirchertach Ua Briain: politics and naval activity in the Irish Sea, 1075 to 1119', in G. MacNiocaill and P. Wallace (eds.), *Keimelia: Studies in Medieval Archaeology and History in Memory of Tom Delaney* (Galway, 1988).

CARMICHAEL, I., *Lismore in Alba* (Perth, n.d.).

CLARK, W., *The 'Lord of the Isles' Voyage: Western Ireland to the Scottish Hebrides in a 16th-century Galley* (Kildare, 1993).

CLOSE-BROOKS, J., *Exploring Scotland's Heritage: The Highlands* (Edinburgh, 1986).

CONWAY, C., *The Story of Mellifont* (Dublin, 1958).

COSGROVE, A. (ed.), *Medieval Ireland, 1169–1534* (*A New History of Ireland*, vol. II; Oxford, 1987).

COSS, P., *The Knight in Medieval England, 1000–1400* (Stroud, 1993).

COWAN, E. J., 'Norwegian sunset – Scottish dawn: Hakon IV and Alexander III', in Reid, *Scotland in the Reign of Alexander III*.

——, 'The historical MacBeth', in W. D. H. Sellar (ed.), *Moray: Province and People* (Edinburgh, 1993).

COWAN, I. B., 'The development of the parochial system in medieval Scotland', *SHR*, xl (1961).

——, *The Parishes of Medieval Scotland* (SRS, 1967).

——, 'Appropriation of parish churches', in McNeill and Nicholson, *Historical Atlas of Scotland*.

——, 'The post-Columban Church', *Scottish Church History Soc. Records*, xviii (1974).

COWAN, I. B. 'The medieval Church in Argyll and the Isles', *Scottish Church History Soc. Records*, xx (1978).

——, and EASSON, D. E., *Medieval Religious Houses: Scotland* (2nd edn, London, 1976).

CRAWFORD, B., *Scandinavian Scotland* (Leicester, 1987).

CROUCH, D., *William Marshal: Court, Career and Chivalry in the Angevin Empire, 1146–1219* (London, 1990).

——, *The Image of Aristocracy in Britain, 1000–1300* (London, 1992).

CRUDEN, S., *The Scottish Castle* (London, 1963).

CUBBON, W. C., 'History of Rushen Abbey, Ballasalla, Isle of Man – 1134 AD', *Proceedings of the Isle of Man Natural History and Antiquarian Soc.*, iv (1932–42).

CURPHEY, R. A., 'Peel Castle summer excursion: June 1979', *Proceedings of the Isle of Man Natural History and Antiquarian Soc.*, ix (1980–2).

DAVIES, R. R., *Domination and Conquest: The Experience of Ireland, Scotland and Wales, 1100–1300* (Cambridge, 1990).

—— (ed.), *The British Isles, 1100–1500: Comparisons, Contrasts and Connections* (Edinburgh, 1988).

DAWSON, J. E. A., 'Argyll: the enduring heartland', *SHR*, lxxiv (1995).

DE GRAY BIRCH, W., 'On the date of foundation ascribed to the Cistercian abbeys of Great Britain', *Journal of the British Archaeological Association*, xxvi (1870).

DICKINSON, W. C., *Scotland from the Earliest Times to 1603*, 3rd edn, revised by A. A. M. Duncan (Oxford, 1977).

DOLLEY, M., *Anglo-Norman Ireland* (Dublin, 1970).

DONALDSON, G., *A Northern Commonwealth: Scotland and Norway* (Saltire Soc., 1990).

DUBY, G., *The Early Growth of the European Economy: Warriors and Peasants from the Seventh to the Twelfth Century* (London, 1974).

——, *The Chivalrous Society* (London, 1977).

——, *The Knight, The Lady and The Priest: The Making of Modern Marriage in Medieval France* (London, 1983).

——, *et al.*, *A History of Private Life*, vol. II: *Revelations of the Medieval World* (Cambridge, Mass., 1988).

DUFFY, S., 'The "Continuation" of Nicholas Trevet: a new source for the Bruce invasion', *Proceedings of the Royal Irish Academy*, xci (1991).

——, 'The Bruce brothers and the Irish Sea world, 1306–29', *Cambridge Medieval Celtic Studies*, xxi (1991).

——, 'Irishmen and Islesmen in the Kingdoms of Dublin and Man, 1052–1171', *Ériu*, xliii (1992).

——, 'Ireland and the Irish Sea Region, 1014–1318' (Dublin University, Ph.D. thesis, 1993).

——, 'The first Ulster Plantation: John de Courcy and the men of Cumbria', in T. D. Barry, R. Frame and K. Simms (eds.), *Colony and Frontier in Medieval Ireland: Essays presented to J. F. Lydon* (London, 1995).

DUFFY, S. (ed.), *A New History of the Isle of Man*, vol. III: *The Medieval Period, 1000–1405* (Liverpool University Press, forthcoming).

DUNBAR, J. G., *The Architecture of Scotland* (London, 1966).

——, 'Kisimul Castle, Isle of Barra', *Glasgow Archaeological Journal*, v (1978).

——, 'The medieval architecture of the Scottish Highlands', in MacLean, *Middle Ages in the Highlands*.

——, and DUNCAN, A. A. M., 'Tarbert Castle: a contribution to the history of Argyll', *SHR*, l (1971).

——, and FISHER, I., *Iona* (RCAHMS, 1983).

DUNCAN, A. A. M., 'The community of the realm of Scotland and Robert Bruce: a review', *SHR*, xlv (1966).

——, *The Nation of Scots and the Declaration of Arbroath* (Historical Association, 1970).

——, *Scotland: The Making of the Kingdom* (Edinburgh, 1975).

——, 'The Scots' invasion of Ireland, 1315', in Davies, *British Isles*.

——, 'The War of the Scots, 1306–23', *Trans Royal Hist. Soc.*, 6th ser., ii (1992).

——, and BROWN, A. L., 'Argyll and the Isles in the earlier Middle Ages', *PSAS*, xc (1956–7).

DUNN, J. A., *History of Renfrew* (Paisley, n.d.).

FAWCETT, R., *Scottish Castles and Fortifications* (Edinburgh, 1986).

——, *Scottish Abbeys and Priories* (London, 1994).

FERGUSSON, J., *Alexander the Third* (London, 1937).

FLEMING, D. F., '*Milites* as attestors to charters in England, 1101–1300', *Albion*, xxii (1990).

FOJUT, N., PRINGLE, D., and WALKER, B., *The Ancient Monuments of the Western Isles: A Visitor's Guide to the Principal Historic Sites and Monuments* (Edinburgh, 1994).

FOSTER, S., *Picts, Gaels and Scots* (Edinburgh, 1996).

FRAME, R., 'The Bruces in Ireland', *Irish Historical Studies*, xix (1974).

——, *The Political Development of the British Isles, 1100–1400* (Oxford, 1990).

FREKE, D., 'History', in V. Robinson and D. McCarroll (eds.), *The Isle of Man: Celebrating a Sense of Place* (Liverpool, 1990).

FRIELL, J. G. P., and WATSON, W. G. (eds.), *Pictish Studies: Settlement, Burial and Art in Dark Age Northern Britain* (Oxford, 1984).

FRYDE, E. B., *et al.* (eds.), *Handbook of British Chronology* (3rd edn, London, 1986).

GALLOWAY, W., 'Notice of the chapel dedicated to St Blane at Kingarth in Bute', *Archaeologia Scotica*, v (1890).

GEARY, P., *Furta Sacra: Thefts of Relics in the Central Middle Ages* (rev. edn, Princeton, 1990).

GIFFORD, J., *Highland and Islands* (London, 1992).

GILLIES, H. C., *The Place-Names of Argyll* (London, 1906).

GRAHAM-CAMPBELL, J., *The Viking World* (London, 1980).

GRANSDEN, A., *Historical Writing in England, c.550 to c.1307* (London, 1974).

GRANT, A., *Independence and Nationhood: Scotland, 1306–1469* (London, 1984).

——, 'Scotland's "Celtic Fringe" in the late Middle Ages: the MacDonald Lords of the Isles and the kingdom of Scotland', in Davies, *British Isles*.

——, and STRINGER, K. J. (eds.), *Medieval Scotland: Crown, Lordship and Community. Essays Presented to G. W. S. Barrow* (Edinburgh, 1993).

GRANT, I. F., *The Economic History of Scotland* (London, 1934).

——, *The Lordship of the Isles* (Edinburgh, 1935).

——, and CHEAPE, H., *Periods in Highland History* (London, 1987).

GREGORY, DONALD, *History of the Western Highlands and Isles of Scotland from AD 1493 to AD 1625* (2nd edn, London and Glasgow, 1881).

GROOME, F. H., *Ordnance Gazetteer of Scotland: A Survey of Scottish Topography* (new edn, London, 1895).

GWYNN, A., and HADCOCK, R. N., *Medieval Religious Houses: Ireland* (London, 1970).

HAYES-MCCOY, G. A., *Scots Mercenary Forces in Ireland (1565–1603)* (Dublin and London, 1937).

HECHTER, M., *Internal Colonialism: The Celtic Fringe in British National Development, 1536–1966* (London, 1975).

HELLE, K., 'Norwegian foreign policy and the Maid of Norway', *SHR*, lxix (1990).

HENDERSON, I., *The Picts* (London, 1967).

HERBERT, M., *Iona, Kells and Derry: The History and Historiography of the Monastic Familia of Columba* (Oxford, 1988).

HILL, B. D., *English Cistercian Monasteries and their Patrons in the Twelfth Century* (Chicago, 1968).

HOLLISTER, C. W., *The Military Organization of Norman England* (Oxford, 1965).

HUDSON, B. T., 'Gaelic princes and Gregorian reform', in B. T. Hudson and V. Ziegler (eds.), *Crossed Paths: Methodological Approaches to the Celtic Aspect of the European Middle Ages* (Lanham, N.Y., and London, 1991).

——, *Kings of Celtic Scotland* (Westport, Conn., and London, 1994).

——, 'Kings and Church in early Scotland', *SHR*, lxxiii (1994).

INNES, C., *et al.* (eds.), *Origines Parochiales Scotiae: The Antiquities, Ecclesiastical and Territorial, of the Parishes of Scotland* (Bannatyne Club, 1851–5).

JACKSON, K., *The Gaelic Notes in the Book of Deer* (Cambridge, 1972).

JOHNSON, SAMUEL, *A Journey to the Western Islands of Scotland*, ed. P. Levi (Harmondsworth, 1984; with Boswell, *Tour to the Hebrides*).

JONES, G., *A History of the Vikings* (rev. edn, Oxford, 1984).

KEEN, M., *Chivalry* (New Haven and London, 1984).

KINVIG, R. H., *A History of the Isle of Man* (2nd edn, Liverpool, 1950; 3rd edn, Liverpool, 1975).

KIRBY, D. P., 'Moray in the twelfth century', in McNeill and Nicholson, *Historical Atlas of Scotland*.

LAING, H., *Descriptive Catalogue of Impressions from Ancient Scottish Seals* (Bannatyne and Maitland Clubs, 1850).

LAING, L., and J., *The Picts and the Scots* (Stroud, 1993).

LAMONT, W. D., *The Early History of Islay* (Dundee, 1966).

——, *Ancient and Medieval Sculptured Stones of Islay* (Edinburgh and London, 1968).

——, 'Alexander of Islay, son of Angus Mór', *SHR*, lx (1981).

LAWRENCE, C. H., *Medieval Monasticism: Forms of Religious Life in Western Europe in the Middle Ages* (2nd edn, London, 1989).

LEWIS, A. R., and RUNYAN, T. J., *European Naval and Maritime History, 300–1500* (Bloomington, Indiana, 1985).

LEWIS, A. W., *Royal Succession in Capetian France: Studies on Familial Order and the State* (Cambridge, Mass., and London, 1981).

LINDSAY, M., *The Castles of Scotland* (London, 1986).

LINKLATER, E., 'The Battle of Largs', in *Orkney Miscellany*, v (1973).

LOGAN, F. D., *The Vikings in History* (2nd edn, London and New York, 1991).

LOYN, H. R., *The Vikings in Britain* (London, 1977).

LUSTIG, R., 'The Treaty of Perth: a re-examination', *SHR*, lviii (1979).

LYDON, J., 'The Scottish soldier in medieval Ireland: the Bruce invasion and the galloglass', in G. G. Simpson (ed.), *The Scottish Soldier Abroad, 1247–1967* (Edinburgh, 1992).

LYNCH, M., *Scotland: A New History* (Edinburgh, 1992).

MACDONALD A., and A., *The Clan Donald* (Inverness, 1896–1904).

MACDONALD, C., *The History of Argyll* (Glasgow, 1950).

MACDONALD, D. J., *The Clan Donald* (Loanhead, 1978).

MACDONALD, HUGH, *History of the Macdonalds*, in *Highland Papers*, vol. I, ed. J. R. N. Macphail (SHS, 1914).

MCDONALD, R. A., 'The death and burial of Somerled of Argyll', *West Highland Notes and Queries*, 2nd ser., viii (Nov. 1991).

——, 'Kings and Princes in Scotland: Aristocratic Interactions in the Anglo-Norman Era' (Guelph University, Ph.D. thesis, 1993).

——, 'Matrimonial politics and core-periphery interactions in twelfth- and early thirteenth-century Scotland', *Journal of Medieval History*, xxi (1995).

——, 'Images of Hebridean lordship in the twelfth and early thirteenth centuries: the seal of Raonall MacSorley', *SHR*, lxxiv (1995).

——, 'Scoto-Norse kings and the reformed religious orders: patterns of monastic patronage in twelfth-century Galloway and Argyll', *Albion*, xxvii (1995).

——, 'Causa Ruine Regni Insularum': Somerled MacGillebrigde and the rise of a new dynasty in the Isles, *c.*1100–1164', in S. Duffy (ed.), *A New History of the Isle of Man*, vol. III: *The Medieval Period, 1000–1405* (Liverpool University Press, forthcoming).

MCDONALD, R. A., and MCLEAN, S. A., 'Somerled of Argyll: a new look at old problems', *SHR*, lxxi (1992).

MCEWEN, A. B. W., 'The death of Reginald son of Somerled', *West Highland Notes and Queries*, 2nd ser., vi (1990).

MACGIBBON, D., and ROSS, T., *Castellated and Domestic Architecture of Scotland* (Edinburgh, 1887–92).

——, *The Ecclesiastical Architecture of Scotland* (Edinburgh, 1896–7).

MACINNES, J., 'West Highland sea power in the Middle Ages', *TGSI*, xlviii (1972–4).

——, 'Clan sagas and historical legends', *TGSI*, lvii (1990–2).

MACKAY, A. J. G., 'Notes and queries on the custom of Gavelkind in Kent, Ireland, Wales, and Scotland', *PSAS*, xxxii (1898).

MACKENZIE, W. C., *History of the Outer Hebrides* (Paisley, 1903).

——, *The Highlands and Islands of Scotland: A Historical Survey* (Edinburgh and London, 1937).

MCKERRAL, A., 'West Highland mercenaries in Ireland', *SHR*, xxx (1951).

——, 'A chronology of the Abbey and Castle of Saddell, Kintyre', *PSAS*, lxxxvi (1951–2).

——, *The Clan Campbell* (Edinburgh and London, 1953).

MACKINLAY, J. M., *Ancient Church Dedications in Scotland: Scriptural Dedications* (Edinburgh, 1910).

MACLEAN, L. (ed.), *The Middle Ages in the Highlands* (Inverness, 1981).

MCNAMEE, C., *The Wars of the Bruces: Scotland, England and Ireland, 1306–1328* (East Linton, 1997).

MCNEIL, T. E., *Anglo-Norman Ulster: The History and Archaeology of an Irish Barony, 1177–1400* (Edinburgh, 1980).

MACNEILL, E., 'Chapters of Hebridean history I: the Norse kingdom of the Hebrides', *The Scottish Review*, xxxix (1916).

MCNEILL, P., and NICHOLSON, R. (eds.), *An Historical Atlas of Scotland, c.400–c.1600* (St Andrews, 1975).

MCNEILL, P. G. B., and MACQUEEN, H. L. (eds.), *Atlas of Scottish History to 1707* (Edinburgh, 1996).

MACQUARRIE, A., 'Kings, lords and abbots: power and patronage at the medieval monastery of Iona', *TGSI*, liv (1984–6).

——, *Scotland and the Crusades, 1095–1560* (Edinburgh, 1985).

——, and MACARTHUR, E. M., *Iona Through the Ages* (2nd edn, Society of West Highland and Island Historical Research, 1992).

MAGNUSSON, M., *Viking Expansion Westwards* (London, 1973).

——, *Hakon the Old – Hakon Who?* (Largs and District Historical Soc., 1982).

MARSDEN, J., *Sea-Road of the Saints: Celtic Holy Men in the Hebrides* (Edinburgh, 1995).

MARTIN, F. X., 'Diarmait Mac Murchada and the coming of the Anglo-Normans'; 'Overlord becomes feudal lord, 1172–85'; 'John, Lord of Ireland, 1185–1216': all in Cosgrove, *Medieval Ireland*.

MARTIN, MARTIN, *A Description of the Western Islands of Scotland circa 1695* (1703; repr. Stirling, 1934).

MATHESON, W., 'Traditions of the MacKenzies', *TGSI*, xxxix–xl (1942–50).

MAYHEW, N., 'Alexander III – a silver age? An essay in Scottish medieval economic history', in Reid, *Scotland in the Reign of Alexander III*.

MEGAW, B. R. S., 'The ship seals of the kings of Man', *Journal of the Manx Museum*, vi, no. 76 (1959–60).

——, 'Norseman and native in the Kingdom of the Isles: a re-assessment of the Manx evidence', *Scot. Stud.*, xx (1976).

METCALFE, W. M., *A History of the County of Renfrew* (Paisley, 1905).

MIKET, R., and ROBERTS, D. L., *The Mediaeval Castles of Skye and Lochalsh* (Isle of Skye, 1990).

MILLAR, H. B., 'The Castle of Fraoch Eilean, Loch Awe, Argyll', *TGAS*, new ser., xv, pt. 3 (1966).

MITCHELL, D., *A Popular History of the Highlands and Gaelic Scotland from the Earliest Times to the 'Forty-Five* (Paisley, 1900).

MONCREIFFE, I., *The Highland Clans* (London, 1967).

MOORE, A. W., 'The connexion between Scotland and Man', *SHR*, iii (1906).

——, *A History of the Isle of Man* (1900; repr. Manx National Heritage, 1992).

MORGAN, M., 'The organization of the Scottish Church in the twelfth century', *Trans Royal Hist. Soc.*, 4th ser., xxix (1947).

MORRIS, C., *The Papal Monarchy: The Western Church from 1050 to 1250* (Oxford, 1989).

MUIR, R., 'The development of sheriffdoms', in McNeill and Nicholson, *Historical Atlas of Scotland*.

MUNRO, R. W. (ed.), *Monro's Western Isles of Scotland and Genealogies of the Clans, 1549* (Edinburgh, 1961).

MURRAY, W. H., *The Islands of Western Scotland* (London, 1973).

——, *The Hebrides* (London, 1966).

NICHOLLS, K., *Gaelic and Gaelicised Ireland in the Middle Ages* (Dublin, 1972).

NICHOLSON, R., *Scotland: The Later Middle Ages* (Edinburgh, 1974).

NICOLAISEN, W. F. H., *Scottish Place Names* (1976, repr. London, 1986).

NICOLSON, A., *History of Skye: A Record of the Families, the Social Conditions and the Literature of the Island*, ed. A. Macleod (Glasgow, 1930, 2nd rev. edn, 1994)

Ó CORRAIN, D., *Ireland Before the Normans* (Dublin, 1972).

Ó CRÓINÍN, D., *Early Medieval Ireland, 400–1200* (London, 1995).

O'DWYER, P., *Céli Dé: Spiritual Reform in Ireland, 750–900* (Dublin, 1981).

——, 'Celtic monks and the Culdee reform', in J. P. MacKey (ed.), *An Introduction to Celtic Christianity* (Edinburgh, 1989).

ORAM, R. D., 'Fergus, Galloway and the Scots', in Oram and Stell, *Galloway*.

ORAM, R. D., 'A family business? Colonisation and settlement in twelfth-and thirteenth-century Galloway', *SHR*, lxxii (1993).

——, and STELL, G. P. (eds.), *Galloway: Land and Lordship* (Edin-burgh, 1991).

ORPEN, G. H., *Ireland Under the Normans* (Oxford, 1911–20).

ORR, W., *Discovering Argyll, Mull and Iona* (Edinburgh, 1990).

OWEN, D. D. R., *William the Lion, 1143–1214: Kingship and Culture* (East Linton, 1997).

PÁLSSON, H., 'Hakonar Saga: portrait of a king', in *Orkney Miscellany: King Hakon Commemorative Number 5* (1973).

PATTERSON, N., *Cattle Lords and Clansmen: The Social Structure of Early Ireland* (2nd edn, London, 1994).

PAUL, J. B. (ed.), *The Scots Peerage* (Edinburgh, 1904–14).

POOLE, R. L., 'The Scottish islands in the diocese of Sodor', *SHR*, viii (1911).

POWER, E., *Medieval People* (10th edn, London, 1963).

POWER, R., 'Magnus Barelegs' expeditions to the West', *SHR*, lxv (1986).

POWICKE, F. M., *The Thirteenth Century, 1216–1307* (2nd edn, Oxford, 1962).

PRESTWICH, M., *Edward I* (London, 1988).

PROCTOR, C., *Ceannas Nan Gaidheal: The Headship of the Gael* (Armadale, 1985).

REEVES, W., *The Culdees of the British Isles* (Dublin, 1864).

REID, N. H. (ed.), *Scotland in the Reign of Alexander III, 1249–1286* (Edinburgh, 1990).

REID, W. S., 'Sea-power in the Anglo-Scottish War, 1296–1328', *The Mariner's Mirror*, xlvi (1960).

REYNOLDS, S., *Kingdoms and Communities in Western Europe, 900–1300* (Oxford, 1984).

——, *Fiefs and Vassals: The Medieval Evidence Re-interpreted* (Oxford, 1994).

RITCHIE, A., *The Picts* (Edinburgh, 1989).

——, *Invaders of Scotland* (Edinburgh, 1991).

——, *Viking Age Scotland* (London, 1993).

——, *Iona* (London, 1997).

RITCHIE, G., and HARMAN, M., *Discovering Scotland's Heritage: Argyll and the Western Isles* (rev. edn, Edinburgh, 1990).

RITCHIE, J. N. G. (ed.), *The Archaeology of Argyll* (Edinburgh, 1997).

RITCHIE, R. L. G., *The Normans in Scotland* (Edinburgh, 1954).

ROBERTS, J. L., *Lost Kingdoms: Celtic Scotland and the Middle Ages* (Edin-burgh, 1997).

ROBERTSON, E. W., *Scotland under her Early Kings* (Edinburgh, 1862).

ROYAL COMMISSION ON THE ANCIENT AND HISTORICAL MONUMENTS AND CONSTRUCTIONS OF SCOTLAND, *Inventory of the Ancient Monuments of Argyll* (Edinburgh, 1971–92).

SCOTT, J. E., 'Saddell Abbey', *TGSI*, xlvi (1969–70).

SCOTT, W. W., 'John of Fordun's description of the Western Isles', *Scot. Stud.*, xxiii (1979).

SELLAR, W. D. H., 'The origins and ancestry of Somerled', *SHR*, xlv (1966).

——, 'Family origins in Cowal and Knapdale', *Scot. Stud.*, xv (1971).

——, 'The earliest Campbells – Norman, Briton or Gael?', *Scot. Stud.*, xvii (1973).

——, 'The Western Isles, *c*.800–1095', in McNeill and Nicholson, *Historical Atlas of Scotland*.

——, 'Marriage, divorce, and concubinage in Gaelic Scotland', *TGSI*, li (1978–80).

——, 'Warlords, holy men and matrilineal succession', *Innes Review*, xxxvi (1985).

——, 'MacDonald and MacRuari pedigrees in MS 1467', *West Highland Notes and Queries*, xxviii (1986).

SEVERIN, T., *The Brendan Voyage* (London, 1978).

SIMMS, K., *From Kings to Warlords* (Woodbridge, 1987).

SIMPSON, W. D., 'The architectural history of Rothesay Castle', *TGAS*, new ser., ix, pt. 3 (1937–40).

——, 'Castle Tioram, Moidart, Inverness-shire; and Mingary Castle, Ardnamurchan, Argyllshire', *TGAS*, new ser., xiii (1954).

——, *Dunstaffnage Castle and the Stone of Destiny* (Edinburgh, 1958).

——, 'Castle Sween', *TGAS*, new ser., xv, pt. 1 (1960).

——, 'Skipness Castle', *TGAS*, new ser., xv, pt. 3 (1966).

——, and DUNBAR, J. G., *Dunstaffnage Castle* (rev. edn, Edinburgh, 1990).

SKENE, W. F., *Celtic Scotland: A History of Ancient Alban* (Edinburgh, 1876–80).

——, *The Highlanders of Scotland*, ed. A. MacBain (Stirling, 1902).

SMALL, A. (ed.), *The Picts: A New Look at Old Problems* (Dundee, 1987).

SMALLEY, B., *Historians in the Middle Ages* (London, 1974).

SMYTH, A. P., *Scandinavian Kings in the British Isles, 850–880* (Oxford, 1977).

——, *Warlords and Holy Men: Scotland, AD 80–1000* (London, 1984).

SOUTHERN, R. W., *Western Society and the Church in the Middle Ages* (Harmondsworth, 1970).

STAPLETON, T., 'A brief summary of the Wardrobe Accounts of the 10th, 11th, and 14th years of Edward II', *Archaeologia*, xxvi (1836).

STEANE, J., *The Archaeology of Medieval England and Wales* (Athens, Georgia, 1984).

STEER, K. A., and BANNERMAN, J., *Late Medieval Monumental Sculpture in the West Highlands* (RCAHMS, 1977).

STIRLING, A. M. W., *MacDonald of the Isles* (New York, 1914).

STRINGER, K. J., 'Periphery and core in thirteenth-century Scotland: Alan son of Roland, Lord of Galloway and Constable of Scotland', in Grant and Stringer, *Medieval Scotland*.

STRINGER, K. J., *The Reign of Stephen: Kingship, Warfare and Government in Twelfth-Century England* (London, 1993).

TABRAHAM, C. J., *Scottish Castles and Fortifications* (Edinburgh, 1986).

——, *Scotland's Castles* (London, 1997).

TRANTER, N., *Argyll and Bute* (London, 1977).

——, *Lord of the Isles* (London, 1983).

TURNER, R. V., *King John* (London, 1994).

VAN DER MEER, F., *Atlas De l'Ordre Cistercien* (Paris and Brussels, 1965).

WADDELL, J. J., 'The chapel or oratory of St Columba at Iona', *TGAS*, new ser., x (1941).

WAINWRIGHT, F. T., *The Problem of the Picts* (Edinburgh, 1955).

WALKER, D., *The Normans in Britain* (London, 1995).

WARD, B., *Miracles and the Medieval Mind: Theory, Record and Event, 1000–1215* (rev. edn, Philadelphia, 1987).

WATSON, W. J., *The History of the Celtic Place-Names of Scotland* (Edinburgh and London, 1926).

WATT, D. E. R., *Fasti Ecclesiae Scoticanae Medii Aevi ad annum 1638: second draft* (SRS, 1969).

——, 'The minority of Alexander III of Scotland', *Trans Royal Hist. Soc.*, 5th ser., xxi (1971).

——, 'Bishops in the Isles before 1203: bibliography and biographical lists', *Innes Rev.*, xlv (1994).

—— (ed.), *Ecclesia Scoticana* (*Series Episcoporum Ecclesiae Catholicae Occidentalis Ab Initio Usque Ad Annum MCXCVIII*, ed. O. Engels and S. Weinferter, series VI, tomus I; Stuttgart, 1991).

WATT, J., *The Church and the Two Nations in Medieval Ireland* (Cambridge, 1970).

——, *The Church in Medieval Ireland* (Dublin, 1972).

WEBSTER, B., *Scotland from the Eleventh Century to 1603* (London, 1975).

WERNER, K. F., 'Kingdom and principality in twelfth-century France', in T. Reuter (ed.), *The Medieval Nobility: Studies on the Ruling Classes of France and Germany from the Sixth to the Twelfth Century* (Amsterdam, 1979).

WILLIAMS, R., *The Lords of the Isles: The Clan Donald and the Early Kingdom of the Scots* (London, 1984).

WILSON, A. J., *St Margaret Queen of Scotland* (Edinburgh, 1993).

YEOMAN, P., *Medieval Scotland* (London, 1995).

YOUNG, A., 'Noble families and political factions in the reign of Alexander III', in Reid, *Scotland in the Reign of Alexander III*.

ZIMMER, H., *The Celtic Church in Britain and Ireland* (London, 1902).

Index